Teaching Students with
Learning and Behavior Problems

Teaching Students with

Published by arrangement with Allyn and Bacon, Inc.

Learning and Behavior Problems

fourth edition

Donald D. Hammill

Nettie R. Bartel

 5341 Industrial Oaks Boulevard   Austin, Texas   78735

Library of Congress Cataloging-in-Publication Data

Hammill, Donald D., 1934–
    Teaching students with learning and behavior problems.

    Rev. ed. of: Teaching children with learning and behavior problems. Canadian ed. c 1984.
    Includes bibliographies and indexes.
    1. Learning disabilities—Addresses, essays, lectures.   2. Learning disabled children—Education—United States.   3. Learning disabled children—Education—United States—Addresses, essays, lectures.
I. Bartel, Nettie R.   II. Hammill, Donald D., 1934–
Teaching children with learning and behavior problems.
III. Title.
LC4704.H35   1986   371.9   85-30803
ISBN 0-89079-116-3

5341 Industrial Oaks Boulevard
Austin, Texas 78735

Composition buyer: Linda Cox
Production coordinator: Helyn Pultz
Editorial-production service: Lifland et al., Bookmakers
Cover coordinator: Linda K. Dickinson
Cover designer: Christy Rosso
Interior photos: The Terry Wild Studio

Printed in the United States of America

10 9 8 7 6 5 4 3 2 1   86 87 88 89 90

Contents

5

Correcting Handwriting Deficiencies *by Donald D. Hammill*   155

6

Problems in Mathematics Achievement *by Nettie R. Bartel*   179

Preface

All teachers, whether they teach regular or exceptional students, frequently encounter youngsters at the elementary or secondary level who are not responsive to instruction or who are disruptive in class. These students may evidence problems in reading, arithmetic, language, or writing or in social adjustment or motivation. Most of them are probably the victims of poor teaching, insufficient background experience, and/or inadequate motivation. No students are immune to the debilitating effects of these three factors; bright or retarded, sound or crippled, stable or difficult students can be affected at one time or another.

Over the years the schools have evolved numerous alternatives for handling below-average learners. Psychological services, special education classes, and remedial programs have been provided. With this proliferation of specialized educational services, teachers have become increasingly dependent upon noninstructional personnel to assist them in teaching students with school-related problems. Thus educational assessment has become the responsibility of the school psychologist; slow learners are shunted off to the "retarded" class; poor readers are referred to the remedial reading specialist; and troublesome students eventually are placed in classes for the "emotionally disturbed." The great majority of difficult pupils, however, remain in the regular class under the supervision of the teacher, who is expected to meet their individual needs.

It appears that many students presently enrolled in special education classes will be integrated into regular classes within the next few years. The trend toward isolating problem children, which was so prevalent during the past few decades, is being reversed as educators recognize that special class placements bring few benefits to mildly handicapped children. Educators and others find the special-class solution philosophically objectionable in the 1980s. School systems are not likely to return these students to the educational mainstream without making some provisions on their behalf. These provisions will probably take the forms of resource rooms, consultants, tutors, and itinerant programs.

Teachers are currently responsible for the achievement of many students who are difficult to teach, and in the future they will probably be responsible for more of these students. Unfortunately, many teachers lack the information that would enable them to cope with these students. A number of elementary and secondary education teacher-training programs fail to sufficiently familiarize their students with basic assessment procedures, diagnostic and prescriptive teacher techniques, and remedial materials and methods. Yet knowledge of a wide variety of remedial and developmental instructional approaches and activities is necessary to accommodate the disparate educational needs of non-achieving pupils.

With these ideas in mind, we have written this book for teachers. Our intention was (1) to succinctly review the roles and duties of teachers in the management of students with school-related problems; (2) to provide teachers with a series of discussions that focus on these school-related difficulties (for example, reading, spelling, arithmetic, handwriting, and behavior); (3) to provide along with these discussions basic information regarding appropriate assessment techniques and instructional methods; and finally (4) to provide teachers with suggestions for specific materials and sources.

It was not our intention to present and discuss all the possible evaluation devices and instructional methods that are available to teachers today. This would have been a monumental effort, and one that we have neither the energy nor the experience to undertake. Instead, we have shared with the reader those exceptional approaches and ideas with which we have had some direct personal experience. We have also included several new programs that appear to be promising, although we have not used them.

We are not necessarily endorsing the materials or methods described here; rather, we have tried to provide information on representative techniques to enable teachers to choose materials appropriate for their pupils. Teachers are urged to evaluate the effectiveness of their selections in their own classrooms, as research on the efficacy of most programs is inadequate or nonexistent.

Some special comment should be made about this fourth edition, which is a major revision of our work. First, we have checked to make sure that all tests and methods referred to are still popular and available. Second, we have refocused the book exclusively on the school-aged student. Two chapters on language and perception included earlier were deleted from this edition because their contents related primarily to preschool education. In their stead, two new chapters were added—one on life-skills education and one on general practices appropriate for students of all ages. Topics in this latter chapter include computer use in the schools, tutoring, parent involvement, materials selection, and recommended instructional methods.

Finally, we want to express our deep appreciation to the college instructors who over the years have continued to adopt our book for their classes, and to the teachers who have found our work useful and recommended it to their colleagues. It has been your loyal support, dear readers, that has made this fourth edition possible.

D.D.H.
N.R.B.

chapter 1

Meeting the Special Needs of Students

by Donald D. Hammill and Nettie R. Bartel

Most experienced teachers are able to recognize children and adolescents who seem bright but who fail to make expected gains in a particular skill after repeated exposure to training. If the skill is reading, the teacher may notice that the student reads aloud quite well but has great difficulty with comprehension during silent reading. Another student may become confused when directions are given orally but exhibit comparative superiority in reading and writing. A third youngster may have adequate listening and speech skills but manifest problems when he or she engages in math activities.

Some pupils evidence discrepancies of varying degrees between their estimated intellectual ability and their actual performance; others show marked divergence between the skills in which they excel and those in which they are inadequate or marginal; and others are merely slow in acquiring necessary school behaviors. To a large extent, these problems involve the understanding or the use of spoken or written language and are manifested in difficulty with reading, thinking, talking, listening, writing, spelling, or arithmetic. They may also include behavior problems. The problems range from mild to intense and are occasionally associated with blindness, deafness, psychosis, and/or severe mental defect. For the most part, however, the difficulties are found in mild to moderate degree in individuals who are otherwise "normal."

In the past, school personnel have been quick to confuse a student's school problem with a diagnostic label. Students who performed inadequately in the classroom tended to be labeled "retarded," "disturbed," "learning disabled," or "deprived," when their problems in fact were reading, writing, or mathematics. Although it is recognized that students exist for whom these labels are appropriate, teachers should be cautioned that labels have been applied to students in a rather indiscriminate fashion and that an uncounted number of pupils have been misdiagnosed and misplaced. Such terms have little utility for the classroom teacher who must devise instructional techniques that are effective for individual students, especially those with mild to moderate problems.

In practice, an educational program must be prepared by a teacher in response to an individual student's educational needs and behaviors, not in response to a diagnostic label or definition the student may or may not satisfy. The nature of the program that is prepared will reflect in large part the teacher's (and the school's) philosophy and attitudes regarding a number of educational matters. We direct the remainder of this chapter to a delineation of these factors and to a discussion of the issues that relate to them.

We have found it helpful to organize our thinking about these educationally important factors in terms of an instructional model, which is presented in Figure 1–1. Although in practice the elements of the model are quite interrelated, for discussion purposes we have separated them arbitrarily into three basic parts: (1) the assumptions that influence instruction, (2) the components that are involved in instruction, and (3) the cycle that is used to implement instructional programs.

ASSUMPTIONS INFLUENCING INSTRUCTION

The program that the teacher elects for each student will necessarily reflect his or her assumptions and beliefs about the purpose of education, the nature of learning, and the role of the student, the teacher, and even society in the schooling process. These assumptions are rarely made explicit as far as teachers are concerned; yet they govern almost all the decisions that a teacher makes. These assumptions include the answers (implicit or explicit) to such questions as these: What are the schools for? What is this particular student supposed to get out of school? How is this student supposed to fit into society ultimately? What is the nature of the world and of the role of the student and the teacher within it? Let us briefly turn to this last question first.

A perusal of the many approaches to educating the student with learning and behavioral problems presented in this book will quickly lead the reader to the conclusion that the last question posed in the previous paragraph has not been answered. The various approaches are quite obviously based on differing, even inconsistent, assumptions about the nature of the world and of the student and the teacher within it. For example, among the approaches reviewed, one

Figure 1-1. Instructional Sequence Model

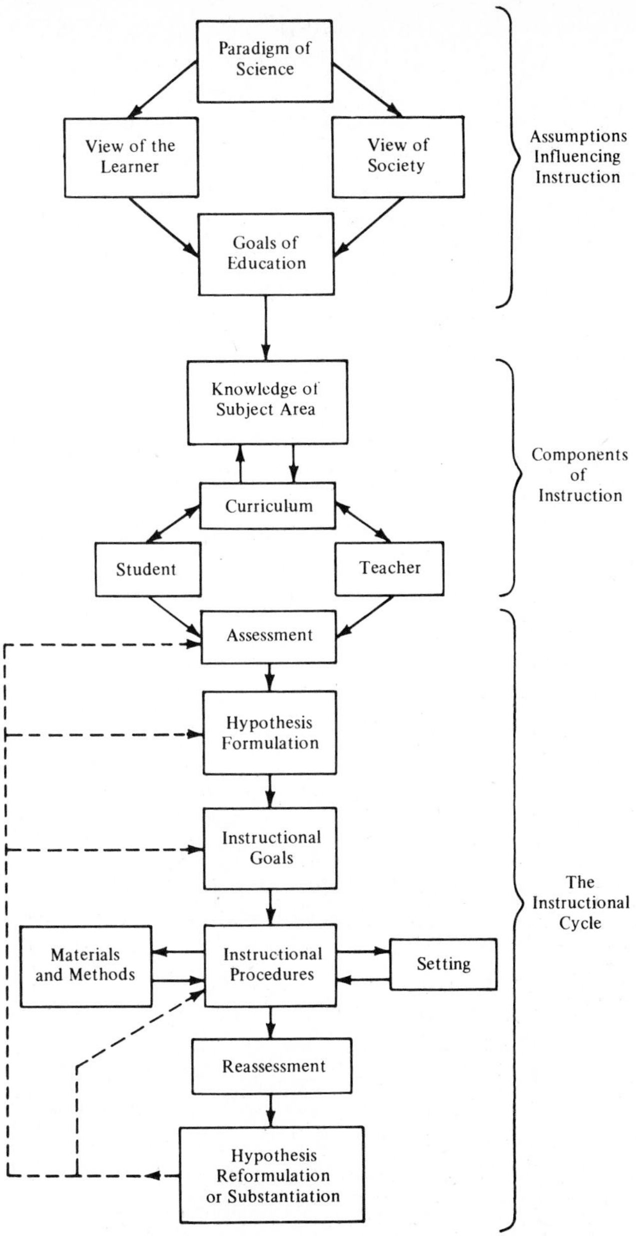

Source: Adapted from N. R. Bartel, D. N. Bryen, and H. W. Bartel, Approaches for alternative programming. In E. L. Meyen, G. A. Vergason, and R. J. Whelan (eds.), *Alternatives for Teaching Exceptional Children* (Denver, Colo.: Love Publications, 1975), p. 354.

will see evidence of a world view that is highly mechanistic and predictable. For such a perspective, the machine is the most appropriate metaphor. Here the student is seen as a relatively passive component in a setting that is arranged so that events (instructional happenings) impinge on him or her in such a way that fully predictable outcomes will come about. The teacher serves as the master technician who engineers the learning environment in such a way that the most desirable results will occur. The act of learning, then, is something that happens to the child as a result of the application of predetermined forces. It follows that the ideal curriculum for such a viewpoint is "teacher-proof." That is, the program is packaged in such a way pedagogically and substantively that the teacher cannot interfere with the learning process. Similarly, the program is designed so that the probabilities are great that the learner will emit the desired responses, and only the desired responses.

The contrasting position is that the essence of the world is not static and controllable, but on the contrary is in continuous transition from one state to another by means of progressive differentiation. This view leads one to think of students, even students with learning and behavioral problems, as active individuals who not only make predetermined "correct" responses, but also interact with, and change, their learning environment. Thus, learning is not merely the quantitative accumulation of objective facts but an active cognitive construction and transformation of reality.

That these issues have not been resolved in the education of students with learning problems is evident in the competing curricula. On the one hand, one sees widespread use of programmed materials, which promise precision, ease of measurement, and ready accountability. Clearly, the implicit assumption is that the curriculum developer has access to society's knowledge store and has arranged this knowledge in appropriate bits and sequences to which the learner need only be exposed following prescribed procedures. The behavior of both the teacher and the student is predictable. Seen from this orientation, the effective teacher is one who is able to move the learner quickly through the prescribed components of the curriculum with minimal obtrusion stemming from teacher or learner idiosyncracies.

On the other hand, the alternative world view is noted for its open-endedness and unpredictability. Here curriculum designers and implementers frequently follow some variation of the Piagetian notion of assimilation and accommodation. That is, they acknowledge that the learner is shaped repeatedly by the realities of the world and that he or she returns the favor by continuously moving to reshape those world realities. To them, education is not getting learners to make predictable responses, but seeing to it that they are progressively being changed by and changing their environment. Clearly, these underlying assumptions have major implications for the choices that a teacher makes in instructional planning and implementation.

COMPONENTS OF INSTRUCTION

The choices that the teacher must make are further complicated by additional decisions that must be made concerning the components of instruction. As can be seen in Figure 1–1, the teacher's job is to bring the student and the learning task into some kind of proximity with each other. However, even this seemingly simple responsibility turns out to be complicated.

It has long been taken for granted in educational circles that pupils and curricular materials cannot be randomly matched to each other. That is, if one is teaching social studies to a group of second-graders, one cannot simply walk down to the school library and pull any text from the social studies section of the shelves and assume that it will meet the learners' needs. There is general agreement that the teacher should consider such factors as the age of the children, their overall developmental level, and their interests in selecting materials. Conversely, just because a teacher is fond of a particular reading series or spelling book does not mean that it can be used effectively with the group of students being instructed.

This brings us to a most interesting question and one that will surface repeatedly throughout this book. Just what are the learner's characteristics that a teacher should take into account in selecting instructional materials? Conversely, just what are the curricular characteristics that a teacher must reckon with in determining their potential effectiveness with a student? A perusal of the educational research literature quickly leads one to conclude that each of an almost infinite array of characteristics—ranging from whether or not the student went through a creeping stage to whether the student's father lives in the home—has been thought by someone to be a significant variable that should be taken into account by the teacher. By no means does everyone agree on what to look for. Obviously, if the teacher is ever going to have any time to do any teaching, he or she must select from an almost endless range of pupil behaviors those that have sufficient implications for instruction to be worth noting and reporting.

The situation with respect to variability among curricular approaches is similar. Thus, to use an example from beginning reading, serious claims have been made that picture words, words using a unique alphabet, or words printed in different colors, to name a few, should be considered by the classroom teacher for teaching reading to certain students. Is the teacher to assume that letter-color aptitude, for example, is a significant student characteristic that should be measured and related to the use of color in the curriculum?

When one considers the possible permutations in the infinite range of potential student characteristics that could be measured and matched to an almost infinite range of curriculum characteristics, the problem becomes staggering indeed. This book represents an effort to reduce the teacher's task to more manageable proportions. We have tried to indicate the most promising aspects of the student's functioning to consider in instructional planning. We have drawn heavily from developmental psychology, particularly the work of Piaget, Bruner, and Gagné.

On the curriculum side, some observations are also in order. We note that curricula may be said to spread themselves on a continuum ranging from (a) wholistic, open-ended approaches that rely heavily on the student's ability to learn inductively and incidentally to (b) approaches that are narrow in focus—specific and prescribed. Since the question of appropriate curriculum is a derivative of the larger one of world view, it is not surprising that the curriculum question is also unresolved.

It is probably fair to say that many of the newer approaches that have been found to be most successful with students who have learning and behavioral problems are found at the prescriptive end of the scale, and the reader will find such approaches heavily represented in the chapters of this book. One could probably make a case that the boys and girls for whom this book is written are precisely those for whom the more widely used unstructured holistic educational approaches have been unsuccessful. That is, they are the youngsters who have failed to learn intuitively, inductively, and incidentally. The generalizations, concepts, cognitive structures, and facts that other students seem to pick up without any specific instruction have, for some reason, not been acquired by these students. It is for that reason that we have included throughout the book so many references to prescriptive teaching approaches. However, we caution the reader that no instructional system or program has been devised to date that can anticipate all the learning possibilities that occur in the classroom. No program can preplan every possible utterance or action of the teacher or pupil.

When using any of the many structured approaches described in the subsequent pages, teachers should watch for those unique teaching/learning interactions that cannot be fully planned in advance. Furthermore, we caution teachers against making the presumptions that the only significant learning is that which the teacher has decided on ahead of time and that everything that is important can be reduced to a paper-and-pencil test or lesson. The highly structured approaches have been at their best in teasing out the subelements of such complicated tasks as decoding words and sentences and arithmetic computation. They have been much less successful in helping teachers develop ways of teaching and measuring reading comprehension and arithmetic understanding. The problem that faces the classroom teacher, however, is that she or he cannot sit still, letting time go by, while the theoreticians and the experts decide whether, for example, the reading act is a unitary phenomenon or can be validly broken into subelements.

The seeming inability of many learners to master content that is presented in the traditional way has led to numerous efforts by educators to present the content in a different format or medium or in the same format but in different-sized chunks. This breaking down of a body of content into its component parts or steps has become known as "task analysis," "learning hierarchies," or the "diagnostic approach." In each instance, the specific step presented to the student is based on what he or she has previously mastered and is "tailored" in such a way that he or she has a high likelihood of mastering the task. Although the specifics of the procedures recommended by the various proponents of task analysis vary, several general commonalities characterize the approach. All advocates of task analysis recommend the differentiation of tasks into micro units or subordinate subskills or lower-level topics that the learner can master one step at a time. Only when the student has demonstrated success on one task is the next task in the hierarchy presented. The teacher does not have to undertake a complete task analysis for every bit of classroom instruction. Most curricular guides, if well organized and well differentiated, can be used as rough task analytic outlines. In fact, a good scope-and-sequence chart can serve many of the functions of a task analysis.

Having reviewed in some detail the assumptions influencing instruction and the components of instruction, we turn next to a consideration of the sequential nature of the instructional process itself.

THE INSTRUCTIONAL CYCLE (THE INDIVIDUALIZED EDUCATIONAL PLAN)

The various stages of the instructional cycle coincide to a great extent with what has become known as the Individualized Educational Plan (IEP). The IEP is a requirement of the federal Education of All Handicapped Children Act (P.L. 94–142), which mandates that every handicapped student must have an individually planned and implemented educational program. Although, legally speaking, the IEP is required only for handicapped students, we assert that it is equally appropriate for every student, handicapped or not, who has been singled out to receive special instruction or services. The elements of the IEP include the assessment of the student, the formulation of long-range goals and short-term objectives, a description of the proposed educational intervention with specification of type and duration of each aspect of instruction, and an evaluation of the effort. These elements are closely related to the steps specified in the instructional cycle of our model (Figure 1–1). Because the IEP will be required for all handicapped students, no matter what their educational setting, and because the IEP concept is implicit in subsequent chapters of this book, we offer the following as a general overview, which is adaptable to each of the subsequent chapter contents. Specific and abundant procedures for generating IEPs are available in the book *Developing Individualized Education Programs* (Fiscus and Mandell, 1983). Topics covered include referral/screening, goal setting, programmatic evaluation, and parent/teacher meetings; useful case histories are also provided.

Assessment

Before developing and implementing instructional plans for students, teachers must assemble a critical body of knowledge about each student's problem. This includes knowing the kind of problem manifested, the degree of its severity, the specific ability and subject matter strengths and weaknesses, the attitudes that the student has toward learning and self-worth, and the many other factors that may cause or contribute to the disability.

At one time or another, the teacher will need to know the answers to the following questions. These particular questions relate to reading, but similar ones can be formulated that pertain to writing, math, behavior, etc.

Does Susan read significantly below her peers?

At what level does she read?

After a semester of remedial reading, how much improvement did she make?

What is the average reading level of the students in her class or school?

Given her performance, does she qualify for placement in a special class?

Which of her particular skills are deficient?

Where should instruction begin?

What and how should she be taught?

To answer these and other equally important questions, teachers will have to interpret data drawn from many sources. Some information may help the teacher reach a diagnosis in terms of physical, emotional, social, and environmental conditions. Other information may help the teacher decide just what skills should be taught, the order of their presentation, and the best methods of instruction. In collecting this information, teachers will have to employ many diverse assessment techniques, to interpret results from several points of view, and to know when to use standardized or nonstandardized techniques.

Assessment Techniques

A variety of assessment techniques are available for teachers. Of these, the most frequently employed are testing, evaluating students' products, direct observation, interviewing, analytic teaching, and reviewing school records.

Testing. A test is any instrument or systematic procedure that measures a sample of behavior. Tests are used to answer the question "How well does the individual perform, either in comparison with others or in comparison with a domain of performance skills?" Tests include all teacher-made tests, checklists, and rating scales.

Product Evaluation. All procedures that are used to assess students' products are considered to be assessment tools. The products, such as speech and oral reading samples, essays, or math papers, can be checked for errors, rated on overall quality, or evaluated according to levels, with scope-and-sequence charts or developmental scales as guides.

Direct Observation. A considerable amount of useful information can be obtained from direct observation. Targeted students can be watched carefully in classrooms or at play and their behavior noted. Observation is a valuable tool when the teacher wants to verify the existence of behavioral problems.

Interviewing. The interview is actually a conversation that is directed to a definite purpose other than satisfaction in the conversation itself. Much useful information can be obtained from interviewing parents, teachers, age-mates, and the students themselves.

Analytic Teaching. Analytic teaching is accomplished through an ongoing process of teaching the student and evaluating his or her responses to dynamic instructional activities and tasks. Sometimes it is called prescriptive, diagnostic, or clinical teaching. For example, a teacher might use an analytic teaching procedure to assess the depth of John's knowledge about colors. To do this, the teacher must evaluate John's responses to a series of tasks that are specifically prepared to yield answers relating to the following questions.

1. Can John match the basic colors (place red chips together, blue chips together, and so forth)? If not, what colors does he have difficulty in matching?
2. If asked to point to the red chip, then to the blue chip, and so forth, can John select the correct chip from among others of different colors?
3. If the teacher points to the red chip, then to the blue chip, and so forth and says "What color is this?" does John answer correctly?

These three questions all relate to the general question of whether or not John can recognize colors, but they also provide different kinds of information about the level of his knowledge, the particular colors he does not know, and how to begin to teach him. First he learns to discriminate among the colors, then he learns the labels (receptive language), and finally he uses the labels in speech (expressive language).

Review of Records. In a complete evaluation, one must not forget to review the cumulative records in the school office. They are a good source of background information about the student and his or her progress through school.

Methods of Interpreting Assessment Information

Regardless of which techniques are used to obtain assessment data, their results can be interpreted from a norm-, criterion-, or non-referenced point of view.

Norm-Referencing. In norm-referenced interpretations, a student's performance is compared to some average made by people who comprise a normative (referent) group. The interpretation may be applied to the findings of highly standardized tests and reported quantitatively, as in the example "Bill's IQ is 85, indicating an intellectual performance of one standard deviation below the mean of the population that is his age."

In cases where statistically prepared norms are available, the results will be reported as percentiles, age/grade equivalents, standard scores, and quotients. All these normative statistics permit a person's performance to be described in terms of its discrepancy from the known average performance of people his or her age. This average is learned by administering the procedure to a large, representative referent sample, called the standardization population.

Norm-referenced interpretations can also be applied to assessment results derived from observation or other nontest procedures. Here, the examiner's experience serves as a substitute for statistically derived normative tables. Such interpretations appear to be relatively subjective, as in the example "Of all the kids her age I have ever known, she is without doubt the meanest." In short, norm-referenced interpretations deal with what a person does relative to other people and the criteria for the judgments are based on either statistical or experiential data.

Criterion-Referencing. In criterion-referenced interpretations, a student's performance is considered in terms of a particular domain of specified skills, and no reference is made to the relative performance of others. The interpretation can be reported quantitatively, as in the example "William can spell *carriage* 75 percent of the time in a test situation" or, simply, "Sally scored 20 points in the game and made the team." Criterion-referenced interpretation deals with what a person does without reference to the performance of others.

Nonreferencing. In nonreferenced interpretation, no attempt is made to relate results to either the performance of others or any particular skill domain. Instead nonreferenced interpretations are attempts to learn what strategies or systems students use to solve problems and reach answers. This type of interpretation leads to such statements as "James used the mnemonic device H-O-M-E-S to help recall the names of the Great Lakes" or "Because Mary tries to spell words just as she pronounces them, she misspells many words."

Standardized and Nonstandardized Techniques

Three elements comprise standardization: (1) set administration procedures, (2) objective scoring criteria, and (3) a specified preferred frame of reference for interpreting results. If these elements have been handled properly, a technique will pass the two "proofs" of adequate standardization; i.e., its results will demonstrate reliability and validity. Techniques that have adequate reliability and validity are called standardized (formal); techniques that do not have these qualities are called nonstandardized (informal).

The advantages of standardized procedures are obvious. If procedures are followed properly, they yield objective results. The degree to which the examiner can have confidence in the results is known and documented by reliability and validity research. Also, guidelines are provided for the proper interpretation of the results. Because of these advantages, standardized procedures are often required by law or school policy, especially where diagnosis and placement into special education programs are the purposes of the assessment.

The advantage of nonstandardize ' procedures lies in their flexibility. For example, their administration and scoring can be adapted to meet the special requirements of individual students; answers can be probed to learn more about the nature of a student's problem or knowledge; and they can be used to study areas for which standardized procedures are not available. However, the value of using such procedures is a function of the examiner's competence.

Assessment plays an important role in the education of problem learners, and considerable skill is required to assess students properly. Fortunately several comprehensive sources are available to those readers who desire more information on this topic. In particular, we recommend the books by Hammill (1987), McLoughlin and Lewis (1986), and Salvia and Ysseldyke (1985).

Long-Range Goals and Short-Term Objectives

Once the teacher has analyzed a student's performance and has identified those areas of functioning that need strengthening, goals and objectives for that student can be developed. As noted previously, the specific goals that are established will be heavily affected by the teacher's assumptions concerning the nature of the student and by his or her beliefs about the overall goals of education. Thus, the teacher who states in the IEP that a long-range goal is for the student to become familiar with certain classic English poems is manifesting a belief that the job of the schools is to transmit culture. Similarly, the teacher who states that a long-range goal is for the student to attain a fifth-grade reading comprehension level is expressing a belief that a purpose of education is to help the student develop functional adult competencies. A third type of goal might be even more open-ended, in that the student may be expected to become a more creative citizen or in some way to positively affect his or her environment.

Short-range objectives are also required in the IEP and should be derived from the long-range goals. Objectives serve an important communication function in that, if well expressed, they convey a picture of the behaviors the student will perform after instruction is completed. Several additional criteria characterize well-written objectives. For example, the desired behavior should be stated in terms that are objective and measurable. Furthermore, the conditions under which the student is supposed to perform should be described. Additional information about objectives that relate to the various areas of pupil performance are addressed in the chapters that follow.

Instructional Materials, Procedures, and Settings

Once the objectives have been specified, the teacher is faced with the task of selecting appropriate instructional materials and methods. In addition, an educational setting that enhances the student's likelihood of meeting the objectives must be selected. These two considerations are addressed next.

Materials and Procedures

The selection and implementation of the most effective materials for a given student is based directly on the observed abilities and problems that he or she manifests. For example, in the arithmetic area, a student's initial profile might appear as shown in Figure 1–2. The student's profile in this graph is interpreted to indicate that he or she is having a great deal of difficulty in multiplication (he or she has not yet been exposed to division), and a further weakness is apparent in his or her lack of understanding of place value.

The next task for the teacher is to explore further the student's trouble in multiplication and place value. To consider the multiplication example only, the teacher might probe as indicated in Figure 1–3. In the second level of this graph, immediately below the student's characteristics, is sketched the profile of a multiplication program that should be maximally effective with the student. Note, for example, that the program is very strong in presenting multiplication as an array of rows and columns (precisely where the student is weakest), pays little attention to multiplication as repeated addition (which he or she has already mastered), and emphasizes the role of zero and multiplying by multiples of ten (both areas in which he or she is very weak).

Figure 1–2. Graph of Arithmetic Ability

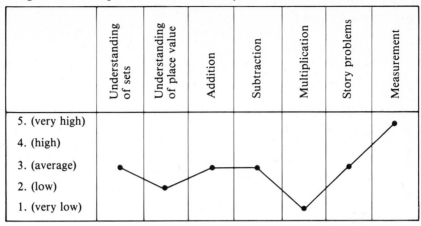

Figure 1–3. Graph of Multiplication Ability

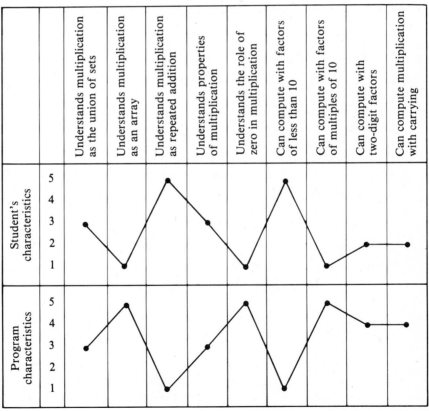

The teacher will not find ready-made programs for every profile of abilities and disabilities that might be discovered in the classroom. The teacher will have to adapt, modify, and improvise. Sometimes the two profiles—learner characteristics and program characteristics—will not fit well. In that case, it is still important for the teacher to sketch the interface, so that he or she will be cognizant of potential problems and be able to anticipate program failures. In some cases the teacher will be at a loss as to how to plan a program that fits a particular student's needs. In those cases, the teacher should plot the student's profile in the area of difficulty and consult with the nearest regional Instructional Materials Center and possibly acquire the appropriate materials there. A perusal of the many approaches suggested in the subsequent chapters of this book for arithmetic, reading, spelling, and writing should also provide ideas for the teacher who is faced with the difficult but crucial task of matching student variables to program variables.

The lengthy, time-consuming procedures spelled out here should not be used every time the teacher is faced with an instructional decision. However, we are aware that in every classroom there are certain students who have particular difficulty in given subject areas. With these students, previous efforts at remediation usually have yielded little improvement. Ultimately, the time spent in detailed diagnosis and planning is time well spent for these students, and the pinpointing of areas of difficulty is well worth the extra effort involved.

To some extent the selection of instructional materials reflects an individual teacher's subjective preferences in style, format, and response mode. However, an awareness of certain guidelines can facilitate intelligent curricular decision making. These guidelines have to do with three basic aspects involving material selection: design, method, and practicality.

Design. Curriculum design is concerned with the overall organization of the school experiences of a student. Specific questions that might be posed as questions of design are the following:

1. Is the material organized into subject areas such as reading, arithmetic, and social studies, or is it organized in terms of "experiences" or "units" that cut across traditional subjects? Which approach makes the most sense for the student under consideration?

2. If organized in terms of subject areas, is the material ordered in hierarchical, sequential steps? Are there sequences related to known facts in child development (e.g., the Piagetian stages of cognitive development)? Is the order of sequences logically related to such order as exists within the subject area itself (e.g., in arithmetic, multiplication should be taught before division because multiplication skills are required in the operations of division)? Ideally, instructional materials should incorpo-

rate both what is known about child development and what is known about the structure of the discipline itself.

3. What criterion is required for the student to proceed from one step to the next? Is mastery of a preceding task a prerequisite to going on to a subsequent task? Is some kind of prerequisite external "readiness score" required before entry into the program or before going on to new units? If so, do these readiness scores bear a manifest relationship to the material they are supposed to make the learner ready for? In general, the closer the readiness task is to the actual required skill, the more effectively it predicts success. For example, ability to walk a balance beam has much less "face validity" as a reading readiness predictor than, say, being able to distinguish d from b.

4. A further consideration underlying the design of materials has to do with its rationale. Is there implicit evidence that sound teaching and/or learning principles were involved? For example, have the authors and producers accounted for motivational factors? Is there any utilization of reinforcement (tangible rewards, social approval, or immediate feedback to the student)? Are basic skills incorporated as a basis for further learning? Is there any research evidence on soundness of the rationale (i.e., are there basic or applied studies supporting the approach)?

A well-designed program has clearly defined objectives for each program component. In any given lesson, the teacher should be able to state unequivocally what the purpose of the lesson is. How clear are the objectives for the materials under consideration? Are the objectives precise enough for the teacher to ascertain whether or not they have been reached? Are the objectives compatible with the learning experiences of the student in other subject areas (e.g., do they permit coordination between social studies and reading)?

Method. Questions of method are variations of the question "What do the teacher and the pupils have to do to successfully use the materials?" One set of these questions concerns the "who" of the instructional process. Can the students be instructed as one large group? If not, can provisions be made for occupying the other members of the class productively? Can the material be adapted for either a tutoring, small-group, or large-group situation? Must the teacher be actively involved in all phases of the instruction, or can the youngsters work on their own some or all of the time? To use the materials, what does the teacher have to do or say? Are the instructions too complicated? Is it physically possible for the teacher to do what is required (e.g., position figures on the flannelboard while reading verbatim instructions, and at the same time walk up and down the aisles to check each student's response)? Is there a balance between teacher-doing and pupil-doing, and between teacher-talk and pupil-talk? Are a variety of responses elicited from the pupils (e.g., oral and written responses, manipulation, painting, demonstrating)? Are several sensory modalities, either simply or in combination, involved? Is there undue penalty for a student who is deficient in one response (e.g., the student who cannot use his or her hands or has difficulty in oral expression)? Are the required responses related to the desired learning? For example, if the desired outcome is silent reading comprehension, is the student required to read silently and tested on mastery, or is he or she required to "word-call" orally?

Is the material sufficiently flexible to permit adaptions that facilitate learning? For example, can the student who has a sight problem still learn through listening and touch? Is there a way that students can serve as each other's tutors, to relieve pressure on the teacher? Can the material readily be broken into smaller steps or supplemented with other materials, for those students who have difficulty?

Can the material be individualized, both in terms of rate presentation and in terms of intensity? That is, can the rapid learner move through the material quickly and the slow learner more deliberately? Are there provisions for the student who is making virtually no incorrect responses to skip unnecessary examples or pages? Conversely, does the material incorporate an opportunity for the student who is making many errors to relearn the material, perhaps through a different format or presentation?

Is the material sufficiently flexible to allow switching to another approach if that should appear desirable? Some programs are so unique that switching to another is impractical because of the material's limited ability to generalize to other areas. For example, if a teacher decides to use a reading program with a unique orthography, he or she must be aware of the fact that this is a long-term decision and difficult to change. One cannot switch orthographies every few months without seriously hampering a student's growth in reading. Similarly, certain programmed programs in reading and arithmetic are so unique that there are really no alternatives to which the student can reasonably be switched if it becomes necessary to do so for reasons such as program failure.

Practicality.   Finally, there are some practical considerations that need to be taken into account in instructional material selection. First, how attractive is the material? Will a youngster want to use it because of its appeal, effective use of color, format, motivational devices, attractive visual arrangement, uniqueness, or variation in presentation? Are the materials practical and durable? Is the price reasonable? Are there any hazardous elements present? Can the material be used independently, or does it require close supervision? Is the quality of drawings or photographs adequate? Can the materials be brought out, used, and reassembled for storage in a reasonable length of time? Are the materials reusable, or must new kits, sets, or workbooks be purchased for each additional student? Is use of materials or the grading of the students' responses unnecessarily boring or laborious for the teacher?

The teacher will quickly find that no one program, no matter how excellent, will work with all students, and some programs will not work with any students. For this reason, a teacher needs to have access to many approaches, involving a variety of different formats, strategies, and modalities. Based on knowledge of the needs of a particular learner, the teacher can make intelligent decisions regarding the how, what, and when of instruction. This knowledge is particularly imperative, since few products have been widely tested before they are offered to the public. The materials are beautifully packaged, widely advertised, and sold in large quantities, usually long before there is evidence to support their value. Efficacy research follows the release of commercial materials by three to five years, if ever. Therefore, teachers almost always are required to use unvalidated programs. There exists no "consumer's report" for teachers, no book that can be consulted to point out shortcomings, limitations, or strengths of the various materials. It is strictly a "buyer, beware" market.

However, many of the teaching methods commonly used in the schools have existed for years, and a body of research has accumulated about many of them. The teacher, therefore, is well advised to undertake a library investigation of the particular method he or she wants to implement to see what success others have had with the program. *Educational Index*, *Dissertation Abstracts*, *Mental Retardation Abstracts*, and *Special Education Abstracts* are profitable initial sources of information. Many companies have assembled data on their programs and will provide it on request; of course, one should not expect to find anything critical from this source.

Use of a particular method should not necessarily be avoided because research on it does not exist. The teacher could use it on an experimental basis. For example, the teacher can test pupils in arithmetic, implement the unvalidated program for several months, and then retest the pupils to see if the program was indeed profitable. If the pupil performance could be compared to that of a control group, the results of the study would be made considerably more creditable.

Because of our recognition of the importance of instructional materials and methods to good educational practice, we have devoted a major part of each of the following chapters to descriptions of widely used programs, methods, and materials. Where information is available regarding the effectiveness of the approaches that are described, it too is presented. In addition, a lengthy section dealing specifically with selecting and analyzing methods has been included in the final chapter of this book.

The Educational Setting

Although this book does not purport to deal with the management difficulties of profoundly retarded, psychotic, autistic, aphasic, dyslexic, or severely sensory-impaired students, the techniques presented can be adapted to ameliorate the students' school-related problems. For these students, the instructional setting is likely to continue to be the special class or the large or small residential facility. Actually, the number of students for whom such placements are appropriate is quite small. The overwhelming majority of students who evidence problems are in need of remedial education designed to enable them to function in the regular class as soon as possible. There are several models that can be employed in the schools to provide pupils with needed services.

The Regular Classroom.   Most students who develop difficulties in school can be successfully managed by their regular teacher; their problems tend to be of a mild and easily corrected variety. The regular classroom is by far the most desirable setting for students to receive remedial help, and the classroom teacher is usually the best person to direct the remedial lessons. In this way, the learner remains with peers and does not have to suffer the indignity of leaving the room to obtain corrective help elsewhere. However, often the teacher-pupil ratio is too high, the teacher lacks the experience, or the pupil's problem is too obdurate to be ameliorated in the regular classroom setting. Alternatives must then be sought.

The Special Class.   Before 1950, the most frequently employed alternative for dealing with students with behavioral and/or educational problems was the self-contained special class. Many arguments set forth in defense of this placement are apparently reasonable. It is often argued that students placed in these classes receive the benefits of specially trained teachers, special materials and methods, smaller classes, and individualized instruction. In fact, this is rarely the case. Until recently, untrained teachers were the rule rather than the exception; although the class enrollments were smaller than in regular classes, there did not seem to be greater individualization of instruction; and the teachers seemed to use much the same approach toward classroom management and selection of materials that was used in the regular class.

Research indicates that students placed in special classes achieve in schoolwork no better than, and often not as well as, similar students left in the regular class. Findings regarding the effects of such placements on self-concept and adjustment are equivocal at the present time.

Special classes exist in assorted types and are restricted to students diagnosed as having a specific condition, such as mental retardation, emotional disturbances, or learning disability. For the most part, students placed in these settings are more similar to typical students than they are different from them. Although they may be poor readers or difficult to cope with, there is little justification for subjecting them to such a drastic measure as isolation from the regular class.

Because of the added stigma that inherently goes with placement in a self-contained class, the segregation from peers, and the doubtful benefits to be derived, this alternative should be used with considerable caution and viewed as a last resort. For readers who are interested in additional references concerning the use of the special class for handling children with learning or behavior problems, the work of Dunn (1968), Christopolos and Renz (1969), and Iano (1972) is strongly recommended.

The Special School. The special school for students with various learning problems is the natural extension of the self-contained class. Here the student not only is segregated from peers but also is removed from the regular school premises completely. The student may attend the special school and return home after classes or may be in residence at the school. The advantage of such a placement is the student's immersion in a total remedial program. In addition to the expense involved, the pro and con arguments are basically the same as those advanced regarding the special class. This placement should be viewed as a last possible alternative for students who cannot be accommodated in any other setting.

The Resource Room. The resource room is a promising alternative to self-contained facilities. This model permits the pupil to receive instruction individually or in groups in a special room outfitted for that purpose. The emphasis is on teaching needed specific skills. At the end of the lesson, the learner returns to the regular classroom and continues his or her education there. In this way, the student is based in the regular class with peers and leaves only for periods of time during the school day. There are several variations of the resource room model that deserve some mention.

1. *The categorical resource room.* Categorical resource rooms are operated in the same way as resource rooms; however, to qualify for placement, the pupil must satisfy a designated special education category or definition, such as retarded, disturbed, or learning disabled. Readers who are interested in implementing this variation of the resource room model are referred to the work of Glavin, Quay, Annesley, and Werry (1971) with emotionally disturbed children; of Sabatino (1971) with learning disabled children; and of Barksdale and Atkinson (1971) with mentally retarded children.

2. *The noncategorical resource room.* This variation is highly recommended. Students who are referred to the resource room are not labeled by category, and programs are designed for them on the basis of instructional, emotional, and behavioral need. Even "gifted" youngsters can be accommodated. In addition to the fact that the students involved remain in the regular classroom for most of the day, there are distinct advantages to this alternative. They include: (a) handicapped students do not have to be bused to the nearest school where there is an appropriate categorical class; (b) the number of students who can be seen daily is at least two-and-a-half times the number seen in the self-contained class; (c) the room serves all students in the school and is not limited to special-education-type students; and (d) the close communication between resource room and regular teacher allows for cooperative handling of the student and his or her problem. Readers interested in the dynamics of setting up a noncategorical resource room are referred to *The Resource Room: Rationale and Implementation* (Hammill and Wiederholt, 1972).

3. *The itinerant program.* The problems handled by the itinerant program may be either disability-based or noncategorical. The program is constructed around mobile resource rooms, and the teacher is not "housed" in any one school. Its advantage lies in its mobility, but it has serious limitations. They include the following: (a) since the teacher is not attached to a particular school, it is difficult for him or her to become fully accepted in any of the schools in which he or she operates; (b) much teacher time is spent in transit; and (c) transportation of materials is a chronic problem.

Readers who desire a comprehensive account of the operation of resource programs are referred to *The Resource Teacher: A Guide to Effective Practices* by Wiederholt, Hammill, and Brown (1983). In this volume, the authors describe in detail the types of resource programs that can be implemented in the schools; define the role of the resource teacher relative to assessment, instruction, and consultation; and outline the procedures to be followed in setting up a program. In addition, they review the kinds of teacher activities that help students improve in reading, math, spoken language, spelling, handwriting, written expression, and behavior.

Reassessment and Hypothesis Reformulation

In the instruction model (Figure 1–1), the last stage pertains to the evaluation of pupil progress and its use in reformulating educational goals and objectives and/or in revising instructional procedures. This activity is also an important part of the IEP. The program evaluation should be continual, occurring periodically throughout the year, and the findings should be incorporated immediately into instructional action by accelerating, attenuating, modifying, or even discontinuing the student's program. It should be clear to teachers and parents alike that maximum accountability can be derived only from an evaluation plan that provides ongoing feedback. It is not in the interests of the student to be evaluated only at the end of the year, when it is too late to do anything if objectives have not been met.

Naturally, the evaluation plan should be developed in such a way that it permits the answering of the question "Were the long-term goals and short-term objectives for this student actually achieved?" Because at the present time there exists no comprehensive test package that adequately tests students in all areas of functioning, the plan will have to have several dimensions, including the use of both standardized and informal assessment techniques. Also, direct observation of the student's performance may be used. If the objectives are precisely stated in such terms as "The student will be able to correctly read aloud the first ten words of the Dolch Sight List with 90 percent accuracy in three minutes," the objective itself becomes the evaluation plan. There should be little question as to whether or not the student has achieved this particular objective; it can be easily established by direct observation.

It should be clear that the various elements of our instructional model, and of the IEP as well, are interrelated and depend on one another for consistency and for effectiveness. Each aspect of the teaching-learning process directly affects, and is affected by, every other aspect. The cyclical, interrelated nature of the elements is implicit in the model.

chapter 2

Teaching Students Who Have Reading Problems

by Nettie R. Bartel

More time in the school day is devoted to the teaching of reading than to any other school subject. Yet more students are characterized as having reading problems than any other kind of school difficulty. "Why Johnny can't read" is a problem that has thus far eluded the best efforts of many individual teachers, concerned parents, local school districts, and even Presidential commissions.

One reason that so many different people want to ensure that students learn to read is that reading is involved in every school subject, especially those in the upper grades. It becomes increasingly difficult for students to be successful in any subject area if their reading problems are not remedied.

Furthermore, inadequate reading skill can eventually interfere significantly with an individual's capacity for economic independence and with his or her general knowledge of the world. Although much information is communicated nowadays through television, print remains the medium through which most persons seek and find jobs, read maps and other documents, and engage in certain recreational activities. For most people, printed materials provide the only access to information that is available around-the-clock to the user. The importance of reading continues to hold with the increasing availability of computers as an information source. Virtually all commercial and home uses of computers (with the exception of computer games) require print literacy as a basic user skill. Thus, individuals who cannot read will find themselves at an even greater disadvantage in our increasingly computerized society.

Almost every classroom teacher has encountered students who cannot or do not read. Some of these students appear limited in ability; others appear confused, reluctant, or resistant. Regardless of the nature of the problem, we take the position that virtually every student can learn to read if the difficulty is carefully diagnosed and an intervention is planned that is based on a firm understanding of what the reading act entails. This chapter was prepared to help teachers design and implement needed procedures.

The first section of this chapter deals with the nature of reading, giving emphasis to current theories, the role of comprehension, and the types of problems encountered in the school. The second section deals with assessment techniques recommended for determining the appropriate level of individuals, as well as specific areas of weakness in reading. The third section covers how to teach a student with a reading problem.

The information presented in this chapter should be regarded as a starting point. Teachers should take this initial information and, using their experiences, resources, and knowledge, continue to develop and refine materials to best suit the teaching situation. The teacher must be aware that unanticipated needs will arise that must be met. By careful planning and organization, the teacher can build a file of materials, both commercial and teacher-made, that will be readily available for use when the need arises. Just as students grow in reading skill, teachers must grow in their acquisition of the skills for teaching reading and in their knowledge of the subject.

THE NATURE OF READING

In order to attempt to improve reading skills of students, one must first understand what reading is. Such an understanding is not easily acquired, for there are many competing conceptions about the nature of reading. The nature of reading becomes a significant issue in that a teacher's ideas about it have direct implications for the kind of instruction in reading he or she will undertake. Three topics are dealt with in this section: current theories about reading, the developing emphasis on the role of comprehension in reading instruction, and the types of reading problems encountered in the schools.

Current Theories about Reading

The major competing positions on the nature of reading can be characterized as "bottom-up" models, "top-down" models, and interactive models that combine the features of both. In general, the models that have been characterized as bottom-up emphasize that reading begins with letters on a page—letters that the reader must distinguish and organize as words, sentences, and, finally, meaningful paragraphs. On the other hand, the top-down models emphasize that the act of reading begins not with letter or word recognition, but with the mind of the reader already set to hypothesize, sample, and predict about the nature of what he or she is about to read. Interactive models hold that an efficient reader moves back and forth, or simultaneously attends to both what's in his or her mind (predicting or hypothesizing) and what's on the page (attending to specific letters and words).

Why is it important for teachers to have a clear sense of the nature of reading? The absence of a theory of reading leaves teachers vulnerable to parents who demand a specific reading approach for their child or to publishers who aggressively promote particular reading materials. Lack of an understanding of the nature of reading leads teachers to religiously follow lessons in a basal reader without knowing why they are engaging in certain instructional procedures; worse still, it deprives them of a perspective from which the progress or lack of progress of a particular student can be viewed.

Historically, most reading approaches developed for problem readers have been from the bottom-up orientation. This is somewhat understandable, insofar as this orientation has lent itself more readily to the differentiation of decoding subskills—subskills that seem to be more easily taught than the global comprehension strategies that seem to be identified with the top-down model.

Our position is that an interactive model most adequately describes the reading process (Rumelhart, 1977; Samuels, 1981), particularly for the early stages of learning to read. As the learner becomes more proficient in reading, he or she can give increasing attention to comprehension and relatively less attention to scrutinizing individual letters and words. (See Figure 2–1 for a graphic example of how the beginning reader must switch back and forth between decoding and comprehending while the fluent reader can simultaneously attend to both, with the emphasis on comprehension.)

The identification of words is a constructive act in which the output is greater than, and different from, the input. That is, the reader does not merely "transcribe" the written word into spoken form, but brings something quite apart from the printed page to the word identification act. That "something" is his or her own knowledge, ideas, experiences, and hypotheses. A good reader uses semantic, syntactic, and visual cues to recognize words and sentences and to get the "sense" of the passage. Word identification is constructive and integrative, with the reader melding together bits of visual, syntactic, and context information to derive meaning. In the fluent reader, the process is enormously efficient; the reader uses just enough visual cues to "fill in," that is, to confirm or disconfirm the ideas that he or she is developing about the passage. Let us

Figure 2-1. A Developmental Model of Reading: Beginning stage shows attention alternating between decoding and comprehending. Fluent stage shows attention divided between decoding and comprehending, with both processes occurring simultaneously. The thin line indicates that just a small portion of attentional resources is allocated to decoding; the thick line indicates that a major portion of attentional resources is on comprehension.

Beginning stage: Decoding (alternating attention)

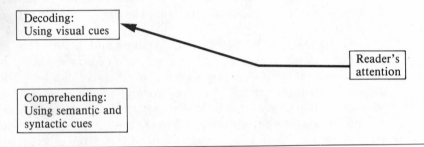

Beginning stage: Comprehending (alternating attention)

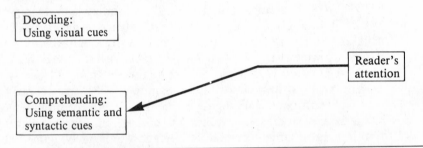

Fluent stage: Simultaneous attention

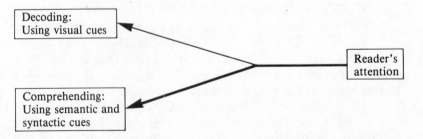

Source: Adapted from Samuels, 1981, p. 16.

take a hypothetical example to see how a reader uses visual, semantic, and syntactic cues. Let us suppose that a second-grader, Tommy, is confronted with the following paragraph to read:

Little Fox and His Friends

Once there was a little fox who didn't like the dark. One morning, before the sun came up, Little Fox woke up all alone. His mother had gone hunting in the forest.

Simply by reading, or by being told what the story is about, Tommy can develop some expectancies about the content. He can, for example, expect to read about other animals. He can expect that the story will have words that refer to life in the forest. Particularly, if the teacher introduces the store carefully, using a directed reading activity format, the child will have some questions, expectancies, or hypotheses cued for him.

Tommy also has other information available to him. By second grade, he has had a lot of experience with his language (presumably English). This experience can help him as he begins to read the paragraph. If he has been exposed to stories such as fairy tales, he will know that the word right after the first word "Once" will probably be "upon" (for "Once upon a time . . .") or "there" (for "Once there was . . ."). Now, although the word "there" in isolation is frequently difficult for second-graders, the cognitively and linguistically active child can be enormously helped in the reading task by, in this case, his prior knowledge of the way stories often begin and by his knowledge of the syntax of the English language.

The next word that may give Tommy difficulty is "didn't." The main cues that he can use here are syntactic and visual. By the second grade, Tommy's knowledge of English is such that he knows when he hears a sentence such as "Once there was a fox who . . ." that the next word will tell something about what the fox did or did not do. This knowledge, coupled with his understanding of the acoustic sound of /d/, the initial letter, may provide enough information for him to "guess" or "hypothesize" the correct word. If he guesses correctly, without too long a hesitation to break his train of thought, the next word, "like," will probably be easy for him. If he had to pause to ponder over "didn't," "like" will be more difficult, because he does not have the string of words "Once there was a little fox who didn't . . ." to help him figure out "like." We could continue our hypothetical analysis, showing how a wrong guess slows the child down and interferes with the cues of meaning and syntax.

According to K. S. Goodman (1976), the best readers are those who can "guess" correctly most of the time, with a minimum use of cues. F. Smith (1971) has shown the significance of interaction and balance among the various types of cues—context, syntax, and visual. Smith makes the point that there are a very large number of cues potentially available to the reader—if he or she had to use all of them, the reading act would be very slow indeed. However, since the cues are so redundant, the good reader selects and uses only a few. The effective use of context cues or of syntactic cues takes some of the interpretative load off the graphic cues so that even if the beginning reader is not completely sure of all the distinctive features of a given letter or word, he or she needs only a little extra help to figure out the word. If the reader is uncertain, however, about each of the areas that could potentially help—context or semantics, syntax, and graphic—he or she will slow down in the reading; and because of normal memory limitations, semantic and syntactic cues will fade rapidly. Although it is true that semantic and syntactic information can help with the visual, it is also true that unless some visual cues are interpretable by the student, the semantic and syntactical help will quickly be lost.

Little imagination is needed to see the potential reading problems that would be encountered by a student who was unfamiliar with the distinguishing features of the letters of the alphabet and who also was unsure of the content that he or she was supposed to read. When this situation is compounded with unfamiliarity with standard English syntax, as is the case with many students growing up in the inner cities of our nation, it is easy to see why so many students have reading problems. Such learners are indeed triply handicapped, in that they cannot "trade" one type of information—semantic, syntactic, or graphic—for another, the way proficient readers do. It is ironic, indeed, that the process that will ultimately make it possible for the student to gain a knowledge of the world—reading—is in its initial stages itself heavily dependent on such knowledge.

Teachers who are not sure about the need to provide additional informational "prompting" for beginning readers are urged to consider their own reading behavior when confronted with reading material that is unfamiliar and perhaps highly technical. In such a situation, all of us slow down in rate; we go back over the material; we skip over words, hoping we can make some sense out of them on the basis of the rest of the passage. One way or another we try to narrow down what the author is saying, to answer the questions in our minds. As F. Smith (1971) put it: "All information acquisition in reading, from the identification of individual letters or words to the comprehension of entire passages, can be regarded as the reduction of uncertainty" [p. 12].

A number of individuals have attempted to schematically portray the act of reading and its relationship to cognitive structure and to language processes (e.g., Carroll, 1978; K. S. Goodman, 1976; Ruddell, 1976; Rumelhart, 1977; J. Williams, 1977), but such efforts have not accounted for all the variables involved in reading. Doehring and Aulls (1979) suggest that cognitive and language skills, motivation and cultural backgrounds, level of reading skill acquisition, reading strategy, the influence of instruction, and the properties of the text should all be considered. It may be the case, as they suggest, that different variables are operative during the successive stages of learning to read, as indicated in Table 2–1. In addition to these variables, recent research (e.g., Mosenthal and Na, 1980) suggests that classroom environment is a factor that affects children's reading behavior.

Today virtually no reading authorities seriously contend that the reading act is passive, rather than active (J. P. Williams, 1973). There is apparent consistency in adherence to the position that reading is a complex cognitive skill, the goal of which is obtaining information. However, if one examines textbooks on the teaching of reading, one finds that much more space is devoted to topics such as "phoneme-grapheme correspondence" than to consideration of the teaching of complex information processing and comprehension skills. The methodology of teaching reading has simply not kept up with the changing viewpoint concerning the cognitive, constructive aspects of the reading act. This chapter is evidence of that very point. Currently, there are many more ways available to the teacher who wishes to assess a student's word-attack skills than there are to the teacher who is interested in measuring a student's comprehension skills in anything other than the grossest fashion. The typical scope-and-sequence chart accompanying many reading series invariably shows much greater differentiation of the "decoding" skills as opposed to the "understanding" skills. The scope-and-sequence chart shown as Table 2–11, which is

Table 2–1. Variables That Interact During Reading Acquisition

Stage of Acquisition	Variables
Pre-Reading	Language Skills Cognitive Skills Cultural Variables
Stage 1 Beginning Reading	Text (including language structure) Reading Skills Language Skills
Stage 2 Transitional Reading	Cognitive Skills Instruction Motivation Cultural Variables
Stage 3 Proficient Reading	Text Reading Skills Cognitive Skills Motivation Cultural Variables

Source: Reprinted with permission of National Reading Conference, Inc. from D. G. Doehring and M. W. Aulls, The interactive nature of reading acquisition, *Journal of Reading Behavior*, 1979, *11*, 27–40.

adapted from a well-known text on reading and learning disabilities (Kaluger and Kolson, 1978), exemplifies this point very well. Several taxonomies of comprehension skills are available (an excellent one is presented in the next section), but there are few published accounts on how to translate these aspects of comprehension into teaching procedures.

The Developing Emphasis on the Role of Comprehension in Reading

The simple view of the reading process that was fashionable in some circles in the 1960s and that underlies a number of reading programs has a good deal of initial appeal. Teaching only observable, easily measured reading skills makes it easy to specify precisely what the student can and cannot do. Objectives can be clearly stated, and it can be determined whether they have or have not been met. Such a clearly defined, observable, and easily measured set of skills is clearly appealing to the teacher of a student who has a reading problem. Unfortunately, there is much more to the reading act than learning to say "cat" when presented with the letters c-a-t. Accordingly, it is to comprehension that we turn next.

In recent years, published materials have expanded to include many different aspects of comprehension. This represents a welcome shift from the previous lack of attention to teaching comprehension skills. Most of the new materials regard comprehension as a set of differentiated skills.

There are at least three broad areas of comprehension:

1. Literal—understanding the primary, direct (literal) meaning of words, sentences, or passages.
2. Inferential—understanding the deeper meanings that are not literally stated in the passage.
3. Critical—passing judgment on the quality, worth, accuracy, and truth of the passage.

Barrett has differentiated comprehension skills even further in *Taxonomy of Cognitive and Affective Dimensions of Reading Comprehension* (see Clymer, 1968). The basic, paraphrased outline of the taxonomy follows.

1.0. *Literal comprehension.* Literal comprehension focuses on ideas and information that are explicitly stated in the selection.
1.1. *Recognition* requires the student to locate or identify ideas or information explicitly stated in the reading selection.
  1.11. Recognition of details
  1.12. Recognition of main ideas

1.13. Recognition of a sequence
1.14. Recognition of comparisons
1.15. Recognition of cause-and-effect relationship
1.16. Recognition of character traits

1.2. *Recall of details.* Recall requires the student to produce from memory ideas and information explicitly stated in the reading selection.
1.21. Recall of details
1.22. Recall of main ideas
1.23. Recall of a sequence
1.24. Recall of comparisons
1.25. Recall of cause-and-effect relationship
1.26. Recall of character traits

2.0. *Reorganization.* Reorganization requires the student to analyze, synthesize, and/or organize ideas or information explicitly stated in the selection.
2.1. Classifying
2.2. Outlining
2.3. Summarizing
2.4. Synthesizing

3.0. *Inferential comprehension.* Inferential comprehension is demonstrated by the student when he or she uses the ideas and information explicitly stated in the selection, intuition, and personal experiences as a basis for conjectures and hypotheses.
3.1. Inferring supporting details
3.2. Inferring main ideas
3.3. Inferring sequence
3.4. Inferring comparisons
3.5. Inferring cause-and-effect relationships
3.6. Inferring character traits
3.7. Predicting outcomes
3.8. Interpreting figurative language

4.0. *Evaluation.* The purposes for reading and teacher's questions, in this instance, are responses by the student that indicate that he or she has made an evaluative judgment by comparing ideas presented in the selection with external criteria provided by the teacher or other sources or with internal criteria provided by the student.
4.1. Judgment of reality or fantasy
4.2. Judgment of fact or opinion
4.3. Judgment of adequacy and validity
4.4. Judgment of appropriateness
4.5. Judgment of worth, desirability, and acceptability

5.0. *Appreciation.* Appreciation involves all the previously cited cognitive dimensions of reading, for it deals with the psychological and aesthetic impact of the selection on the reader.
5.1. Emotional response to the content
5.2. Identification with characters or incidents
5.3. Reaction to the author's use of language
5.4. Imagery

This taxonomy gives some idea of the complexity of reading comprehension. Because of the integral nature of comprehension in the reading act, a subsequent section of this chapter will deal specifically with how to teach it more effectively. Before reading instruction can take place, however, the teacher needs to know the nature of reading difficulty that a given student may have. Accordingly, we next look at types of reading problems.

Types of Reading Problems

Ideally, students read at a level commensurate with their mental age, *not* their chronological age or grade placement. Unfortunately, many students for one reason or another do not read at their mental age level. Students with reading problems are often labeled as "developmental," "corrective," "retarded," or "remedial." Sometimes more complicated and threatening labels are attached—"strephosymbolic," "dyslexic," "brain injured," and so on. The list could go on *ad nauseum*. It should be pointed out that these words have no precise (i.e., no generally accepted) meaning among professionals working in the field. For example, "developmental" may refer to a class (or to a student) taught using regular class methods; sometimes the use of the term is limited to students who are performing at a level commensurate with their ability; sometimes it is used with students who are working far behind their expectancy but are still being taught by regular class methods. A "corrective" class may be one in which the students are functioning below expectancy but do not appear to have any associated learning problems (brain damage, specific learning disabilities, etc.); "corrective" may also refer to any student who is one to two years behind expectancy regardless of the presence or absence of any associated learning problems. To some professionals, "remedial" students have associated learning problems; to others, the term is applied to all students who are more than two years behind expectancy in reading. Because of this confusion, we rarely use any of these terms; but if these terms are used in schools for any purpose, we do recommend that teachers become familiar with their local definitions.

Although teachers should be familiar with these medical and psychological terms, and the conditions they represent, they should keep in mind that knowledge of the terms or the conditions is not particularly helpful in teaching the student to read. In fact, most of the reading problems found in the classrooms are not of a highly clinical nature; rather, they have a relatively obvious cause.

The types of reading problems that a teacher identifies will be related to the view that the teacher holds about the nature of reading. If the teacher believes that reading consists of saying the word "look" in response to seeing the letters l-o-o-k, and nothing more, he or she will not identify as a problem the fact that the child may not understand what it means to "look."

Our interactive view of the nature of reading leads us to identify the reading problems listed in Table 2–2. Obviously, not every poor reader will exhibit *all* of the problems.

Some students may experience temporary lags in reading development due to external causes and a few may have serious word-learning problems. A stu-

Table 2–2.   Comparison Between Good and Poor Readers

What the Good Reader Does	*What the Poor Reader May Do*
Notes the distinctive features in letters and words	Fails to notice distinctions between b and d, or was and saw, or m and n, or the configuration of other letters and words; focuses only on certain characteristics, e.g., beginnings of words
Predicts the endings of words (e.g., "righ?"), phrases (e.g., "once upon a _____ "), or sentences (e.g., "the fire _____ed") with feasible hypothesis	Cannot predict reasonable or possible endings of words, phrases, or sentences
Expects what he or she reads to make sense in terms of his or her own background	Fails to relate reading content to his or her own background
Reads to identify meaning rather than to identify letters or words	Reads to identify individual letters or individual words, or reads because he or she has to
Shifts speed and approach to the type and purpose of reading	Approaches all reading tasks the same way
Formulates hypotheses or expectations about the way the passage will develop an idea	Cannot/does not develop expectations or predictions concerning the direction or main idea of a passage
Takes advantage of the graphic, syntactic, and semantic cues in a passage to speed reading and improve comprehension	Becomes bogged down in attempting to decipher the passage on a letter-by-letter or word-by-word basis

Source: Portions of this table are adapted from C. R. Cooper and A. R. Petrosky, A psycholinguistic view of the fluent reading process, *Journal of Reading*, 1976, 20, 184–207.

dent may fall behind in reading due to an extended absence from school, a temporary failure in vision (which can be corrected by appropriately prescribed glasses), a temporary failure in hearing (for example, a tonsillectomy sometimes causes a temporary loss of hearing), a constant change in schools, a radical change in the reading program (from a basal approach to an augmental alphabet approach such as i/t/a), or poor teaching. In such cases, nothing is wrong with the student's central nervous system; the student is not mentally retarded, nor is he or she emotionally disturbed. If appropriate steps are taken through the careful assessment of the student's needs and proper instruction is provided, the difficulty can usually be overcome by using appropriate materials designed for the student's instructional level. Most of these problems can be handled in the ongoing classroom situation.

A few students evidence severe reading problems and experience great difficulty in attaching meaning to word or wordlike symbols when taught by the usual visual-auditory techniques. Often these students need specialized word-learning techniques similar to those presented in the section of this chapter titled Examples of Specific Remedial Techniques in Reading.

ASSESSING READING PROBLEMS

In order to effectively teach a student with reading problems, a teacher needs to learn more about the student's strengths and weaknesses in reading. First of all, the teacher needs to obtain a general picture of the student's overall level of reading performance. Then, additional assessment must be done to explore the nature of the student's difficulties. A number of useful techniques are available for obtaining this information, many of which are described in this section. Their use by teachers will result in a precise picture of the level and nature of a student's reading performance.

A discussion of assessment must be introduced with a word of caution. Overtesting can be as undesirable as no testing at all. A full clinical evaluation of a student's reading problems may take as long as two days to complete. Yet very few students need this kind of detailed work. A few teachers who have been exposed to some formal training in the evaluation of reading, as in a graduate course, may become overzealous and feel that every student needs to be given an informal reading inventory, an interest inventory, an attitude scale, an associative learning test, a test of memory span, and so on. Actually, all this testing can consume too many hours that could better be devoted to instruction. A good rule to follow is to test minimally to find out where to initiate instruction and to identify areas of strength and weakness. Then, through analytic or clinical teaching, the teacher can continue to uncover the student's needs and to meet them with appropriate instruction as they arise.

Establishing a Reading Level

Teachers often need to estimate quickly the reading level of a particular student or class of students. Two popular ways of doing this involve the use of informal oral reading and informal reading inventories.

Informal Oral Reading

Although today "round robin" reading is generally condemned as a teaching method, the procedure does enable the teacher to quickly identify those students who need immediate attention. Each student is asked to read a short passage from a book to determine whether he or she can pronounce the words successfully. If the student has trouble with more than five running words out of every hundred, reads in a word-by-word manner, reads too slowly, or exhibits other difficulties, it is likely that the material is too difficult.

The oral reading should be carried out in a nonthreatening manner and the teacher should note the more severe cases of reading failure without drawing embarrassing attention to the reader. The teacher can accomplish this in a small-group situation by prefacing the lesson by saying, "This is a new reading book; this morning I want to find out if it is the right book for this group." If this approach is not deemed advisable, then the teacher can call on each student to read on an individual basis while the rest of the group is engaged in some other activity. In cases where this approach does not give enough information to establish an individual's reading level, an informal reading inventory may be administered.

Informal Reading Inventory

A complete, informal reading inventory (IRI) is usually regarded as a clinical instrument used by reading specialists, but on occasion a teacher may want to use it. Readers who desire a detailed description of these procedures are referred to the discussion of informal inventories by Johnson and Kress (1969). Although informal reading inventories are too time-consuming for classroom administration, they can provide precise and valuable information about an individual student's reading difficulty. In the event that a teacher desires a detailed evaluation, he or she should probably request that an informal reading inventory be administered by the reading specialist. Botel (1966), Newcomer (1986), Silvaroli (1973), and Sucher and Allred (1971) have developed informal reading inventories that are available commercially.

Initially a student is given a word-recognition test beginning at the preprimer level. The student is given tests until he or she misses 50 percent of the words on the flash presentation on two successive levels. Starting with the last level at which the student received 100 percent on the flash presentation in the

Table 2–3. Criteria for Various Levels

Level	Word Recognition in Context (percent)	Comprehension (percent)	Observable Behavior
Independent	99	90	No signs of frustration or tension
Instructional	95	75	No signs of frustration or tension
Frustrational	Below 90	Below 50	Signs of frustration and/or tension
Hearing capacity		75	

word-recognition test, the student reads two selections (one oral and one silent) at each level and answers questions concerning each selection. When he or she falls below 90 percent in word recognition, below 50 percent in comprehension (average of oral and silent selection), or is qualitatively frustrated, the child stops reading. Then the examiner reads aloud one selection at each level until the child is unable to answer 50 percent of the questions asked about the material. Levels for word recognition in context and comprehension are computed for each level using the generally accepted criteria shown in Table 2–3.

Of the commercially available inventories, the one by Newcomer (1986), *The Standardized Reading Inventory,* is unique. Unlike other authors, Newcomer has given her test a creditable statistical base by providing research evidence of its reliability and validity. In addition, she has conformed the inventory to the leading basal reading series used in the schools today. Thus, the independent, instructional, and frustrational reading levels that are identified by giving the test roughly correspond to similar levels in the teaching series, making it possible for the teacher to move directly from assessment results to appropriate instructional levels in a particular basal series.

Measuring Attitudes Toward Reading

If the student's attitude toward reading is not a positive one, the teacher may want to explore this area further. Several instruments for measuring attitudes toward reading are available, among them a student self-report inventory (Estes, Estes, Richards, and Roettger, 1981), a paired-activities attitude scale (Gurney, 1966), and an observational checklist (Powell, 1972). Tests of attitudes toward reading should be used in conjunction with other indicators of attitude toward school in general. Paper-and-pencil tests alone sometimes reveal more about what the child thinks the teacher wants him or her to say than about the "true" attitude toward reading (Vaughn, 1980).

Analyzing Specific Reading Skills

A number of strategies are available to the teacher who wishes to probe specific skill levels in reading. Three of these will be described in this section. First, the use of standardized, norm-referenced tests will be discussed because they provide a quick objective way of documenting competence in a wide variety of reading skills, including vocabulary and passage comprehension, word recognition, phonics, alphabet knowledge, and oral reading rate. The discussion next turns to teacher-made word-recognition tests and then to teacher-made reading comprehension tests. A fourth approach, analysis of oral reading miscues, is treated separately in a subsequent section because of its special relationship to comprehension.

Standardized Norm-Referenced Reading Tests

A number of commercially prepared standardized norm-referenced reading tests are available. All of them assist the teacher in identifying difficulties in word-attack; most of them also assess comprehension problems. The best known of these tests are summarized in Table 2–4. All of the listed tests are intended for individual administration.

Teacher-Made Word-Recognition Tests

In general, word-recognition tests serve three purposes. First, they serve as an indication of a student's sight vocabulary; second, they give clues to the word-attack skills that the student uses to work out unfamiliar words; and third, they give some indication of where to initiate reading instruction with the child. The words for the following sample lists have been taken from basal reader glossaries, the Durrell List, the Thorndike List, and other word lists. Word-recognition tests are easily constructed and administered. It must be remembered that they only measure a student's sight vocabulary and word-attack skills. This kind of test does not measure meaning or comprehension. Therefore, word-recognition tests, if used alone, may place the student above his or her true instructional level. This is because many students can "read" a passage glibly and then not be able to recall the most obvious literal information included in the text. "Oh, I read it; I didn't know that I was supposed to remember anything," has been said by more than one student to a puzzled teacher who cannot understand how a child can word-call so well but not understand or retain any of the thoughts expressed in the passage.

A number of commercially prepared word-recognition lists are available. Some of these are arranged by difficulty level by grade (e.g., LaPray and Ross,

Table 2–4. Standardized Norm-Referenced Reading Tests

Test (and Publisher)	Grade Levels	What the Test Measures
Diagnostic Reading Scale (CTB/McGraw-Hill)	1–8	Word recognition, phonics, reading comprehension
Durrell Analysis of Reading Difficulty (Psychological Corporation)	1–6	Word and letter recognition, blending, spelling, listening, and recall
Formal Reading Inventory (Pro-Ed)	1–12	Silent reading comprehension and oral reading miscues
Gates-McKillop-Horowitz Reading Diagnostic Tests (Teachers College Press)	1–6	Oral reading, word and phrase perception, syllabication, letter names and sounds, blending
Gray Oral Reading Test (Pro-Ed)	1–Adult	Oral reading rate, accuracy and comprehension
Stanford Diagnostic Reading Test (Psychological Corporation)	1–Adult	Vocabulary, auditory discrimination, phonics, syllabication, comprehension
Test of Early Reading Ability (Pro-Ed)	Pre–2	Alphabet knowledge; comprehension; conventions of print
Test of Reading Comprehension (Pro-Ed)	2–12	Vocabulary, paragraph comprehension; syntactic reading. Supplemental tests of "school language" and vocabularies of science, social studies, and math
Woodcock Reading Mastery Tests (American Guidance Services)	K–12	Word identification, attack, and comprehension; also passage comprehension

Pre = preschool; K = kindergarten.

1969); others are compilations of words most typically found in basal readers (e.g., D. D. Johnson, 1971). Teachers may also develop their own lists of words from the reading materials that they are using. Usually twenty to twenty-five words from the word lists or glossaries found in most basal readers are used. The words can be chosen at random or by dividing the total number of words by 20 or 25 and taking every nth word; for example, if there are 375 words in the word list, divide 375 by 25. Since the answer is 15, take every fifteenth word from the list. This can later be refined to measure a number of phonic skills. (Do not overload the list with compound words or words of two syllables or have a large group of words at any one level that follows the same phonic or structural pattern.)

The words can be printed on oaktag in individual lists. The lists can be presented in a number of ways. The words can be read orally from the list by the student. The words can be flashed by using two 3-by-5-inch index cards, or a slot can be cut in an index card wide enough to show one word at a time. The flash technique quickly exposes each word, but requires some practice on the part of the person presenting it. To flash a word, the teacher holds the two index cards together immediately above the first word on the list. The lower card is moved down to expose the word and the upper card is moved down to close the opening between them. The complete series of motions is carried out quickly with about a one-second exposure, and the student sees the word only briefly. If the student responds correctly on the flash presentation, the examiner goes on to the next word. If, however, the student gives an incorrect response, the process is repeated untimed, and the word is reexposed. No cues are given, but the student has an opportunity to reexamine the word and apply whatever analysis skills he or she has learned to help deduce the word. By carefully recording the student's responses in this untimed presentation, the teacher can get some idea of the student's word-attack skills as a basis for further instruction. Betts (1956) recommends that a child should achieve a flash score of approximately 95 percent at a given reading level before continuing to the next level.

Figure 2–2 provides an example of a teacher-constructed word-recognition test for a third-grade student. In this case, the word-recognition test shows that the student, when given sufficient time, does have the ability to do some word analysis. However, it is apparent that the student will need additional work with the "r" blends (stranger, branches), the digraph "ch" (branches, which), and suffixes in general.

By carefully recording the student's responses, the teacher can assess weaknesses in word-attack skills. Of course, *every* error should not be treated as a significant problem. However, when the student has been administered several levels, patterns usually emerge. For example, if a fifth- or sixth-grader misses many words at the preprimer levels, he or she probably has not established a basic sight vocabulary. At levels beyond this, the student may miss initial consonants, final consonants, endings, or make other errors. A list of some of the common word-attack errors is given in Table 2–5.

Teacher-Made Reading Comprehension Tests

After estimating an appropriate instructional level for word recognition, the teacher may want to determine the student's reading-in-context and comprehension skills. The directions for developing an informal test to tap these areas are presented in some detail in the following outline. The teacher should use personal judgment in deciding how much of this test to administer. For some

Figure 2–2. Word Recognition—Flash/Untimed

Stimulus Word (Third-Grade Level)	Flash	Untimed
1. another		
2. places	✓	
3. helpful		
4. thousand		
5. wishes	✓	✓
6. supper	super	
7. November		
8. stranger	✓	✓
9. branches	✓	✓
10. between		
11. decided		
12. quickly	✓	✓
13. haunted	✓	✓
14. mystery		
15. which	✓	✓
16. understand		
17. picture		
18. first	✓	fr...
19. clothes		
20. Monday		

Code: Blank denotes correct response,
    check denotes no response,
    words or letters denote incorrect attempt.

Name of Child _Betsy Fisher_ Date _1/10/85_ Class _3_

Table 2–5. Common Word-Attack Errors

Problem	Example	
	Text Says	Student Reads
1. Omission of letters in a word	grown	gown
	furniture	funiture
2. Insertion of letters into a word	sight	slight
	chimney	chimaney
3. Substitution of consonants in a word (initial, medial, final)	nice	mice
	fright	flight
	lad	lab
4. Substitution of medial vowels	hat	hot
	dog	dug
5. Reversal of letters in a word	saw	was
	there	three
6. Addition of endings	sheep	sheeps
	gave	gaved
7. Omission of endings	friends	friend
	bark	bar
8. Syllable omission	visiting	visting
	trying	trine

students, only one or two levels will have to be administered to ascertain whether the student's comprehension level is equal to his or her skills in word recognition. In other cases, the teacher may desire a more comprehensive probe of the student's skills.

1. Selection of a standard basal series
    a. Choose any series that goes from preprimer to the sixth level.
    b. Select materials that the child has not previously used.
2. Selection of passages from the basal reader
    a. Choose a selection that makes a complete story.
    b. Choose selections of about 50 words at the preprimer level; 100 words at the primer, first, and second levels; and 100–150 words at the upper levels.
    c. Choose two selections at each level: plan to use one for oral reading and one for silent reading, and take the selections from the middle of the book.
3. Construction of questions
    a. Build five questions for each selection at the preprimer level; six questions for each selection at primer, first, and second levels; and ten questions for each selection at level three and above.

    b. Avoid "yes" and "no" questions.

    c. Include vocabulary in the questions that is at the same level as vocabulary in the selection.

    d. Construct three kinds of questions at each level in about the following percentages: factual, 40 percent; inferential, 40 percent; vocabulary, 20 percent.

4. Construction and preparation of test

    a. Cut and mount the selections on oaktag; *or*

    b. Note the pages in the book, put the questions on separate cards, and have the student read the selection from the text itself.

Since the student's word-recognition level would have been determined by one of the previously mentioned word-recognition tests, the teacher can begin this test of comprehension one or two levels below the student's instructional level in word recognition. The student is asked to read the first selection aloud, the teacher noting errors in the oral reading.

Table 2–6 shows the types of errors or miscues that are frequently noted as students read aloud. A common way of coding these is shown to the right.

Analyzing Oral Reading Miscues[1]

The assessment procedures described to this point will provide teachers with a number of ideas for instruction. However, each classroom has within it a small number of boys and girls whose reading problems are so persistent that additional, more intensive analysis is required. This statement is based on the belief that students' errors or miscues are not random or capricious, except in the most unusual circumstances. On the contrary, such miscues occur in systematic patterns that can be identified by careful analysis of students' oral reading. A major goal of such qualitative miscue analysis is to derive ideas on what strategies the student is using that result in the obtained performance patterns. Once the teacher has detected the pattern of the miscues presented by the child, he or she can develop hypotheses concerning the particular ineffective or inefficient strategies being utilized by the child and appropriate instructional efforts can follow.

The complete and comprehensive analysis of each oral reading miscue of a particular child would be too time-consuming for everyday classroom use. For example, the complete coding of the miscues of an average reader would call for approximately 2000 separate decisions. Although such detailed analyses may

---

[1]We use the term "miscue" rather than "error" for much the same reasons as those articulated by K. S. Goodman (1969); that is, the term "miscue" is less judgmental and avoids the implication that good reading cannot involve departures from the printed text (expected responses).

Table 2–6. Coding Errors

Type of Error or Miscue	Example
Omissions of letter, word(s), punctuation	Jane and Bob (were) riding.
Reversals	/saw\
	He /called\ loudly./
Substitutions	~~thank~~ think
Dialect difference	(d) be He ~~has~~ gone
Insertion of words or letters	old strange∧man
Nonword substitution	(s)tran The ~~train~~
Word-by-word reading or long pauses	down/the/street
Repetition that corrects a previously incorrect word	(c) Saturday Today is Sunday
Repetition that abandons a previously correct word	(ac) Saturday Today is Sunday
Repetition of incorrect substitution	(uc) Saturday Today is Sunday
Student asks for assistance	He |called|

be necessary for research purposes, we believe that a less detailed analysis can provide the classroom teacher with necessary and valuable insight. Teachers interested in the more comprehensive program for oral miscue analysis are referred to K. S. Goodman (1969), Y. M. Goodman (1972), and Weber (1968, 1970).

A word of caution on the use of miscue analytic procedures is appropriate. Good readers do not maximally utilize every cue presented in the printed page; that is, they do not make letter-by-letter discriminations, attending to each feature of each letter or even each word. In fact, some authorities (K. S. Goodman, 1969; F. Smith, 1971) have made strong cases that the really effective and efficient reader is one who is able to derive meaning from the printed page with a minimum use of cues. Thus a good reader forms hypotheses about how the sentence, the paragraph, and the story will end. Subsequent reading behavior serves to confirm or disconfirm those hypotheses, which then become part of the "meaning" derived from the page, or become modified, respectively. Accordingly, teachers should not be overly concerned if, on occasion, a student emits a response that is at variance with the printed page. The teacher is properly concerned, however, when the miscues are of such a nature and frequency that the child's comprehension is impaired. Miscue analysis can help the teacher discover what faulty strategies and consistently misleading patterns or rules the student uses that interfere with the reading performance.

Table 2–7 presents the common miscue types. They are of interest to the teacher, but they provide insufficient detail as to the strategies that underlie their use. We suggest that teachers use Table 2–8 to further refine their examination of how the student responds to graphic symbols. In actual practice, teachers will find that the overwhelming number of miscues are substitutes of one kind or another (D'Angelo and Wilson, 1979). Hence a closer look at substitution miscues (Table 2–8) is warranted.

Table 2–7.   Analysis of Oral Reading Miscues: Response Types

Response Type	Description	Example*
Omission	The student omits a word or words.	the big red ball/the big ball
Insertion	The student adds a word or words.	the big ball/the big red ball
Sequence or order	The student makes a response that is expected elsewhere in the text—either immediately preceding or following (horizontal miscue), or immediately above or below the stimulus word (vertical miscue)	John and Harry found the dog/John and Harry found the Harry
Substitution†	The student substitutes a word other than that in the text. (If the child makes a substitution on the first occurrence of the stimulus word, then on later occurrences makes the expected response, no further analysis is required—see self-correction below.)	The dog ran/The dog red
Sounding out	The student makes several tentative partial responses, voiced or unvoiced.	Patty will play/Patty will p—
Self-correction	The student makes any of the above response types, then spontaneously corrects the miscue.	That is good/What is—that is good
Dialect	The student makes any of the above, but in accordance with the rules of his or her dialect.	The boys were scared/The boy be scared

*In each example, the printed text or expected response precedes the diagonal line; the student's miscue or the observed response follows.

†For more detailed analysis of substitutions, see Table 2–8.

Table 2–8. Analysis of Substitution Miscues

Type of Substitution Analysis*	Example†	Hypothesis or "What the Teacher Does Next"
I. Graphic analysis		
a. No discernible similarity (no shared letters)	king/lady	Probe whether the student is just guessing. Student may have virtually no word-attack skills (test further with commercial or teacher-made word-analysis test).
b. Words similar in overall configuration	leg/boy	Student may be utilizing configural clues—this is a strength that needs to be built on and supplemented with other word-analysis skills.
c. Reversal of single letter	bad/dad	Recheck student's ability to discriminate between b and d, also between other pairs, such as p and q. Provide left-right activities, also specific exercises for discrimination training. See also section on grammatical appropriateness.
d. Reversal of two or more letters	was/saw	Provide activities as indicated in I.c.
e. Beginning letters similar	play/plant	Student is correctly utilizing initial consonant blend cue. He or she needs to be encouraged to utilize middle and ending graphic cues, also to attend to context. Check other initial letters.
f. Middle letters similar	good/food	Same as I.e except with middle letters.
g. Ending letters similar	that/what	Same as I.e except with ending letters; also extra exercises with "wh" and "th" letters.
h. Single letter omission, deletion, or substitution	very/every	Student needs to be encouraged to look at entire word, also needs help on using syntactic and semantic cues.
i. Similar root word; suffix/prefix miscue	toys/toy	Check for presence of dialect; then use activities dealing with singular and plural; also encourage attention to word endings.
II. Syntactic analysis		
a. Beginning position in sentence	The boy ... Who ...	Check whether student can discriminate between these words when they occur later in the sentence; if so, he or she is relying heavily on syntactic cues (which is good), but needs more help on word-analysis skills.
b. Middle or ending position in sentence	Mary ran far/ Mary ran fast	Student is using syntactic and semantic features of the sentence (good); needs help as in I.e.
c. Grammatical appropriateness (substituted word has same rate of occurrence as stimulus word? Sentence grammatical up to and including miscue?)	John found his pet/John found his play	Student relying on initial letter cue (good), but is not showing grammatical awareness. Does student have mastery of oral language? If so, further testing and activities with cloze technique and "guess the end of the sentence game" might be used.

(continued)

Table 2–8   *Continued*

Type of Substitution Analysis*	Example†	Hypothesis or "What the Teacher Does Next"
III. Semantic analysis		
a. Stimulus word and child's response unrelated or only partially related	Peter could/ Peter cold	Student is using fairly sophisticated word-analysis skills (teacher can build on this), but needs sequential sentence speaking and reading opportunities. Other activities as in II.c.
b. Meaning of student's response acceptable in sentence, but not related to stimulus sentence or paragraph	Jerry went home/Jerry went away	Student is thinking about the internal meaning of the sentence (good), but is not relating it to the meaning of the story. Student lacks word-analysis skills.

*Category types are not mutually exclusive.
†In each example, the printed text or expected response precedes the diagonal line; the child's miscue or the observed response follows.

Table 2–8 has been organized to indicate that most students' reading substitutions fall readily into graphic, syntactic, and semantic categories. These categories are, of course, not mutually exclusive; any printed word has graphic, syntactic, and semantic characteristics; and a child may use faulty strategies that apply to these characteristics singly or in combination.

An additional point about Table 2–8 is worth making. It is not accidental that the miscue characteristics are analogous to the aspects of language—phonology, syntactics, and semantics. We point this out again to underline the intimate relationship of the reading act to the student's language proficiency.

In performing a miscue analysis, teachers structure the situation much as they would in administering an informal reading inventory. In fact, if adequate protocols have been kept from a previous administration of an IRI, the teacher may be able to perform usable analyses without asking the student to read orally again. If no IRI protocols are available, the teacher asks the student to read several paragraphs at the instructional level, marking a double-spaced copy with an appropriate code. The miscues emitted by the student are then subjected to an analysis as follows. Using Table 2–7, the teacher categorizes the types of responses made by the student. Special note is made of the student's efforts at "sounding out" (these efforts are invaluable in helping the teacher derive hypotheses concerning the student's word-attack strategies; in fact, the student should be encouraged to "sound out" for this reason), self-correction (which similarly provides valuable insight into how the child monitors personal performance, and whether he or she utilizes feedback effectively), and dialect considerations. This latter issue will not be further explicated, except to say that the student's dialect will affect the interpretation given to graphic, syntactic, and semantic miscues; in fact, the presence or absence of a dialect will determine whether certain departures from the expected responses should be considered miscues at all.

Next, each miscue is analyzed according to its graphic, syntactic, and semantic characteristics. By noting the relative proportion of miscues in each category, the teacher can form a rough idea of whether the student's difficulty is more of the word-analysis type (mostly graphic miscues) or whether the child has linguistic or cognitive difficulty in forming hypotheses about the meaning of the material being read (such difficulty showing up more in syntactic and semantic miscues). We strongly urge teachers to attend closely to this latter miscue type, for it is our belief that linguistic and cognitive aspects of reading have been generally ignored by teachers.

After completing the miscue analysis, the teacher will find it useful to summarize the results on a record sheet such as the one presented in Figure 2–3. The use of this record sheet should make it apparent at a glance where the student's faulty strategies seem to cluster. The teacher will then have a sound basis for be-

Figure 2–3. Sample Record Sheet for Oral Reading Miscues

Name _____ Age _____ Grade _____ Date _____
Sample of Reading Material on Which Analysis Is Based _____
Number of Words in Sample _____

Response Type Number of Occurrences	*Response Type Number of Occurrences*
Omission _____	Sounding Out _____
Insertion _____	Self-Correction _____
Sequence _____	Dialect _____
Substitution _____	

Substitution Analysis

Graphic analysis
  a. No similarity _____
  b. Configuration _____
  c. Single-letter reversal _____
  d. Several letters reversed _____
  e. Beginning letters similar _____
  f. Middle letters similar _____
  g. Ending letters similar _____
  h. Single-letter miscue _____
  i. Root word _____
Total graphic miscues _____

Syntactic analysis
  a. Beginning position _____
  b. Middle or ending position _____
  c. Grammatical appropriateness _____
Total syntactic miscues _____

Semantic analysis
  a. Meaning unrelated _____
  b. Story meaning distorted _____
Total semantic miscues _____

ginning instruction designed to build on strengths and to redress weaknesses. The student's reading protocol should be readily available as instruction is planned.

A new technique for looking at students' miscues is provided by Wiederholt (1985) in the *Formal Reading Inventory: A Method for Assessing Silent Reading Comprehension and Oral Reading Miscues.* The test's standardization is extensive and includes numerous studies of reliability and validity. The norms are based on a large, nationally representative sample of students from grades one through twelve.

In using this test, the teacher first finds a student's silent reading comprehension level by having him or her read passages of increasing difficulty from a series of stories and answer literal, inferential, critical, and affective questions about their contents. The student's performance is reported as percentiles and standard scores. Next, three passages are selected from an equivalent form of the test. The student's silent reading comprehension level is used as a criterion; one of the selected passages is at the student's reading level, and the other two are easier and more difficult, respectively.

The three passages are read orally by the student, while the teacher records specific departures from the text. The types of departures noted are (1) meaning similarities, (2) function similarities, (3) graphic-phonemic similarities, and (4) self-corrections. The test's four forms allow teachers to pre- and post-test students on their silent reading comprehension and their oral reading miscues.

TEACHING THE STUDENT WHO HAS A READING PROBLEM

The previous section has described how to identify the levels and types of difficulties in reading that a student may have. Once the teacher has a clear picture of the student's reading problem, the task becomes that of developing teaching strategies that are feasible and effective. Such strategies will be implemented on a trial basis; if the student makes progress, the strategy should be continued. If discernible learning does not occur, however, it is appropriate to return to a previous point in the instructional cycle (see Chapter 1)—that is, to retest the student with a view to generating an alternative hypothesis as to which approach might work with that student.

This may sound as if the teaching of reading is largely a matter of trial and error. It is true that the research has not yet been able to show precisely which kind of reading approach works best with a student exhibiting certain learning styles or modality preference. However, it is also true that there now exists a significant body of research and knowledge about useful overall instructional principles in reading, basal reading series intended for classroom use, and spe-

cial remedial approaches intended for use with remedial or handicapped learners. It is to these topics that we turn next.

Instructional Principles in Teaching Reading

Even though much remains to be learned, the task of teachers is to use the
knowledge that is available in their instructional procedures. The following
section is based on current literature on the nature of learning difficulties and
on our present understanding of what constitutes effective teaching practices.

Teach Reading Strategies to the Student

The instructional principles in this section are based on the view that many students with learning problems fail to deploy cognitive resources efficiently and
effectively. This means that they are generally inattentive, inactive, and unable
to generate appropriate learning strategies without outside help. The difficulties are as much in the executive or monitoring (metacognitive) functions as in
the performance (cognitive) functions. Although they use different terminology,
e.g., "academic strategy training," "cognitive behavior modification," "self-
monitoring," or "metacognitive training," a growing number of theorists and researchers are now coming to this point of view (see, for example, Deshler,
Warner, Schumaker, and Alley, 1983; Leon and Pepe, 1983; Lloyd, Hallahan, Kosiewicz, and Kneedler, 1982; Loper, Hallahan, and Ianna, 1982; Meichenbaum,
1977).

What all these approaches have in common is the need to teach the student
a sense of self-awareness in terms of his or her cognitive strategies for problem
solving. The student is made aware of how to structure his or her thinking when
engaging in decoding or comprehension tasks. Self-instruction, it is believed,
plays a central role in the performance of many problem-solving tasks. Such
self-instruction may take the form of internalized language and may play a key
regulatory role in human behavior.

Students with learning problems are at a disadvantage in knowing how to
go about a task that requires attention and memory but, when trained on an
adult-generated strategy, can satisfactorily perform the task or solve the problem. The general sequence is to teach the student task-specific strategies in isolation, then have the student practice those strategies in controlled or assisted
situations, and finally have the student apply the strategies in a new learning
situation.

Initially, a comprehensive diagnostic assessment of the student is undertaken in the reading area to establish levels of functioning in areas of weakness
requiring intervention (see the previous section on assessment). Once these lev-

els are established, the cognitive behavior modification, or strategy training, is begun. The following stages are implemented:

Stage 1—The teacher demonstrates the technique, verbalizing the self-instructional strategy and reading the passage out loud.

Stage 2—The teacher and the student together utilize the strategy, overtly verbalizing each stage and orally reading the passage in question.

Stage 3—The student verbalizes the strategy but reads silently for the next reading passage.

Stage 4—The student whispers the strategy and reads silently the next reading passage.

Stage 5—The student covertly uses the strategy and reads the passage silently.

If at any point the student has less than 90 percent comprehension on questions asked after the reading, he or she goes back to an earlier stage of instruction until that criterion is reached. If after three attempts, the criterion is not reached, the student is placed in a lower reading level.

Use Task Analysis to Organize and Sequence Instruction

Frequently, the teacher will find that a student is deficient in a word-analysis or comprehension skill that had been previously taught. In such cases, it is helpful to analyze the skill in question to determine if it can be broken into component parts that can be separately and successfully taught to the student. Such an approach is called task analysis. In undertaking a task analysis of a given reading skill, the first step is to state clearly the objective of the task. This objective then needs to be scrutinized on the basis of the following criteria:

1. *Significance.* How important is it for the student to master this skill? Is it basic or trivial? Is it necessary?
2. *Relevance.* How relevant is this skill to the other things the student needs to learn or has learned?

Having determined that the task to be taught is a significant and relevant one, the teacher then identifies the subskills that are necessary for performing the target task. Once the subskills have been delineated, the teacher asks, "What does the student have to be able to do to perform each of the subskills?" The answer to this question leads to the development of sub-subskills. This procedure is repeated until the teacher arrives at a subskill level where the student is able to perform the tasks. This type of analysis is called a *descending* analysis, because it starts with a target task and works backward to subsidiary tasks. The

Figure 2–4.   Descending Task Analysis

Teacher Does

Step I - Statement of Target Task

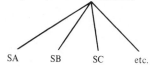

Step II - Statement of Subskills

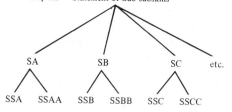

SA   SB   SC   etc.

Step III — Statement of Sub-subskills

SA   SB   SC   etc.

SSA   SSAA   SSB   SSBB   SSC   SSCC

Continue further differentiation
into subskills until a level is
achieved where the student can
perform all the tasks.

Teacher Asks

Is it significant?

Is it relevant?

Are these subskills necessary
for performing target tasks?

Are these subskills sufficient
for performing target tasks?

Are these subskills relevant
for performing target tasks?

Are there any missing or
redundant subskills?

Can the student perform any of
these tasks?

Are these sub-subskills necessary
for performing subskill tasks?

Are these sub-subskills sufficient
for performing subskill tasks?

Are these sub-subskills relevant
for performing subskill tasks?

Are there any missing or
redundant sub-subskills?

Can the student perform any of
these tasks?

procedure of developing a descending task analysis is outlined in Figure 2–4. When the teacher finds a level at which the student can perform all the tasks, the teacher reviews these tasks with the student. Actual instruction begins at the next higher level.

The following section presents a sample work-attack task analysis (Figure 2–5) and a comprehension analysis task (Figure 2–6). Note that these task analyses are developed in terms of the generalizations (or rules) that the student must be able to utilize in order to perform the task. The generalization at each level is enclosed in a box.

Word-Attack Task Analysis.   In this example, Figure 2–5, the objective is to help the student master the necessary skills, so that when the student sees a "y" preceded by a consonant at the end of a word, he or she will know what sound is represented by that "y." Using a descending task analysis, this target skill has

Figure 2-5.   Example of Word-Attack Task Analysis

Target Skill Level

> When I meet another word that ends in *y* with a consonant before it: in a one-part word, the *y* will probably have the "long i" sound; in a two-or-more-part word, the *y* will probably have the "long e" sound.

Known words about which subskill level generalizations have been made

dry	funny	city
shy	berry	happily

Observations necessary

All are one-part or two-or-more-part words.
When I say the one-part words, each has a "long i" sound at the end.
When I say the two-or-more-part words, each has a "long e" sound at the end.
When I look at these words, each has a *y* at the end with a consonant before it.

Subskill Level

> When I meet another one-part word that ends in *y* with a consonant before it, *y* will probably have a "long i" sound.

known words about which subskill level generalizations have been made

my	cry
dry	shy
fly	

Observations necessary

All are one-part words.
When I say these words, each has a "long i" sound at the end.
When I look at these words, I see a *y* at the end with a consonant before it.

> When I meet a two-or-more-part word that ends in *y* with a consonant before it, the *y* will probably have a "long e" sound.

Known words about which subskill level generalizations have been made

funny	many	city
silly	pony	happily
foggy	berry	elementary

Observations necessary

All are two-or-more-part words.
When I say these words, each has a "long e" sound at the end.
When I look at these words, each has a *y* at the end with a consonant before it.

Sub-subskill Level

> When I see another one-part word that ends in *y* with a consonant before it, it will probably rhyme with . . .

> When I see another two-part word that ends in *any*, it will probably rhyme with . . .

> When I see another two-part word that ends in *erry*, it will probably rhyme with . . .

> When I see another two-part word that ends in *illy*, it will probably rhyme with . . .

> When I see another two-part word that ends in *itty*, it will probably rhyme with . . .

> When I see another two-part word that ends in *oggy*, it will probably rhyme with . . .

> When I see another two-part word that ends in *ony*, it will probably rhyme with . . .

> When I see another two-part word that ends in *unny*, it will probably rhyme with . . .

Level at which child can perform all tasks and make all required generalizations

Known words

my	cry	shy
by	dry	why
	try	
	fry	

Known words

many	berry (very)	silly	kitty (city)	foggy	pony	funny
any	ferry	hilly	witty	soggy	Tony	bunny
	merry	Willy	gritty	groggy		sunny
	Sherry	frilly				
	Perry					

Observations necessary

All are one-part words.
When I say these words, they all rhyme.
When I look at these words, I see a *y* at the end with a consonant before it.

Observations

All are two-part words.
All have *any*, *erry*, *illy*, *itty*, *oggy*, *ony*, or *unny* at the end and rhyme within those various rhyming elements.

Source: Adapted from S. Tobia, B. Elliot, and C. Rubenstone, Unpublished manuscript developed under the direction of M. S. Johnson at Temple University Laboratory School, Psychology of Reading Department, Philadelphia, 1978.

52

been broken down into subskills and sub-subskills. The student is first tested on all tasks at the lowest level of the task analysis, or the sub-subskill level. Does the student know each set of one- and two-part words? Can the student make the indicated observations? If the student does not know the words or is unable to make the observations, he or she is taught to do so. Then the student is encouraged to make the generalizations shown in the boxes at the sub-subskill level. Only when the student can make these generalizations does the teaching move up to the next level—the subskill level. The procedures of testing and teaching words, observations, and generalizations are repeated at this level. When the student demonstrates mastery at the subskill level, he or she is ready to be exposed to tasks at the target skill level. When the student can make the generalization enclosed in the box at the top of Figure 2–5, the program is complete. The student can successfully figure out the sounds of the "y" at the end of one- and two-part words.

Comprehension Task Analysis.   In this example, Figure 2–6, the objective is to get the student to the point where he or she will be able to use temporal sequence clues to determine the logical order of a series of events in a story. Here again, a descending task analysis has been developed to show the levels of prerequisite tasks necessary to successfully perform the target task.

Some comments are necessary to provide perspective for this task analysis. First, sequence "clue words" have been categorized as "exact" and "nonexact." The categorizing of these clue words should help the student draw conclusions about the use of the clue words in determining sequence, since exact words (first, last) require a slightly different approach than do nonexact words (next, later).

Furthermore, the model presented in Figure 2–6 focuses only on the exact words (except at the target task level, which draws both categories together). The approach to teaching for the two categories is virtually the same. The main difference lies in the need for elaborate use of context clues when dealing with nonexact words. This technique does become evident in target task level procedures.

Additionally, at the sub-subskill level, only one subgroup of exact words is illustrated (again because it is the same basic procedure for all subgroups). Numerical clue words, such as first and second, are the focus of the procedures. Although most students come to school already familiar with the concept behind these words, it is necessary to review them in relation to the reading and sequencing task.

Finally, it should be noted that interpretative skills, background experience, and semantic knowledge are necessary in utilizing both the exact and nonexact words. Therefore, the developmental level of the student should be considered before a target skill such as this one is presented.

Figure 2–6. Example of Comprehension Task Analysis

Target Skill Level

When I meet any clue words or phrases that tell me *when*, I can use them to determine sequence.

Subskill Level

Known words about which Level 2 generalizations have been made
Baseline words—"exact" and "nonexact" clues

Observations necessary
All words or phrases tell me *when*.
Some words are "exact" clue words and some are "nonexact".

When I meet any "exact" clue words or phrases that tell me *when*, I can use them to determine sequence.

When I meet any "nonexact" clue words or phrases that tell me *when*, I can use them to determine time order.

Observations necessary
All are words or phrases that tell *when*.
All are "nonexact" clue words or phrases.

Known words about which Level 1 generalizations have been made
Baseline words—"exact" clues

Observations necessary
All are words or phrases that tell *when*.
All are "exact" clue words or phrases.

Known words
Baseline words—"nonexact" clues

When I meet . . . I know they tell me *when*, and I can use them to determine time order.

When I meet . . . I know they tell me *when*, and I can use them to determine time order.

When I meet . . . I know they tell me *when*, and I can use them to determine time order.

When I meet . . . I know they tell me *when*, and I can use them to determine time order.

Sub-Subskill Level

When I meet . . . I know they tell me *when*, and I can use them to determine time order.

Known words

first
second
third
fourth
fifth
etc.

Known words

today
tomorrow
yesterday

last
finally
etc.

Known phrases (words)

in the beginning
day before yesterday
at the end
next to last
etc.

Known words

next
then
after
now

before
later
etc.

Known phrases

by then
last week
later that day
etc.

Level at which child can perform all tasks and make all required generalizations

Monday	January	noon
Tuesday	February	midnight
Wednesday	March	
Thursday	April	1978
Friday	May	etc.
Saturday	June	
Sunday	July	
	August	6:00
	September	6:15
	October	7:30
	November	etc.
	December	

Source: Adapted from S. Tobia, B. Elliot, and C. Rubenstone, Unpublished manuscript developed under the direction of M. S. Johnson at Temple University Laboratory School, Psychology of Reading Department, Philadelphia, 1978.

Teach Specific Reading Skills Directly

The term "direct instruction" has been used in a number of different ways—to denote a specific instructional program as well as to describe a teacher-student orientation that is characterized by " . . . an academic focus, precise sequencing of content, high pupil engagement, careful teacher monitoring and specific corrective feedback to students" (Duffy and Roehler, 1982, p. 35). Such an instructional style puts a heavy demand on the teacher—the teacher actually teaches, as opposed to merely arranging the learning environment, or monitoring seatwork, or correcting seatwork or other assignments. In direct instruction, the teacher explains, models, demonstrates, and leads. Direct instruction means the teacher is centrally involved in the act of teaching and directly in command of, and responsible for, instructional activities.

Direct instruction of reading skills requires that the teacher have objectives for a lesson clearly in mind before starting a lesson (see Chapter 1 for points to keep in mind in formulating objectives). The precise delineation of objectives and subobjectives requires that the learning task be broken down into constituent parts so that instruction toward each objective can proceed in an orderly and sequential fashion. For this reason, direct instruction almost always requires the use of task analysis (which was described in the preceding section). Here we will consider how the teacher actually directly teaches the skills and subskills identified in the task analysis.

The research on direct instruction has been generally supportive of its use. It has been most widely used for teaching word-analysis skills (e.g., Idol-Maestas, 1981; Pany, Jenkins, and Schreck, 1982). More recently, reading comprehension skills have been targeted for direct instruction; the results also are promising (Baumann, 1984; Hare and Borchardt, 1984).

In general, direct instruction follows a number of steps that are adaptable to the particular lesson being taught. These steps are

1. *Introduction.* The teacher states the purpose of the lesson.
2. *Direct instruction.* The teacher does the actual teaching—states, manipulates, explains, requests, demonstrates.
3. *Teacher-directed application.* The students do several examples under the direct guidance of the teacher.
4. *Independent practice.* The students work individually or in groups to reinforce, consolidate, and generalize their skills.

We have provided a detailed example from Baumann (1984) to demonstrate each of the stages of direct instruction.

Sample Lesson Employing a Direct Instruction Paradigm[2]
(Lesson 2: Main Ideas and Details in Paragraphs—Implicit)

Introduction: "Remember last time when we learned how to find main idea sentences right in paragraphs? We called these main idea sentences *topic sentences.* Today you will learn how to find main ideas in paragraphs that do not have topic sentences; that is, paragraphs which actually do have main ideas in them, but paragraphs in which the main ideas are not stated. You will learn how to figure out these unstated main ideas by looking at the details in the paragraph and determining what all these details are talking about, and that will be the main idea. This is an important reading skill because many paragraphs have unstated main ideas, and if you can figure out what these main ideas are, you will understand and remember the most important information in the material you read."

Example: "Look at the example I have on this transparency."

My father can cook bacon and eggs real well. He can also bake cakes that taste wonderful. He cooks excellent popcorn and pizza. The thing he cooks best of all, however, is hamburgers barbecued on the grill.

"Follow along with me silently as I read the paragraph aloud." (Teacher reads paragraph.) "Notice that there is no single sentence that states the main idea; that is, there is no topic sentence. Rather, the entire paragraph consists of a series of details. That does not mean that there is not a main idea in this paragraph, however, for there is. What we will learn how to do today is to inspect paragraphs like this one that contain an unstated main idea and then figure out what that main idea is."

Direct Instruction: "Let's examine this same paragraph on the transparency and see if we can determine its main idea. Remember in our last lesson, we learned to figure out the topic of a paragraph—the one or two words that tell what a paragraph is about? What would be the topic of this paragraph? Would it be 'father cooking'?" (Student response.) "All right, the topic of the paragraph is 'father cooking.' Now let's list on the board all the ideas that tell about father cooking. Who can help us begin?" (Students respond by stating the four detail sentences in the paragraph, and the teacher writes them on the board in a numbered list.) "Very good. These are the ideas that tell us about father cooking, and we learned already that we can call these ideas *supporting details.* If supporting details go with a main idea, let's inspect these details and see if we can figure out what the main idea of this paragraph is." (Teacher rereads the supporting details on the board.) "Now what would be a main idea sentence we could come up with that goes with all these details?" (Teacher writes student responses on the board.) "Yes, there are several different ways of saying what the main idea is: 'Father can cook many different things' or 'Father is a good cook.' But the main idea tells us about all the details in the paragraph; that is, the biggest, most important, idea in the paragraph."

"Now look at this transparency. Who can tell me what it is?" (Student response.) "Yes, it is a table. Let's use this table to help us understand how main ideas and details go together. Just as a table is supported by its legs, so too, a

[2]Reprinted with permission of James Baumann and the International Reading Association.

main idea is supported by details. So let's put the main idea on the table and the supporting details on each of the legs. Who can help us get going? Let's start with the details on the legs." (Students respond and teacher writes details on table legs.) "Now let's put the main idea on the top of the table." (Teacher writes main idea on table top.) "Just as the legs of this table support the table top, so too, the details in this paragraph support the main idea of the paragraph. When you try to figure out the main idea of a paragraph, think of a table and legs to help you understand how supporting details and main ideas relate to one another, or go together." (Teacher then works through a second example paragraph in a similar fashion.)

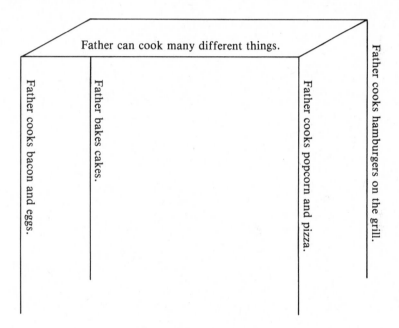

Teacher-Directed Application: "I have a work paper we will complete together." (Teacher distributes work paper.) "Look at the paragraph after Number 1. Read this paragraph to yourself silently, and see if you can figure out the main idea. There is no topic sentence in this paragraph, so you will have to use the supporting details to determine what the main idea is. Then darken the letter that goes with the sentence you think best states the main idea of this paragraph." (Students complete exercise.) "All right, how did you do? Who can tell us what the main idea is?" (Student response.) "Correct, answer choice c, 'Animals help people in many different ways' is the main idea. Who can tell us what the supporting details are for this main idea?" (Student response.) "Good, now let's try Exercise 2. Read this paragraph to yourself silently and then write what you think the main idea of the paragraph is on the line below the paragraph. Think of the table and legs idea to help you." (Students complete exercise.) "Who can tell us what the main idea is . . ." (Teachers and students proceed through the remaining exercises in a similar manner. If students have difficulty with the exercises, the teacher provides additional instruction.)

UNSTATED MAIN IDEAS AND DETAILS IN PARAGRAPHS
GROUP EXERCISE

1. Horses can carry people. Mules pull heavy loads. Dogs lead blind people across streets. Sheep give us wool, and cows give people milk to drink.
   (a) Animals give us many different foods to eat.
   (b) Horses and mules do heavy work for people.
   (c) Animals help people in many different ways.
   (d) Dogs and cats are good companions for people.

2. Mother likes to read mystery stories. Dad enjoys reading science fiction. My sister Kim likes to read joke books, and my little brother Thomas only likes to read comic books. But I enjoy reading nature books about wild animals.

   _____

3. Eohippus, the ancestor of the modern horse, lived fifty million years ago. Because the eohippus grazed on foliage, its teeth were very different from the teeth of the modern horse, which are adapted to eating grass. This "dawn horse" also had four toes on each of its front feet and three toes on each of its hind feet. Horses of today, however, have only one highly developed toe, covered by a hoof, on each foot.

   _____

4. Modern treasure hunting began in the northwestern United States in the late 1960s. Today, nearly one million people participate in this exciting hobby. Armed with metal detectors, these present-day adventurers track through old dumps, beaches, and schoolyards in search of lost "treasure." About 3,000 small businesses cater to the amateur treasure hunter, selling an estimated 600,000 metal detectors each year.

   _____

Independent Practice: "The final thing you will do in this lesson is to complete a work paper on your own." (Teacher distributes exercise.) "On this paper are some paragraphs for which you must figure out the main ideas, since there are no topic sentences in any of the paragraphs. For Number 1, the directions tell you simply to circle the statement that is the best main idea, and for Number 2, to write a main idea sentence for each paragraph. When completing these exercises, try to remember how to figure out the main idea by thinking of a statement that tells about the details in the paragraph; you also might want to use the table and legs idea to help you. Work carefully and do your best."

UNSTATED MAIN IDEAS AND DETAILS IN PARAGRAPHS
INDEPENDENT PRACTICE

1. Read the following paragraphs and circle the letter of the statement that best tells the main idea for each paragraph.

Some dinosaurs were huge animals that were much larger than elephants. Some dinosaurs were small animals no larger than a chicken. Many dinosaurs, however, were middle-sized and about as big as a cow or horse.

(a) Some dinosaurs were chickens.
(b) All dinosaurs were huge, large animals.
(c) Dinosaurs were of different sizes.
(d) Dinosaurs were fearful, large animals.

Many dogs guard peoples' houses and stores. Some dogs are seeing-eye dogs and help blind people move around safely. Some dogs with keen noses are used to hunt criminals. But most dogs are just good friends for people.

(a) Dogs help blind people.
(b) Dogs help people in different ways.
(c) Dogs are good friends.
(d) Dogs hunt people and guard houses.

Many people are aware that the giraffe is the tallest animal on earth, but few realize that despite its long neck, the giraffe has the same number of neck bones that humans have—only seven. Also, many people think that giraffes have no voice. This is not true. Although giraffes rarely use their voice, they have vocal cords and are quite capable of making noises when they choose to. The "horns" that grow on their heads are not really horns at all. Instead, they are simply bumplike growths covered by skin and hair. Some giraffes even have three or four of these "horns," not the two most people think they have.

(a) Giraffes are tall animals with a real voice and bumplike horns.
(b) Giraffes can make sounds, even though people think they cannot.
(c) Giraffes and humans are alike in several ways.
(d) Giraffes are strange and surprising animals.

2. Each of the following paragraphs have unstated main ideas. Read each paragraph and try to figure out what a good main idea statement would be. Then write this statement on the line below each paragraph.

My mother wore bedroom slippers this morning. Then she put on running shoes for jogging. After jogging, she put on her old shoes to work in the garden. After lunch, she put on her new sneakers to play tennis. This evening she wore fancy high heels when she and Dad went out to dinner.

_____

Pumpkins, of course, can be made into pies. But pumpkins can also be used to make soup and cake. Some people roast pumpkin seeds and eat them. Probably most people use pumpkins to make Jack-o-Lanterns for Halloween.

_____

A person with a metal detector will usually find things like bottle caps, tin cans, or perhaps a nickle or dime. But sometimes a person with a metal detector, if he or she is lucky, will find an old silver dollar or a valuable ring or piece of jewelry. Some people have found old coins worth very much money, perhaps $100 or $200. And a few lucky persons have found an entire treasure chest filled with gold and jewels.

We owe the word "sandwich" to the person who invented it—John Montague, the Earl of Sandwich. Louis Braille, who was blinded at the age of three, had to learn to read, from large, clumsy letters. He found these difficult to use, so he invented a system of raised dots which later became known as "braille." The German engineer Rudolf Diesel invented an internal combustion engine that would run on cheap crude fuel. Of course, now this engine is known as a "diesel" engine.

Teach Comprehension by Asking Appropriate Questions

As mentioned earlier, merely being able to recognize words is insufficient for receiving communication from the printed page. Understanding what the words, sentences, and paragraphs mean is the main purpose of reading. It follows, then, that the teaching of comprehension skills is a major objective for every teacher.

The use of questions to improve comprehension can help students understand and remember what they read. Asking the student questions *before* he or she reads a passage, as in a directed reading activity, helps the student focus attention on the information in the text that will help him or her answer the questions. However, this approach can direct the student's attention away from those parts of the narrative that do not contain information needed to answer questions. If, on the other hand, the student is told that he or she will be questioned *after* reading a passage, the student may try to remember as much as possible about all of the passage. The teacher must ascertain whether the student can attend to the passage without the need for specific guidance.

Ruddell (1976) has developed a model of teacher questioning that facilitates moving the pupil's thinking from the literal or factual memory level toward the higher cognitive processes. These sequential steps have been summarized by Singer (1978), as shown in Table 2–9.

Student responses to inferential, as opposed to factual, questions tend to be longer and more complex and utilize the higher cognitive processes (C. T. Smith, 1978). Furthermore, the quality of pupil responses can be improved by encouraging the student to delay the response for a few seconds, to take some "think-time" before trying to answer the teacher's questions (Gambrell, 1980).

Table 2–9.   Teacher-Student Interaction in Questioning Strategy

Teacher-Student Interaction	
Who Talks	*Function*
Teacher	Question
Student	Response

Questioning Strategy		
Type	*Purpose*	*Question*
Focusing	Initiate discussion or refocus on the issue.	What did you like best about story? What was the question we started to answer?
Controlling	Direct or dominate the discussion.	First, would you review the plot?
Ignoring or rejecting	Maintain current trend in discussion. Disregard a student's interest.	Would you mind if we don't go into that now?
Extending	Obtain more information at a particular level of discussion.	What other information do we have about the hero?
Clarifying	Obtain a more adequate explanation. Draw out a student.	Would you explain what you mean?
Raising	Have discussion move from factual to interpretative, inferential, or abstraction and generalization level.	We now have enough examples. What do they have in common? (Abstract) Was it always true for his behavior? (Generalization)

Response Level
Factual or literal (what the author said)
Interpretative (integration of ideas of inference)
Applied (transfer of ideas or judgment that idea is subsumed under broader generalization)
Evaluative (using cognitive or affective criteria for judging issue)

Source: H. Singer, Active comprehension: From answering to asking questions, *The Reading Teacher*, May 1978, 903. Reprinted with permission of the author and the International Reading Association.

Teacher-posed questions serve a valuable purpose in focusing the student's attention on the material and in helping the student learn the type of questions to ask about a reading passage. The ultimate goal in reading for comprehension is not to read to answer someone else's questions, but to learn to ask appropriate questions for oneself as one reads. As noted in an earlier part of this chapter, the good reader develops hypotheses or questions as he or she reads, then reads on to see if the questions are answered the way he or she thinks they will be. Singer (1978) has called this process "active comprehension," and it occurs before, during, and after reading. Getting students to develop self-questioning skills has been found to be particularly helpful to students of low verbal ability (André and Anderson, 1978–79). This approach is consistent with the section of this chapter that deals with teaching reading strategies.

Teaching students to generate their own questions entails the following procedures:

1. The teacher provides models of good questions (following Ruddell, 1976; or some other strategy designed to elicit higher-level thinking).
2. The teacher phases out the questioning and, depending on the ages of the pupils, uses a picture, a title, an introductory paragraph, or another device to encourage the students to begin asking questions.
3. The questions generated by the students are used to set the purposes for reading and to encourage speculation about the main idea of the passage or story.
4. The students read the text to a point where their initial speculation is answered or intensified. At this point the teacher encourages further questioning by the students. Depending on the passage, these questions may concern generalizations, concepts, predictions of plot resolution, interpretation, character development, or making inferences.

The last two steps are repeated until the passage is completed. Throughout, the teacher's role is one of eliciting student questions, encouraging students to recognize answers to their own questions, and guiding students to ask higher-level questions.

Teach Fluency through Sustained Silent Reading and Repeated Reading

One goal of reading instruction is to develop students' desire to read. Yet frequently, reading instruction is so intensive, so structured, and so "hard" that students have little or no opportunity to read material of their choice. To encourage students to develop a desire to read, as well as to consolidate learned reading skills, many teachers have relied on techniques involved in sustained silent reading (SSR) and repeated reading.

Sustained Silent Reading (SSR).   Many teachers incorporate a period of sustained silent reading (SSR) into each school day. The method for doing this is summarized below and is based on the work of Cline and Kretke (1980), Gambrell (1978), McCracken and McCracken (1978), Minton (1980), and Moore, Jones, and Miller (1980). In large part, the success of an SSR program depends on the following procedures, which should be performed *before* the program is implemented.

1. Advertise and promote SSR well before attempting to implement it. Use bulletin boards, book displays, and letters to parents, as well as reading aloud to the class and sharing thoughts about good books with pupils.

2. Assemble reading materials of many different topics, types, and difficulty levels. Include books, news magazines, newspapers, or other appropriate reading material.

3. Develop the rules for implementing SSR. This includes deciding what time of day it should take place and where students may engage in SSR (at desks, on mats, in reading nook, in library, etc.). For very young children, the SSR period might be only five minutes in length; older pupils enjoy reading for fifteen to twenty minutes. The rules for SSR should make clear that material selection occurs *before* the actual reading time begins.

A few precautions will enhance the probability of success for an SSR program.

1. Ensure that *everyone*, especially the teacher (no grading of tests!), reads silently and without interruption during SSR.

2. Do not allow changes of reading material during the period.

3. Reluctant or resistant readers may sit quietly at their desks; they may not walk around the room or otherwise interrupt the readers.

4. There are no book reports, questions to answer, or other follow-up activities to SSR.

5. There should be a means of sharing what has been read with the teacher or other pupils for those who wish to do so. Bulletin boards, informal commenting, or a special weekly time for promoting books may be used.

6. If possible, invite parents or other school personnel to participate in SSR when possible.

In general, SSR promotes students' reading skills and improves their attitudes toward reading. These findings are most consistent when the teacher unfailingly participates in SSR and when a good selection of reading materials is available.

Repeated Reading.   Repeated reading is another technique that has been promoted as a way of improving the performance of students in oral reading fluency and in comprehension. Most often the technique takes the form of having the student repeatedly read orally a selection of approximately 200 words while simultaneously listening to a taped version of the same material. Sometimes, before the actual oral reading, students listen to the tape or the teacher, with or without "following along" in the printed text. The procedures are repeated, with the student working independently in a corner of the room, until some criterion of speed and accuracy is reached. At this point the teacher listens to the student read orally; if the criterion (usually eighty-five words per minute) has been reached, new and slightly more difficult materials are prescribed.

Sometimes this technique is combined with other techniques. For example, Bos (1982) used repeated reading together with the neurological impress method (a technique in which teacher and student read aloud together, with the teacher sitting behind the student and reading slightly faster and louder than the student) and reported improvement in word recognition and comprehension.

The advantages and disadvantages of this approach have been reviewed by Moyer (1982). In a recent study with learning disabled children (Rashotte and Torgesen, 1985), it was found that increases in reading fluency with the repeated reading technique depend on the amount of shared words among stories. When stories have relatively little shared vocabulary, little generalization occurs, and repeated reading is no more effective for improving reading speed than an equivalent amount of nonrepetitive reading.

Classroom Approaches to Reading Instruction

Table 2–10 summarizes the various approaches to the teaching of reading that are used often in regular classroom settings. In a subsequent section, we will address reading approaches that are more commonly used in resource rooms or other more intensive, clinical-type settings. Classroom approaches are used for regular developmental reading programs. They can also be adapted for the amelioration of specific reading problems in one student or a group of students with similar difficulties. In addition to the overview of selected available reading programs given in Table 2–10, two other related topics are dealt with in this section. First, procedures to be used in selecting materials at appropriate reading levels are discussed. Second, a discussion of the role of scope-and-sequence charts to basal series and reading instruction is presented, along with an example of such a chart adapted from Kaluger and Kolson (1978).

Selecting Materials at Appropriate Level for Students

No matter which of the preceding approaches is selected as being the most appropriate for a particular student, it is necessary to identify materials that match the student's instructional level. Reading texts and sometimes textbooks in such subjects as social studies are clearly designated by grade level of difficulty. For the secondary level, however, and for supplementary or trade books at all levels, teachers need to be able to assess the difficulty level, or readability, of the material.

One way that readability can be assessed is through the use of one of the readability formulas that have been developed (e.g., E. Fry, 1977). Basically these readability formulas are based on the finding that text with longer words and sentences is generally harder to read than text with shorter words and sentences.

Table 2–10. Classroom Reading Approaches

Type of Approach	Where Available	Advantages/Disadvantages/ Special Comments
Complete Basals. These usually consist of reading texts, teacher's manual, and supplementary materials such as workbooks. They are often sequenced in a series from K to Grade 6 or 8. The instructional approach is one of introducing a controlled sight vocabulary coupled with an analytic phonics emphasis.	Holt Basic Reading Ginn 720 Series American Book Company Readers Scott, Foresman Reading Houghton Mifflin Reading Program MacMillan Series E Lippincott Basic Reading Pathfinder (Allyn and Bacon)	1. Basals lend themselves well to the three-reading-group arrangement; less well to individualizing 2. Content usually designed for the "typical" child; often not appealing to inner-city or rural children 3. Basals are generally well sequenced and comprehensive; attend to most aspects of developmental reading 4. Most have complete pupil packets of supplementary materials, saving teacher searching time 5. Basals are sufficiently detailed and integrated that successful use is possible for a teacher lacking in confidence or experience
Synthetic Phonics Basals. Similar to above in some ways, but emphasis is on mastering component phonics skills, then putting together into words.	Open Court Reading Program Lippincott's Basic Reader Series DISTAR I, II, III Swirl Community Skills Program (SW Regional Laboratory)	1. Same as above 2. Evidence is that a synthetic approach to word-attack is rarely utilized by good readers
Linguistic Phonemic Approaches. Vocabulary that is used is highly controlled and conforms to the sound patterns of English (e.g., Nan, Dan, man, fan, ran, etc.). Most programs contain children's texts, teacher's manual, and supplementary materials.	Let's Read (Bloomfield) SRA Basic Reading Series Merrill Linguistic Readers Programmed Reading (Webster, McGraw-Hill) SRA Lift-Off to Reading Palo Alto Program (Harcourt, Brace, Jovanovich)	1. Content and usage in stories (especially early ones) sometimes contrived because of controlled vocabulary 2. Same as for Complete Basals

(continued)

Table 2–10 *Continued*

Type of Approach	*Where Available*	*Advantages/Disadvantages/ Special Comments*
Individualized Reading. Each child reads materials of own choice and at own rate. Word recognition and comprehension skills are taught as individual children need them. Monitoring of progress is done through individual teacher conferences. Careful record-keeping is necessary.	Trade books of many different types, topics, and levels	1. Children are interested in content 2. Individualized reading promotes good habits of selection of reading materials 3. An extensive collection of books is needed for students to make choices 4. Teacher needs comprehensive knowledge of reading skills to make sure all are covered 5. Required record-keeping can be cumbersome
Diagnostic-Prescriptive Programs. These consist of entry-testing and exit-testing of skills related to specific skills. Students who pass entry test go on to other needed areas. Reading objectives fully stated.	*Print* Wisconsin Design for Reading Skill (National Computer Systems) Fountain Valley Reading Support System (Richard Zweig) Ransom Program (Addison-Wesley) *Nonprint, Computer-Assisted* Stanford University CAI Project Harcourt Brace CAI Remedial Reading Program	1. Skills are usually well sequenced 2. Pupils work at own pace 3. Learning may be boring, repetitive, or mechanistic 4. Programs provide for on-going assessment and feedback 5. Programs de-emphasize the language basis of reading (interaction and communication with other people) 6. Only those skills that lend themselves to the format are taught
Language Experience Approach. This approach is based on teacher's recording of child's narrated experiences. These stories become basis for reading. May be based on level of group or individual child. Stories are collected and made into a "book."	Teacher-made materials	1. Relationship to child's experience is explicit 2. Approach firmly establishes reading as a language/communicative act 3. Approach provides no systematic skill development (left up to the teacher to improvise) 4. Approach can reinforce only at child's existing level, rather than pushing him or her on 5. Usage is highly adaptable to pupils with unique needs and backgrounds

Klare (1976) found that readability is significantly related to comprehension, but readability formulas do have their shortcomings. Irwin and Davis (1980) have recognized these shortcomings and have attempted to address them in their *Readability Checklist* (see Figure 2–7). It should be noted that their checklist is divided into two major components—"Understandability" and "Learnability." This checklist is recommended for use because each item has been included on the basis of empirical evidence linking that question to reading, understanding, and retention.

Scope-and-Sequence Charts

Most authors of classroom basal series provide a scope-and-sequence chart or table that outlines the major skill areas considered in their programs and the specific instructional activities that are taught, in order of presentation. Scope-and-sequence charts can be used to build individual educational programs for problem students or to identify content for teacher-made tests.

For example, if a commercially prepared word-attack test indicates that a student is having trouble with initial consonant blends, the teacher should consult a scope-and-sequence chart to establish whether the student is at about the place in the program where the blends are usually taught. On the chart we have provided (Table 2–11), the initial blends *st, pl, bl, br, tr, dr, gr,* and *fr* appear as skills to be taught near the end of first grade. The blends *cr, sn, sl, pr,* and *cl* are not taught until the beginning of the second grade; the blends *thr, gl, squ, apr,* and *str* are typically taught in the latter half of second grade. So, depending on where the student is in the program, the teacher will construct a test with the appropriate items. The skill should be tested in a variety of ways—including the ability to discriminate one blend from another, such as between the spoken words "brown" and "frown." The student might be presented with pictures of such items as "clown" and "crown" and be asked to point to the one for which the teacher says the name. Or the student can be asked to circle all the pictures on a page that start with "pl." Other ideas for format can be found in workbook pages and in the suggested exercises of a good basal reading series. Note that the activities for testing the students are very similar to the activities for teaching them. In fact, the teacher should think of each day's instruction as a test/teach/test sequence, with each element of instruction being based specifically on the prior "test" results. This cyclical test/teach/test paradigm is especially adaptable to instruction in word-attack skills.

One word of caution is in order in using the scope-and-sequence chart we have provided, or any chart found in a basal series. At the present time, the sequencing of these skills (i.e., which skills should be taught in first grade, which in second, and so on) are based on the judgment of "experts" and on tradition. Such sequences or hierarchies of skills have not yet been validated (Bourque,

Figure 2–7. Readability Checklist

This checklist is designed to help you evaluate the readability of your classroom texts. It can best be used if you rate your text while you are thinking of a specific class. Be sure to compare the textbook to a fictional ideal rather than to another text. Your goal is to find out what aspects of the text are or are not less than ideal. Finally, consider supplementary workbooks as part of the textbook and rate them together. Have fun!

Rate the questions below using the following rating system:

5—Excellent
4—Good
3—Adequate
2—Poor
1—Unacceptable
NA—Not applicable

Further comments may be written in the space provided.

Textbook title: _____

Publisher: _____

Copyright date: _____

Understandability

A. ____Are the assumptions about students' vocabulary knowledge appropriate?

B. ____Are the assumptions about students' prior knowledge of this content area appropriate?

C. ____Are the assumptions about students' general experiential backgrounds appropriate?

D. ____Does the teacher's manual provide the teacher with ways to develop and review the students' conceptual and experiential backgrounds?

E. ____Are new concepts explicitly linked to the students' prior knowledge or to their experiential backgrounds?

F. ____Does the text introduce abstract concepts by accompanying them with many concrete examples?

G. ____Does the text introduce new concepts one at a time with a sufficient number of examples for each one?

H. ____Are definitions understandable and at a lower level of abstraction than the concept being defined?

I. ____Is the level of sentence complexity appropriate for the students?

J. ____Are the main ideas of paragraphs, chapters, and subsections clearly stated?

K. ____Does the text avoid irrelevant details?

L. ____Does the text explicitly state important complex relationships (e.g., causality, conditionality, etc.) rather than always expecting the reader to infer them from the context?

M. ____Does the teacher's manual provide lists of accessible resources containing alternative readings for the very poor or very advanced readers?

N. ____Is the readability level appropriate (according to a readability formula)?

Learnability
Organization

A. ____Is an introduction provided for in each chapter?

B. ____Is there a clear and simple organizational pattern relating the chapters to each other?

Figure 2–7 *Continued*

C. ____Does each chapter have a clear, explicit, and simple organizational structure?

D. ____Does the text include resources such as an index, glossary, and table of contents?

E. ____Do questions and activities draw attention to the organizational pattern of the material (e.g., chronological, cause and effect, spatial, topical, etc.)?

F. ____Do consumable materials interrelate well with the textbook?

Reinforcement

A. ____Does the text provide opportunities for students to practice using new concepts?

B. ____Are there summaries at appropriate intervals in the text?

C. ____Does the text provide adequate iconic aids such as maps, graphs, illustrations, etc. to reinforce concepts?

D. ____Are there adequate suggestions for usable supplementary activities?

E. ____Do these activities provide for a broad range of ability levels?

F. ____Are there literal recall questions provided for the students' self-review?

G. ____Do some of the questions encourage the students to draw inferences?

H. ____Are there discussion questions which encourage creative thinking?

I. ____Are questions clearly worded?

Motivation

A. ____Does the teacher's manual provide introductory activities that will capture students' interest?

B. ____Are chapter titles and subheadings concrete, meaningful, or interesting?

C. ____Is the writing style of the text appealing to the students?

D. ____Are the activities motivating? Will they make the students want to pursue the topic further?

E. ____Does the book clearly show how the knowledge being learned might be used by the learner in the future?

F. ____Are the cover, format, print size, and pictures appealing to the students?

G. ____Does the text provide positive and motivating models for both sexes as well as for other racial, ethnic, and socioeconomic groups?

Readability analysis

Weaknesses

1) On which items was the book rated the lowest?

2) Did these items tend to fall in certain categories?

3) Summarize the weaknesses of this text.

4) What can you do in class to compensate for the weaknesses of this text?

Assets

1) On which items was the book rated the highest?

2) Did these items fall in certain categories?

3) Summarize the assets of this text.

4) What can you do in class to take advantage of the assets of this text?

Source: J. W. Irwin and C. A. Davis, Assessing readability, the checklist approach, *Journal of Reading,* November 1980, 129–130. Reprinted with permission of the authors and the International Reading Association.

Table 2–11.   Typical Scope-and-Sequence of Reading Skills Usually Taught at the Elementary Level

	Word-Study Skills	Comprehension Skills

First Grade — Preprimer Stage	A. Word meaning and concept building
	B. Picture clues
	C. Visual discrimination
	D. Auditory skills
	   1. Initial consonants —e.g., *b, c, d, f*
	   2. Rhyming elements
	E. Structural analysis
		A. Associating text and pictures
		B. Following oral directions
		C. Understanding main idea
		D. Understanding details
		E. Understanding sequence
		F. Drawing conclusions
		G. Seeing relationships

First Grade — Primer Stage	A. Review, reteach, or teach all skills not mastered and expand vocabulary
	B. Context clues
	C. Phonetic analysis
	   1. Initial consonants
	   2. Rhymes
	   3. Learning letter names—*n, l, p, d, g, r, c*
	D. Structural analysis
		A. Understanding all those skills listed at preprimer level
		B. Forming judgments
		C. Making inferences
		D. Classifying

First Grade — First Reader	A. Review all previous skills
	B. Phonetic analysis
	   1. Final consonants
	   2. Initial blends—*st, pl, bl, br, tr, dr, gr, fr*
	C. Structural analysis
	   1. Verb forms—*ed, ing*
	   2. Compound words
		A. Reviewing all previously taught skills
		B. Recalling story facts
		C. Predicting outcome
		D. Following printed directions

Table 2–11   *Continued*

Word-Study Skills	*Comprehension Skills*

Book One
 A. Review and practice all first-grade skills
 B. Phonetic analysis
   1. Rhyming words visually
   2. Consonants
     a. Initial—*j*
     b. Final—*x, r, l*
     c. Blends—*cr, sn, sl, pr, cl*
     d. Digraphs—*ai, oa*
 C. Structural analysis
   1. Plural of nouns—adding *s* and *es*
   2. Variant forms of verbs
     a. Adding *es, ing*
     b. Doubling consonants before adding *ing* or *ed*
	A. Reviewing all previously taught skills
	 B. Making generalizations
	 C. Seeing relationships
	 D. Interpreting pictures

Book Two
 A. Review all previously taught skills
 B. Recognize words in alphabetical order
 C. Phonetic analysis
   1. Consonant blends—*thr, gl, squ, apr, str*
   2. Phonograms—auditory and visual concepts of *ar, er, ir, ow, ick, ew, own, uck, ed, ex, ouse, ark, oat, ound*
   3. Vowel differences
     a. Vowels lengthened by final *e*
     b. Long and short sounds of *y*
     c. Digraphs—*ee, ea*
     d. Diphthongs—different sounds of *ow*
 D. Structural analysis
   1. Contractions—*it's, I'm, I'll, that's, let's, don't, didn't, isn't*
   2. Variant forms of verbs—dropping *e* before adding *ing*
   3. Plural forms of nouns—changing *y* to *ies*
	A. Practicing and using all previously taught skills
	 B. Making inferences
	 C. Seeing cause-and-effect relationships

Second Grade (spanning both Book One and Book Two rows)

(continued)

Table 2-11   *Continued*

Word-Study Skills	*Comprehension Skills*

Book One

A. Review all previously learned skills
B. Word meaning
   1. Opposites
   2. Adding *er, est* to change meaning of words
   3. Words with multiple meanings
C. Phonetic analysis
   1. Consonants
      a. Hard and soft sounds—*c, g*
      b. Recognizing consonants
      c. Digraphs—*ck*
   2. Vowels
      a. Silent vowels
      b. Digraphs—*ai, ea, ou,* etc.
D. Structural analysis
   1. Contractions
   2. Possessive words
   3. Suffixes—*en, est, ly*
   4. Variant forms of verbs
E. Alphabetizing—first letter
F. Syllabication—up to three-syllable words

Comprehension Skills (Book One):
A. Practicing all skills previously learned
B. Detecting mood of situation
C. Relating story facts to own experiences
D. Reading pictorial maps
E. Skimming

Book Two

A. Review all previously learned skills
B. Word meaning
   1. Homonyms—*dew, do; sea, see;* etc.
   2. Synonyms—*throw, pitch; quiet, still; speak, say;* etc.
C. Phonetic analysis
   1. Consonants—hard/soft sounds of *g, c*
   2. Vowels
      a. Diphthongs—*ou, ow, or,* etc.
      b. Sounds of vowels followed by *r*
D. Structural analysis
   1. Plurals—change *f* to *v* when adding *es*
   2. Contractions—*doesn't, you'll, they're*
   3. Suffixes
   4. Prefixes—*un* changes meaning of words to the opposite
E. Alphabetizing—using second letter
F. Syllabication
   1. Between double consonants
   2. Prefixes and suffixes as syllables
G. Accent—finding emphasized syllables

Comprehension Skills (Book Two):
A. Practicing all previously learned skills
B. Solving problems

(Left margin: Third Grade)

Table 2–11   *Continued*

Word-Study Skills	*Comprehension Skills*

A. Word meaning
  1. Antonyms
  2. Synonyms
  3. Homonyms
  4. Figures of speech
  5. Sensory appeals in words
B. Word analysis
  1. Phonetic analysis
    a. Consonants
     (1) Silent
     (2) Two sounds of *s*
     (3) Hard and soft sounds of *c* and *g*
     (4) Diacritical marks
      (a) Long sound of vowels
      (b) Short sounds of vowels
     (5) Applying vowel principles
      (a) Vowel in the middle of a word or syllable is usually *short*
      (b) Vowel coming at the end of a one-syllable word is usually *long*
      (c) When a one-syllable word ends in *e*, the medial vowel in that word is usually *long*
      (d) When two vowels come together, the first vowel is usually *long* and the second vowel is *silent*
  2. Structural analysis
    a. Hyphenated words
    b. Finding root words in word variants
    c. Prefixes—*dis, re, un, im*
    d. Suffixes—*ly, ness, ment, ful, ish, less*
    e. Syllabication
     (1) When a vowel is followed by one consonant, that consonant usually begins the next syllable
     (2) When a vowel sound in a word is followed by two consonants, this word is usually divided between the two consonants
    f. Accent
	A. Practicing all previously learned skills
	B. Reading for comprehension
	C. Finding the main ideas
	D. Finding details
	E. Organizing and summarizing
	F. Recalling story facts
	G. Recognizing sequence
	H. Reading for information
	I. Reading creatively
	  1. Classifying
	  2. Detecting the mood of a situation
	  3. Drawing conclusions
	  4. Forming judgments
	  5. Making inferences
	  6. Predicting outcomes
	  7. Seeing cause-and-effect relationships
	  8. Solving problems
	J. Following printed directions
	K. Skimming

Fourth Grade

(continued)

Table 2–11 *Continued*

Word-Study Skills	Comprehension and Study Skills

<table>
<tr><td valign="top">

Fifth Grade

A. Antonyms—review and practice
B. Expand vocabulary
C. Review figures of speech and introduce new ones to enrich vocabulary
D. Homonyms—review and introduce new ones
E. Synonyms—review and introduce new ones to expand vocabulary
F. Use of dictionary and glossary
G. Phonetic analysis
  1. Review consonant sounds
  2. Review pronunciation of diacritical marks
  3. Review phonograms
H. Structural analysis
  1. Compound words
  2. Words of similar configuration
  3. Prefixes, review and introduce *in-, anti-, inter-, mis-*
  4. Suffixes, review and introduce *-sp, -or, -ours, -ness, -ward, -hood, -action, -al*
  5. Syllabication
  6. Application of word analysis in attacking words outside the basic vocabulary

</td><td valign="top">

A. Continuing development in the following areas:
  1. Understanding main idea
  2. Understanding sequence
  3. Reading for details
  4. Appreciating literary style
  5. Drawing conclusions
  6. Enriching information
  7. Evaluating information
  8. Forming opinions and generalizing
  9. Interpreting ideas
  10. Using alphabetical arrangement
  11. Using dictionary or glossary skills
  12. Interpreting maps and pictures
  13. Skimming for purpose
  14. Classifying ideas
  15. Following directions
  16. Outlining
  17. Summarizing
  18. Reading for accurate detail
  19. Skimming
B. Introducing
  1. Discriminating between fact and fiction
  2. Perceiving related ideas
  3. Strengthening power of recall
  4. Using encyclopedias, atlas, almanac, and other references
  5. Using charts and graphs
  6. Using index and pronunciation keys
  7. Reading to answer questions and for enjoyment of literary style

</td></tr>
</table>

Table 2–11 *Continued*

	Word-Study Skills	*Comprehension and Study Skills*	*Locating and Using Information (Study Skills)*

Sixth Grade	A. Word meaning
	  1. Antonyms—review and practice
	  2. Homonyms—develop ability to use correctly
	  3. Classify words of related meaning
	  4. Enrich word meaning
	  5. Review use of synonyms
	  6. Use of context clues in attacking new words
	  7. Expand vocabulary
	  8. Become aware of expressions that refer to place and time and develop skill in interpreting such expressions
	  9. Use dictionary and glossary
	B. Word analysis
	  1. Phonetic analysis—review consonant sounds, diacritical marks, and vowel sound principles
	  2. Structural analysis
	    a. Review compound and hyphenated words
	    b. Review prefixes and introduce *trans-, pre-, fore-, ir-, non-*
	    c. Review suffixes and introduce *-able, -ance, -ence, -ate, -est, -ent, -ity, -ic, -ist, -like*
	    d. Review principles of syllabication
	    e. Review accented syllables
	    f. Apply word analysis to words outside the basic vocabulary
		A. Continuing development in the following areas
		  1. Understanding main ideas
		  2. Understanding sequence
		  3. Reading for details
		  4. Appreciating literary style
		  5. Drawing conclusions
		    a. Predicting outcomes
		    b. Forming judgments
		    c. Seeing relationships
		  6. Extending and enriching information
		  7. Interpreting pictures
		  8. Evaluating information
		  9. Interpreting ideas
		  10. Using facts to form opinions, generalizing
		B. Introducing the skills of
		  1. Enriching imagery
		  2. Discriminating between fact and fiction
		  3. Strengthening power of recall
			A. Reviewing skills in the following
			  1. Arranging alphabetically
			  2. Using dictionary and glossary
			  3. Using encyclopedia, almanac, and other references
			  4. Interpreting maps and pictures
			  5. Skimming for a purpose
			  6. Classifying ideas
			  7. Following directions
			  8. Summarizing
			  9. Outlining
			  10. Reading for accurate detail
			  11. Using index and pronunciation keys
			  12. Using charts and graphs
			B. Introducing the following skills
			  1. Using facts and figures
			  2. Using headings and type style—especially italics
			  3. Using an index
			  4. Using the library
			  5. Using a table of contents
			  6. Taking notes
			  7. Reading informational material
			  8. Reading poetry

Source: Adapted from G. Kaluger and C. J. Kolson, *Reading and Learning Disabilities,* Second Edition (Columbus, Ohio: Charles E. Merrill, 1978).

1980). Hence, the teacher cannot be *certain* that Skill A must be mastered before Skill B is introduced or even that the mastery of Skill A will facilitate the learning of Skill B. For this reason, the teacher should use discretion in making decisions for a particular student.

Special Remedial Approaches

The following teaching techniques are often used in schools or classes that specialize in children with reading disabilities. A regular classroom teacher would not usually be expected to use any of these clinical approaches in their entirety. However, they can be modified and adapted to meet the needs of specific children.

The Fernald (VAKT) Approach

If a child has a severe word-learning difficulty, and visual-auditory approaches have been unsuccessful, a modification of the Fernald (1943) Word Learning Technique is recommended. Although several authors refer to Fernald's remedial technique for teaching disabled readers as a kinesthetic method, the system is actually multisensory, involving four modalities simultaneously—visual, auditory, kinesthetic, and tactile (or VAKT). The approach is cognitive, for the words learned always originate with the reader and have contextual or meaningful association.

Fernald, who opened a clinic school at UCLA in 1920, was concerned with the emotional components of failure to learn. "The child who fails in his school work is always an emotional problem" (1943, p. 7). The circular aspect of this dilemma was approached in two ways: by analyzing the problem and by reconditioning the student. Both are positive approaches to remediation that call the learner's attention to what he or she has already learned and assure the student that one can learn any words that one wants to learn. To maintain a positive learning climate the following are avoided: (1) emotionally laden situations, (2) the use of methods associated with previous failure, (3) embarrassing situations, and (4) references to the learner's problems. Poor readers are divided into two groups: total or extreme disability, and partial disability. The VAKT method is used with children from both groups when the disability is failure to recognize words.

Perception of the word as a whole is basic to the Fernald method. For example, Sara begins remediation by story writing, initially about anything of interest, and later concerning her various school subjects. Sara "asks" for any word she does not know. It is written for her, learned by her, and used immediately in her story. What she has written is typed so that she may read it while its content is still fresh in her mind. For children with extreme disability, almost every word is necessarily taught.

Stage I uses a multisensory approach. When Sara requests a word, it is written or printed for her with black crayon in blackboard-size script on a piece of heavy paper. She traces the word with firm, two-finger contact (tactile-kinesthetic), and says the word aloud in syllables (auditory) as she traces. She sees the word while she is tracing (visual), and hears it as she says it (auditory). She repeats the process until she can write the word correctly twice, without looking at the sample. When tracing or writing, she always writes the word as a unit, without stopping. If she errs, Sara begins again with the first step. Copying a word by alternately looking at the sample and writing a few letters is forbidden. After the lesson, the words are filed alphabetically, to provide a record or source of the words learned.

After a period of tracing, the tactile phase is discontinued and Stage II is begun. Here Sara learns a new word by following the looking, saying, and writing steps of Stage I. Vocabulary is still learned in context and involves VAKT. There is no arbitrary time limit for the tracing period and usually the student tends to drop tracing of his or her own accord.

Stage III dispenses with the kinesthetic mode, and Sara learns a new word merely by looking at the sample and saying it to herself.

Stage IV is achieved when Sara has the ability to recognize new words by their similarity to words or to parts of words that she has already learned (i.e., when she can generalize her reading skills). Teaching phonics is not considered necessary, for this generalizing process presumably occurs without phonetic analysis. At this stage the student reads to satisfy her curiosity.

The amount of reading necessary before discontinuing remediation and returning the student to the regular classroom reading situation depends on the educational level he or she must reach. Older students spend more time in Stage IV, and they do not return to the regular instructional setting until they are able to read well enough to make progress at their own instructional level.

In addition to those already stated, Fernald holds several principles:

1. Students are never read to; they must do their own reading.
2. The student never sounds out words, unless he or she does it while scanning a paragraph for unknown words before beginning to read that paragraph.
3. At any stage, material must be suited to the child's age and intelligence.

Careful scheduling is important, as the teacher cannot plan to work with one child unless all of the other children are involved in some purposeful activity. The student's resentment at being taken away from gym or art also might outweigh any positive accomplishment. It should be emphasized that the Fernald approach (VAKT) is basically a word-learning technique, and the child should have directed reading instruction in a group, or individually, to develop comprehension skills.

The Gillingham (Orton) Phonics Approach

This remedial, phonics-oriented reading program (Gillingham and Stillman, 1970) is based on the theoretical work of Orton. The systematic approaches to reading, spelling, and writing are adapted to all levels from age six through high school. This "alphabetic system" is based on the premise that children who fail to read by group methods do so because group programs rely on visual-receptive strength. In contrast, Gillingham's training system stresses auditory discrimination abilities with supplementary emphasis on kinesthetic and tactile modalities. Although phonetic methods help the child to synthesize what he or she sees with what he or she hears, visual perception is used minimally.

Gillingham's synthetic approach is essentially a formal skill-building program. Teachers are encouraged to follow the manual to attain success. The entire program is built on eight basic linkages that form the association of auditory, visual, and kinesthetic stimuli. Once the student has mastered basic sound production, he or she is introduced to phonograms (one letter or a group of letters that represents a phonetic sound). Once the phonograms have been mastered, they are used in drill procedures.

The teaching procedure begins with the introduction of the short "a" sound plus several specified consonant sounds. When these have been learned by the method above, blending is begun. Several phonogram cards are placed side by side. Individual sounds are produced in succession and with increasing speed until a fluid rate is achieved. The day following the initiation of the blending procedure, word analysis begins. This is achieved on an auditory level with the teacher sounding the word, and the student identifying the letters he or she hears. This process leads directly to the simultaneous oral spelling process, in which the teacher says the word, the student says the word, names the letters, then writes the letters as he or she names them. This procedure is always used in the production of phonetically pure words.

One of the stipulations of the early program is that the student is given no other printed materials. If the student remains in a regular class while receiving remedial help, all other subject material must be presented auditorially. After blending has been established with all of the phonetic sounds, a reader or primer may be introduced. Books are carefully screened to ensure that all words included are phonetic and thus suitable for blending. The student is then introduced to basic phonetic rules, including syllabication and accent (all of which are included in the manual). When the student is able to synthesize and analyze any combination of phonetic syllables, nonphonetic syllables are introduced and memorized as whole syllables.

Gillingham's program for developing skills combines the use of phonetic study as well as experiences and language stories. Tracing, copying, and dictation are used simultaneously to achieve different purposes. Tracing is useful in learning the formation of letters and establishing a letter sequence for spelling.

Copying develops visual memory; after practicing, the students must produce a model that has been removed from sight. The purpose of dictation is to lengthen the auditory attention span and promote the association between auditory stimuli and visual imagery.

Initially, Gillingham felt that students who were capable of learning by visual methods should do so. However, in "Correspondence" (1958), she noted the difficulties students have with spelling and concluded that the kinesthetic and auditory stimuli provided in her program would prevent such difficulties. Therefore, she advised that all students be exposed in the "Alphabetic System."

The success of this system seems dependent on its use with children whose auditory discrimination is unimpaired. It is essential that the student's strengths as well as weaknesses be diagnosed. To extend its effectiveness, meaningful interpretations and activities must be introduced despite the admonitions of Gillingham.

Both Dechant (1964) and Gates (1947) have been critical of this system. Their concerns center on the lack of meaningful activities, the rigidity of the teaching procedures, and the tendency to develop labored reading. If valid, these points would certainly limit the usefulness of the system as a total reading program. Interestingly, Harris (1968) noted that even though this approach has been used for many years, he had been unable to locate any comparative research on it.

DISTAR I, II, III

The Direct Instructional System for Teaching Arithmetic and Reading (DISTAR) (Engelmann and Bruner, 1973, 1974, 1975) is a highly structured program that was originally developed for young culturally disadvantaged children. It has since been revised and reorganized so as to be suitable for handicapped students from beginning to more advanced reading levels (six levels in all).

The program consists of lessons based on carefully sequenced skill hierarchies that entail the following:

1. The teacher uses games, flash cards, chalkboard, wall charts, etc., to present a fully scripted lesson.
2. The students (individually and in unison as a group) provide the desired response.
3. Correct responses are immediately reinforced by the teacher.
4. Additional skill practice is provided.
5. The teacher evaluates the degree of mastery of individuals and the group on criterion-referenced tasks and tests.
6. Children are regrouped as necessary, depending on their performance.

The companion *Corrective Reading Program* is designed for older students who have not yet learned to read. It consists of two strands: decoding, which follows the regular DISTAR format; and comprehension, which presents real-life situations for adolescents.

Edmark Reading Program

The Edmark program (Bijou, 1977) was designed especially for lower functioning handicapped students for whom full adult literacy might not be a reasonable goal. It is designed to teach a survival sight vocabulary of 150 functional words. The program consists of several hundred lessons that use stories and student activities. The emphasis is on word recognition and word comprehension rather than on sentences. Readers who want a complete description of the program are referred to V. L. Brown's (1984) comprehensive review.

Examples of Specific Remedial Techniques in Reading

The following list of remedial techniques can aid the teacher in helping certain students overcome specific difficulties in reading. The teacher should carefully file remedial activities so that they can be used again and again. In a few years it is possible to collect a significant number of specific exercises that can be used for individual follow-up to a group reading lesson.

Problem Area	*Suggested Remedial Activity*
I. General word recognition (basic sight vocabulary)	1. The picture dictionary. The student makes a scrapbook that is indexed with the letters of the alphabet. Pictures can be drawn or cut out of magazines. As the student learns a word, he or she pastes a picture on the page that has that letter. For example, the word "car" would go on the C page. This has advantages over commercial picture dictionaries because it contains the words that the student is learning and because the student makes it. It is most useful with nouns.

Problem Area

Front   Back

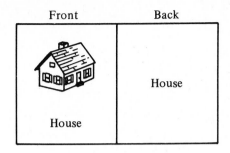

House   House

Front   Back

Run   Rat
               Rub
               Run

Suggested Remedial Activity

2. Picture cards and tracing. On one side of the card a picture is placed with a word underneath it; on the other side the word is printed. The teacher presents the card with the word and picture side up and pronounces the word. Next the student pronounces the word. Then the student pronounces and traces the word until he or she can recognize the word without seeing the picture. The words can be reviewed from time to time and used as an independent drill. This procedure is most useful with nouns.

3. Matching words with pictures. This exercise can be used with words other than nouns. For example, a clear picture of a child running can be used to help teach the word "run." On the back of the card, the picture is reproduced. The student is given three words and must match the word and the picture.

4. Labeling. Labels can be attached to the door, closet, window, pictures, bulletin board, and other things in the room so that the student will begin to associate the written symbol with the object.

5. Tachistoscope. To make a tachistoscope, the teacher can cut a piece of oaktag or cardboard to a 5-by 8-inch size. The top and bottom are folded down about ½ inch to hold the word cards. A window is cut in the center to expose the word and a shutter is attached to the outside. Word cards can be

Problem Area   *Suggested Remedial Activity*

made with basic sight vocabulary words on them. These can be flashed by quickly opening the shutter. If the student misses a word, it can be reexposed so that the student will be able to apply word-attack skills.

6. Phrase cards. Short phrases, then longer phrases should be introduced. These can be used in the tachistoscope exercise.

II. Reversals
   A. Word

1. The word is placed on a 5- by 8-inch card in crayon. The pupil is asked to say the word, trace it, and say it again. The student should do this a number of times and then be given an opportunity to read it in a sentence.

2. The teacher can hold up a card that is covered with a sheet of paper. The sheet of paper is then moved to the right so that the letters are exposed in the proper sequence.

3. The teacher can use a card with the word printed on it and the first letter lightly colored.

4. The teacher can place some design (e.g., a diamond) to call the student's attention to the first letter.

   B. Letters

1. The letter should be placed on a 3- by 5-inch card. The student should first trace it until he or she is ready to write it correctly, and then practice writing it. This can also be done at the chalkboard.

2. Pictures illustrating words that begin with the letters the child reverses. For example, for the letters "b" and "d," pictures of a boat and a duck can be used. The picture of

Problem Area

Suggested Remedial Activity

the duck would be placed to the left of the "d." The picture of the boat would be placed next to the lower part of the "b" and to the right of it.

3. Stories may be used to differentiate letters frequently reversed:
This is b
b is on the line
b is tall like a building
b looks to the right

III. Initial sounds
Note: Teacher's manuals of readiness and primary-level reading books may have more suggestions.

h	ard
	and
	ouse

1. The teacher can dictate a series of three or four words that begin with the same sound. The student writes the letter that represents the initial sound.

2. On 3- by 5-inch index cards, the teacher places a letter on the left side and three or four phonograms on the right. The student is asked to give the initial sound and then the whole word.

3. Picture dictionary. See item 1 under General word recognition.

4. Rotating wheel. Two cardboard circles, one smaller than the other, can be fastened together so that they rotate freely. Common phonographs are placed on the larger wheel, initial consonants are placed on the smaller one. As the larger circle is rotated, initial consonants can be combined with phonograms.

IV. Final sounds
Note: Teacher's manuals from linguistically based reading series have many suggestions for developing this skill.

1. A rhyming book can be made to illustrate word families.

2. The teacher asks the student to give a rhyming word for the one the teacher has just pronounced. These can be placed on the chalkboard and the parts that sound alike can be underlined.

Problem Area

b	
l	
m	end
s	

V. Medial vowel sounds

VI. Endings

VII. Context clues

We ride to school on a (bus).
At night I go to (bed).

Suggested Remedial Activity

3. Cards can be made with an initial consonant on the left and an ending on the right. The student blends the initial sound with the ending to make new words.

1. Practice exercises should be developed to make the student focus attention on the medial vowel sound in the word. For example:
    a. The cat sat on a (rig, rog, rug).
    b. The cat sat on a r__g.

2. Key cards can be made with the vowel colored to call attention to the sound
    b*a*t   b*e*t   b*i*t   b*o*t   b*u*t
    (Because "bot" is a nonsense word, the student may remember it for its uniqueness.)

1. Three columns of words can be placed on cards (or the chalkboard), and the student asked to pick out the one that has a different ending from the other two.

1. This teaches the student to anticipate meanings. If a new word, such as "toys," is to be introduced, the teacher writes a sentence like "Jim saw many _____ in the window of the store." The student is asked what Jim might have seen that starts with a "t." (The teacher should read the sentence and have the student simply respond with the word "toys.")

2. The teacher writes a sentence on the chalkboard containing only one word that the student does not know the meaning of but can infer through the context. The student is asked to read the sentence silently. When the student has read

Problem Area

Suggested Remedial Activity

it, the teacher asks if he or she knows what the last word is. If the student is having difficulty, further questions can be structured until he or she can infer the right word.

Mary is wearing a new
    dress.
    bless.
    class.
I carry my home. I like to live in water. I am in this room. What am I?

3. Sentences can be constructed with a number of choices. The student underlines the correct one to complete the sentence.

4. The teacher or the students make up riddles. These can be put on spirit-duplicating masters or on the chalkboard. The students must infer the meaning from the context.

VIII. Letter discrimination

put	*hat*
porch	hold
ball	hot
pot	pot
doll	hat
pass	have

1. The teacher places a list of words on the chalkboard and the student underlines the words that begin with the same letter as the first one.

IX. Phonemic and word discrimination

1. The teacher says that he or she is going to read a list of words. Most of them will begin alike (e.g., boat). Every time the student hears a word that does not begin like boat, he or she should clap hands.

2. The student is told to shut his or her eyes. Pairs of words are read and the student must tell if they sound exactly alike or are different.

3. Step 2 is followed with exercises on beginning sounds.

4. Step 2 is followed with exercises on final sounds.

5. The teacher pronounces a word and its beginning sound. The student is asked to give some more

Problem Area	*Suggested Remedial Activity*
	words that begin with the same beginning sound.
	6. Step 5 is followed with exercises on ending sounds.
X. Compound words	1. The student is given a list of compound words to separate.
	2. The teacher gives the student two lists of words and asks him or her to draw lines from the right column to the left to make compound words.
XI. Root words	1. The teacher presents a list of words with variant endings and the student circles the root word.
	2. The teacher presents the student with a list of words and a list of endings. The student is asked to make up as many *real* words as he or she can using the endings.
XII. Suffixes	1. The teacher writes a sentence on the chalkboard with a derived form of a word in it. The student finds the root word and then explains how it alters the meaning of the whole word or what the meaning of the suffix is.
	a. The teacher should start with words that do not change their spelling when a suffix is added.
	b. Spelling variations can be introduced one at a time, with practice provided before another one is added.
XIII. Prefixes	1. The teacher writes sentences on the chalkboard that contain words with prefixes. The student is asked to locate the root word. The student then explains what the new word means.
Jim locked the door. Jim __ locked the door.	2. The teacher writes sentences on the chalkboard. Each sentence is

Problem Area   *Suggested Remedial Activity*

written twice but in the second one space is left for a prefix on one word. The student is asked to think of a prefix that can be added to make the sentence mean the opposite.

XIV. Vocabulary development

1. The teacher should use any opportunities to introduce new words in discussion and call attention to them, e.g., "The sign over the main door of the school says 'exit.' What do you think it means?"
2. A modified crossword puzzle can be developed. For early grades, the first letter should be given.
3. Students can develop their own crossword puzzles.
4. The students can be asked to give words that they associate with the stimulus word, e.g., *volcano:* hot, lava, mountain, etc. The relationships among the words given are then discussed.

XV. Classification

1. The teacher prepares a list of words that can be separated into general classifications and asks the student to group them, e.g., *vegetables—house—transportation:* carrot, floor, car, airplane, tomato, helicopter, door, potato, train.
2. Lists of three or more words can be prepared. The student crosses out the one that doesn't belong.

XVI. Sequence

1. The teacher can cut up or draw a series of pictures that make a complete story when arranged in the proper sequence. The student arranges the pictures.
2. Strips of paper can be made with single sentences on each. The student arranges them to tell a complete story.

Problem Area	*Suggested Remedial Activity*
	3. The teacher writes out directions for making something in a scrambled order. The student numbers the steps in the order in which they should happen.
	4. Comic strips can be cut apart; the student puts them back together in appropriate sequence.
XVII. Following directions	1. The student is given a picture with specific directions as to how it should be colored and then completes it.
	2. The teacher gives a student a series of oral directions and asks him or her to carry them out in the order in which they were given. Directions should be simple at the start and gradually become more complex.
XVIII. Main ideas	1. After reading the students a short story, the teacher writes a list of phrases on the chalkboard. Students are asked to pick out the one that best tells the main idea. (In some cases, the phrases must be read to the students.)
	2. The teacher reads a story to the students and asks them to make up a title and tell why it is a good one.
	3. Exercises similar to 1 and 2 above can be done but with the student reading the story and completing the exercise independently.
	4. Older students may be asked to choose details from the story that support the main idea. Diagrams may be used to represent this:

Main Idea

Early humans discovered fire in different forms.

Problem Area	Suggested Remedial Activity

Supporting Details
lightning hot lava of spark from
volcanoes   stones
rubbed
together

XIX. Cause-effect

1. The teacher performs actions such as turning the light switch off. Students are asked what happened and why to establish the cause-effect relationship.
2. As part of a story activity, the teacher reads a causal statement and asks the students to give the effect.
3. The student is asked to match causes with effect.

XX. Comparison/contrast

1. After a student is shown two pictures that have some similarities to each other, he or she tells how they are alike and different.
2. The teacher can explain how two characters in a story are alike or different.
3. Older students may make a comparison/contrast chart.

chapter 3

Problems in Written Composition

by Donald D. Hammill

Writing is a highly complex method of expression involving the integration of eye-hand, linguistic, and conceptual abilities. Because of its complexity, it is one of the highest forms of communication and hence is usually the last to be mastered. As an expressive form of a graphic symbol system used for conveying thoughts, ideas, and feelings, writing may be considered to be "the other side of the coin" from reading, which is the receptive form of that system.

The term *writing* refers to a variety of interrelated graphic skills, including: (1) *composition*, or the ability to generate ideas and to express them in an acceptable grammar, while adhering to certain stylistic conventions; (2) *spelling*, or the ability to use letters to construct words in accordance with accepted usage; and (3) *handwriting*, or the ability to execute physically the graphic marks necessary to produce legible compositions or messages. For convenience, in this book we have arbitrarily divided the material on writing into three chapters. The first of these chapters will deal with problems relating to composition; the next chapter will handle spelling difficulties; and the third chapter will discuss the problems of legibility.

The present chapter, then, will discuss the nature of written composition, means by which it can be assessed, and instructional considerations and procedures for improving ability in this important area.

THE MAJOR ELEMENTS IN WRITTEN COMPOSITION

Written composition includes at least three interrelated elements: a cognitive component, a linguistic component, and a stylistic component. When these are combined with two additional elements, handwriting and spelling, the result is the comprehensive concept of the entire writing process. A brief description of each of the components involved in composition follows. With minor exception, these descriptions are essentially the same as those observed by Hammill and Larsen (1983).

Cognitive Component

The cognitive component refers to the ability to write logical, coherent, and sequenced written products. The actual piece may be a creative story, a personal or professional letter, an essay, or a factual accounting of events; however, regardless of its content, the passage must be formulated in such a way that it is readily understandable to a reader. Maturity in a written product is usually signaled by the use of titles, paragraphs, definite endings, character development, dialogue, or humor, or the expression of some philosophical or moral theme. The cognitive component is not as easily defined as are the other components, but a product that is immature in its development of expression is frequently "sloppy" in the presentation of ideas, disjointed in thought sequence, lacking in theme, or simply difficult to understand. Because the cognitive aspects of writing are often vague and subjective, teachers have tended to overlook this aspect of writing. This is regrettable, for if a person does not write conceptually, effective written communication is virtually impossible.

Linguistic Component

The linguistic component refers to the use of serviceable syntax and semantic structures. The selection of suitable words, tenses, plurals, subject-verb correspondences, and cases is essential to good writing. Particular vocabulary items and grammatical forms will vary somewhat from person to person, social class to social class, geographical area to geographical area, and ethnic group to ethnic group. In most cases, the particular grammars and vocabularies employed by different individuals are equally efficient in conveying a writer's meaning. For example, one person may write "I grew a lot this year," while another might write "I growed a lot this year." Even though the two individuals are using different grammatical rules in expressing the past tense of "grow," the sentences that are generated convey identical thoughts. Linguistically speaking, neither rule is right or wrong. If some people consider one form to be "better" than another, the reasons are likely to be rooted in sociological factors and personal preference.

Yet if writers wish to be "accepted" by the majority of readers who encounter their passages, some standards of linguistic usage must be maintained.

Relative to this point, Otto and Smith (1980) note that today there are at least five levels of English usage: the illiterate, the homely, the informal standard, the formal standard, and the literary. Illiterate usage, characteristic of individuals out of the cultural mainstream, is rarely accepted in the classroom and is targeted for correction; e.g., "he done," "didn't have no," "them books." The homely level is more acceptable to most people than the illiterate but is not quite as acceptable as standard forms of English. These homely forms, often regional in nature, are usually tolerated but rarely sanctioned by the school; e.g., confusion between "lie" and "lay," and "like" and "as." Informal standard English is the level of colloquial speech and writing used by most educated persons. It is employed in conversations and correspondence with friends and relatives but generally not with strangers or in formal situations. The grammatical forms characteristic of this level are intended for everyday use and are considered by most individuals to be both functional and acceptable. Otto and Smith suggest that this level should be the language of the classroom and the goal for most elementary students. The final two levels, formal standard English and the literary, are reserved for special occasions and purposes. Both are characterized by the absence of colloquial expressions, more than usual attention to the tone of the words, and agreement in number, tense, and case; e.g., "I *shall* be there." The structure used at the literary level raises the use of the English language to an art form; e.g., "Fourscore and seven years ago . . ." (literary form) for "Eighty-seven years ago . . ." (informal standard form).

Stylistic Component

The stylistic component refers to the use of "accepted" fashions or rules established for punctuation and capitalization. The rules governing punctuation and capitalization must be learned by students before they can write effectively. In most instances, children quickly recognize that capital letters are used to give stress to words of special significance and that commas separate thoughts within a sentence.

Many of the rules governing the use of style are arbitrary in nature, based in tradition, and do not necessarily facilitate meaning. Consider, for example, the placement of the period in relation to the quotation marks in the following sentence: Mary said, "I saw the boy." Whether the period is placed inside or outside of the quotation marks does not affect the meaning of the sentence. Other rules, however, are essential to understanding the sense of sentences and passages. For example, the meaning of the sentence "In reading, comprehension will be impaired greatly by poor vocabulary development" is altered considerably if the comma is omitted. Without the comma between "reading" and "comprehension," the sentence has no rational meaning.

Figure 3–1.   A Model of Written Language

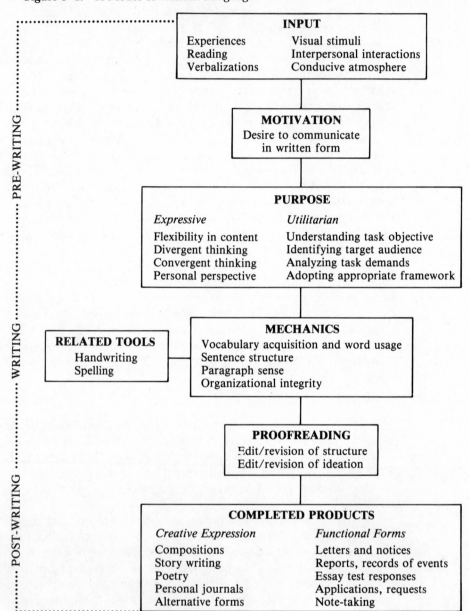

Source: E. A. Polloway, J. R. Patton, and S. B. Cohen, Written language for mildly handicapped students, *Focus on Exceptional Children,* 14, 3 (1981), 4.

Obviously, efficient and consistent use of the rules of punctuation and capitalization enhances the quality of a written product. In some instances, it is an absolute necessity for conveying the meaning of written communications.

Polloway, Patton, and Cohen (1981) position writing within a personal and social context. In their model (see Figure 3–1), the cognitive, linguistic, and stylistic elements are called *mechanics* and are but one aspect of a multifaceted writing experience involving pre-writing and post-writing stages as well as the writing act itself. This model is of value to teachers because it focuses attention on the importance of considering the following factors before planning remedial programs: (1) the student's prior experiences, motivations, and needs, (2) the status of the student's current writing skills, and (3) the creative and functional products that are possible.

ASSESSING DIFFICULTIES IN WRITTEN COMPOSITION

Two important goals of assessment in written composition are (1) to identify individuals who are unable to write well enough to meet the minimum standards required for their personal daily needs and (2) to inventory their specific instructional needs. To accomplish these goals, teachers must know which skills are critical in writing and must have mastered the standardized and informal techniques required to do an instructionally relevant evaluation. This section is devoted to discussion of these important topics.

Informal Assessment of Writing Skills

The teacher begins the effort to assess written composition by deciding which skills are to be evaluated and in what order they are to be assessed. The teacher will find it easier to make these decisions if he or she has available a scope-and-sequence chart such as the one in Table 3–1.

In this chart, the scope is represented by capitalization, punctuation, vocabulary, word usage, sentence construction, grammar, and paragraph construction. These are the major aspects in the writing curriculum. The specific skills and the order in which they are to be assessed (or taught) are covered in the sequence. In this particular case, the skills in the sequence are grouped according to grade levels.

The entries in the chart suggest the breadth of skills that can be assessed by the teacher but do not indicate the precise evaluation procedures to be used. For performing evaluations, teachers must rely on subjective interpretation of students' written-work samples, on criterion-referenced tests that they have constructed for their own use, and on teacher-made checklists.

Table 3–1. Scope and Sequence of Composition Skills

	Grade 1	Grade 2	Grade 3
Capitalization	The first word of a sentence The child's first and last names The name of the teacher, school, town, street The word *I*	The date First and important words of titles of books the children read Proper names used in children's writings Titles of compositions Names of titles: Mr., Mrs., Miss	Proper names: month, day, common holidays First word in a line of verse First and important words in titles of books, stories, poems First word of salutation of informal note, such as Dear First word of closing of informal note, such as Yours
Punctuation	Period at the end of a sentence that tells something Period after numbers in any kind of list	Question mark at the close of a question Comma after salutation of a friendly note or letter Comma after closing of a friendly note or letter Comma between the day of the month and the year Comma between the name of the city and the name of the state	Period after abbreviations Period after an initial Use of an apostrophe in a common contraction such as isn't, aren't Commas in a list
Vocabulary	New words learned during experience Choosing words that describe accurately Choosing words that make you see, hear, feel	Words with similar meanings; with opposite meanings Alphabetical order	Extending discussion of words for precise meanings Using synonyms Distinguishing meanings and spellings of homonyms Using the prefix *un* and the suffix *less*
Word Usage	*Generally in oral expression* Naming yourself last Eliminating unnecessary words (my father he) Using *well* and *good* Verb forms in sentences: is, are did, done was, were see, saw, seen ate, eaten went, gone came, come gave, given	*Generally in oral expression* Avoiding double negatives Using *a* and *an*; *may* and *can*; *teach* and *learn* Eliminating unnecessary words (this here) Verb forms in sentences: rode, ridden took, taken grow, grew, grown know, knew, known bring, brought drew, drawn began, begun ran, run	Using *there is* and *there are*; *any* and *no* Using *let* and *leave*; *don't* and *doesn't*; *would have*, not *would of* Verb forms in sentences: throw, threw, thrown drive, drove, driven wrote, written tore, torn chose, chosen climbed broke, broken wore, worn spoke, spoken sang, sung rang, rung catch, caught

Grade 4	Grade 5	Grades 6, 7, and 8
Names of cities and states in general Names of organizations to which children belong, such as Boy Scouts, Grade Four, etc. Mother, Father, when used in place of the name Local geographical names	Names of streets Names of all places and persons, countries, oceans, etc. Capitalization used in outlining Titles when used with names, such as President Lincoln Commercial trade names	Names of the Deity and the Bible First word of a quoted sentence Proper adjectives showing race, nationality, etc. Abbreviations of proper nouns and titles
Apostrophe to show possession Hyphen separating parts of a word divided at end of a line Period following a command Exclamation point at the end of a word or group of words that make an exclamation Comma setting off an appositive Colon after the salutation of a business letter Quotation marks before and after a direct quotation Comma between explanatory words and a quotation	Colon in writing time Quotation marks around the title of a booklet, pamphlet, the chapter of a book, and the title of a poem or story Underlining the title of a book Period after outline Roman numeral	Comma to set off nouns in direct address Hyphen in compound numbers Colon to set off a list Comma in sentences to aid in making meaning clear Comma after introductory clauses
Dividing words into syllables Using the accent mark Using exact words that appeal to the senses Using exact words in explanation Keeping individual lists of new words and meanings	Using antonyms Prefixes and suffixes; compound words Exactness in choice of words Dictionary work; definitions; syllables; pronunciation; macron; breve Contractions Rhyme and rhythm; words with sensory images Classification of words by parts of speech Roots and words related to them Adjectives, nouns, verbs—contrasting general and specific vocabulary	Extending meanings; writing with care in choice of words and phrases In writing and speaking, selecting words for accuracy Selecting words for effectiveness and appropriateness Selecting words for courtesy Editing a paragraph to improve choice of words

Agreement of subject and verb
Using she, he, I, we, and they as subjects
Using bring and take
Verb forms in sentences:
  blow, blew, blown
  drink, drank, drunk
  lie, lay, lain
  take, took, taken
  rise, rose, risen
  teach, taught, taught
  raise, raised, raised
  lay, laid, laid
  fly, flew, flown
  set, set, set
  swim, swam, swum
  freeze, froze, frozen
  steal, stole, stolen
	Avoiding unnecessary pronouns (the boy he)
	Linking verbs and predicate nominatives
	Conjugation of verbs, to note changes in tense, person, number
	Transitive and intransitive verbs
	Verb forms in sentences:
	  am, was, been
	  say, said, said
	  fall, fell, fallen
	  dive, dived, dived
	  burst, burst, burst
	  buy, bought, bought
	Additional verb forms: climb, like, play, read, sail, vote, work
		Homonyms: its, it's; their, there, they're; there's, theirs; whose, who's
		Using parallel structure for parallel ideas, as in outlines
		Verb forms in sentences:
		  beat, beat, beaten
		  learn, learned, learned
		  leave, left, left
		  light, lit, lit
		  forgot, forgotten
		  swing, swung, swung
		  spring, sprang, sprung
		  shrink, shrank, shrunk
		  slide, slid, slid

(continued)

Table 3–1 *Continued*

	Grade 1	Grade 2	Grade 3
Grammar	Not applicable	Not applicable	Nouns: recognition of singular, plural, and possessive Verbs: recognition
Sentences	Writing simple sentences	Recognizing sentences; kinds: statement and question Composing correct and interesting original sentences Avoiding running sentences together with *and*	Exclamatory sentences Using a variety of sentences Combining short, choppy sentences into longer ones Using interesting beginning and ending sentences Avoiding run-on sentences (no punctuation) Learning to proofread one's own and others' sentences
Paragraphs	Not applicable	Not applicable	Keeping to one idea Keeping sentences in order; sequence of ideas Finding and deleting sentences that do not belong Indenting

Grade 4	Grade 5	Grades 6, 7, and 8
Noun: common and proper; in complete subject Verb: in complete predicate Adjective: recognition Adverb: recognition (telling how, when, where); modifying verbs, adjectives, other adverbs Pronoun: recognition of singular and plural	Noun: possessive; object of preposition; predicate noun Verb: tense; agreement with subject; verbs of action and state of being Adjective: comparison; predicate adjective; proper adjective Adverb: comparison; words telling how, when, where, how much; modifying verbs, adjectives, adverbs Pronoun: possessive; object of preposition Preposition: recognition; prepositional phrases Conjunction: recognition Interjection: recognition	Noun: clauses; common and proper; indirect object Verb: conjugating to note changes in person, number, tense; linking verbs with predicate nominatives Adjective: chart of uses; clauses; demonstrative; descriptive; numerals; phrases Adverb: chart of uses; clauses; comparison; descriptive; *ly* ending; modification of adverbs; phrases Pronoun: antecedents; declension chart—person, gender, case; demonstrative; indefinite; interrogative; personal; relative Preposition: phrases Conjunction: in compound subjects and predicates; in subordinate and coordinate clauses Interjection: placement of in quotations
Using command sentences Complete and simple subject; complete and simple predicate Recognizing adjectives and adverbs; pronouns introduced Avoiding fragments of sentences (incomplete) and the comma fault (a comma in place of a period) Improving sentences in a paragraph	Using a variety of interesting sentences: declarative, interrogative, exclamatory, and imperative (*you* the subject) Agreement of subject and verb; changes in pronoun forms Compound subjects and compound predicates Composing paragraphs with clearly stated ideas	Developing concise statements (avoiding wordiness or unnecessary repetition) Indirect object and predicate nominative Complex sentences Clear thinking and expression (avoiding vagueness and omissions)
Selecting main topic Choosing title to express main idea Making simple outline with main idea Developing an interesting paragraph	Improving skill in writing a paragraph of several sentences Selecting subheads as well as main topic for an outline Courtesy and appropriateness in all communications Recognizing topic sentences Keeping to the topic as expressed in title and topic sentence Using more than one paragraph Developing a four-point outline Writing paragraphs from outline Using new paragraphs for new speakers in written conversation Keeping a list of books (authors and titles) used for reference	Analyzing a paragraph to note method of development Developing a paragraph in different ways: e.g., with details, reasons, examples, or comparisons Checking for accurate statements Using a fresh or original approach in expressing ideas Using transition words to connect ideas Using topic sentences to develop paragraphs Improving skill in complete composition—introduction, development, conclusion Checking for good reasoning Using bibliography in report based on several sources

Source: Adapted from W. Otto and R. J. Smith, *Corrective and Remedial Teaching* (Boston: Houghton Mifflin, 1980); H. Greene and W. Petty, *Developing Language Skills in the Elementary School* (Boston: Allyn and Bacon, 1967).

Consider the case of a second-grader suspected of having a writing problem involving composition. If the individual conducting the evaluation were interested in the pupil's mastery of capitalization, he or she would first consult the chart to identify the capitalization forms that are characteristically taught in school between kindergarten and the end of the second grade. Examples of the student's written work could then be evaluated in terms of which forms have been acquired by the student, which forms have been insecurely mastered, and which forms are missing altogether. The main problem with the analysis of work samples is that the samples selected for evaluation may not adequately represent the student's writing weaknesses and strengths. For example, in executing spontaneous written products, such as essays or stories, some children write only sentences that contain the grammatical forms that they know how to use. Therefore, error analysis of their work may result in a distorted view of the skills that they have and have not acquired. Put another way, if error analysis is to work well, the writing assignments that are to be evaluated must include adequate opportunities for all types of errors to occur and to be observed. Because errors may or may not appear in spontaneously written products, the teacher may want to use additional procedures.

The teacher could generate a sentence (i.e., a test item) that contains the particular element being evaluated (e.g., the capitalization of proper names, the use of a colon to separate the hour from minutes, or the use of a comma to set off introductory clauses). Presumably, one or two sentences would be developed to correspond with each item on the chart. Next, the sentences would be typed in such a manner that the specific element being tested were left unpunctuated (or punctuated incorrectly). The list of sentences could then be presented to the student, who would be asked to correct any errors that he or she recognized in the sentences. Example sentences might include:

1. The boy's name was bill.
2. School is out at 3 30.
3. After the movie was over Mary went to the store.

In the first sentence, students who strike out the "b" and replace it with a "B" are telling the teacher that they understand the capitalization rule that pertains to first names. Those who insert a semicolon after "Mary" on the third sentence, who see nothing wrong with the sentence, or who place a comma after "movie" are showing that they do not know how to apply the rule concerning the punctuation of introductory clauses. The educational implications of the students' performance on such a criterion-reference device are obvious—the students need to be taught the forms that they do not know and then given ample, meaningful opportunities to practice their newly acquired knowledge.

If the criterion-referenced approach is attempted, special care should be taken to make sure that the vocabulary used in the sentences is well known to the students being evaluated. A student who does not comprehend the meaning of a written sentence certainly cannot be expected to punctuate it properly. If the teacher has any reason to suspect that the student cannot read the sentences, the student should be asked to tell in his or her own words what the sentence means. If he or she is unable to do this, the sentence should be reworded utilizing an appropriate vocabulary.

The teacher also will want to adhere very closely to the developmental sequence found in Table 3–1, for it indicates the order in which grammatical forms are usually taught in the schools. For example, with respect to the three sentences above, the table indicates that it is (1) during kindergarten and first grade that students learn that the first and last names of a person are capitalized, (2) during fifth grade that students learn that colons separate hours from minutes, and (3) between fourth and sixth grades that students learn that commas are used to set off an introductory clause. This information is of considerable value for teachers who must prepare special programs for individual students, because it enables them to sequence both the goals that underlie training and the activities that are to be used to ameliorate deficiencies in the most desirable way.

The assessment of the content of a composition is considerably more difficult, although the problems are hardly unsurmountable. The experienced teacher can probably read an essay and score it properly according to the criteria specified in the Carlson Analytical Originality Scale (Carlson, 1979) (see Figure 3–2). This scale requires that the teacher rate the written content on five dimensions—its story structure, novelty, emotion, individuality, and style.

Of course, since the ratings tend to be subjective, they are only as good as the talent and experience of the individual doing the evaluation. Therefore, it is important to take a few precautions to minimize the evaluator's subjectivity and to increase his or her reliability. Whoever is designated to evaluate the quality of the ideas expressed in students' written work should take steps to calibrate the judgments by acquiring a set of "internalized norms." This can be done by standardizing the topics of the written pieces that are to be assessed. For example, if the examiner is called upon most often to assess the work of children in grades three through six, he or she should select three topics, e.g., "My Favorite Television Show," "The Place I'd Most Like to Visit," "The Person I Admire Most," and have a sample of ten to twenty representative students at each grade level write a short composition on each topic. Reading approximately sixty essays all on the same topic will usually equip the examiner with a better-than-intuitive knowledge of what constitutes average, below-average, and above-average quality with regard to a given topic and will probably enable the examiner to complete Carlson's scale items with greater accuracy.

Figure 3–2. Carlson Analytical Originality Scale Scoring Key for Scoring Original Stories

Name of child _____   Name of teacher _____

Story type _____   Total score on scale _____

Scale Division A—Story Structure
1. Unusual title   0 1 2 3 4 5
2. Unusual beginning   0 1 2 3 4 5
3. Unusual dialogue   0 1 2 3 4 5
4. Unusual ending   0 1 2 3 4 5
5. Unusual plot   0 1 2 3 4 5

Scale Division B—Novelty
6. Novelty of names   0 1 2 3 4 5
7. Novelty of locale   0 1 2 3 4 5
8. Unique punctuation and
   expressional devices   0 1 2 3 4 5
9. New words   0 1 2 3 4 5
10. Novelty of ideas   0 1 2 3 4 5
11. Novel devices   0 1 2 3 4 5
12. Novel theme   0 1 2 3 4 5
13. Quantitative thinking   0 1 2 3 4 5
14. New objects created   0 1 2 3 4 5
15. Ingenuity in solving
    situations   0 1 2 3 4 5
16. Recombination of ideas in
    unusual relationships   0 1 2 3 4 5
17. Picturesque speech   0 1 2 3 4 5
18. Humor   0 1 2 3 4 5
19. Novelty of form   0 1 2 3 4 5
20. Inclusion of readers   0 1 2 3 4 5
21. Unusual related thinking   0 1 2 3 4 5

Scale Division C—Emotion
22. Unusual ability to express
    emotional depth   0 1 2 3 4 5
23. Unusual sincerity in ex-
    pressing personal problems 0 1 2 3 4 5
24. Unusual ability to identify
    self with feelings of others 0 1 2 3 4 5
25. Unusual horror theme   0 1 2 3 4 5

Scale Division D—Individuality
26. Unusual perceptive
    sensitivity (social and
    physical environment)   0 1 2 3 4 5
27. Unique philosophical
    thinking   0 1 2 3 4 5
28. Facility in beautiful writing 0 1 2 3 4 5
29. Unusual personal experience 0 1 2 3 4 5

Scale Division E—Style of Stories
30. Exaggerated tall tale   0 1 2 3 4 5
31. Fairy tale type   0 1 2 3 4 5
32. Fantasy-turnabout of
    characters   0 1 2 3 4 5
33. Highly fantastic central
    idea of theme   0 1 2 3 4 5
34. Fantastic creatures, objects,
    or persons   0 1 2 3 4 5
35. Personal experience   0 1 2 3 4 5
36. Individual story style   0 1 2 3 4 5

Source: R. K. Carlson, *Sparkling Words: Two Hundred Practical and Creative Writing Ideas* (Geneva, Ill.: Paladin House Publishers, 1979).

Standardized Tests of Writing

In addition to informal procedures, teachers can use standardized tests to measure written composition, especially when the purposes for testing require the quantification of results. Almost all achievement test batteries commonly used in the schools today include at least one subtest that measures some aspect of composition. (See Comprehensive Test of Basic Skills, California Achievement Tests, Stanford Achievement Tests, Metropolitan Achievement Tests, SRA

Achievement Series.) These tests are helpful in screening but have limited diagnostic value. For the most part, they test only word usage ability (grammar) and do this using contrived (unnatural) testing formats. They do not involve the analysis of students' spontaneously composed stories.

The Test of Written Language (Hammill and Larsen, 1983) is a standardized test of written composition that can be used for diagnostic purposes. The TOWL was standardized on a fourteen-state sample of 3,418 school-aged students attending grades two through twelve. Normative data are available for students between the ages of 7-0 and 18-11. The battery is made up of six subtests, the results of which yield information about:

1. *Word usage*—the use of standard verb tenses, plurals, pronouns, and other grammatical forms
2. *Style*—the use of generally accepted conventions regarding punctuation and capitalization
3. *Spelling*—the ability to phonetically spell regular and irregular words
4. *Thematic maturity*—the ability to construct a meaningful story on a given theme
5. *Vocabulary*—the level of words used in a spontaneously composed story
6. *Handwriting*—the legibility of the written story

With the exception of Spelling and Handwriting, these subtests tap aspects of written composition.

The TOWL results can be used to identify students who have problems in writing, especially when those problems involve composition; to pinpoint specific areas of deficiency; and to conduct research. The results can be recorded on the Profile Sheet to facilitate interpretation (see Figure 3–3).

TEACHING WRITTEN COMPOSITION

The focus of this four-part section is how problem learners are taught writing. The first part provides the reader with important general considerations in teaching composition; the second part describes the language-experience approach; the third part outlines the kinds of remedial activities that can be used; and the fourth part describes commercially available teaching packages.

Considerations for Composition Instruction

Composition refers to the syntactic and semantic aspects of a student's written product. Skill in composition is manifested in the ability to capitalize and punctuate, to use vocabulary and grammatical forms, and to construct sentences and

Figure 3–3. Example of TOWL Summary Sheet

Name: _Laurel L._   Male ☐ Female ☑

	Year	Month	Day
Date tested	78	12	6
Date of Birth	68	2	1
Age	10	10	5

TOWL

TEST OF WRITTEN LANGUAGE

Donald D. Hammill & Stephen C. Larsen

School: _Harris Elementary_   Grade: _5th_

Examiner's Name: _M._ (FIRST) _Bagley_ (LAST)

Examiner's Title: _School Psychologist_

SECTION I   RECORD OF SCORES

SUBTESTS	Raw Scores	% iles	Std. Scores
I Vocabulary	9	50	10
II Thematic Maturity	2	25	8
III Spelling	2	5	5
IV Word Usage	8	9	6
V Style	1	2	4
VI Handwriting	3	9	6

Sum of Standard Scores = 39

Written Language Quotient (WLQ) = 76

SECTION II   OTHER TEST SCORES

NAME	DATE	STD. SCORE	TOWL EQUIV.
WISC VS	10-78	95	95
WISC PS	10-78	100	100
WISC FS	10-78	96	96
Reading CTBS	5-77	4 (stanine)	93½
Math CTBS	5-77	4 (stanine)	93½
Language CTBS	5-77	3 (stanine)	85
TOLD-I	9-78	93	93

SECTION III   PROFILE OF SCORES

SECTION IV   OBSERVATIONS

Reprinted by permission of Pro-Ed.

paragraphs. Obviously, a certain level of competence in all these abilities is essential if a student is to use writing as a means of self-expression. Before attempting to remedy problems in any of these areas, teachers must first be aware of (a) the goals of individualized instruction in writing, (b) the best time to begin teaching composition, and (c) the scope and sequence of the specific skills to be taught.

Goals of Individualized Instruction

The goals of instruction in composition are threefold. The first goal is to teach students at least the minimum competencies that they will need to succeed in the school curriculum. The second goal is to instruct them in those forms of writing in which ability will be required for success outside the school (letter writing, completion of forms, note-taking, etc.). The third goal is to teach them to express their creativity in writing poetry, fantasies, and stories. Each of these goals is important, and the teacher should keep them all in mind when planning an intervention program for a particular student.

The Start of Instruction in Writing

Barenbaum (1983) provides an overview of a continuing controversy about when writing instruction should begin. In this dispute, the conventional wisdom and the research literature are at odds. Most school programs in language arts are based on the idea that listening and speaking abilities are taught first, reading next, and writing last. Yet Emig (1977) points out that this sequence is not necessary and perhaps not even desirable.

The notion that writing should follow reading is challenged strongly by numerous researchers, including Britton (1978), Graves (1978), and Moffett (1973). Chomsky (1971) goes so far as to suggest that writing naturally precedes reading. Given the state of the literature on this matter, it seems safe to conclude that writing should be taught simultaneously with reading, from the beginning of a student's school experience.

Scope and Sequence for Skills in Written Composition

In teaching written expression, the teacher must have a clear understanding of the theoretical basis and the specific sequence of skills that make up the instructional program that is to be used. The teacher can use this information as a guide for assessing a student's strengths and weaknesses in that program and also as a framework for planning short- and long-term objectives. The easiest way to obtain the needed knowledge about a particular approach is to prepare and study a scope-and-sequence chart in which the skills and conceptual ideas incorporated in the program are depicted. Fortunately, the authors of many programs provide teachers with scope-and-sequence data for their materials.

The theoretical constructs (i.e., the major aspects of the curriculum) are represented in the scope of the chart, and the skills of a particular construct and the order in which they are to be taught are displayed in the sequence. An example of a scope-and-sequence chart that is useful for assessment and remedial purposes in writing was presented in Table 3–1. This chart serves as a guide for identifying the skills that need to be taught, for deciding the order in which the skills are to be introduced, for recording an individual's progress, and for facilitating systematic instruction.

The procedures for using a scope-and-sequence chart to assess skills in writing have already been described. After using these procedures to determine which skills a particular student lacks, the teacher can plan an appropriate course of instruction.

The Language-Experience Approach to Teaching Composition

In general, teachers usually use a variation of the language-experience approach to teach conceptual writing. With this technique, the teacher's knowledge of a particular youngster's background and interests serves as the basis of instruction. The teacher begins by recording a student's verbal description of objects and events on a chart or board. Contents of the chart are discussed with the student, and his or her attention is directed to the various mechanical and compositional aspects of written expression, as well as to the relationships existing between the student's experiences and both oral and written language. Gradually, the student assumes more and more responsibility for the writing of personal expressions. At first, the student is asked to write only those words that the teacher knows are well within his or her speaking vocabulary. Eventually, the student is asked to write complete compositions reflecting thoughts about some interesting topic or experience. The theme of these essays can be provided by the teacher or, as is more often the case, by the student.

At all times, the student is encouraged to write creatively; the emphasis of instruction is always on the quality of ideas expressed and on motivation for writing. In time, the more mechanical and rule-governed aspects of writing are introduced, but care is taken to make sure that the increased curricular focus on these skills does not interfere with the student's desire to write creatively. This approach to the teaching of conceptual writing is most effective when it is integrated with the teaching of other areas in the language arts curriculum (reading, spelling, penmanship, etc.). Readers who want more information on using the language-experience approach to teach writing are referred to Parts II and III of Fernald (1943); Chapters 6, 8, and 9 of J. Smith (1967), and Chapters 7–9 of Burns and Broman (1983).

Proofreading, the reading of a written product for the purpose of identifying errors, is an integral part of all approaches to teaching composition, including the language-experience method. Students are usually taught to proofread soon after they begin to read and write original compositions. Students can proofread their own work, the work of other pupils, or special pieces containing selected errors that have been composed by the teacher. Regardless of the material to be proofread, students will find the following questions designed by Burns and Broman (1983, p. 232) to be helpful guides to developing proofreading ability.[1]

1. As the teacher (or another pupil) reads the sentence, listen and look at each group of words to be sure it is a good sentence. Make sure that you have no run-on sentences.
2. Listen and look for mistakes in punctuation. Be sure that you have put in punctuation marks only where they are needed. Did you end sentences with the mark required?
3. Listen and look for mistakes in word usage. Be sure that you have said what you mean and that each word is used correctly. Is there any incorrect verb or pronoun usage?
4. Look for mistakes in capitalization. Did you capitalize the first word and all important words in the title? Did you begin each sentence with a capital letter?
5. Look for misspelled words. Use the dictionary to check the spelling of any word about which you are not sure.
6. Check legibility of writing and items such as margins, title, indents, etc.

Specific Remedial Activities in Writing

Once a suitable scope-and-sequence chart has been developed and a student's skill deficiencies have been identified, the teacher is ready to choose instructional activities that are appropriate to the student's needs and situation. The activities described in the remainder of this chapter are representative of those that can be used to teach punctuation, capitalization, vocabulary, word usage, grammar, and sentence and paragraph construction. When applied to students with problems in writing, these activities should be used in conjunction with the language-experience approach discussed earlier.

---

[1]P. C. Burns and B. L. Broman, *The Language Arts in Childhood Education,* 5th ed., p. 232. Copyright © 1983 by Houghton Mifflin Company.

Punctuation and Capitalization

The strategies for teaching punctuation and capitalization are basically similar. For example, to teach skills in either area, the teacher (1) utilizes the language-experience approach to collect passages of the student's written work, (2) calls attention to each place in the essay where punctuation or capitalization is required, (3) discusses the need to use the skill to enhance meaning, (4) shows how to use the required skill properly, (5) provides activities for practice, and (6) arranges an opportunity for the pupil to demonstrate competence in spontaneous writing. To facilitate instruction in punctuation and capitalization, the teacher may want to use variations of the following activities. For example, students can:

1. Match items on a list of punctuation marks with possible functions (stop, yield, etc.). *Examples:* period = stop; comma = yield.
2. Punctuate and/or capitalize written passages. *Example:* billys cat was lost but it was found quickly.
3. Proofread the work of their classmates and underline possible errors. The papers can be returned to the classmates for correction, or the students who did the proofreading may correct the errors.
4. Write passages dictated by the teacher. The sentences dictated should involve various examples of punctuation and capitalization.
5. Be taught to listen for drops in the teacher's voice when he or she is dictating. These drops indicate the end of a sentence or the need for a comma. Young students can clap their hands when they recognize a point where a punctuation mark should be placed.
6. Be asked to write sentences demonstrating a particular kind of form. *Example:* Write a sentence as if you were talking to Mr. Smith (quotation marks).

Vocabulary, Word Usage, and Grammar

The related areas of vocabulary, word usage, and grammar can often be taught simultaneously. A student's vocabulary is the supply of words that he or she comprehends and uses in speaking and writing. The goal of vocabulary-development activities is to increase this supply of words in number and complexity. Word usage refers to the appropriateness of the child's selection of vocabulary in terms of accepted standards. Finally, grammar is the way in which words are structured or organized to form a complete thought. An example will illustrate these differentiations more clearly:

I am not going to school.   (The basic sentence)
I am not *attending* school.   (Improvement due to vocabulary)
I *ain't* going to school.   (Unacceptable usage—ain't)
I am going *not* to school.   (Incorrect organization of words—
     grammatical error)

One of the most important issues in the consideration of vocabulary, word usage, and grammar is the student's oral language and past experiences. In no instance should the teacher expect a student's written composition to reflect a vocabulary, a usage pattern, or a grammar that the child does not use in speaking. Therefore, it is important for the teacher dealing with these aspects of written expression to allow the student to utilize those forms with which he or she is familiar. For example, when experience charts are prepared, the student's own words and structure should be recorded. An attempt to remedy problems in written language must be preceded and accompanied by remediation in oral language.

The following list is an accumulation of suggested activities to increase *vocabulary* skills. They are drawn from Greene and Petty (1967), Burns and Broman (1983), Otto and Smith (1980), and our own experience.

1. List on the board new words encountered in classroom and out-of-school activities.
2. Read stories, descriptions, poems, etc., aloud to the students and follow up with group discussions.
3. Have a student go on "word hunts" outside the classroom. Most students will enjoy collecting words from billboards, warning signs, traffic signs, etc. These words may be used as the student's weekly spelling list.
4. Discuss and use words appearing in reading material.
5. Let the student keep a list of words that he or she likes or wants to use. As an alternative, the student can write new words on an index card and file them with others in a "word box."
6. Make lists or charts of special-interest words, such as those related to football, television, and cooking.
7. Build words from root words by adding prefixes, suffixes, etc.
8. List words that rhyme with others and discuss their meanings.
9. Suggest topics for oral written expression whereby students must employ the new vocabulary items.
10. Utilize word games, such as Scrabble.
11. Find synonyms and antonyms for new words.

12. Have students take turns bringing in new words for the day.
13. Use dictionary drills and emphasize proper use of reference books.

It is important for the teacher interested in remedying word-usage problems to select only a few items to attack at any one time. Following is a list by Pooley (1960) of goals related to word usage[2]:

1. The elimination of all baby-talk and "cute" expressions.
2. The correct uses in speech and writing of *I, me, he, him, she, her.*
3. The correct uses of *is, are, was, were* with respect to number and tense.
4. Correct past tenses of common irregular verbs such as *saw, gave, took, brought, bought, stuck.*
5. Correct use of past participles of the same verbs and similar verbs after auxiliaries.
6. Elimination of the double negative: *we don't have no apples,* etc.
7. Elimination of analogical forms: *ain't, hisn, hern, ourn, theirselves,* etc.
8. Correct use of possessive pronouns: *my, mine, his, hers, theirs, ours.*
9. Mastery of the distinction between *its,* possessive pronoun, and *it's,* contraction of *it is.*
10. Placement of *have* or its phonetic reduction to *v* between *I* and a past participle.
11. Elimination of *them* as a demonstrative pronoun.
12. Elimination of *this here* and *that there.*
13. Mastery of use of *a* and *an* articles.
14. Correct use of personal pronouns in compound constructions: as subject (*Mary and I*), as object (*Mary and me*), as object of preposition (to *Mary and me*).
15. The use of *we* before an appositional noun when subject; *us* when object.
16. Correct number agreement with the phrases *there is, there are, there was, there were.*
17. Elimination of *he don't, she don't, it don't.*
18. Elimination of *learn* for *teach, leave* for *let.*

[2]R. C. Pooley, Dare schools set a standard in English usage? *English Journal,* 49 (1960), 179–180. Copyright © 1960 by the National Council of Teachers of English. Reprinted by permission of the publisher and the author.

19. Elimination of pleonastic subjects: *my brother he; my mother she; that fellow he.*

20. Proper agreement in number with antecedent pronouns *one* and *anyone, everyone, each, no one*. With *everybody* and *none*, some tolerance of number seems acceptable now.

21. The use of *who* and *whom* as reference to persons (but note, *Who did he give it to?* is tolerated in all but very formal situations; in the latter, *To whom did he give it?* is preferable).

22. Accurate use of *said* in reporting the words of a speaker in the past.

23. Correction of *lay down* to *lie down.*

24. The distinction between *good* as adjective and *well* as adverb, e.g., *He spoke well.*

25. Elimination of *can't hardly, all the farther* (for *as far as*), and *Where is he (she, it) at?*

The teacher can utilize this list in targeting the particular usages to be attacked.

The most important factor in correcting word usage and grammatical errors is to provide ample opportunity for the student to utilize the correct forms in oral expression. The following list provides some suggested activities to increase efficiency in word usage:

1. Provide frequent opportunities for practice. Repetition should be emphasized.

2. Utilize the tape recorder in oral language activities.

3. Provide usage activities throughout the day, not only during a language time.

4. Rephrase students' incorrect usage in situations where correction will not prove embarrassing.

5. Have students clap, etc., when they hear a usage error in a selection.

6. Give students opportunities to mark incorrect usage in written expressive tasks.

7. Play games involving substitution of correct usage for incorrect usage in sentences.

8. Dramatize characters in plays utilizing different usage forms.

9. Attend primarily to those usage forms that are most socially unaccepted.

Grammatical skills can be enhanced through most of the approaches mentioned for vocabulary and word usage. Initial instruction in the various grammatical structures is best provided through oral and written examples and repetition. After giving instruction in the simple sentences and questions using the noun + verb, noun + verb + noun, etc., the teacher will want to include instruction, group activities, and games that involve experimentation with noun and verb phrases and, later, clauses. For example,

The dog ran.
The big dog ran.
The big gray dog ran.
The big gray and white dog with a red collar . . .
. . . ran over the hill.
. . . ran over the green hill toward them.

Exercises such as these can often be extended into the absurd, not only incorporating new vocabulary but also providing for enjoyable class interactions. Burns et al. (1971, p. 21) provide the following twelve items in which students should be instructed so that they can manipulate grammatical structures and patterns to create sentence variations.[3] They are a useful guide in sequencing of instruction.

1. Elements (as adverbs) can be recorded:
   Marie stood by quietly.   Quietly Marie stood by.
2. Indirect objects can be rearranged:
   He gave a ball to John.   He gave John a ball.
3. The use of "there" provides an alternative:
   A visitor was upstairs.   There was a visitor upstairs.
4. Adjectives can be used:
   The cat is dirty.   The dirty cat . . . (or The cat that is dirty . . .)
5. Possessives can be formed:
   Bill has a dog.   The dog is gentle.
   Bill's dog is gentle.
6. Comparisons can be made:
   John is strong.   Tom is stronger.
   Tom is stronger than John.
7. Relatives (such as *that, which, who, whom*) can be utilized:
   The girl played the piano.   The girl is my sister.
   The girl who played the piano is my sister.
8. Appositives can be employed:
   Clara is my youngest sister.   She went to California.
   Clara, my youngest sister, went to California.
9. Noun phrase complements may consist of a "that clause"; infinitive clause ("for . . . to"); or gerundive clause (genetive or possessive form):

---

[3]P. C. Burns, B. L. Broman, and A. L. L. Wantling, *The Language Arts in Childhood Education*, p. 21. Copyright © 1971 Houghton Mifflin Company. Used by permission.

That Bill arrived late bothered Sue.
For Bill to arrive late bothered Sue.
Bill's having arrived late bothered Sue.

10. Coordination:
The phone rang.   No one answered it.
The phone rang, but no one answered it.

11. Subordination:
The man was strong.   He was tall.   He was handsome.
The man was strong, tall, and handsome.

The wind was strong.   The leaves fell to the ground.
The leaves fell to the ground because (as, since, when) the wind was strong.

12. Sentence connection:
I am not going to the movie.   I am going to the dance.
I am not going to the movie; however, I am going to the dance.

Activities employed to help students with learning problems develop grammatical skills will primarily be oral. Some examples of suggested activities are listed below:

1. Repeat and expand or elaborate student's utterances to form more complete or complex sentences.
2. Give students ample opportunities to participate orally in class:
   —describing objects or events
   —retelling a story
   —discussing an experience or activity.

In the list by Burns et al., items 5–8 and 10–12 involve some type of sentence combining. When used as an instructional technique, sentence combining has been shown to be extremely effective in enhancing students' ability to write syntactically (Hunt and O'Donnell, 1970; Mellon, 1969; O'Hare, 1973) as well as to read with comprehension (Combs, 1977).

The sentence-combining technique is easy to use, especially with older children, who find it motivating. In part this is because there is no one correct way to combine sentences; many combinations are equally acceptable.

A resource for all who would plan sentence-combining activities is the *Sentence Combining: A Composing Book* by Strong (1973). The following examples of the technique are from his work.[4]

---

[4]W. Strong, *Sentence Combining: A Composing Book*, pp. x, 7. Copyright © 1973, Random House.

Main Drag, Saturday Night

1. The cars come cruising up Broadway.
2. The cars are glittering.
3. The paint is harsh.
4. The paint is metallic.
5. The paint is highly waxed.

The student is told:

1. As you combine sentences, listen to them; say them aloud in several ways; experiment with new structures.
2. In the beginning, at least, write out all the transformations you can think of for each cluster; then choose the one you like best.
3. In a special notebook, write out the final transforms for each string; use the notebook daily.
4. Compare your transforms with those of the other students; discuss which transformations sound best; try to figure out why.
5. Look for the patterns that show up over and over as you make your combinations; you'll also see patterns of spelling and punctuation as you work.
6. Go beyond the lists that are given in the text by following the Suggestions; in other words, *keep writing*.

Examples of how students may combine the first five sentences in the "Main Drag, Saturday Night" series into two sentences follow. The emphasis is on forming transformations, not on combining the sentences into a single correct way.

Transformation 1
The glittering cars come cruising up Broadway. Their paint is harsh, metallic, and highly waxed. . . .

Transformation 2
The cars that glitter come cruising up Broadway. Their metallic paint is harsh and highly waxed. . . .

Sentence and Paragraph Construction

To be competent in forming written sentences and paragraphs, students have to coordinate all the skills involved in punctuation, capitalization, vocabulary, word usage, and grammar. In addition, they must organize content. West (1966) has prepared a list of problems that are commonly associated with students' sentence construction. These include fragments, run-on sentences and comma splices, sentences that are too simple or too complex, misplaced or dangling modifiers, pronouns without proper referents, lack of variety in sentence structure, pronoun-antecedent and subject-verb disagreement, overuse of expletives and passive voice, and tense-sequence problems. The teacher should attend to each of the errors individually by applying and/or adjusting instructional activities such as those that follow.

1. Ask students to arrange a string of written words to form a sentence.
   Examples:
   fast   the   dog   black   ran
   The   black   dog   ran   fast

2. Ask students to mark errors in given sentences or mark, correct, and re-write the incorrect portions.

3. Ask students to complete partially written sentences. *Examples:*
   Mary went to the store to buy _____.
   Mary went to the store to buy _____, _____, and _____.
   Mary went _____.

4. Do much group work in composing (e.g., preparing experience charts, writing letters to classmates, etc.).

5. Begin conceptual writing instruction with one-word composition, progress to simple sentences, and gradually increase the number and complexity of the sentences used in the exercises.

6. Encourage and provide opportunities for students to dictate letters and stories.

7. Utilize dictation and proofreading exercises in the writing program.

8. Give students a group of written statements comprising both complete sentences and fragments; ask them to select those that are fragments.

9. Ask students to underline subject and verb as clues to finding complete sentences and fragments.

10. Have students match predicate and verb phrases.

11. Give students an outline or form for a sentence to be constructed. *Examples:*
    Noun   *Verb*   *Noun*   *Noun*
    John   gave   Bill   the ball

12. Have students practice using connectives, such as *and, but, for, which, when, because,* etc. *Examples:*
    Willie was tired, _____ he got up early this morning.
    Susie ran well, _____ Judy won the race.

Once a student can compose complete sentences, the teacher should begin instruction on paragraph formation. Four major points should be stressed in teaching students to write paragraphs: the content to be expressed, the topic sentence, the order and flow of sentences and ideas within the paragraph, and the concluding sentence. Activities for each are provided below.

1. Collect statements made by students during a discussion, write them on the board, and ask the students to select those that go together.
2. Let students order the statements selected above.
3. Give students paragraph selections in which they must locate inappropriate sentences.
4. Give students paragraphs that contain appropriate but poorly sequenced sentences; have the students rearrange the sentences into a more meaningful order. Before assigning this task the teacher may want to first check whether the young pupil can tell an experience in sequence or arrange comic strips and tell a story from the frames.
5. Utilize opportunities, such as class or school newspapers, to motivate students to compose.
6. Employ dictation and proofreading activities.
7. Introduce students to the concept of outlining.

In conclusion, teachers should be ever mindful that in using any of the activities described in this chapter, care must be taken to ensure that students are required to perform only those tasks in which they can experience some degree of success. As the student succeeds, the complexity of the tasks can be increased gradually until he or she has mastered the targeted skills or areas completely.

We conclude this section by referring the reader to *Evaluating and Improving Written Expression* (J. K. Hall, 1981). This practical guide for teachers is advertised as "a step-by-step approach to analyzing and building writing skills, from idea to finished composition." Teachers and others who assess and teach written composition—as well as handwriting and spelling—will not be disappointed in this work. The book is replete with activities designed to develop creative and practical writing, organizational skill, sentence structure, and mature vocabulary.

Commercially Available Programs

In recent years, interest in written composition has increased markedly. Because of this increased interest, several comprehensive programs for training abilities in expressive writing have become available commercially. In general these programs include sequenced lessons, systematic activities, teacher manuals, and student workbooks. To a considerable extent, they incorporate many of the informal activities described in the previous section. Two of the programs are discussed here as examples of the kinds of programs that are now available. The first program is intended as a developmental approach to teaching writing to beginning learners; the other program is intended for remedial use.

Expressive Writing 1 and 2

Engelmann and Silbert's (1983) *Expressive Writing* program was designed for beginning writers who read at or above the third-grade level. The core of the program is 50 forty-five-minute lessons, each of which provides for practice in mechanics (punctuation and capitalization), sentence writing, paragraph writing, and editing. The teacher presents a lesson using instructions found in the *Teacher Presentation Book* (a teacher's manual); the students execute the lesson in space provided in their *Student Workbook*.

Consider Lesson 29 as an example. The lesson has four parts, each dealing with a different skill: editing run-ons, editing *was* to *did*, introducing sequence in paragraphs, and writing a paragraph that reports on an event.

1. Editing run-ons. Students are given a series of run-on sentences to correct (e.g., "A girl bought an old bike from a friend and the bike had rust on its handlebars and wheels and the girl and her friend fixed up the bike.")
2. Changing *was* to *did*. Students are asked to rewrite a passage so that all the sentences tell what a person or thing did, not what a person or thing was doing. For example, "One boy was falling down" is changed to "One boy fell down."
3. Introducing sequence in paragraphs. Students are shown a series of related pictures that depict a story. A paragraph accompanying the pictures tells the story depicted. Each element in the story is read aloud in sequence and associated with the picture.
4. Writing a paragraph that reports an event. Students are shown four story-related pictures about a rodeo and a box containing fourteen printed words related to the rodeo theme. Students are asked to write a paragraph that reports what happened. They are directed in composing their paragraph, e.g., they are told to indent, to start with "The cowboy," to tell what he did in the picture, etc.

At the end of the lesson, students are given the opportunity to self-evaluate aspects of their work. Other lessons vary in content but are similar in format to this one.

Basic Writing Skills

Gleason and Stults (1983a, 1983b) have produced two sets of remedial activities. One set is for developing the sentence skills of students who read and spell at or above the third-grade level and who have problems in this area. The other set is for teaching style to students in grades seven through twelve who use little capitalization or punctuation in their daily writing. Both programs have a teacher's manual and a series of reproducible student worksheets.

The *Sentence Development* (Gleason & Stults, 1983a) program has thirty-one lessons that follow a consistent format. Lesson 8, for example, begins with the teacher's writing six statements on the board. One of them is a complete sentence that has been punctuated properly; the others either are fragments or have stylistic errors in them. The student is asked to answer three questions about each statement: Is it a sentence? Does it begin with a capital? Does it end with a correct end mark? Next, the students write five sentences about a picture depicted on their worksheet (see Figure 3–4). Students check each sentence by answering the questions at the bottom of the worksheet. Then a second picture is shown to the students, who respond by writing sentences. Afterwards, they proof their sentences for errors.

The *Capitalization and Punctuation* (Gleason & Stults, 1983b) program has forty lessons. Each lesson deals with a different element and follows a fairly consistent format. For example, Lesson 15 deals with putting commas in the date. First, a series of sentences is read from the worksheet. Each sentence contains a punctuation error involving dates (e.g., "You will get paid on Friday June 3."). The proper punctuation of each sentence is discussed. Second, a set of unpunctuated sentences is provided (e.g., "will grandpa arrive by monday january 26") and the student rewrites them, putting in the proper punctuation. Third, students are given the opportunity to generate five sentences that contain dates and proof their own work.

Needless to say, these commercial programs are highly sequenced, organized, and instructionally efficient. But teachers must monitor student writing that is not integral to the special program in order to ensure that the skills being taught are being used in everyday writing and in other school-related writing.

Computer Programs

The role of computers in composition instruction has been expanding. Several software packages have been developed recently for use at the elementary and middle school levels, the purpose of which is to assist students in acquiring desirable composition skills. Chief among these are *The Banks Street Writer* (1982, Scholastic), *Quill* (1984, Heath), *Story Maker* (1981, Bolt, Beranek, & Newman), and *Story Tree* (1984, Scholastic). These programs engage students in

Figure 3–4. Sample *Sentence Development* Lesson

Lesson 8

Name _____

Date _____

Part A

1. _____

   _____

2. _____

   _____

3. _____

   _____

4. _____

   _____

5. _____

   _____

Proof your sentences.   1   2   3   4   5

1. Is it a sentence?   — — — — —

2. Does it begin with a capital?   — — — — —

3. Does it end with a period?   — — — — —

149

Figure 3–4 *Continued*

Lesson 8　　　　　　　　　Name _____

　　　　　　　　　　　　　　　　Date _____

Part B: Mastery Quiz

Directions: Look at the picture. Write five interesting sentences about what's happening in the picture. Proof your sentences.

1. _____

　 _____

2. _____

　 _____

3. _____

　 _____

4. _____

　 _____

5. _____

　 _____

150

---

creative story-writing exercises; teach them to take notes, express ideas, and organize material; and imitate many of the pre-writing activities employed by teachers. H. L. Burns (1984, p. 22) summarizes what computer writing programs can do as follows:

1. A program can ask the question.
2. A program can clarify the question.
3. Good software can define the dimensions of the question.
4. The software can call attention to the essay's purpose.
5. It can purposefully distract (for incubation's sake).
6. It can rephrase the question.
7. It can create random metaphors.
8. Invention programs can offer research questions.
9. A program can print a copy of the dialogue so a student can later evaluate the answers.

Readers who are interested in the potential of computers for writing instruction are referred to the cogent discussions of S. K. Miller (1985). In a two-part article published in *Direct Instruction News*, Miller traces the history of the microcomputer era, describes the writing software currently available, and summarizes recent research in the area.

chapter 4

Improving Spelling Skills

by Donald D. Hammill

Spelling is the forming of words from letters according to acceptable usage. Although words can be spelled orally, as in the traditional spelling bee, their written form is by far the more important, because students use it when writing essays for teachers, notes to friends, correspondence to relatives, or grocery lists for themselves.

It is surprising that proficient spelling, although highly prized, is often an unattained outcome of language arts instruction. Most students are taught by means of a schoolwide program and readily become fluent spellers. However, many others, with comparable mental ability and interest, do not learn to spell adequately. When deficiencies are first observed, the teacher should immediately take steps to help the student overcome the problem. The teacher should first seek the answers to several pertinent questions:

1. Does the student have sufficient mental ability to learn to spell?
2. Are the student's hearing, speech, and vision adequate?
3. What is the student's general level of spelling ability?
4. Are there areas of specific weakness in spelling?
5. What systems, techniques, or activities might be used to remedy difficulties?

Answers to the first two questions relate to a student's "readiness" or "capacity" for spelling. If teachers are unsure about the status of a student's intellectual or sensory abilities, a referral to the school psychologist or nurse may be in order. Procedures for answering the other three questions are provided in the remainder of this chapter. This chapter is designed to help teachers to better understand spelling skills and to acquire information about appropriate assessment techniques and various developmental and remedial teaching programs directed toward improvement in spelling.

ASSESSING SPELLING SKILLS

Three types of assessment techniques are discussed—tests with norms, tests with criterion-referenced items, and other procedures. Tests with norms are superior by far when the teacher is asking the question "What is the general level of spelling ability?" For inventorying a student's spelling errors and patterns and for getting information needed to plan an individual remedial program, tests designed for criterion-referenced interpretation and other less standardized (informal) procedures are unsurpassed.

Norm-Referenced Spelling Tests

Most teachers are familiar with normed tests of spelling, because all popular group-administered achievement batteries used in schoolwide testing programs include a spelling subtest, e.g., the Metropolitan Achievement Tests and the Iowa Test of Basic Skills. Teachers who work in special education are aware that all popular individually administered achievement batteries used to qualify students for special services also include a spelling subtest, e.g., the Diagnostic Achievement Battery, the Wide-Range Achievement Test, and the Peabody Individual Achievement Test.

Another test of spelling that has national norms and an interesting format is the Test of Written Spelling (TWS) (Larsen and Hammill, 1986). This device is composed of 100 words that were chosen because they appear in each of the ten spelling series that are used most often in the schools. Fifty of these words are "predictable" in that their spelling is consistent with certain phonological (i.e., phoneme-grapheme correspondence) rules or generalizations (e.g., had, spring, pile, salute, legal); and fifty words are "unpredictable" in that their spelling conforms to no useful phonological or morphological rules (e.g., people, knew, eight, fountain, community). Test results can be interpreted in terms of the student's mastery of the predictable words, the unpredictable words, or the total number of words.

The test is normed on a nationwide sample of children who share the national characteristics relative to geographic location, sex, and urban-rural residence. Studies indicate that the TWS is reliable (i.e., internally consistent) at all grade levels between one and twelve (coefficients in the 80s and 90s), and that its results correlate strongly with the spelling subtests of the Wide-Range Achievement Test, California Achievement Test, and SRA Achievement Series.

In general, the normed tests with the most complete standardizations are useful mostly for telling examiners who the poor spellers are. They offer little information that a teacher can use to plan individual programs. On the other hand, the tests that attempt to provide a more complete analysis of an individual's spelling ability tend to have inadequate standardizations. The teacher, therefore, has to choose between using a test that has a comparatively sound research base but offers little instructionally relevant information and using a test that attempts to tap more components of spelling but has no reported reliability.

The teacher should be selective in the type of tests used and should consider the following three suggestions:

1. Know what the test measures and what its limitations are before giving it to the student; for example, the types of students used for the standardization and norms and the reported reliability and validity of the test.

2. Be prepared to supplement the test where possible with other less standardized measures.

3. Use other evaluation techniques whenever specific information about the student's spelling abilities is required, and as a guide to planning a remediation program.

Criterion-Referenced Spelling Tests

Normed tests such as those just mentioned usually contain statistically selected items because they are built to be relatively short, highly reliable measurement devices. Tests built with criterion-referencing in mind, on the other hand, include a broad spectrum of items, reflecting most, if not all, of the elements that make up the skill being measured. Builders of criterion-referenced measures are not unduly concerned with the statistical characteristics of the items being chosen. The purpose of criterion-referencing in educational practice is not to determine where the student stands relative to other students but to identify those components of the ability being assessed in which the student needs training.

This type of assessment helps the teacher to determine a student's instructional level and also measures progress toward the task goal. The following advantages to this approach are suggested by Westerman (1971). Tests designed for criterion-referencing:

1. Indicate the skills the student has and those the student needs.

2. Provide an objective measure of progress as the student moves from task to task.

3. Are based upon what content is to be taught and who is to learn it if they are designed by the teacher.

The teacher can choose from many tests that allow a criterion-referenced interpretation. Two of these will be presented in this book, Kottmeyer's (1959) Diagnostic Spelling Test and C. R. Cohen and Abrams's (1976a, 1976b) Spellmaster instruments.

The Diagnostic Spelling Test

The Diagnostic Spelling Test, which is presented in Figure 4–1, is administered using a dictation format; e.g., the examiner says to the students, "Not. He is *not* here," after which they write the word "not." After the student has completed the test, the number of correct spellings is totaled and first interpreted in a norm-referenced fashion using the data offered just below the heading "Directions for Diagnostic Spelling Test." The results are next interpreted in a criterion-referenced manner. For example, if the student misspelled "not," it is likely that he or she has not yet mastered the phonological rule governing the short vowel /o/. Analysis of the student's errors on the test should result in the development of a relatively data-based remedial program.

The Spellmaster Tests

A second criterion-referenced approach, Spellmaster, was designed by Cohen and Abrams (1976a, 1976b). In addition to sorting out good and poor spellers, Spellmaster can identify the elements that students need to learn. This is accomplished by administering grade-sequenced tests "in which the elements within each word, rather than the whole word, are scored right or wrong" (p. 6). Regular words, irregular words, and homonyms are assessed.

An example of how the tests are scored and interpreted is provided in Figure 4–2. In this example, Test 5 has been given to Lee N. This particular test is designed to assess mastery of words whose sounds can be spelled in more than one way; e.g., *mean*, not *meen* or *mene*. Both visual recall and phonic ability are required to spell these words. Lee misspelled item 13, *Poodle*, as *podel*. Since he had trouble with the medial vowel and the final ending sound, the *oo* and *le* elements corresponding to item 13 at the right of the figure were circled, a sign that they should be targeted for further study or remediation. In a companion volume, Cohen and Abrams (1976b) suggest efficient and practical techniques for correcting spelling errors.

Other Assessment Procedures

Information gleaned by assessing a student's actual spelling behavior will be of considerable value to teachers in planning individualized programs of study.

Figure 4–1. Kottmeyer's Spelling Test

DIRECTIONS FOR KOTTMEYER'S SPELLING TEST

Give list 1 to second or third graders.
Give list 2 to any pupil who is above Grade 3.
Grade Scoring, List 1:
  Below 15 correct: Below second grade
  15–22 correct: Second grade
  23–29 correct: Third grade
Give List 2 Test to pupils who score above 29.

Grade Scoring, List 2:
  Below 9 correct: Below third grade
  9–19 correct: Third grade
  20–25 correct: Fourth grade
  26–29 correct: Fifth grade
  Over 29 correct: Sixth grade or better
Give List 1 Test to pupils who score below 9.

LIST 1

Word   *Illustrative Sentence*

1. not—He is *not* here.
2. but—Mary is here, *but* Joe is not.
3. get—*Get* the wagon, John.
4. sit—*Sit* down, please.
5. man—Father is a tall *man*.
6. boat—We sailed our *boat* on the lake.
7. train—Tom has a new toy *train*.
8. time—It is *time* to come home.
9. like—We *like* ice cream.
10. found—We *found* our lost ball.
11. down—Do not fall *down*.
12. soon—Our teacher will *soon* be here.
13. good—He is a *good* boy.
14. very—We are *very* happy to be here.
15. happy—Jane is a *happy* girl.
16. kept—We *kept* our shoes dry.
17. come—*Come* to our party.
18. what—*What* is your name?
19. those—*Those* are our toys.
20. show—*Show* us the way.
21. much—I feel *much* better.
22. sing—We will *sing* a new song.
23. will—Who *will* help us?
24. doll—Make a dress for the *doll*.
25. after—We play *after* school.
26. sister—My *sister* is older than I.
27. toy—I have a new *toy* train.
28. say—*Say* your name clearly.
29. little—Tom is a *little* boy.
30. one—I have only *one* book.
31. would—*Would* you come with us?
32. pretty—She is a *pretty* girl.

LIST 2

Word   *Illustrative Sentence*

1. flower—A rose is a *flower*.
2. mouth—Open your *mouth*.
3. shoot—John wants to *shoot* his new gun.
4. stood—We *stood* under the roof.
5. while—We sang *while* we marched.
6. third—We are in the *third* grade.
7. each—*Each* child has a pencil.
8. class—Our *class* is reading.
9. jump—We like to *jump* rope.
10. jumps—Mary *jumps* rope.
11. jumped—We *jumped* rope yesterday.
12. jumping—The girls are *jumping* rope now.
13. hit—*Hit* the ball hard.
14. hitting—John is *hitting* the ball.
15. bite—Our dog does not *bite*.
16. biting—The dog is *biting* on the bone.
17. study—*Study* your lesson.
18. studies—He *studies* each day.
19. dark—The sky is *dark* and cloudy.
20. darker—This color is *darker* than that one.
21. darkest—This color is the *darkest* of the three.
22. afternoon—We may play this *afternoon*.
23. grandmother—Our *grandmother* will visit us.
24. can't—We *can't* go with you.
25. doesn't—Mary *doesn't* like to play.
26. night—We read to Mother last *night*.
27. brought—Joe *brought* his lunch to school.
28. apple—An *apple* fell from the tree.
29. again—We must come back *again*.
30. laugh—Do not *laugh* at other children.
31. because—We cannot play *because* of the rain.
32. through—We ran *through* the yard.

(continued)

Figure 4–1 *Continued*

	LIST 1		LIST 2
Word	*Element Tested*	*Word*	*Element Tested*
1. not			*ow-ou* spellings
2. but		1. flower	of *ou* sound, *er*
3. get	Short vowels	2. mouth	ending, *th*
4. sit			spelling
5. man		3. shoot	Long and short
6. boat	Two vowels		*oo, sh*
7. train	together	4. stood	spelling
8. time	Vowel-consonant *-e*	5. while	*wh* spelling,
9. like			vowel-consonant
10. found	*ow-ou* spelling of	6. third	*th* spelling,
11. down	*ou* sound		vowel before *r*
12. soon	Long and short *oo*	7. each	*ch* spelling, two
13. good			vowels together
14. very	Final *y* as short *i*		
15. happy		8. class	Double final
16. kept	*c* and *k* spellings of		consonant, *c*
17. come	the *k* sound		spelling of *k*
18. what	*wh, th, sh, ch,* and		sound
19. those	*ng* spellings and	9. jump	
20. show	*ow* spelling	10. jumps	Addition of *s, ed,*
21. much	of long *o*	11. jumped	*ing; j* spelling of
22. sing		12. jumping	soft *g* sound
23. will	Doubled final	13. hit	Doubling final
24. doll	consonants	14. hitting	consonant before
25. after	*er* spelling		adding *ing*
26. sister		15. bite	Dropping final *e*
27. toy	*oy* spelling of *oi*	16. biting	before *ing*
	sound	17. study	Changing final *y*
28. say	*ay* spelling of long	18. studies	to *i* before ending
	a sound	19. dark	
29. little	*le* ending	20. darker	*er, est* endings
30. one		21. darkest	
31. would	Nonphonetic	22. afternoon	Compound
32. pretty	spellings	23. grandmother	words
		24. can't	Contrac-
		25. doesn't	tions
		26. night	Silent *gh*
		27. brought	
		28. apple	*le* ending
		29. again	
		30. laugh	Nonphonetic
		31. because	spellings
		32. through	

Source: Reprinted from *Teacher's Guide for Remedial Reading* by William Kottmeyer, © 1959, with permission of Webster/McGraw-Hill, Inc.

Figure 4-2. Lee N.'s Performance on Spellmaster's Test 5

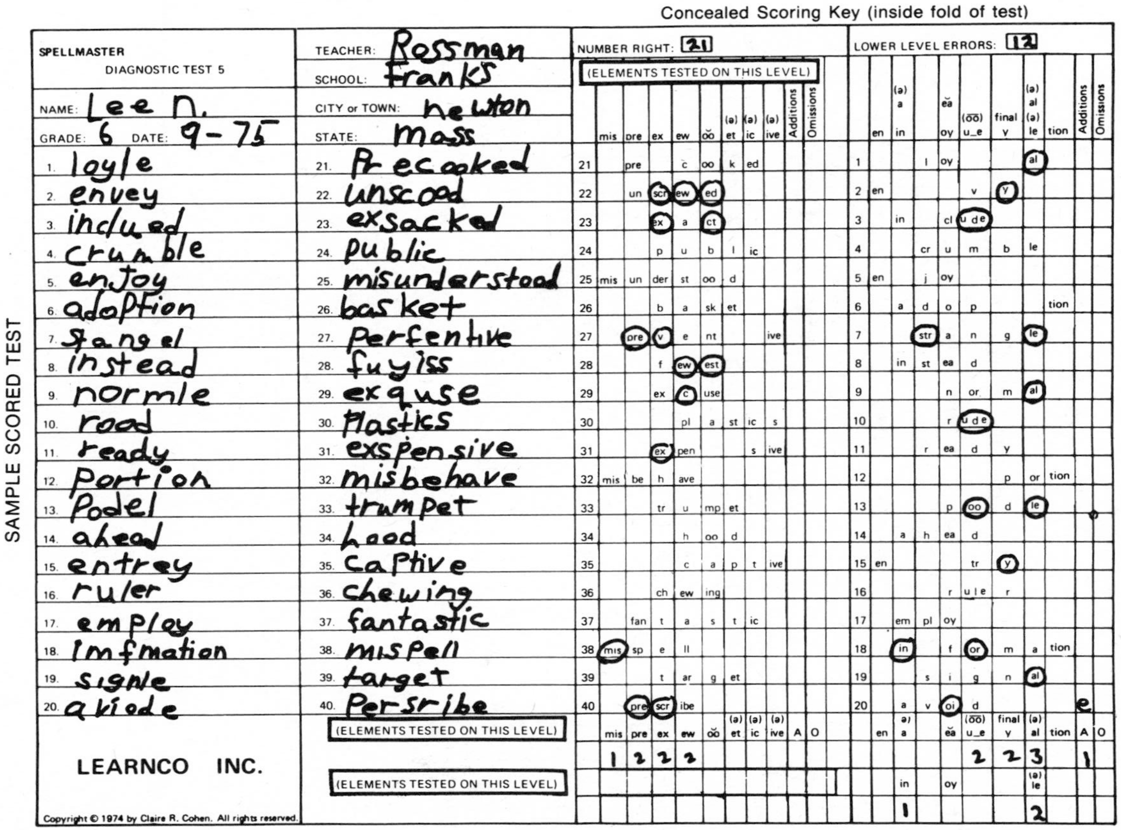
SAMPLE SCORED TEST
Concealed Scoring Key (inside fold of test)
SPELLMASTER
DIAGNOSTIC TEST 5
NAME: Lee N.
GRADE: 6 DATE: 9-75
TEACHER: Rossman
SCHOOL: Franks
CITY or TOWN: newton
STATE: mass
1. loyle
2. envey
3. inclued
4. crumble
5. enjoy
6. adoption
7. stangel
8. instead
9. normle
10. road
11. ready
12. Portion
13. Podel
14. ahead
15. entrey
16. ruler
17. employ
18. Imfmation
19. signle
20. aviode
21. Precooked
22. unscood
23. exsacked
24. public
25. misunderstood
26. basket
27. Perfentive
28. fuyiss
29. exquse
30. Plastics
31. exspensive
32. misbehave
33. trumpet
34. hood
35. captive
36. chewing
37. fantastic
38. mispell
39. target
40. Persribe
(ELEMENTS TESTED ON THIS LEVEL)
(ELEMENTS TESTED ON THIS LEVEL)
LEARNCO INC.
Copyright © 1974 by Claire R. Cohen. All rights reserved.
NUMBER RIGHT: 21
(ELEMENTS TESTED ON THIS LEVEL)
mis pre ex ew ŏŏ (ə) et (ə) ic (ə) ive Additions Omissions
21 pre c oo k ed
22 un scr ew ed
23 ex a ct
24 p u b l ic
25 mis un der st oo d
26 b a sk et
27 pre v e nt ive
28 f ew est
29 ex c use
30 pl a st ic s
31 ex pen s ive
32 mis be h ave
33 tr u mp et
34 h oo d
35 c a p t ive
36 ch ew ing
37 fan t a s t ic
38 mis sp e ll
39 t ar g et
40 pre scr ibe
mis pre ex ew ŏŏ (ə) et (ə) ic (ə) ive A O
1 2 2 2
LOWER LEVEL ERRORS: 12
en (ə) a in ĕa oy (ōō) u_e final y (ə) al (ə) le tion Additions Omissions
1 l oy al
2 en v y
3 in cl u de
4 cr u m b le
5 en j oy
6 a d o p tion
7 str a n g le
8 in st ea d
9 n or m al
10 r u de
11 r ea d y
12 p or tion
13 p oo d le
14 a h ea d
15 en tr y
16 r u le r
17 em pl oy
18 in f or m a tion
19 s i g n al
20 a v oi d e
en ə/a ĕa (ōō) u_e final y (ə) al tion A O
2 2 3 1
in oy (ə) le
1 2

Reprinted by permission.

This evaluation is based primarily on the teacher's direct observation of a student's behavior in a variety of spelling situations and on an analysis of many samples of spelling work. In short, assessment is directed, structured, and/or analytic observation.

Brueckner and Bond[1] have systematized informal observations by suggesting the following guidelines for teachers to use:

1. Analysis of Written Work, including Test Papers
   a. Legibility of handwriting
   b. Defects in letter forms, spacing, alignment, size
   c. Classification of errors in written work, letters, or tests
   d. Range of vocabulary used
   e. Evidence of lack of knowledge of conventions and rules
2. Analysis of Oral Responses
   a. Comparison of errors in oral and written spellings
   b. Pronunciation of words spelled incorrectly
   c. Articulation and enunciation
   d. Slovenliness of speech
   e. Dialect and colloquial forms of speech
   f. Way of spelling words orally:
      (1) Spells words as units
      (2) Spells letter by letter
      (3) Spells by digraphs
      (4) Spells by syllables
   g. Rhythmic pattern in oral spelling
   h. Blending ability
   i. Giving letters for sounds or sounds for letters
   j. Technique of word analysis used
   k. Quality and error made in oral reading
   l. Oral responses on tests or word analysis
   m. Analysis of pupil's comments as he states orally his thought process while studying new words
3. Interview with Pupil and Others
   a. Questioning pupil about methods of study
   b. Questioning pupil about spelling rules

---

[1]L. J. Brueckner and G. L. Bond, The diagnosis and treatment of learning difficulties. In E. C. Frierson and W. B. Barbe (Eds.), *Educating Children with Learning Disabilities* (New York: Appleton-Century-Crofts, 1955). Reprinted by permission.

      c. Questioning pupil about errors in convention
      d. Securing evidence as to attitude towards spelling

4. Questionnaire
      a. Applying checklist of methods of study
      b. Having pupil rank spelling according to interest
      c. Surveying use or written language

5. Free Observation in Course of Daily Work
      a. Securing evidence as to attitudes towards spelling
      b. Evidence of improvement in the study of new words
      c. Observing extent of use of dictionary
      d. Extent or error in regular written work
      e. Study habits and methods of work
      f. Social acceptability of the learner
      g. Evidences of emotional and social maladjustment
      h. Evidences of possible physical handicaps

6. Controlled Observation of Work on Set Tasks
      a. Looking up the meanings of given words in dictionary
      b. Giving pronunciation of words in dictionary
      c. Writing plural forms and derivatives of given words
      d. Observing responses on informal tests
      f. Estimating pupil scores when using a variety of methods studying selected words

For each student with a spelling problem, a careful analysis of errors should be made to discern whether a pattern of errors exists. For analysis and error tabulation, the teacher should use both lists of spelling words written from dictation and uncorrected continuous prose, such as a story a student has made up. Edgington has provided a sample of types of errors that exist in students' spelling work:[2]

Addition of unneeded letters (*dressses*)
Omissions of needed letters (*hom* for *home*)
Reflections of child's mispronunciations (*pin* for *pen*)
Reflections of dialectical speech patterns (*Cuber* for *Cuba*)
Reversals of whole words (*eno* for *one*)

---

[2]From R. Edgington, But he spelled them right this morning, *Academic Therapy*, 3 (1967), 58–59. Used with permission of the author and publisher (Academic Therapy Publications, San Rafael, California).

Reversals of vowels (*braed* for *bread*)

Reversals of consonant order (*lback* for *black*)

Reversals of consonant or vowel directionality (*brithday* for *birthday*)

Reversals of syllables (*telho* for *hotel*)

Phonetic spelling of nonphonetic words or parts thereof (*cawt* for *caught*)

Wrong associations of a sound with a given set of letters (*u* has been learned as *ou* in *you*)

"Neographisms," or letters put in a word which bear no discernible relationship with the word dictated.

Varying degrees and combinations of these or other possible patterns

Of course, it is useful for teachers to know which words the student cannot spell. Therefore, each student who has difficulty in spelling should have his or her own list of frequently misspelled words. Since some words are more likely to be misspelled than others, the teacher should at some time assess the student's performance on the following list of 100 demons, or commonly misspelled words.[3] Teachers should select words from the list that correspond to the student's grade level.

ache	climbed	hungry	onion
afraid	course	husband	passed
against	double	its	peaceful
all right	easier	it's	perfectly
although	eighth	kitchen	piano
angry	either	knives	picnic
answered	enemy	language	picture
asks	families	lettuce	piece
beautiful	fasten	listening	pitcher
because	fault	lose	pleasant
beginning	February	marriage	potato
boy's	forgotten	meant	practice
buried	friendly	minute	prettiest
busily	good-bye	neighbor	pumpkin
carrying	guessed	neither	purpose
certain	happened	nickel	quietly
choose	happily	niece	rapidly
Christmas	here's	ninety	receive
clothes	holiday	ninth	rotten

[3]From A. Kuska, E. J. D. Webster, and G. Elford, *Spelling in Language Arts 6* (Ontario, Canada: Thomas Nelson & Sons (Canada) Ltd., 1964). Reprinted by permission of the publisher, Thomas Nelson & Sons (Canada) Limited.

safety	shining	straight	through
said	silence	studying	valentine
sandwich	since	success	whose
scratch	soldier	taught	worst
sense	squirrel	their	writing
separate	stepped	there's	yours

In addition to knowing which of the demons a student cannot spell, the teacher should know which of the most commonly used words a student cannot spell. Horn (1926) found that 100 words comprise 65 percent of all the words written by adults and that only ten words (*I, the, and, to, a, you, of, in, we,* and *for*) account for 25 percent of the words used. Doubtlessly, many students are considered poor spellers because they cannot spell correctly the words on Horn's list. Poor spellers can improve noticeably and quickly if they are taught systematically the words on the list that they can't spell. Horn's list is provided below, in order of frequency.[4]

1. I	21. at	41. do	61. up	81. think
2. the	22. this	42. been	62. day	82. say
3. and	23. with	43. letter	63. much	83. please
4. to	24. but	44. can	64. out	84. him
5. a	25. on	45. would	65. her	85. his
6. you	26. if	46. she	66. order	86. got
7. of	27. all	47. when	67. yours	87. over
8. in	28. so	48. about	68. now	88. make
9. we	29. me	49. they	69. well	89. may
10. for	30. was	50. any	70. an	90. received
11. it	31. very	51. which	71. here	91. before
12. that	32. my	52. some	72. them	92. two
13. is	33. had	53. has	73. see	93. send
14. your	34. our	54. or	74. go	94. after
15. have	35. from	55. there	75. what	95. work
16. will	36. am	56. us	76. come	96. could
17. be	37. one	57. good	77. were	97. dear
18. are	38. time	58. know	78. no	98. made
19. not	39. he	59. just	79. how	99. glad
20. as	40. get	60. by	80. did	100. like

[4]From Ernest A. Horn, *A Basic Writing Vocabulary: 10,000 Words Most Commonly Used in Writing,* University of Iowa Monographs in Education, First Series, No. 4, Iowa City, Iowa, 1926.

TEACHING STUDENTS TO SPELL

Since students vary considerably in intellectual capacity and specific areas of weakness, spelling programs and remedial techniques should also vary with regard to level, theoretical orientation, vocabulary, manner of presentation, and format. The teacher cannot expect that a single spelling series will be suitable for all pupils. Therefore, he or she should have knowledge of an assortment of instructional alternatives. This section will review briefly several developmental and remedial systems as well as a few game activities that can facilitate spelling competence if employed effectively.

Developmental Methods

A long-standing and sometimes confusing controversy exists among authorities regarding the teaching of spelling. [See Yee (1966) for a detailed discussion of the topic.] Teachers should be aware of this debate because many of the spelling materials and methods used today reflect the controversy. Simply put, the conflict centers on the relative merits of using rules to enhance spelling competence. Some educators recommend the teaching of spelling rules that utilize a phonetic or sound-letter approach (Hanna & Moore, 1953; Hodges & Rudorf, 1965). They have found support in the work of Hanna, Hanna, Hodges, and Rudorf (1966), who programmed a computer with rules and then made it "spell" 17,000 words, which it did with remarkable accuracy. It spelled 50 percent of the words correctly; 37 percent were spelled with only a single error. A review of this project is in Hanna, Hodges, and Hanna (1971).

Other educators point out that English spelling forms are linguistically so irregular that spelling should be taught using almost no rules whatsoever. Still others suggest the limited use of teaching of rules (Archer, 1930; Horn, 1957). Spelling instruction, following this latter view, should involve a gradual accumulation of necessary and practiced words and include the introduction of rules whenever warranted.

Whatever the merits of the arguments may be, most of the developmental spelling series in common use today seem to adhere to the idea that American English spelling is sufficiently rule-governed that a basic linguistic approach, to be discussed shortly, can be utilized. Justification for this statement is based on the detailed survey of spelling instructional methodologies reported by Hammill, Larsen, and McNutt (1977). They contacted a nonselected group of 100 third- through eighth-grade teachers and asked them to specify the particular methods that they used to teach spelling. In all, these teachers were instructing 2956 students in twenty-two states.

The three basal spelling series used most often by teachers in this sample were *Silver Burdett Spelling* (1983), used with 26.0 percent of the students; *The*

Riverside Spelling Program (Wallace, 1984), used with 16.7 percent of the sample; and *Basic Goals in Spelling* (Kottmeyer & Claus, 1984), used with 14.2 percent of the students. [Since the Hammill et al. (1977) study was completed, the names and authors of some of the series have been changed. Current editions of the series are referenced in this paragraph and discussed later in this section.] Various other spelling programs were employed with 29.6 percent of the student sample; the teachers reported that 13.4 percent of the children were receiving no specific spelling instruction.

The authors of the three most-used basal spelling series in this sample all maintain that their method of teaching spelling is based on "linguistic theory." Linguistics, the study of language, may be subdivided into four discrete but related topics: (1) phonology, study of speech sounds; (2) morphology, study of the meaningful units of speech; (3) syntax, study of the rules that govern sentence formation or word order; and (4) semantics, study of the process by which a global understanding is gained from the presented language. Although linguistic theories usually encompass all four areas of study, when they are applied to teaching spelling, two elements appear to receive a majority of the emphasis: phonology and morphology. A more specific explanation of these two areas follows.

The term "phonology" is derived from the word "phoneme," which means a group of sounds so similar that they are considered equivalent. Although there may be slight variations in the production of a phoneme, for all intents and purposes it is a single speech sound represented by various letters or groups of letters. There are approximately thirty-six phonemes in our language. Graphemes are the letter or combination of letters that represent a phoneme. For example, the phoneme /k/ may be represented by the grapheme "k," "c," or "ck."

The term "morphology" is derived from the word "morpheme," which refers to the smallest units of meaningful speech. A morpheme may be a word (e.g., *boy*, because it cannot be broken into smaller units that yield meaning) or even a single letter (e.g., the plural marker /z/ in boys). Morphology includes the study of the inflections and changes in words that alter their meanings (e.g., prefixes and suffixes).

Although each of the three most-used basal spelling series utilizes aspects of linguistic theory, the series are not identical. A brief description of the three spelling series follows.

The words for each unit in the *Silver Burdett Spelling* (1983) series are divided into basic lists and enrichment lists which are topical or thematic in organization. The basic words constitute approximately 90 percent of the words most students use in their daily writing, with each group or list focusing on one particular spelling pattern. The patterns generally are phonological (e.g., short *a* words) or morphological (e.g., prefixes that mean "not") in nature. In addition to providing general spelling lessons, *Silver Burdett Spelling* integrates many skills from a language arts curriculum (e.g., dictionary skills) and contains various enrichment or extension activities for the more able student.

   Basic Goals in Spelling (Kottmeyer & Claus, 1984) also presents basic word lists and word lists for enrichment. The basic words were chosen because research revealed that they are commonly used in the writing vocabulary of students at each level. Although morphological relationships are included, the stress according to the series authors is on sound-symbol relationships, indicating the importance of phonology. The authors of the programs stress the importance of allowing the students to observe similarities of sound and spelling in words and to formulate generalizations, or rules, on their own, rather than stating spelling rules for the students to memorize.

   Wallace (1984) reports that in the *Riverside Spelling Program* presented words are grouped according to their particular spelling patterns: rhyming patterns (bit, fit, hit), nonrhyming patterns (did, dig, dip), and vowel-changing patterns (pat, pet, put). The words of the core vocabulary comprise 80 percent of the spelling needed by an elementary student, and the upper levels stress words that are important to adult living. Emphasis is placed on integrating various communication skills (e.g., speaking and listening skills, dictionary investigation, and composition). An example lesson is shown in Figure 4–3. This lesson, number 19 from the Level 4 book, is fairly representative of those included in other series.

Remedial Techniques for Spelling

Many students exposed to the traditional, classroom-based spelling programs reviewed in the previous section do not reach expected levels of achievement. With these students, the teacher may decide to try a remedial approach. With students who are targeted for remedial training, the teacher may find it useful to consider the general suggestions offered by Petty and Jensen (1980). In addition to encouraging the development of favorable attitudes toward spelling and good study habits, they recommend the following activities for teaching the "slow speller."

1. Emphasize the importance of the words the student is to learn. Teach a minimum list and make certain that the words on it are as useful as possible.
2. Teach no more words than the pupil can successfully learn to spell. Success is a motivating influence, and the poor speller has probably had much experience with failure in learning to spell the words in the weekly lessons.
3. Give more than the usual amount of time to oral discussion of the words to be learned. In addition to making certain the children know the meanings of the words, ask questions about structural aspects of the words.

Figure 4–3. Example Lesson from the *Riverside Spelling Program*

Lesson 19

second	*garden*	*uncle*
across	*alive*	*settle*
example	*bottle*	*approach*
table	*apple*	*alert*
able	*lion*	*robin*
simple		

Answer the questions.

1. Which spelling words use *a* to spell /ə/?

   across   approach

   alive   alert

2. Which spelling words contain /ən/ as in *children?*

   second   lion

   garden   robin

3. What are three different ways to spell /ən/?

   on   en   in

4. Which spelling words end in /əl/ like *circle?*

   example   bottle

   table   apple

   able   uncle

   simple   settle

5. What letters spell /əl/ in the words you

   just wrote? le

82   Lesson 19   Patterns That Spell /ə/, /ən/, /əl/

TEACHING NOTES
Remind students that each vowel letter can spell the schwa
sound.

Figure 4–3 *Continued*

Context

Write spelling words to complete the story.

My __(1)__ from Detroit came to spend a few days with us because he might __(2)__ in our city. I really like him and wanted to do something special for him. So I planned to serve lunch in the __(3)__ one day. I set the __(4)__ for two. In the middle, I put a small __(5)__ of water with two roses from our garden. I decided to make a __(6)__ meal so that I would be __(7)__ to prepare it all myself. I served soup, crackers, chicken sandwiches, __(8)__ juice, and fruit. My uncle really liked my cooking. He had a __(9)__ bowl of soup and another sandwich.

I like our garden. I feel very __(10)__ there because there are so many things happening. If I am __(11)__, I can see many things going on. For __(12)__, we watched a __(13)__ building its nest in the tree __(14)__ from us while we ate. The growing leaves in the garden tell us about the __(15)__ of summer.

Before my uncle left, he gave me a T-shirt with a picture of a __(16)__ on it because he knows that I like the Detroit Lions football team. He also invited me to visit him this summer.

1. uncle
2. settle
3. garden
4. table
5. bottle
6. simple
7. able
8. apple
9. second
10. alive
11. alert
12. example
13. robin
14. across
15. approach
16. lion

83

TEACHING NOTES
Context Explain that each spelling word can be used only once on this page.

Figure 4–3 *Continued*

Dictionary

1. Read the paragraph. Complete the statements.

> Roberto wanted to write the saying "through /thik/ and thin." He needed to use the dictionary to find out how to spell /thik/.

a. The consonant digraph he heard at the beginning of /thik/ is spelled ___th___ .

b. The vowel sound he heard was /i/. He knew that /i/ can be spelled ___i___ as in *pin* or ___y___ as in *gym*.

c. The consonant sound he heard at the end of /thik/ was /k/. He knew that /k/ can be spelled ___c___ as in *cat*, ___k___ as in *king*, ___ch___ as in *chorus*, or ___ck___ as in *back*.

d. By checking his Spelling Dictionary, he found that /thik/ is spelled ___thick___ .

2. Check your Spelling Dictionary to write each word.

a. /chans/ ___chance___   c. /chik′ ən/ ___chicken___

b. /plas′ tik/ ___plastic___   d. /traf′ ik/ ___traffic___

Handwriting

1. If *a* looks like *o*, *alive* will look like *olive*. Write a row of the letter *a* and a row of the letter *o*.

a _____

o _____

2. Write these pairs of words so that each word is clear.

a. bath—both   _____   _____

b. same—some   _____   _____

84

TEACHING NOTES

Dictionary Remind students that they will be using a sound-by-sound strategy to help them locate in the dictionary words that they don't know how to spell. Point out to students that in each of the respellings presented in the exercise, the very first dictionary symbol has only one spelling. Mention that the spelling for this initial sound is the first important clue in spelling the word. Then refer students to the pronunciation key in the Spelling Dictionary and, if necessary, help them sound out the other symbols in each respelling.

Figure 4–3 *Continued*

Checkup

Write a spelling word to match each clue.
Then complete the sentences.

1. bird   2. fruit   3. easy   4. living
5. big cat   6. watchful   7. place for growing things

1. robin _____   4. alive _____   6. alert _____

2. apple _____   5. lion _____   7. garden _____

3. simple _____

The letters _____le_____ can spell /əl/. Three ways of

spelling /ən/ are _____in_____, _____on_____, and _____en_____.

Challenge

Write the answers to these riddles. Some answers have
/əl/ spelled by *le*. Some answers have /ən/ spelled by
in, en, or *on.* Look at the scrambled letters for clues.

1. I float through the air just barely there.
   I am a _____. (b b b e u l)

   1. bubble _____

2. I am something you might bake in the shape of a
   small, round cake. I am a _____. (f u n f i m)

   2. muffin _____

3. I can be on a sweater or a shirt; I can even be
   on jeans or a skirt.
   I am a _____. (t u b t o n)

   3. button _____

4. You might have to puzzle over me a second or two;
   I might be hard or easy, but I'm usually fun to do.
   I am a _____. (d e r d i l)

   4. riddle _____

Let's Write

A fable is a story made up to teach a lesson. One
well-known fable is "The Hare and the Tortoise."
Usually, the lesson is summed up in one sentence
at the end of the fable. Make up your own fable.
Proofread your fable when you finish.

TEACHING NOTES
Let's Write Before students begin, you might ask a volunteer to recall the fable of "The Hare and the Tortoise." Then
ask another volunteer to explain the lesson of the fable. After
students have finished proofreading, they might enjoy compiling and reproducing a class booklet of their fables.

*Challenge/Spelling
Plus* exercises for
Unit Four can be
found at the back
of this book.

To assess student
progress, use *Lesson 19
Test Yourself* found on
page 185 at the back
of the book.

Practice Tests for
85   Unit Four can be
found at the back
of this book.

---

4. Pay particular attention to pronunciation. Make certain the pupil can pronounce each word properly and naturally.

5. Strengthen pupils' images of words by having them trace the forms with their index fingers as you write them on the board.

6. Note bad study habits. Show how the habit is harmful and may prevent success in spelling.

7. Check and perhaps modify the child's method of individual study.

8. Provide a wide variety of writing activities that necessitate using the words learned. (pp. 456–457)

Remedial programs differ considerably from the developmentally oriented classroom basal series in that the student is taught on a one-to-one basis or in small groups. Also, multisensory, particularly kinesthetic, elements are frequently incorporated into the training activities. The programs about to be described are suitable for students of all ages, including adolescents and adults.

Fernald's Multisensory Approach

Fernald's (1943) multisensory approach, discussed in Chapter 2, is reported to be highly successful with some students. The student traces the letters (tactile-kinesthetic), sees the tracing (visual), says the letters aloud (vocal), and hears what he or she says (auditory). For this reason, the approach is often referred to as the VAKT (visual-auditory-kinesthetic-tactile) technique.

Fernald's techniques are usually reserved for clinical use with students who have serious problems in spelling. This is unfortunate, for although the activities are highly individualized, they can easily be adapted to work in a regular classroom as well as in a remedial group. Fernald recommends that when teaching remedial spelling, teachers adhere strictly to the following procedures:

1. The word to be learned is written on the blackboard or on paper by the teacher.

2. The teacher pronounces the word very clearly and distinctly. The students pronounce the words.

3. Time is allowed for each student to study the word.

4. When every student is sure of the word, it is erased or covered and the student writes it from memory.

5. The paper is turned over and the word written a second time.

6. Arrangements are made so that it is natural for the student to make frequent use, in written expression, of the word he or she has learned.

7. The student is allowed to get the correct form of the word at any time when he or she is doubtful of its spelling.

8. If spelling matches (spelling "bees") are used, they are written instead of oral.

In her book, Fernald described in detail just how each of these steps is to be carried out, what verbal instructions are given to the student, and how spelling vocabulary lists are used to select the "foundation" words that should be taught first. Of all the approaches to the remedial teaching of spelling, this one is perhaps the most popular.

Slingerland's Alphabetic Approach

The original alphabetic approach to spelling was developed by Gillingham and Stillman (1970) and is known by several names, including the Gillingham, the Orton-Gillingham, and the Gillingham-Stillman method. The technique stresses the building of sounds into words through the application of visual, auditory, and kinesthetic associations. Students link a sound with a letter, establish a visual memory pattern for a particular word, and then reinforce that pattern by writing the word. This linkage is accomplished by a four-step cover-and-write procedure:

1. Students see a word and say it out loud.
2. They write the word twice (more often if necessary) while looking at it.
3. They cover the word and write it once again.
4. They check the correctness of their spelling by looking at it.

Beth Slingerland's adaptation of this method is particularly useful in remediating moderate to severe cases of a type commonly found in school situations. Aho's (1967) description of the adaptation is reproduced below.[5]

> The children should be shown each letter as it is being taught or reviewed, given the name, the sound as *heard* and *felt* in a key word, and then in isolation, the teacher listening for individual weaknesses or errors as *each* child repeats.
>   The children then trace a correctly formed large-sized pattern of the letter, using the first two fingers or the wrong end of a pencil and naming the letter as it is traced.
>   After the "feeling" of the letter form is fairly secure, the children copy it and continue tracing lightly with a relaxed hand so the whole arm motion can be felt from the shoulder, the teacher giving help with correct letter forms if needed.

[5]From M. Aho, Teaching spelling to children with specific language disability, *Academic Therapy*, 3, 1 (1967), 46–50 (Novato, Calif.: Academic Therapy Publications). Reprinted by permission. (Footnote has been renumbered.)

The children are then taught the letter's sound. A knowledge of the teacher's correct use of sounds is essential here.[6]

When all have mastered the letter form and sound, the children should (1) name the letter as it is being formed, *h*; (2) give the key word *house*; and (3) give the sound /*h*/.

Large key cards should be placed on the wall for the child's quick and easy reference when he is in doubt or before he makes a "guessing mistake."

The letters may be grouped for similar movement patterns:

Manuscript:

b	f	h	k	l	t	p			
a	c	d	g	o	qu	s	e		
i	j	m	n	r	u	y	v	w	x	z

Cursive:

b	f	h	k	l	e			
a	e	d	g	o	qu			
i	j	p	r	s	t	u	w	(y)
m	n	v	x	y	z	(w)		

Spelling should now begin with letters as single elements of sound.

The teacher may ask: "What consonant says /*h*/?" One child answers: "*H* (forming the letter in the air as he names it), *house*, /*h*/." The children repeat, then write the letter on paper. Later the response may be simply, "*H*, /*h*/."

To further develop automatic response, say: "Make *b*," "Make *a*," "Make /*f*/," the children writing, naming, tracing, and making the next letter as directed. A rhythm should be kept in directing, leaving no lapses of time between directions.

Patterns should be made for tracing and practicing difficult letter connections, such as *br*, *os*, *wr*, etc. The large-spaced paper used to begin with may be reduced to smaller spaces after the children gain the "feel" of the sequential movement pattern necessary for the automatic formation of letters.

This adaptation classifies all words into three kinds for spelling. Children should become aware of these approaches to enable them to determine the method for study which gives them self-confidence.

Green-Flag Words are short vowel, purely phonetic words that can be spelled as soon as the letters and sounds of the letters required have been taught. However, unless a child speaks correctly (and this means teacher awareness, control, and direction of speech practice) even these will not be accurately phonetic for him. Unstudied Green-Flag words may be written from dictation following the pattern which is learned in the primary grades:

• Child repeats the word named by the teacher.
• Child hears and gives the vowel sound.
• Child names the vowel, forming the letter in the air as he names it.
• Child spells the word orally, writing each letter in the air as he names it.
• Child writes the word on paper. At times he retraces if needed.

---

[6]Sally B. and Ralph de S. Childs, *Sounds of English* (Cambridge, Mass.: Educators Publishing Service), phonograph record.

Red-Flag Words are non-phonetic or irregular and must be "learned as wholes" because every sound cannot be heard. (While giving practice, the words are listed on the board accordingly as Red-Flag or Green-Flag words.) The phonetic parts should be noted and the difficult parts are underlined or stressed. In *laugh*, only the *l* is easy. The *augh* has to be learned as a whole. In *could, would,* and *should,* the beginning and ending sounds can be heard, but the *oul* must be learned, so the entire word is learned by this procedure:

- Child copies the word.
- The teacher checks for correct spelling and letter forms.
- Child traces over the letter lightly, naming each letter as it is formed.
- When he feels he has learned the word, he closes his eyes and tries writing the word in the air. He is encouraged to realize that if his hand stops, his brain is no longer directing his hand, so he hasn't learned the word and must do more tracing. He may also try writing the word and checking it with the correct pattern.
- The teacher may give the final checkup by dictating as words, in phrases, or as part of the dictation lesson.

Yellow-Flag Words, or ambiguous words, can be spelled in more than one way as far as the vowel or consonant sound is concerned. Spelling of these words begins after the vowel digraphs, diphthongs, and phonograms are introduced. (They will have been used for reading a considerable time before they are introduced for spelling unless given as "learned words.") From now on, spelling becomes more complicated.

Children in the third and fourth grades, having had training in this way, should acquire the ability to recall all the ways of spelling a given vowel or consonant sound that they have been taught:

/ā/	/ē/	/ī/	/ō/	/ū/	/o͞o/	/ĕ/	/ou/
a	e	i	o	u	u	e	ou
a-e	a-e	i-e	o-e	u-e	u-e	ca	ow
ai	ee	igh	oa	ew	ew		
ay	ea	ie	ow				
eigh	ie						
ea	y						

/c/	/au/	/i/	/oi/		/ch/	/j/
c	au	i	oi	er	ch	j
k	aw	y	oy	ir	tch	dge
ck				ur		

Practice should be given, in studying, in how to listen for or take note of the vowel sound and then to make a selection.

- Child repeats the word given by the teacher. (*Grain.*)
- Child hears and gives the vowel sound, /ā/. After working with the different ways that spell /ā/, the children will discover that /ā/ followed by a consonant sound could be *ai, a-e,* or *eigh;* that *ay* usually occurs at the end of a word or syllable, and that *ea* is found in only a few words.
- After generalizing, the child makes a selection and asks the teacher, "Is it *a-e?*" The teacher answers: "It would make the correct sound but it is not used in this word." The child thinks again and asks: "Is it *ai?*" The reply is: "Yes, in this case it is."
- Child repeats the word.
- Child spells the word, naming each letter as he writes it in the air.

In this way, the teacher serves as the dictionary while the children get the practice which precedes intelligent dictionary technique.

- Children repeat and write *grain* on paper.
- Children trace for study.

Additional related words may be given for further practice; for example, *trail, grave, snake, gray,* etc. Mixed groups of words with the vowel sound of /ā/ may be given to be worked out and placed under the correct heading (for example, *chain, tray,* etc.) either as independent seat work or as the teacher dictates for organizational practice on paper.

Words for spelling should begin with simple three-letter phonetic short vowel words, progressing in difficulty as the children gain skill; for example, *lap, cast, pack, lash, chat, grasp, branch,* etc. After the "vowel concept" of short *a* is well understood, short *i* will be another sound to open the throat. (The secret of success is in very thorough teaching and the opportunity to "over-learn" the *a,* the *i,* and then discrimination.) Then the other vowels may be included. Continue with the following as the children are ready:

- Words with letter combinations, such as *ink, ank, ing, ong,* etc.
- Adding suffixes or endings and their meanings to words (no rules), for example, *ing, s* or *es, er, est, ed, less, ness, ly, y,* etc.
- Words where the short vowel sound is made long as in vowel-consonant-e words, such as *pan, pane, rip, ripe,* etc.
- Words containing vowel digraphs, diphthongs, and phonograms.
- Words of two or more syllables (over-emphasizing each syllable when pronouncing them). For example, *poppin, butter, fragment, lumber, fiddle, bumble, title, rifle, pavement, dictate,* etc.
- Words doubling the final *f, l, s;* words doubling the final consonant before adding an ending (1-1-1 rule), and words dropping the silent *e* (which requires special teaching not included in this paper).

Phrase writing carried into sentences should begin early.

- Use phonetic words in simple phrases; for example, *grab the bat,* etc.
- Begin with a root word, carry it into phrases, and then into simple sentences. This should be dictated by the teacher. Put underlined words on the board to be copied if they haven't been taught:

Camp
camping   camps   camped   camper
to *go* camping   to camp *out*   camped and camped
I like to camp.   I like to go camping.   Do you like to go camping?

- Use any non-phonetic word, repeating it in different phrasing:

Laugh
laughing at that
a laughable matter
laughed and laughed

- The teacher should ask questions to give meaning:

List
What *did* Mother do? Listed the toys.
What *does* she do? Lists the toys.
What is she *doing?* Listing the toys.

- Use root words, dropping the silent *e* or doubling the final consonant, after the procedure for this more difficult spelling has been well structured.
- Write answers to questions. For a one-part question, the teacher should write: "Have you been to the zoo?" The child copies the question and writes: "Yes, I have been to the zoo."

For a two-part question, the teacher should write: "What city do you live in? In what state is it?" The child writes: "I live in Renton. Renton is in the state of Washington." Or, "I live in the city of Renton which is in the state of Washington."

Through structured dictation lessons, these children gain feeling for form, arrangement, sentence construction, continuity, and organization of thoughts which is carried over into individual creative writing. The material used should be made by the teacher and children, but with teacher-controlled guidance to insure the right words for their level of learning, organization, and overall planning.

After the teacher writes the story in cursive on a large sheet of paper so it can be seen about the room, the children copy it, the teacher checking before study to prevent incorrect practice. Any errors made in copying are bracketed to discourage erasing and untidy papers and to encourage the children to "stop and think" before writing.

Words that are too hard to be learned at this time are underlined. These will be written where they can be seen when the final dictation is given. (These may be used for extra work for those able to learn them, too.) The children should note the Green-Flag, Red-Flag, and Yellow-Flag words to determine the method of study.

The teacher should guide directed study in various ways:

- Special practice in writing phonetic words in and related to the story.
- Learning non-phonetic words.
- Adding suffixes and prefixes and their meanings. (Using rules.)
- Writing ambiguous words from the story and giving additional related words under correct headings as far as vowel sounds are concerned.
- Giving phrases from the story for a check.
- Playing games using ambiguous words with the teacher serving as the dictionary.
- Spelldown—requiring the correct response used for oral spelling.

When the weekly study is over, all evidences of study are removed and the teacher dictates the story sentence-by-sentence and phrase-by-phrase. (pp. 46–50)

Proff-Witt's Tutorial Program

The *Speed Spelling* (1978) and the *Advanced Speed Spelling* (1979) programs by Proff-Witt incorporate multisensory elements found in the Fernald and Slingerland approaches. These elements are organized into a systematic, highly sequenced, and linguistically oriented tutorial program for use with students in grades one through twelve.

The carefully ordered daily lessons, each of which is designed to teach a specific aspect of spelling, form the core of the program. As an example, Lesson 14.4, Prefixes—dis-, mis-, is shown in Figure 4–4. All lessons take about twenty

Figure 4–4. Example Lesson from the *Speed Spelling* Program

14.4 Prefixes — dis-, mis-

OBJECTIVE	WHAT TUTOR SAYS	WHAT STUDENT DOES	WHAT TUTOR SAYS/DOES IF STUDENT IS RIGHT	WHAT TUTOR SAYS/DOES IF STUDENT IS WRONG
Given a list of words, student (S) says 20 words per minute with 2 errors or less.	A. **Read these words.** B. **I am going to time you for 1 minute. Keep reading the words until the minute is over. Ready, read.**	A. Reads words. B. Reads words.	A. **Good reading!** B. Count and chart the number of words right and wrong in 1 minute on Word Reading graph.	A. (1) **Listen** (say sounds of the word) (2) **Sound it out with me** (say sounds together) (3) **Sound it out by yourself** (student says sounds) (4) **What word?** (student says word)
When tutor says words, S writes 12 words in 1 minute with 2 errors or less.* Grades 1-3: write 10 words with 1 error or less.*	A. **Write these words as I say them.** B. **I am going to time you for 1 minute. Keep writing the words as I say them until the minute is over. Ready . . . .**	A. Writes words. B. Writes words.	A. **Good spelling!** B. Count and chart the number of words right and wrong in 1 minute on Word Writing graph.* Write words missed on the Tutor Record Sheet.	A. See "How to Study" in the SPEED SPELLING *Student Book.*
When tutor reads 2 sentences, S writes the words of the sentences with no spelling errors.	A. **Write this sentence . . . .** (Choose 2 sentences. Read each 2 times slowly as S writes.)	A. Writes sentence.	A. **Good writing!** Count and chart the number of sentences with no spelling errors on the Sentence Writing graph.	A. Have S write the sentence the right way 1 time.

Word List

disband	misfire	displease	distaste	4
distrust	dislike	misdeal	misuse	8
mistake	misspell	disown	mislead	12
disobey	misprint	misconduct	disorder	16

Dictation Sentences**

The group must disband.
Tom showed disrespect for his father.
That mistake is a misprint.
Our gun will misfire.
Did she disobey the order?
They dislike a mismatched outfit.

* When the S passes (writes 12 words in 1 minute with 2 or less errors), write the date on the Skills Checklist in the *Student Book.* Have teacher give *Cycling Test 13.0a.*

Source: J. Proff-Witt, *Speed Spelling.* Published by C. C. Publications, Inc., Tigard, Oregon, 1978, 800-547-4800.

minutes to complete and consist of three parts: word reading, word writing, and sentence writing.

Students who can read the words listed in the lesson but who misspell some of them when writing are taught the misspelled words according to a five-point study plan that is described in the student booklet that accompanies the lessons. Students are told to do the following (Proff-Witt, 1978):

1. Copy the word.
2. Say each letter sound as you trace the letters. Then say the whole word. Do this three times.
3. Say each letter sound as you use your finger to write the letters in your hand. Then say the whole word. Do this three times.
4. Say each letter sound as you write the letters on paper with your eyes closed. Then say the whole word. Do this three times.
5. Test yourself to see if you can write the word the right way.

Shaw's Self-Teaching Approach

Shaw (1971) has formulated a teaching system for the self-motivated older student or the adult who wishes to improve his or her spelling ability. He reduces spelling remediation to six basic methods:[7]

1. Mentally see words as well as hear them.
2. Pronounce words correctly and carefully.
3. Use a dictionary.
4. Learn a few simple rules of spelling.
5. Use memory devices.
6. Spell carefully to avoid errors.

The relevance of these six strategies is described in detail in his book, along with numerous related training activities.

We conclude this section on training by referring the reader to Hansen's (1978) chapter in *The Fourth R: Research in the Classroom*. In this work, she reviews the research relating to three categories of behaviorally oriented methods for remedying spelling. Although all of these direct teaching procedures are useful, only one is described here because of the limits of space. The "cover-copy-compare" tactic comprises four steps:

---

[7]From p. 14 in *Spell It Right!* Second edition by Harry Shaw (Barnes & Noble Books). Copyright © 1961, 1965 by Harry Shaw. Reprinted by permission of Harper & Row, Publishers, Inc.

. . . first, the student analyzes a word and notes its distinctive features; then, he or she writes the word while saying each letter silently; next, he or she covers the word and writes it once again from memory; finally, the student compares the written word to the original to see if it is spelled correctly. The pupil repeats the process until he or she spells each word correctly without referring to the model. (pp. 108–109)

Game Supplements for Spelling Instruction

The literature is replete with games and other activities reported to be beneficial as supplements to a spelling program. Although games provide for diversification in the method of presentation and help to foster interest in the teaching effort, the experienced teacher knows that they are intended as supplements and not as substitutes for a spelling program. Several examples of spelling games follow.

Tongue Twisters

The objective of Tongue Twisters is awareness of initial consonants.

Directions. Students think of a sentence in which most of the words start with the same letter, e.g., "Funny father."

Examples. Funny father fed five foxes. Polly Page put a potato in her pocket.

Variation. The teacher writes each student's twister on the board.

Directions. The teacher asks, "How are many of these words similar? Draw a line under the similar parts." The teacher then helps the students to see that most of the words start with the same sound and letter.

Bingo

Bingo is a group game for grades three to six.

Directions. Each student folds a paper into sixteen squares. In turn, students are asked to give a word. A scribe writes the word on the board or challenges the donor to spell the word. The students each write the correctly spelled word on any of one of the sixteen squares. When all the squares are filled, a student is selected to come forward. With his or her back to the board, the student spells any one of the words a selected caller gives. Each correctly spelled word enables the students to place a marker on the corresponding Bingo square. The first student to complete a row or a diagonal calls "Bingo" and wins the game. The teacher keeps a list of the words called and checks off the winner. These Bingo squares may be kept for repeated playing.

Treasure Hunt

Treasure Hunt is a team game for grades two to six.

Directions. The teacher selects teams, sets a time limit of two minutes, and writes a base word on the board at the head of each team's column. Each student can write only one word, a new one or a corrected one. At a given sign, the first student from each team races to the board and writes any word that can be made with letters in the base word. Each student races back, hands the chalk to the next student, and goes to the end of the line. The game continues until the teacher calls time. The group with the longest correct list in a specified limit is the winner.

Example. For the given base word *tame*, students might write:

tam
am
me

Anagrams

Students can make anagram or Scrabble games for independent activities.

Variation 1. Words can be made by adding a letter in vertical or horizontal order.

Example. Cat
over
e
r
y

Variation 2. Students start with a common word and change one letter each time the word is spelled. Each player must either have a scribe to record completed words or else record his or her own words. Winners are those who can complete the greatest numbers of correctly spelled words. Teachers act as final judges of correct spelling.

Example. dime—dome—home—hope

Telegraph

The objectives of Telegraph are quick thinking and correct spelling. It is a team game for grade five.

Directions.   A goal of six or ten points is established for winning the game, and a time limit of four slow counts or four seconds for the hesitant speller. Each student is given one or two letters of the alphabet. The teacher pronounces a word to team one. The letters of the telegraph begin to respond in proper order. If the response is correct, the team gets one point and another word to transmit. The opposing side gets a word when

1. a member of the team fails to give a letter in the four-second time limit or by four counts;
2. the completed word is misspelled;
3. someone on the team "helps" to spell the word.

Variation.   For primary grades, letters used or needed for the spelling of the teacher's list may be printed on 2- by 6-inch cards. Each child receives a card. When the teacher pronounces a word, the telegraph letters take their places in the proper order at the front of the room (alternatively, letters may be placed in a chart holder or on the blackboard ledge).

CONCLUSIONS

Several final observations about teaching and remediating spelling seem in order. For the most part these conclusions pertain to the nature of spelling and its relationship to language arts instruction.

Spelling is not a subject that should be taught entirely apart from reading and writing. To be sure, some phoneme-grapheme correspondences, linguistic rules, and a considerable number of different words can be taught in isolation. But no programs are complete enough, no time periods long enough, and no teachers tenacious enough to teach students all of the words they need to know how to spell in life. Therefore, Hodges (1981) suggests that no spelling program by itself is likely to acquaint the student with all the regularities, patterns, and rules that make up English spelling. He goes on to point out that a spelling curriculum can set the stage and point the direction for the student but that ultimately good spelling is a consequence of interaction with written language, especially writing.

This idea is seconded by F. Smith (1983), who suggests that reading, as well as writing, is important to learning to spell. F. Smith would probably consider reading to be more important than writing. He mentions that people can actually spell more words than they ever were taught to spell and more than they are ever called upon to use in writing. He suggests that people learned these words through reading. To him, spelling competence is a natural by-product of learning to read. He speculates:

> I am not asserting that anyone who reads will become a speller because that is not the case. But anyone who is a speller must be a reader. Reading is the only possible source of all the spelling information you have in your head. (1983, p. 193)

If Hodges and F. Smith are correct, the traditional practices in remedial and developmental education of waiting until the student has mastered reading before introducing spelling and of teaching spelling largely in isolation should be avoided. Instead, reading and writing instruction should begin at the same time, and spelling should be introduced as soon as the student is capable of forming letters. Besides being taught through workbooks, sequenced lessons, and skill exercises, spelling should be integrated into a general language arts program as much as possible. It must always be kept in mind that word recognition, reading comprehension, handwriting, punctuation and capitalization style, and spelling go hand in hand. These are all aspects of written language; they necessarily complement and reinforce one another.

chapter 5

Correcting Handwriting Deficiencies

by Donald D. Hammill

No matter how well conceived a composition may be, it is useless if it is so illegible that it cannot be read. At one time or another, we have all had the experience of hastily jotting down a good idea and later being unable to decipher the writing. If we frequently cannot read our own handwriting, consider the dismay of those individuals who occasionally have to read what we write. The frustrations that teachers encounter as a result of attempting to read the all-too-often unreadable compositions of students is but another reason why good handwriting is desirable. Care must be taken in the physical preparation of compositions if they are to be understood. Also, legible handwriting is simply good manners, a courtesy that readers have the right to expect.

This discussion on correcting handwriting deficiencies is divided into two major parts. The first part describes procedures for measuring handwriting and determining specific deficiencies. The second part is devoted to describing activities and programs that are helpful in remedying poor handwriting.

MEASURING HANDWRITING

The discussion pertaining to the measurement of handwriting has three sections: (1) assessing handwriting readiness, (2) assessing general handwriting competence, and (3) assessing specific errors in handwriting.

Assessing Handwriting Readiness

We do not agree with the concept of "handwriting readiness"—at least not as traditionally defined and applied. We doubt, for example, that copying geometric shapes or developing laterality (handedness), ocular control, and visual perception of forms not involving words or letters has much to do with proficiency in handwriting. Much research supports this suspicion (Harris & Herrick, 1963; T. L. Niedermeyer, 1973; Wiederholt, 1971). All the so-called prerequisite, readiness skills can probably be developed naturally without any specific instruction as a consequence of learning to write letters, words, and phrases directly. Since we don't believe these readiness skills need to be developed, we prefer a more direct approach to handwriting assessment, one that can be used to identify young students who are likely to become poor writers later in their school life and to pinpoint the specific areas of writing readiness in which training is needed. To achieve these purposes, the teacher can use the Writing subscale of the Basic School Skills Inventory—Diagnostic (Hammill & Leigh, 1983).

The Basic School Skills Inventory—Diagnostic (BSSI) was developed to measure fundamental school-related skills in young students aged 4-0 through 6-11. It was constructed primarily on the basis of the results of extensive interviews with kindergarten and first-grade teachers. In these interviews, the teachers were asked to describe the actual behaviors that seemed to distinguish children who were "ready" for school from those who were not. The behaviors that related to writing were singled out and used to form the Writing subscale of the BSSI.

The BSSI can be used either in a norm-referenced fashion (i.e., to identify children who are "low in writing readiness" and therefore need special help) or in a criterion-referenced fashion (i.e., to decide what skills are to be taught and in what order). To use the scale, the teacher selects a particular student to be assessed, reads each item carefully, and then, using personal knowledge about the student's classroom performance relative to the item, decides whether or not he or she can do the task. The student is not taken aside and "tested" unless the teacher lacks sufficient familiarity with the pupil's writing behavior to answer the scale items. The items that comprise the subscale are reproduced below.[1]

[1]Reprinted by permission of authors and publisher from The Basic School Skills Inventory—Diagnostic (Austin, Texas: Pro-Ed, 1983).

Writing

Materials: primary pencil
lined primary writing paper
card containing a common word
chalkboard

The items on this subtest measure the child's proficiency in using a pencil and paper for written expression. The items focus on those abilities and skills directly involved in writing letters, words, and sentences. The child may use either manuscript or cursive writing for each of the items.

1. *Does the child write from left to right?*
   To earn a pass on this item, a child should demonstrate some consistent knowledge of left-right progression in writing. Letters or words may be illegible, poorly formed, misspelled, or otherwise inadequate and still be recorded as a pass if, in the execution of her written efforts, the child proceeds in a left-to-right sequence. This sequence does not even have to be on a straight line; diagonal writing is permissible, as long as it is basically left to right.

2. *Can the child write his first name?*
   The intention of this item is to determine whether the child can write (manuscript or cursive) her first name on command. The letters do not have to be properly formed nor does spelling have to be exactly correct. The result must, however, be recognizable as being the child's actual name. Writing one's name from a model is not acceptable here.

3. *When given a common word on a card, can the child copy the word correctly on his own paper?*
   Place a card containing a common word with at least three letters on the child's desk. The pupil must copy the example correctly to receive credit for the item. The letters in the word must be recognizable and in proper order.

4. *When a common word is written on the chalkboard, can the child copy it correctly on her own paper?*
   Copying from the chalkboard is an activity required of pupils throughout the school years. Write a common word containing at least three letters on the chalkboard in the size and type of print you would typically use. While sitting at his usual location in the room, the child must copy the word correctly. The copied word must be correctly spelled, although quality of handwriting is not a consideration on this item.

5. *Can the child write letters upon request by the teacher?*
   Ask the child to write each of the following letters as you say them: *a, b, e, h, m, t.* While the letters do not have to be perfectly formed, all six letters must be clearly legible in order for the child to receive credit.

6. *Can the child write her last name?*
   To receive credit for this item, a child should make a solid attempt at writing his last name. The name may be misspelled and some of the letters may be reversed or poorly formed. The child receives credit for producing a recognizable version of her last name without copying from a model.

7. *When writing, can the child stay on the line?*
   This is a relatively difficult task for many children. In scoring the item, you are concerned with the child's skill at organizing and spacing the letters squarely on the line, not with the legibility or quality of the letters themselves.

8. *When sentences or instructions are written on the chalkboard, can the child copy them correctly on his own paper?*
   Write the following sentence, using the size and type of print you would typically use on the chalkboard: *The dog is brown.* The child must copy the sentence as it appears on the board. Spelling, capitalization, punctuation, and word order must be correct. The child should receive credit even though the letters may be poorly formed and spaced, if the sentence has been properly copied otherwise.

9. *Can the child write simple words dictated by the teacher?*
   Select three simple words that are definitely in the child's vocabulary. Ask the child to write each word after it is dictated. You may repeat words or use the words in context if necessary. To pass the item, the child's effort must yield a recognizable version of each of the three words. However, the words do not have to be correctly spelled, nor do the letters have to be perfectly formed or spaced.

10. *Can the child write simple sentences dictated by the teacher?*
    Create a simple sentence containing no more than four words that are in the child's vocabulary. Ask the child to write the sentence after you say it in a natural, conversational manner. Do not pause between words to enable the child to write each word after it is presented. You may repeat the sentence if the child does not appear to understand or remember it. To receive credit, the child must write each of the words in the correct sequence from left to right. Spelling, capitalization, punctuation, and penmanship should not be considered in scoring the item.

11. *Can the child spell simple words correctly?*
    Ask the child to write each of the following words: *in, cat, make.* Say each word to the child, use the word in a simple sentence, and then repeat the word (for example, "in, The boy is *in* the house, in"). Although the quality of formation of letters is not important, the child must produce clearly recognizable letters in the correct sequences for all three words to pass the item.

12. *Can the child write a complete sentence consisting of at least four words?*
    This item pertains to the child's ability to compose a grammatically and syntactically correct sentence. Ask the child to write a story containing at least four sentences. To receive credit, the child must write at least one complete sentence in which at least four words are used with correct grammar and sentence structure. Spelling, penmanship, capitalization, and punctuation do not have to be correct. However, the child's response must clearly include at least four words used properly as a complete unit containing a subject-predicate relationship.

13. *Does the child share information or ideas with others through meaningful and purposeful writing?*
    To receive credit on this item, the child must demonstrate the ability to use writing skills independently and spontaneously, regardless of level, to communicate with other people. The child may do this, for example, by writing letters to other children, writing stories for family members, writing notes to the teacher or other students, or in any other manner in which the writing activity is self-initiated and self-directed. Writing letters or stories in fulfillment of class assignments should not be counted.

14. *Can the child write a simple story consisting of at least three sentences?*
    To pass this item, the child must be able to independently compose a story
    that contains a minimum of three sentences. Although the sentences do
    not have to be grammatically or syntactically perfect, they must be related
    to some extent in theme or topic. Credit should be awarded even if the rela-
    tionship among the sentences is minimal (for example, "Tom is my brother.
    He is big. He likes ice cream." — In this story, all three sentences relate to
    the topic of Tom). Spelling, capitalization, punctuation, and handwriting
    quality do not affect scoring on this item.
15. *Does the child use correct capitalization and punctuation in writing?*
    Ask the child to write the following two sentences as you dictate them: *I
    have a ball. The ball is red.* Since the purpose of this item is to determine if
    the child possesses beginning skills pertaining to capitalization and punc-
    tuation, you may repeat the sentences, pausing between words if necessary,
    to enable the child to write each word as you say it. The child passes the
    item if he capitalizes the first word in each sentence and places a period at
    the end of both sentences. Scoring of the item is not affected by the child's
    spelling or quality of handwriting.

Four-year-olds who score zero on this scale, five-year-olds who score two
points or less, and six-year-olds who score six points or less should be studied
further. Possibly a program of special early writing activities should be provided.

Assessing General Handwriting Competence

The experienced teacher has no difficulty in identifying students whose handwriting is below average for their age. But new teachers or teachers who wish to
quantify their observations will find the following techniques helpful.

A popular informal device for assessing the cursive and manuscript handwriting of pupils in grades one through twelve is Zaner-Bloser's Evaluation
Scale (1974). To administer this test, the teacher writes a particular sample sentence on the chalkboard. After several practice efforts, the pupils copy the example on a piece of paper. They are allowed two minutes to complete the task.
Papers are collected and assigned to one of three groups ("good," "medium," or
"poor") on the basis of the teacher's judgment. Each paper is then matched
against a series of five specimen sentences that are appropriate to the student's
grade placement. Each of the sentences represents a different quality of penmanship, ranging from "high for grade" to "poor for grade." The use of the specimen sentences permits teachers to make rough estimates about the adequacy of
a student's penmanship compared with that of other youngsters in the same
grade. Two examples of Zaner-Bloser's evaluation sentence charts, one for
manuscript and one for cursive writing, are provided in Figure 5–1.

Figure 5–1. Evaluation Scale for Manuscript and Cursive Writing

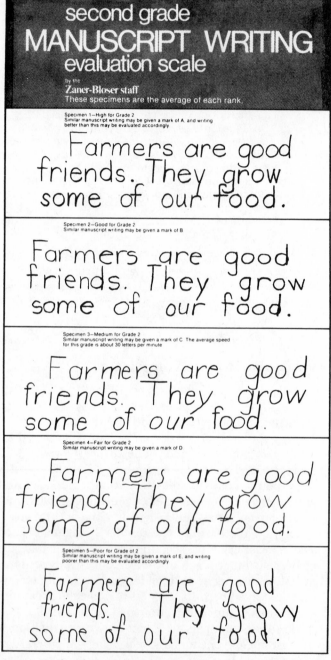

Source: Used with permission from *Creative Growth with Hand-writing.* Evaluation scale, second grade. Copyright © 1974. Zaner-Bloser, Inc., Columbus, Ohio.

Figure 5–1 *Continued*

fifth grade
CURSIVE WRITING
evaluation scale
by the
Zaner-Bloser staff
These specimens are the average of each rank.

Specimen 1—High for Grade 5
Similar cursive handwriting may be marked A. and writing better
than this may be evaluated accordingly

I live in America. It is good to live where you have freedom to work and play. As an American, I support my country and what it stands for.

Specimen 2—Good for Grade 5
Similar cursive handwriting may be marked B

I live in America. It is good to live where you have freedom to work and play. As an American, I support my country and what it stands for.

Specimen 3—Medium for Grade 5
Similar cursive handwriting may be marked C. The standard speed
for this grade is about 60 letters per minute

I live in America. It is good to live where you have freedom to work and play. As an American, I support my country and what it stands for.

Specimen 4—Fair for Grade 5
Similar cursive handwriting may be marked D

I live in America. It is good to live where you have freedom to work and play. As an American, I support my country and what it stands for.

Specimen 5—Poor for Grade 5
Similar cursive handwriting may be marked E. and writing poorer
than this may be evaluated accordingly

I live in America. It is good to live where you have freedom to work and play. As an American, I support my country and what it stands for.

Source: Used with permission from *Creative Growth with Handwriting.* Evaluation scale, fifth grade. Copyright © 1974. Zaner-Bloser, Inc., Columbus, Ohio.

161

On those occasions when a norm-referenced test of overall handwriting is needed, we recommend using the Handwriting subtest from the Test of Written Language (Hammill & Larsen, 1983). Here handwriting ability is estimated by classifying samples of students' spontaneous writing, using graded examples as guides. Norms are based on the analysis of the written products of a national, representative sample of 1700 students attending grades two through eight.

Use of these assessment devices will permit only the grossest evaluation of a student's handwriting. For example, they allow the examiner to determine if the pupil's penmanship skills are seriously behind, level with, or appreciably above those of peers, but they do not yield the kinds of specific information about the child's handwriting that can be used to formulate a remedial program. To derive maximum value from this procedure, teachers must subject the student's written products to a thorough analysis of errors.

Assessing Specific Errors in Handwriting

Having determined, through direct observation or through the use of one of the scales just mentioned, that a problem does exist, the teacher can use Ruedy's (1983) checklist as an initial guide to error analysis (see Figure 5–2). While the student is actively engaged in some writing activity, the teacher observes any problematic habits that might affect the quality of the handwriting (e.g., posture, pencil grip); these are noted on the checklist. Later, the writing sample is evaluated for errors involving letter formation and slant, fluency, spacing, etc.; these too are noted on the checklist.

Although checklists will provide the teacher with some valuable information, they yield no data about the particular letters that are illegible. Therefore, when engaged in a complete analysis of the errors in a student's handwriting, the teacher should keep in mind the work of Newland (1932), who studied the handwriting of 2381 people and analyzed the errors they made. He identified the most common illegibilities in cursive handwriting by elementary-school pupils and classified the errors into twenty-six major groups. Surprisingly, almost half of the illegibilities were associated with the letters *a, e, r,* and *t.* If teachers are familiar with these common errors, they will find it easier to recognize them in their pupil's written work. The ten most common errors were as follows:[2]

1. Failure to close letters (e.g., *a, b, f*) accounted for 24 percent of all errors.
2. Top loops closed (*l* like *t, e* like *i*) accounted for 13 percent.
3. Looping nonlooped strokes (*i* like *e*) accounted for 12 percent.

[2]From T. E. Newland, An analytical study of the development of illegibilities in handwriting from the lower grades to adulthood, *The Journal of Educational Research,* 26 (1932), 249–258.

Figure 5–2. Student Handwriting Evaluation Sheet

	O.K.	Needs Review
1. Performance observation.		
a. pen or pencil is held properly	☐	☐
b. paper is positioned at a "normal" slant	☐	☐
c. writing posture is acceptable	☐	☐
d. writing speed is acceptable	☐	☐
2. Correct letter formation.		
a. closed letters are closed	☐	☐
b. looped letters are looped	☐	☐
c. stick letters are not loops	☐	☐
d. i's and j's are dotted directly above	☐	☐
e. x's and t's are crossed accurately	☐	☐
f. m's and n's have the correct number of humps	☐	☐
g. all lower case letters begin on the line (unless they follow b, o, v, or w)	☐	☐
h. b, o, v, and w end above the line	☐	☐
i. all lower case letters end on the line	☐	☐
j. v's and u's are clearly differentiated	☐	☐
k. connecting strokes of v and y are clearly not ry and ry	☐	☐
l. upper case letters are correctly or acceptably formed	☐	☐
m. numbers are correctly formed	☐	☐
3. Fluency.		
a. writing is smooth, not choppy	☐	☐
b. pencil pressure appears even	☐	☐
c. words appear to be written as complete units	☐	☐
d. letter connection is smooth	☐	☐
4. Letter size, slant, and spacing.		
a. lower case letters are uniform size	☐	☐
b. upper case letters are clearly larger than lower case letters	☐	☐
c. upper case letters are uniform in size	☐	☐
d. tail lengths are consistent and do not interfere with letters on the line below	☐	☐
e. tall letters are a consistent height and are clearly taller than other letters	☐	☐
f. writing is not too small or too large	☐	☐
g. slant of letters is acceptable	☐	☐
h. slant of letters is consistent	☐	☐
i. spacing of letters and words is consistent	☐	☐
5. Student attitude toward writing.		
a. student's opinion of his writing skills	☐	☐
b. "writing is hard"	☐	☐
c. writes too slowly	☐	☐
d. feels good about writing	☐	☐
6. Overall teacher evaluation.	☐	☐

(continued)

Figure 5-2 *Continued*

Teacher Recommendation:
☐ You appear to write smoothly and easily. Your letters are formed correctly. Letter size, slant, and spacing are good. Your writing is neat and legible. It is *not* necessary for you to complete the handwriting exercises.
☐ You appear to write smoothly and easily. You have developed your own writing style which is acceptable, neat and legible. It is *not* necessary for you to complete the handwriting exercises.
☐ You appear to write smoothly and easily. However, your letter formation, neatness, and legibility need some work. Please complete the handwriting exercises.
☐ Writing seems to be difficult for you. You need practice in handwriting skills. Please complete the handwriting exercises.

Source: L. R. Ruedy, Handwriting instruction, *Academic Therapy,* 18, 4 (1983), 427–428 (Novato, Calif.: Academic Therapy Publications). Reprinted by permission.

4. Using straight-up strokes rather than rounded strokes (*n* like *u, c* like *i*) accounted for 11 percent.

5. End-stroke difficulty (not brought up, not brought down, not left horizontal) accounted for 11 percent.

6. Top short (*b, d, h, k*): 6 percent.

7. Difficulty crossing *t:* 5 percent.

8. Letters too small: 4 percent.

9. Closing *c, h, u, w:* 4 percent.

10. Part of letter omitted: 4 percent.

Newland's (1932) research concerning common errors can easily be incorporated into a simple criterion-referenced assessment procedure that can be used to identify the letters that are illegible in a student's writing and to estimate the particular kinds of errors being made in the formation of those letters. The first step is to obtain a sample of the student's ability to write the letters that are most likely to be illegible. To do this, the teacher might have the student write five to ten *a*'s in a row in cursive, then an equal number of *b*'s, *e*'s, *h*'s, *m*'s, *n*'s, *o*'s, *r*'s and *t*'s. These particular letters are selected because the research suggests that they are the ones that are most often produced in a defective, unreadable fashion. The student's paper might look like the following:

An alternative to step 1 might be to take an example of the student's spontaneous or elicited written work and circle the *a*'s, *b*'s, *e*'s, *h*'s, etc. The next step is to evaluate the way a pupil forms letters according to the criteria listed in Figure 5–3. If the manner in which the student forms the letters differs from that suggested in the column marked "right," one can assume that illegibility will be increased. The handwriting examples under the "wrong" column indicate the

Figure 5–3.   Evaluating Formation of Letters

	Wrong	Right
1. *a* like *o*		
2. *a* like *u*		
3. *a* like *ci*		
4. *b* like *li*		
5. *d* like *cl*		
6. *e* closed		
7. *h* like *li*		
8. *i* like *e* with no dot		
9. *m* like *w*		
10. *n* like *u*		
11. *o* like *a*		
12. *r* like *i*		
13. *r* like *n*		
14. *t* like *l*		
15. *t* with cross above		

most common errors made in the formation of the eight letters. These particular errors are often referred to in the language arts literature as the fifteen handwriting demons and are purported to cause or contribute to most of the illegibilities in cursive writing.

The procedures outlined in this section will enable teachers to identify (1) the students who need help in handwriting, (2) the general areas requiring attention (slanting, spacing, etc.), (3) the individual letters being misformed, and (4) the specific kinds of errors causing the illegibilities. It is this kind of information that teachers need to individualize remedial programs.

REMEDYING PROBLEMS IN HANDWRITING

The remainder of this chapter is devoted to discussing how handwriting can be taught to students who exhibit difficulty in developing proficiency in the skill. Three areas are dealt with: (1) background information that relates to the teaching of handwriting in general, (2) specifics pertaining to a remedial program, and (3) classroom approaches for use with normal learners or with writers with mild problems.

Background Information Concerning Handwriting Instruction

Before we describe selected procedures for teaching handwriting, several important points should be made. These points pertain to the management of left-handed writers, the current ideas about cursive and manuscript writing forms, the role of readiness in teaching, a scope-and-sequence guide to writing objectives and instruction, and principles for effective programs.

Left-Handed Writers

Teaching handwriting to left-handed students presents a few special problems, although in general the techniques used with right-handed students will suffice with slight adjustment. Some of the adjustments are depicted later in this chapter in Figure 5–8. Readers are referred to the work of Petty and Jensen (1980) or Polloway and Smith (1982) for thorough discussions of modifications for left-handed learners. Current thinking dictates that a student who is definitely left-handed should be allowed to write with the preferred hand. Forcing the student to use the right hand is not recommended.

Cursive or Manuscript

Often teachers are unsure whether to teach manuscript or cursive initially. Arguments for starting with cursive writing are that it reduces spatial judgment problems for students and that there is a rhythmic continuity and completeness that is not present in manuscript writing. Also, reversals are virtually eliminated with cursive writing. When cursive is taught initially, the need to transfer from one form to the other is avoided. Many problem writers have difficulty transferring to cursive after learning manuscript writing.

Advantages of manuscript writing are that it is supposed to be easier to learn since it consists of only circles and straight lines (Voorhis, 1931). Also, manuscript letters are closer to the printed form used in reading than are cursive letters. Some educators (Plattor & Woestehoff, 1971) believe that students do not have to transfer to cursive writing at all since the manuscript form is readable and just as rapid.

Overall, the research suggests that in most cases it does not matter which style is taught. The common practice, however, is to begin with manuscript and to introduce cursive at about the third-grade level.

The Role of Writing Readiness in Teaching

The concept of handwriting readiness (see p. 156) should be considered carefully before planning an instructional program for any student. Most students are "ready" to begin to write before they reach their sixth birthday and enter school. In point of fact, children usually start reading and writing during the preschool years as a natural consequence of daily interaction with the print that is omnipresent in their environment. Thus, there are probably no true readiness abilities that children must learn before they can learn to write, although there are doubtlessly a few prerequisites. For example, children do not have to be able to scribble circles to be able to learn to write the letter O; but children must be able to see, to grasp a pencil, and to think of an idea before they can learn to write. Of equal importance, they must possess a desire to write. When these abilities are present, formal instruction in writing can begin with every likelihood of success. When these basic abilities are lacking, it is unlikely that they will be developed by a traditional school "readiness" program.

We feel that the most efficient way to teach students to write is directly, with a straightforward approach. They will learn to write in a left-to-right direction, to discriminate one letter from another, and to use a pencil to form legible letters best as a result of practice in writing. Perceptual-motor training, tracing of geometric shapes, walking board exercises, and activities that do not involve letters are off-task and should be avoided—unless, of course, they are being done for their own sake, to improve general eye-hand coordination or to amuse the children. Fortunately, some readiness programs that are available commercially do emphasize the skills of early writing; these should be sought out and used.

A Scope-and-Sequence Chart for Handwriting Instruction

In teaching handwriting, it is often useful to have a scope and sequence of skills in mind. The scope-and-sequence chart enables the teacher to identify skills to be taught and their order of presentation. Graham and Miller (1980) present an eight-level handwriting scope-and-sequence chart. In this chart (presented as Figure 5–4), each level represents approximately one school year. The authors point out that "depending upon the student's characteristics and the severity of the handicapping condition, the rate of progression through the curriculum may be either decelerated or accelerated" (p. 5).

Principles for Effective Programs

We conclude this section with a listing of the principles and conditions that are vital to the preparation of effective programs for poor writers. The items in this list are drawn from the work of Graham and Miller (1980, pp. 5–6). They recommend that handwriting instruction be

1. Taught directly, rather than incidentally.
2. Individualized to each student's needs.
3. Planned, monitored, and modified according to assessment information.
4. Flexible in its use of different techniques.
5. Taught in a short daily period.
6. Done in meaningful contexts when possible.
7. Unaccepting of slovenly work.
8. Dependent on attitudes of student and teacher.
9. Undertaken in a conducive atmosphere.
10. Taught by teachers who can write legibly.
11. Accompanied by self-evaluation.
12. Encouraging a consistent, legible style.

A Specific Remedial Program

After targeting a level and a letter for training, the teacher is ready to intervene. The procedures for teaching handwriting skills necessary for legible writing are

Figure 5–4. Handwriting Scope and Sequence

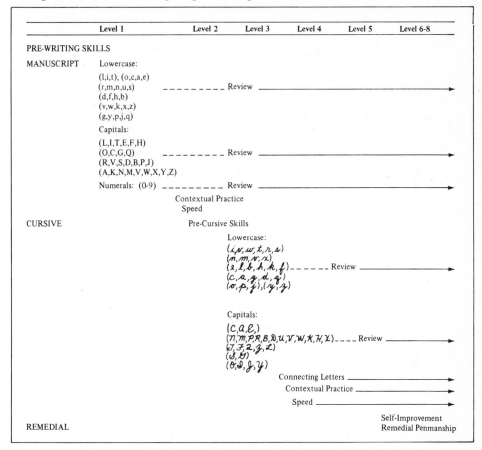

Source: S. Graham and L. Miller, Handwriting research and practice, *Focus on Exceptional Children*, 13 (1980), 6.

subdivided by Reger, Schroeder, and Uschold (1968, pp. 220–224) into four developmental levels.[3] The teacher should begin with Level I and move gradually to Level IV as the pupil masters the skills. It should be noted that although this sequence could be used as a program for all pupils, it is intended for use with students who experience difficulty in handwriting. Most students will respond adequately to one of the developmental systems described later in this chapter.

[3]Material in this section was drawn from *Special Education: Children with Learning Problems* by Roger Reger, Wendy Schroeder, and Kathie Uschold. Copyright © 1968 Oxford University Press, Inc. Used with permission.

Level I—Introductory Movements

Using the chalkboard as a prop, the teacher discusses how the movements of writing are made; for example, "First we go up and then we go down." The teacher demonstrates on the board. Or he or she says, "We go away from our body and then toward our body." The students make the movement at the board, looking at the teacher's model rather than the board as they draw. They say "up" when they are going up and "down" when they are going down. The movements should be rhythmic and free flowing. The students should stand at least six inches from the board.

After the student has had several days of practicing the movement on the board following the procedure above, the auditory clue is eliminated. The student makes the movement on the board in silence, still looking at the model rather than his or her hands. Then the outlined procedures are repeated, this time on paper or large newsprint, using crayon. Reger et al. (1968, p. 221) suggest the movements shown in Figure 5–5.

The teacher will also want to keep in mind Spalding and Spalding's observation (1969) that only the six different pencil strokes shown in Figure 5–6 are necessary for making lowercase manuscript letters. One or two of these movements can be introduced each week in conjunction with Reger's exercises. If a student has difficulty with any of the movements, additional practice should be given as often as possible. Before a new movement is introduced, the previous ones should be reviewed.

Figure 5–5.   Introductory Movements

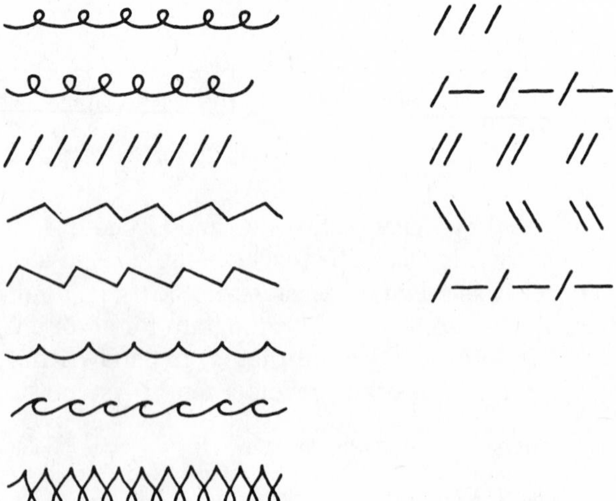

Figure 5–6. Pencil Strokes Needed for Lowercase Letters

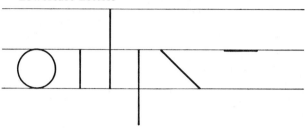

Source: From R. B. Spalding and W. T. Spalding, *The Writing Road to Reading* (New York: William Morrow, 1969), p. 54. Used by permission of the authors and publishers.

Level II—Introductory Movements on Paper

In Level II, the procedures from Level I are repeated, but the student is allowed to look at the paper. It should be kept in mind that: (1) the student should have correct posture when performing the movements; (2) the slant of the paper should be correct, and dependent on the hand used; (3) the hand position should be proper. Teachers can usually find detailed descriptions of the proper positions for writing in the teacher's manuals that accompany the various commercially available writing programs.

The paper used for the first movements on paper should have 1-inch spaces. The letters should be three spaces high initially, then two spaces high, and finally one space high. The teacher can line the paper with felt-tipped markers, using blue for the top line, green for the middle line, and red for the bottom line. This helps the children stay on and within the lines. Serio (1968) is a source of information regarding writing materials, especially pencils and paper with colored lines.

Level III—Movements for Cursive Writing

In Level III, the procedures set forth under Level I are followed, using Spalding and Spalding's (1969) movements shown in Figure 5–7. Spalding and Spalding believe that cursive writing is an adaptation of manuscript and that it is only necessary to teach five connecting strokes. Students begin on the chalkboard and eventually progress to newsprint, using crayon or marker.

Level IV—Movements for Cursive Writing on Paper

In writing letters, students progress from the chalkboard (repeating the procedures stipulated under Level I), to 1-inch-lined paper where three lines have

Figure 5–7. Cursive Writing

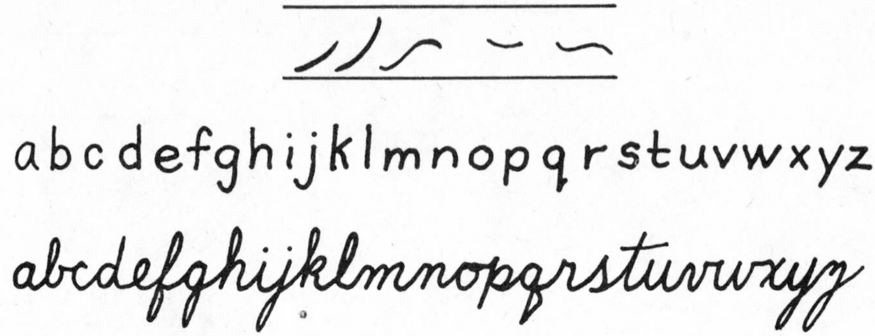

Source: From R. B. Spalding and W. T. Spalding, *The Writing Road to Reading* (New York: William Morrow, 1969), pp. 70–71. Used by permission of the authors and publisher.

been drawn with red, green, and blue markers, and finally to regular-lined paper. Materials for Level IV include overlays on which each letter has been made with felt-tipped marker, blank overlays, and an overhead projector.

In general, the following sequence is appropriate for teaching at this level:

1. The teacher names the letter.
2. The teacher discusses the form of the letter while the student looks at it.
3. The teacher makes the letter for the student on a blank overlay. The different parts of the letter are made with different-colored markers to show the various movements.
4. To show the direction of the letters, such as *s*, *z*, and others, cinematic materials are used. A Polaroid filter mounted on a motorized clear plastic wheel is placed over the transparency. The teacher can thus move the letters from left to right, or right to left, to show the student the direction of the letter.
5. Kinesthetic feel for the form of letters is developed by having students use sunken and raised script letterboards (may be purchased from the American Printing House for the Blind).
6. The student makes the letter while looking at the model.
7. The student keeps his or her eyes on the model, not on the hand.
8. The teacher helps the student compare his or her work with the model.
9. To help the student who has difficulty with the letter, the teacher may give oral clues or hold the student's hand as he or she makes the letter. Some students may need to write the letter in salt or sand (on a salt tray).

10. The student writes the letter on the chalkboard without the model.

11. The student writes the letter on newsprint without a model, eyes averted.

12. The student writes on paper with eyes on the paper.

In this sequence, 1-inch-lined paper should be used, with the writing space divided into three parts (by colored markers). The teacher puts a model of the letter on the student's paper, and the letter form and direction are discussed. If the top line is always blue, the middle line green, and the bottom line red, the teacher can say to the child "Start on the red line, go up to the blue line, come down to the red line." The lines should be dark and heavy so that the student will be able to stay within them.

When the student traces the model of the letter and makes a row of letters, the teacher should watch the student carefully. In this way, the teacher can evaluate the student's success with the letter and decide where he or she needs help. The student is then taught to write within the 2-inch-lined area, next within 1-inch lines, and finally on regular primary paper.

Before each writing assignment, correct habits for writing should be reviewed. The teacher should demonstrate proper positioning of the paper and then check each paper for positioning. Masking tape or marks on the desk can be used to show the student how he or she should position the paper. Writing posture also should be discussed and demonstrated: elbow on the desk, nonwriting hand holding the paper, fingers on the pencil correctly, feet on the floor, head properly tilted.

Of course, paper positions, body positions, and pencil grips are different for left- and right-handed writers. Teachers have to be aware of these differences and help their students to adopt an effective stance. Postures, grips, and positions for left- and right-handed persons are pictured in Figure 5–8.

When the student has succeeded in writing the letters accurately, he or she should be taught to connect letters and then to write simple words. As the student progresses, he or she should be asked to copy simple sentences and then gradually encouraged to attempt to write without copying. It is at this point that handwriting becomes an expressive language ability. The time of the writing period will vary from class to class and from student to student. If one student can tolerate writing only one line, he or she should write only that much. If another student can write a whole page, he or she should be allowed to do so. The sequence just outlined is basically a remedial one and can be supplemented by activities drawn from Gillingham and Stillman (1970), Johnson and Myklebust (1967), and Spalding and Spalding (1969).

The "applied behavioral analysis" technique is particularly productive when specific errors in handwriting have been noted and selected for improvement. For example, the teacher may have decided as a result of observation or

Figure 5–8. Posture, Grip, and Paper Positions for Left- and Right-Handed Writers

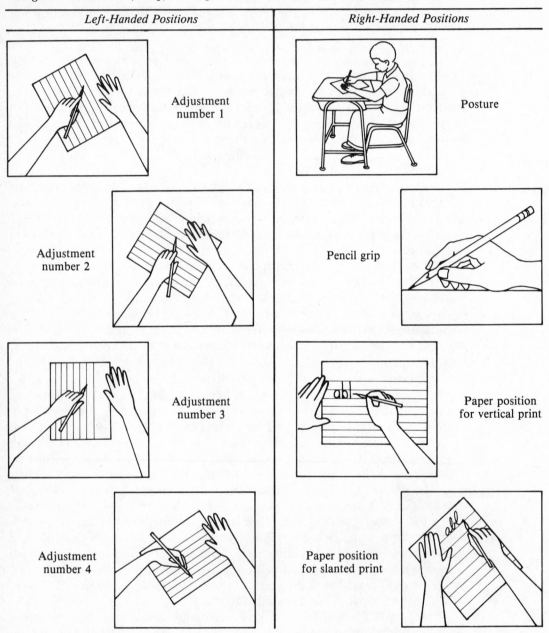

Left-Handed Positions	*Right-Handed Positions*
Adjustment number 1	Posture
Adjustment number 2	Pencil grip
Adjustment number 3	Paper position for vertical print
Adjustment number 4	Paper position for slanted print

Source: S. Graham and L. Miller, Handwriting research and practice, *Focus on Exceptional Children*, 13 (1980), 2, 9, and 12.

testing that the student's difficulty is centered in letter illegibility, improper spacing, sloppiness, slowness, and/or unacceptable slanting. One of these problems, probably the one that is the most annoying to the teacher, can be chosen as the target for retraining and the principles of ABA implemented. The dynamics of managing an ABA program are based on the ideas expressed in the behavior-modification section in Chapter 7. Individuals interested in this approach should read this section mentioned, as well as Lovitt's (1975b) description of how the technique has been used to help improve students' handwriting skills.

Classroom Approaches to Handwriting Instruction

The experienced teacher will recognize readily that the procedures just outlined cannot be used with all the students in a regular class. They are best reserved for use in special remedial classes with an enrollment of six to ten pupils or with those pupils in the regular class who are developing problems in writing. Although this book is primarily concerned with the management of students with problems, an overview of the "developmental" teaching systems is included because such systems can often be used in their entirety or in adapted form with remedial cases.

Three classroom systems are described briefly in this section. The first, *Better Handwriting for You*, is among the most popular in use today. The other two, *D'Nealian Handwriting* and *Cursive Writing Program*, contain particular elements that make their use with remedial cases highly attractive.

Better Handwriting for You

In 1960, four companies, Zaner-Bloser, Palmer, Scale, and Noble and Noble, produced 50 percent of all instructional materials in use in the United States for teaching handwriting. As they are all similar, only one set of materials, that of Noble and Noble, will be described.

The Noble and Noble program, *Better Handwriting for You*, contains a series of eight workbooks and teacher's editions prepared by Noble (1966). Books 1 and 2 present manuscript writing; Books 3 through 8 deal with cursive writing. There is a transitional book between Books 2 and 3 that begins with manuscript and introduces cursive. Throughout, the teacher is given instructions regarding management of the left-handed pupil, correct position for holding the pencil, proper positions for the paper, and correct positions for writing on the chalkboard or at the desk.

In the first book, uppercase and lowercase letters and numbers are introduced. Numbers and arrows are used to teach the sequence and direction of strokes necessary to write the various graphic forms. Models and ample opportunity to copy them are provided in the workbooks. In Books 7 and 8, devices are presented that the pupil can use to evaluate the quality of his or her writing; the child is presented with the 15 handwriting demons previously mentioned, the errors that cause most illegibilities, and the 100 spelling demons discussed in Chapter 4.

D'Nealian Handwriting

The D'Nealian handwriting system (Thurber, 1981) provides the teacher with an alternative to the traditional methods in which the manuscript-cursive choice is accepted as an instructional necessity. In this system, the lower-case manuscript letters closely resemble the corresponding cursive letters. The D'Nealian letter forms are depicted in Figure 5–9. It is obvious that except for *b*, *f*, *r*, *s*, *v*, and *z* the manuscript letters can be easily changed to cursive simply by adding the joining uphill (⤶) and overhill (⤴) strokes. Recommendations are included regarding letter size, spacing and slant, rhythm, and evaluation. Evaluation is unique in that it stresses general legibility, rather than strict adherence to particular letter formations, model perfection, etc. Since the materials provided are not essential, the program is cost effective. For many remedial cases, the D'Nealian approach may well work and should be tried. V. L. Brown

Figure 5–9. D'Nealian Handwriting

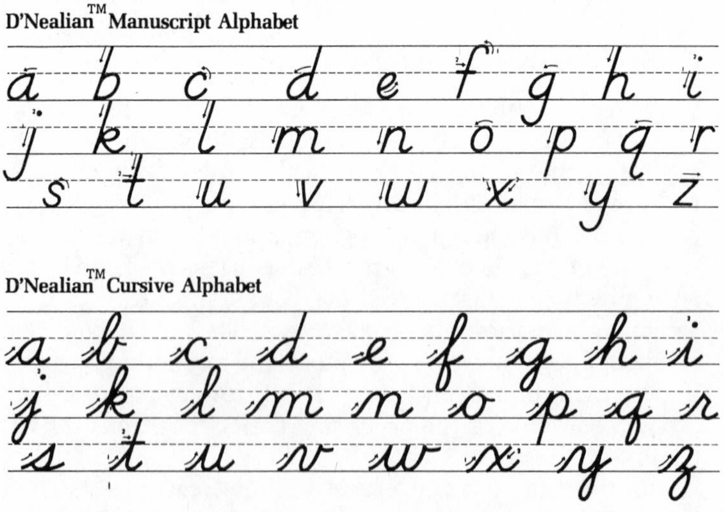

Source: From *D'Nealian™ Handwriting* by Donald N. Thurber. Copyright © 1981 by Scott, Foresman and Company. Reprinted by permission.

(1984b) has provided a detailed description of this program emphasizing its use with special and remedial students.

The Cursive Writing Program

The *Cursive Writing Program* (S. K. Miller & Engelmann, 1980) was designed to teach cursive writing to students who have already mastered manuscript writing. The program teaches how to form letters, construct words, transcribe sentences, and write fast and accurately. There are 140 twenty-minute developmentally sequenced lessons in the program. Materials consist of a teacher's manual and a student workbook containing practice pages. The lessons follow a consistent format—a series of exercises followed by an awarding of points for successful work. An entry test allows for individualization and makes the program suitable for classroom or remedial use.

chapter 6

Problems in Mathematics Achievement

by Nettie R. Bartel

The 1980s have seen an explosion of interest on the part of the public and professionals in the teaching of mathematics. Among the most significant of these recent developments are the national recognition of teacher shortages in mathematics and science, the widespread demand for better mathematics achievement (Gallup, 1982; National Commission on Excellence in Education, 1983), and the increasing recognition of the accelerating impact of technology, especially computers, on current and future generations. All of these factors have placed mathematics in the school curriculum in a position of particular scrutiny and renewed support.

The number of students with difficulty in mathematics is quite large. In the overall school population, the average mathematics performance in students aged nine to seventeen is improving slightly, according to Lindquist, Carpenter, Silver, and Matthews (1983). Yet teachers of learning disabled students report that two out of three of their students require significant remediation in the area of mathematics (McLeod & Armstrong, 1982).

Fortunately, the past few years have been exceptionally promising in terms of the caliber of the research, scholarship, and test development that have occurred in the field. Notable among these has been the sustained work of John Cawley and his associates on the nature of mathematics assessment and instruction (1984); the conceptual work and test development of Fredricka Reisman (Reisman, 1977, 1984; Reisman & Kauffman, 1980); the work in cognitive strategy training; and, finally, the development of improved assessment devices in the mathematics area.

This chapter provides an overview of some preliminary considerations in planning an individualized mathematics program. The next section is concerned with assessing mathematical problems; a third section on instructional methods concludes the chapter.

PRELIMINARY CONSIDERATIONS IN PLANNING AN INDIVIDUALIZED MATHEMATICS PROGRAM

Before any mathematics program can actually be selected or implemented, a teacher needs to raise some preliminary questions. Among these questions are the following: What are the goals of mathematics instruction for this student? Does the student have the requisite cognitive skills to undertake a program that would meet these goals? Why is this student having difficulty in mathematics? Let us consider these questions in turn.

Establishing Goals in Mathematics

A mathematical activity should be undertaken only if it is responsive to some goal or objective that has been established for a particular child or for a group of children. Teachers will find many sources that will help to articulate the goals of the mathematics program: curriculum guides, professional publications, scope-and-sequence charts accompanying commercial materials, Bloom's Taxonomy of Educational Objectives (Bloom et al., 1956), and the landmark 1963 report of the Cambridge Conference on School Mathematics.

For our purposes, we have developed the following set of broad mathematical goals:

1. Development of problem-solving ability, including ability to think convergently, divergently, logically, and creatively and to use computers for problem solving.
2. Development of understanding of basic mathematical concepts and terms.
3. Development of the ability to understand and perform measurements of distance, weight, temperature, quantity, area, speed, volume, and money with conventional and metric units, where appropriate.
4. Development of the ability to perform basic mathematical computations using calculators or computers as appropriate.
5. Development of an understanding of how mathematics computation and concepts are utilized in real-life situations.

This last goal is included in recognition of the fact that, for most persons, mathematics will serve as a tool in daily living. For example, in a study conducted by the author with graduate students in Special Education, newspapers and radio and television news programs were analyzed for prerequisite mathematical understandings. It was found that to fully comprehend such material, individuals needed to understand the following:

1. Money relationships (including large sums)
2. Measurements—temperature, speed, distance, weight or quantity, and area (listed in order of frequency)
3. Time—past, present, future; hour, day, week, month, season, year, and decade
4. Computations with whole numbers, fractions, decimals, and percentages, including ratios

Mathematical Prerequisites

A number of cognitive abilities are needed to learn mathematics. The most basic of these are prerequisite to the acquisition of the most fundamental mathematical understandings; the higher-order cognitive abilities are required before students can master more complex or more abstract mathematical concepts. Reisman and Kauffman (1980) have described the importance of cognitive factors in mathematics learning and schematically portrayed their relationship to mathematic understandings. Their schema are reproduced in Figure 6–1.

Figure 6–1 makes it clear that continued and progressive cognitive growth is needed for a student to make progress in mathematics. The three most elementary kinds of cognitive factors—ability to remember arbitrary associations, ability to understand basic relationships, and ability to make lower-level generalizations—may be thought of as the basis for formal mathematics instruction. If these abilities are not present, students will not understand the mathematics that is being taught to them. Table 6–1 provides examples of how children demonstrate the presence of these cognitive abilities.

Because of their importance, these basic cognitive abilities are briefly described next. The following section on "Prerequisites for More Advanced Mathematics" describes the higher-level concepts, relationships, and generalizations and shows how more advanced mathematics learning is based on earlier mathematics learning.

Prerequisites for Basic Mathematics

Basic to the development of arithmetic-related abilities is the child's ability to classify. *Classification* refers to the grouping of objects according to some com-

Figure 6–1.   Cognitive Factors and Their Relationship to Mathematics Understanding

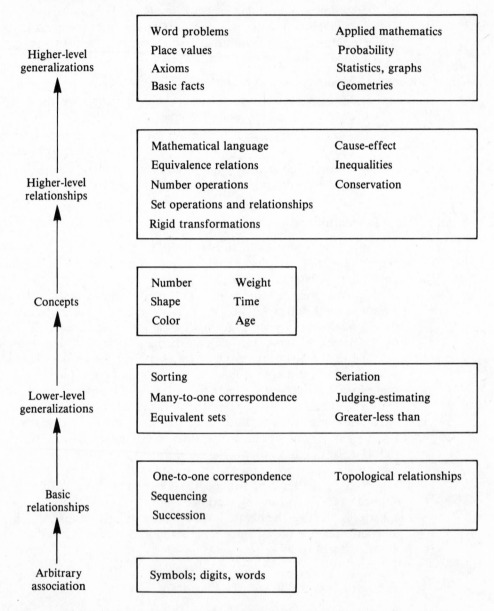

Table 6–1.   Assessment of Prerequisite Cognitive Abilities

| Cognitive Ability | Examples of How Child Demonstrates Ability | | |
	Orally States	Demonstrates with Object	Matches/Selects/Other
Classification			
by function	Can child state why a toy car does not belong in an array of toy furniture?	Can child arrange groups of objects by function, e.g., all transportation by air, land, water?	Can child match pictures of items that "go with" other items by function, e.g., mitten with hand, boot with foot?
by color	Can child state why red block does not belong with blue blocks?	Can child group objects by color?	Can child match objects by color?
by size	Can child state why large flag does not belong in group of small flags?	Can child arrange objects into groups by size?	Can child select "large" or "small" object in group?
by shape	Can child state why circles do not belong in group of squares?	Can child group objects by shape?	Can child identify several circular shaped or rectangular shaped objects in the room?
by several criteria simultaneously	Can child state differences among prearranged groups of blue squares, red squares; blue squares, red circles?	Can child sort objects on basis of simultaneous criteria of size and function, size and shape, color and shape, etc.?	Can child select which one "does not belong" in array employing two criteria at once?
Seriation			
linear	Can child state basis of linear serial array based on increasing size?	Can child arrange objects in order of increasingly intense color?	Can child select item missing in a serial array?
unit	Can child state relationships between sets of 1, 2, 3, 4, etc.?	Can child develop sequence of objects or numerals, based on units in each?	Can child count to 10 or 20? Can child tell which numeral contains more—4 or 6, 3 or 8, etc.?

(continued)

Table 6–1 *Continued*

Cognitive Ability	Examples of How Child Demonstrates Ability		
	Orally States	*Demonstrates with Object*	*Matches/Selects/Other*
Seriation, continued			
temporal	Can child state what he or she did first in a simple task, what last?	Can child follow simple directions, e.g., "First put the block in the box; next put the penny beside the tray"?	Is there informal evidence of child's developing temporal sense—e.g., does child know which task is done after recess without being told?
one-to-one correspondence	Can child state the number of pencils that will be required for a group of three children?	Can child "order" milk for the class lunch based on the number in attendance? Does he or she know how to distribute the milk when it's received?	Can child pair boots or mittens with the owner?
understanding of spatial relations	Can child state which object is over, under, in, or beside with respect to another object?	Can child match geometric objects to openings into which they fit?	Can child distinguish between right and left?
Conservation			
of shape	Can child state if, and why, a ball of clay has the same mass whether rolled into a ball or into a rope?	Can child show that a ball of clay can be made into a rope and back into a ball again?	Can child (a) break clay into smaller pieces and then put it back into a ball and (b) flatten clay like a pancake and then put back into ball?
of liquid	Can child state which glass contains more water?	Can child demonstrate equality by pouring water into a glass?	Can child demonstrate equality by pouring water from one glass into several smaller ones?
of number	Can child state which row has more blocks?	Can child make equal numbers in these rows?	Can child recognize that the number of pencils is the same whether they are packed in a box or scattered on a desk?

mon distinguishing characteristic. In order to classify, the child must be able to discriminate between objects on the basis of some relevant aspect of color, size, shape, or pattern. The ability to make these discriminations is usually attained by a child sometime between the second and the seventh year, during the period that Piaget has called the pre-operations period (Piaget, 1965). Initially motor actions, then internalized behaviors, are utilized in the child's emerging awareness of various classifications (Piaget and Inhelder, 1963). In accordance with the general Piagetian principle that actions precede perceptions, children should be encouraged to enact as many concepts as possible and to manipulate two- and three-dimensional objects in the initial stages of classificatory behavior. During the latter part of this period, acquisition of language is believed to facilitate the ability to classify.

The ability to classify may be assessed a number of different ways. Children may be shown an array of objects, all but one of which share a common characteristic, and asked, "Which does not belong?" For example, "Which does not belong . . . dog, cat, tree, bird?" Since three of the items share the category "animal," the correct answer is "tree." The Sesame Street jingle "One of these things is not like the others; one of these things doesn't belong" is exemplary of the kind of exercise that helps to establish whether a child has learned to classify. It should be recognized that classification tasks vary greatly in difficulty, depending on the salience of the characteristic that must be discriminated.

Learning the concept of *one-to-one correspondence* is essential for subsequently learning to count and mastering addition and subtraction. The concept underlies such seemingly intuitive abilities as placing the correct number of table settings for a given number of people or distributing candies or other treats one or two per child. Whether or not the pupil understands one-to-one correspondence can be quickly established by asking him or her to give each child in a row a piece of paper or to get enough pencils for each child in a reading group. Teaching of the idea of one-to-one correspondence should begin with situations in which there are only two objects in each set. Gradually, the numbers to be corresponded are increased. Only when one-to-one correspondence in a wide variety of settings has been firmly established should the children be instructed in many-to-one correspondence. Initially, items in each set should be identical. Later, children can be asked to match dissimilar objects, such as pieces of bubble gum and pennies. Pictures of objects are introduced only when the youngster has developed a firm grasp of the concept and has demonstrated success with concrete objects.

Seriation, or *ordering,* in its simplest form is accomplished by a two- or three-year-old child who successfully places a series of rings of graduated sizes on a cone. More complex seriation tasks include lining up disks of graduated diameter or height in ascending order. More difficult are tasks that require the child to seriate on the basis of numbers in a series of sets—sets of one, two, or three objects in order. It is apparent that ability to seriate underlies the entire number system. Work in seriation can most meaningfully be done with three-dimensional objects. The Montessori materials, the Stern materials, and the Cuisenaire rods (discussed later in this chapter) offer excellent training in seriation. Lacking any of these materials, the teacher can teach seriation with bottles, crayons, pencils, or cards of varying sizes.

In addition to the linear seriation described above, children also need to become familiar with succession, or sequencing. Sequencing refers to the idea that some things or events or processes precede others in an orderly fashion. Children may initially be introduced to notions of sequencing through awareness of morning and afternoon and through sequencing of classroom activities. The mastery of sequencing is basic to any mathematical operation that has more than one step—such as adding two-place numbers. For this reason, it is important that children firmly grasp this concept before formal mathematics is introduced. (A complete task analysis of sequence is found in Table 2–7.)

The child's *understanding of space* and *topological relationships* has both perceptual and cognitive aspects. A firm grasp of spatial relations is important not only for understanding traditional geometry (geometric forms), but also for understanding sets and fractions and the basic arithmetic processes of addition, subtraction, multiplication, and division. Here again, according to Piaget, motor actions should precede strictly perceptual tasks (Piaget & Inhelder, 1963). Visual-perceptual activities should be supplemented with opportunities for tactual explorations of objects.

Before meaningful formal instruction (counting, adding) in arithmetic can occur, the child must have achieved *flexibility* and *reversibility* of thought, as well as the concept of *conservation.* Flexibility of thought is demonstrated by the child's ability to see that colored geometric shapes can be sorted first on the basis of one criterion, namely color; then another criterion, shape; and finally a third criterion, size. Flexibility also characterizes the conceptual process of observing that an individual or object belongs to several categories and subcategories at once; e.g., a person may be both a mother and a daughter, and two cups of water equals both one pint and half a quart. Flexibility is also necessary for a child to recognize that although 10 equals 5 + 5, it may also equal 4 + 6 or 9 + 1.

Reversibility is essential for the child to grasp the relationship between addition and subtraction; e.g., 5 + 4 = 9 and 9 − 4 = 5. In younger children, reversibility can be readily demonstrated with the Cuisenaire and Stern materials. Only with considerable experience in the manipulation of objects can the child achieve a firm grasp of the concept that no matter how objects are arranged they can always be returned to their original pattern. Thus, if ⦂ · ⦂ is rearranged to ˙.˙.˙, its basic value is still the same, and it can be reversed back.

The concept of conservation, closely related to that of reversibility, refers to the fact that the number of units within an object or set remains the same re-

Figure 6–2. Conservation—Amount of Water in the Two Containers Is the Same; Amount of Clay in the Two Shapes Is the Same

gardless of changes made in the shape of the unit or the arrangement of the set (Figure 6–2). The familiar Piagetian experiments in which the same amount of clay is formed into a ball and a long roll, and the same amount of water is poured into a tall, thin glass and a low, wide glass are examples of conservation. Whether conservation can be directly taught is debatable; however, allowing the child plenty of opportunity to manipulate clay and to rearrange units of sets will permit reinforcement of the notion of conservation.

To assess the child's readiness for formal instruction in mathematics, it is suggested that the teacher engage the child in a set of tasks such as those described in Table 6–1.

Prerequisites for More Advanced Mathematics

Once the student has demonstrated basic readiness for mathematical thinking, higher-level mathematical understandings can be introduced. To do this successfully, the teacher must consider both the student's general intellectual capability and the kinds of mathematics skills he or she has already acquired. For example, a student is not ready for instruction in long division until he or she is capable of higher-level generalizations (a prerequisite cognitive ability) and has mastered the multiplication algorithm (a prerequisite mathematical skill).

Readiness for higher-level mathematical operations was the topic of a study reported by Brownell (1951). The particular type of mathematics task that he investigated was division by two-place divisors. Prior to the study, he identified the mathematics skills that children must have in order to perform the division task. The specific subskills that he considered prerequisite for readiness for two-place divisor division are the following:

1. Multiply a two-place number by a digit:

$$\begin{array}{r} 23 \\ \times\ 6 \\ \hline \end{array}$$

2. Add, to the extent of carrying in multiplication:

$$\begin{array}{r} 48 \\ +48 \\ \hline \end{array}$$

3. Subtract, without and with borrowing:

$$\begin{array}{r} 323 \\ -\ 21 \\ \hline \end{array} \qquad \begin{array}{r} 323 \\ -\ 27 \\ \hline \end{array}$$

4. Divide, in the sense of knowing the algorithm:

$$3 \overline{)\ 7}$$

Next, Brownell developed a Test of Readiness for Division by Two-Place Divisors—a test of skills 1 to 4 above. Using 80 percent correct as a criterion, he concluded that almost half of the children were "not ready" to begin instruction in two-place division. Yet their teachers already had begun such instruction.

This study is illustrative of the need for establishing the criteria for readiness clearly. Whether one is dealing with initial mathematics instruction or with the introduction of a more advanced topic, the teacher's effectiveness and efficiency are enhanced by appropriate timing in the presentation of teaching tasks. The real test of readiness for a given mathematical topic is not whether that topic comes next in the workbook but whether the pupils have mastered the prerequisite skills (as demonstrated in Brownell's study) and the cognitive operations underlying the topic to be introduced.

Establishing Causes for Difficulty in Mathematics

When a student demonstrates difficulty in mathematics performance, the teacher will want to undertake a preliminary appraisal of possible reasons for the problem. This initial appraisal is usually informal in nature and highly subjective. At this point, the teacher is attempting to generate hypotheses about the possible reasons for the difficulty; he or she will then try to confirm these initial hypotheses using more objective means. Depending on what is discovered, the teacher may refine, reformulate, or implement an intervention based on that first hypothesis. Descriptions of some of the more general reasons underlying mathematics difficulty are presented below.

1. *Ineffective instruction* probably accounts for more cases of problems in arithmetic than any other factor. Students who are the victims of poor teaching can frequently be identified by their relatively good performance in arithmetic concepts that are usually acquired incidentally (size relationships or value of coins) compared with their performance in areas that are usually understood as the result of specific instruction ("carrying" in addition or long division). Remediation is usually effective if it is planned on the basis of a diagnosis of specific deficits.

2. *Difficulties in abstract or symbolic thinking* will interfere with the student's ability to conceptualize the relationship between numerals and objects that they represent, the structure of the number system (base of

10), and relationships between units of measurement. Teachers of students with these difficulties frequently turn in frustration from attempting to get the child to master concepts to emphasizing the rote manipulation of numerals. This may create a facade of arithmetic competence when in fact the student does not understand what he or she is doing.

3. *Reading problems* frequently are responsible for the difficulties of those students who perform well on tests of computation or on oral story problems, but who do poorly in typical workbook or standardized test situations in which they must be able to read the problem to understand which mathematical process to perform.

4. *Poor attitudes or anxiety* about mathematics may inhibit the performance of some students. Careful observation on the part of the teacher may provide the first indication that this is at the root of the child's problem. Does the student avoid mathematics? Does the student "play sick" when it is time for mathematical activities? The teacher may also wish to use one of the instruments developed for assessing attitudes toward arithmetic, e.g., the Math subtest of the Estes Attitude Scales (Estes et al., 1981).

ASSESSING MATHEMATICS PERFORMANCE

To engage in appropriate and efficient instruction, the teacher must first employ a set of assessment procedures that permit him or her to have a detailed picture of each student's strengths and weaknesses in mathematics. Most teachers discover quickly that the standardized survey type of mathematics achievement tests yields little information. It is necessary for the teacher to study in depth the areas of difficulty pointed out by the survey test. For example, the student who is shown to be having computational difficulties is given a much more detailed inventory of computational problems. The teacher appraises the student's performance on the various computation tasks to determine the types of errors that trouble the student. Further probing of the student's errors is done through intensive analysis of written work and/or through an oral interview in which the student "thinks out loud" while solving problems.

The entire assessment process can be conceived of as a search on the part of the teacher for the faulty concepts and strategies being used by the student. Initial testing is gross and provides only the most general clues to the teacher. Successive assessment efforts, based on clues obtained from previous testing, help the teacher to zero in on the child's difficulty. Having discovered the problem, the teacher then plans an intervention to correct the difficulty. If the student shows improvement, the teacher may conclude that the problem was correctly identified and followed by appropriate instruction. Continued failure by the student indicates a need for reexamination of the assessment process and/or of the subsequent instruction.

This section provides some details on the assessment of a student's performance in mathematics. The utilization of commercially produced tests as well as teacher-made inventories is considered. Procedures for conducting an oral clinical interview and for analyzing a student's errors in mathematics are described as well.

The Use of Commercially Available Tests

A teacher could establish a student's overall performance level by having him or her "try out" in various mathematics tests, programs, or instructional systems. We believe, however, that it is much more efficient and reliable to administer commercially available standardized tests. These tests will give the teacher a general idea of students' functional level in mathematics and some idea of their performance in mathematical subareas.

One readily accessible body of test information is the results of the group-administered survey tests usually given systematically during the school year. All of these tests, e.g., the Metropolitan Achievement Test, the California Achievement Test, and the Iowa Tests of Basic Skills, include at least one subtest dealing with mathematics. This is also true of the individually administered achievement survey tests, e.g., the Diagnostic Achievement Test, the Wide-Range Achievement Test, and the Peabody Individual Achievement Test. Regrettably, the results of these survey tests have limited utility for the teacher in that they only yield information about students' general level of proficiency.

Of considerably more value to the teacher are the results of individually administered multifaceted test batteries that are designed to produce information about a variety of discrete mathematical skills and competencies (see Table 6–2). These results can be used to inventory a youngster's strengths and weaknesses in mathematical skills and concepts and point the way to areas that should be probed in depth through comprehensive informal analysis.

The authors of a few mathematics programs provide their own placement tests to help teachers establish the student's entry level into the program. Of course, such tests are usually applicable only to that program.

Even for students whose test performance indicates grade-level or near-grade-level functioning, we recommend that the teacher check the errors made by the pupil to see whether the student's performance is reasonably even across the various types of mathematics problems; by excelling in one area, say addition, one can obtain a fairly average score even if performance in another area, say multiplication, is very poor. The analysis of errors and error patterns has been found to be particularly helpful for pupils who are new to the teacher.

Table 6–2. Multifaceted Tests of Mathematics Performance

Test	Skills Measured	Grade Level	Special Features
Basic Educational Skills Inventory in Math (1972)	All mathematical areas	Elementary	Criterion-referenced Keyed to a retrieval system that refers teacher to materials designed to develop skills that the child missed
Diagnostic Test of Arithmetic Strategies (Ginsburg & Mathews, 1984)	1. Addition 2. Subtraction 3. Multiplication 4. Division	Elementary	Assesses strategies
Fountain Valley Teachers Support System in Mathematics (1976)	1. Numbers and operations 2. Geometry 3. Measurement 4. Application 5. Statistics/probability 6. Sets 7. Functions 8. Logical thinking 9. Problem solving	Grades K–8	Criterion-referenced Self-scoring Areas of weakness keyed to math text or program
Key Math Diagnostic Arithmetic Test (Connolly, Nachtman, & Pritchett, 1976)	1. Content 2. Operations 3. Applications	Grades K–6	Convenient and attractive to administer Requires almost no reading or writing
Patterns Recognition Skills Inventory (Sternberg, 1976)	Levels of readiness for all areas of math Reasoning skills	Ages 5–10	Concept-referenced diagnostic inventory Requires no reading by student Developmentally sequenced
Sequential Assessment of Mathematics Inventory (Reisman, 1984)	Eight areas of mathematics	Grade K–8	Organized by topic Available in computer form
Test of Early Mathematical Abilities (Ginsburg & Baroody, 1983)	Both formal and informal aspects of math	Ages 4–9	Norm-referenced Measures basic math prerequisites at preschool level
Test of Mathematical Abilities (V. L. Brown & McEntire, 1984)	1. Vocabulary 2. Computation 3. Information 4. Story problems 5. Attitudes	Grades 3–12	Norm-referenced Includes attitudes

Teacher-Made Assessment Inventories

The teacher's first step in developing an inventory is to choose the content to be assessed. One way to do this is to study the scope-and-sequence chart of the mathematics program that is being used in the school (most mathematics series present these near the beginning of the teacher's manual) or Table 6–3. The table has been organized in such a way as to enable the teacher to quickly identify, on the basis of a student's grade level, what mathematics skills and capabilities he or she should have. For example, if the child is in second grade and is having difficulty with subtraction, the teacher looks in column 2 of part V of the table. The table (based on commonly used commercial texts and curriculum guides) indicates that the child should understand the properties of subtraction, be able to conceptualize subtraction as the inverse of addition, be able to use the number line to subtract, be able to use both vertical and horizontal notation, and be able to subtract up to two-place numbers without regrouping and two-place numbers with regrouping. Of course, the teacher may wish to include more difficult items on the inventory in order to establish whether the student has skills beyond those usually developed in second grade.

The next step is to establish whether the student has the necessary underlying concepts and capacities required for the subtraction tasks. For help with this task the teacher is referred to Figure 6–3, which outlines the general hierarchical interrelationships between and among various areas of mathematical functioning. In each case, the source of an arrow may be considered to be a necessary prerequisite for full mastery of the capability to which the arrow is pointing. Thus, in the subtraction example, the student would need to have evidenced readiness capabilities and mastery of basic mathematical concepts and vocabulary. (For fuller analysis of these categories the reader is referred to the preceding section on Readiness and to the section on Mathematical Concepts in Table 6–3.)

An alternative approach is to conduct a task analysis and/or concept analysis of each of the terminal skills desired in the subtraction area. (For an excellent description of how to proceed with a mathematical task analysis, see also Reisman, 1972, 1977.)

The final step in determining what should go into the inventory is to decide in what form and under what conditions the child is supposed to be able to perform the task. Objectives should be stated in *precise, observable* terms. (See Chapter 1 for a fuller discussion of the stating of objectives.)

Now the teacher is ready to begin to write the actual items. They may be adapted from commercial texts or workbooks, or the teacher may create them. An example of a subtraction inventory, adapted from Burns (1965) and limited to the vertical format, is presented in Table 6–4.

To further probe the student's understanding of concepts underlying subtraction proficiency and to assess ability to perform subtraction problems in a

Table 6–3. Typical Scope and Sequence of Elementary Mathematics

	Grade						
	K	1	2	3	4	5	6
I. Readiness for Mathematics							
Classification	•	•	•	•	•	•	•
One-to-one correspondence	•	•	•	•	•	•	•
One-to-many correspondence				•	•	•	•
Seriation or ordering	•	•	•	•	•	•	•
Space and spatial representation	•	•	•	•	•	•	•
Flexibility and reversibility	•	•	•	•	•	•	•
Conservation	•	•	•	•	•	•	•
II. Mathematical Concepts							
Same, equal, as much as	•	•	•	•	•	•	•
More than, greater, greatest, larger, largest	•	•	•	•	•	•	•
Bigger, biggest, longer, longest	•	•	•	•	•	•	•
Less than, fewer, fewest, smaller, smallest	•	•	•	•	•	•	•
Shorter, shorter, most, least	•	•	•	•	•	•	•
Enough, not enough, more than enough	•	•	•	•	•	•	•
Left, right		•	•	•	•	•	•
Above, below, up, down, next to, between		•	•	•	•	•	•
Putting together, add, plus		•	•	•	•	•	•
Take apart, take away, subtract, minus		•	•	•	•	•	•
How many in all? How many are left?		•	•	•	•	•	•
Odd, even			•	•	•	•	•
Open, closed		•	•	•	•	•	•
=, >, <			•	•	•	•	•
Factors, primes, multiples							•
III. Sets							
Definition	•	•	•	•	•	•	•
Elements of sets	•	•	•	•	•	•	•
Kinds of sets							
Identical	•	•					•
Equal and equivalent	•	•					•
Unequal and nonequivalent						•	•
Empty set		•	•	•	•	•	•
Union of sets (addition)		•	•	•	•	•	•
Subset (subtraction)		•	•	•	•	•	•
Intersection of sets						•	•
IV. Whole Numbers							
Abstracting idea of cardinal number from equivalent set	•	•	•	•	•	•	•
Counting: one through ten	•	•	•	•	•	•	•
Concepts and counting: numbers above ten		•	•	•	•	•	•
Concept of zero	•	•	•	•	•	•	•
Skip counting by twos, threes, fives, tens		•	•	•	•	•	•
V. Operations on Whole Numbers: Addition and Subtraction							
Properties							
Closure and nonclosure		•	•	•	•	•	•
Commutativity and noncommutativity		•	•	•	•	•	•
Associativity and nonassociativity		•	•	•	•	•	•

(continued)

Table 6–3 *Continued*

	K	1	2	3	4	5	6
Inverse relation of addition and subtraction		•	•	•	•	•	•
Ways of conceptualizing							
Union of sets or forming of subsets		•	•	•	•	•	•
Number line		•	•	•	•	•	•
Addition and subtraction with zero		•	•	•	•	•	•
Addition and subtraction with horizontal notation		•	•	•	•	•	•
Addition and subtraction with vertical notation		•	•	•	•	•	•
Addition and subtraction without regrouping							
One-place numbers	•	•	•	•	•	•	•
Two-place numbers		•	•	•	•	•	•
Three-place numbers			•	•	•	•	•
Numbers with more than three digits				•	•	•	•
Addition and subtraction with regrouping							
Two-place numbers			•	•	•	•	•
More than two-place numbers				•	•	•	•
Column addition		•	•	•	•	•	•
VI. *Operations on Whole Numbers: Multiplication and Division*							
Properties							
Commutativity of multiplication			•	•	•	•	•
Associativity of multiplication				•	•	•	•
Distributive property of multiplication and division over addition				•	•	•	•
Inverse relation of multiplication and division				•	•	•	•
Ways of conceptualizing							
Union of sets or partitioning into equivalent sets			•	•	•	•	•
Repeated addition or successive subtraction			•	•	•	•	•
Arrays			•	•	•	•	•
Number line				•	•	•	•
Multiplication and division with horizontal notation			•	•	•	•	•
Multiplication and division with vertical notation			•	•	•	•	•
Use of zero in multiplication and division			•	•	•	•	•
"One" as the identity element			•	•	•	•	•
Multiplication and division with 10's, 100's, etc.				•	•	•	•
Computation without regrouping							
One-place factor or divisor, one-place sums, dividends			•	•	•	•	•
One-place factor or divisor, two-place sums or dividends			•	•	•	•	•
Computation with regrouping							
One-place factor or divisor, two- or three-place sums or dividends				•	•	•	•
Two-place factors or divisors, any number sums or dividends					•	•	•
Three- or four-place factors or divisors							•
Multiple multiplication				•	•	•	•
VII. *Fractions*							
Definition		•	•	•	•	•	•

Table 6–3 *Continued*

	K	1	2	3	4	5	6
Ways of conceptualizing							
Number line				•	•	•	•
Arrays or subsets				•	•	•	•
Geometric figures		•	•	•	•	•	•
Computation							
Addition and subtraction of simple fractions with common denominators				•	•	•	•
Addition and subtraction of simple fractions with mixed denominators					•	•	•
Addition and subtraction of mixed fractions with common denominators				•	•	•	•
Addition and subtraction of mixed fractions with mixed denominators						•	•
Multiplication and division							•
Decimal fractions							•
VIII. *Measurement*							
Measurement of length (inch, foot, yard, mile, metric)		•	•		•	•	•
Measurement of area (English and metric units)					•	•	•
Measurement of weight (ounce, pound, ton, metric units)					•	•	•
Measurement of liquids (cup, pint, quart, metric units)	•	•	•	•	•	•	•
Dry measures (quart, peck, bushel, metric units)				•	•	•	•
Measurement of quantity (dozen, gross)				•	•	•	•
Measurement of temperature (Fahrenheit, Celsius)				•	•	•	•
Measurement of time (clock, calendar)	•	•	•	•	•	•	•
Measure of money (coins, paper bills)		•	•	•	•	•	•
IX. *Geometry*							
Geometric shapes (circle, square, rectangle, triangle)	•	•	•	•	•	•	•
Spatial relationships	•	•	•	•	•	•	•
Point, line, line segment, ray, intersection						•	•
Parallel line, curved line, straight line						•	•
Radius, diameter						•	•
Angles, arc degrees							•
Closed-line plane, open-line plane						•	•
Area and perimeter						•	•
Three-dimensional shapes (sphere, cube, cone)						•	•

Figure 6–3.   Summary Scope and Sequence in Typical Elementary Mathematics

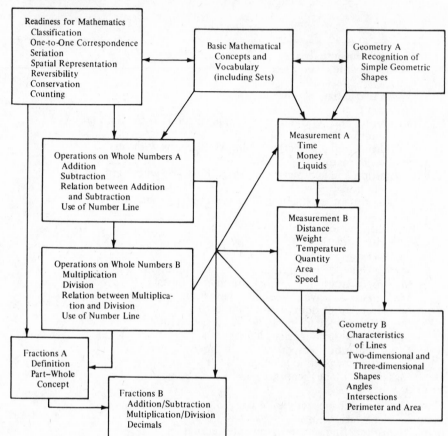

variety of formats and contexts, Burns (1965) has suggested a series of follow-up exercises. These are presented in Figure 6–4.

The Oral Interview (Clinical Mathematics Interview)

All existing evidence shows that most computational errors are caused by students' problems with number facts or by their use of faulty algorithms. Causes of difficulty with number facts can usually be discovered and confirmed by examination of a student's written work. However, to establish the faulty rules or strategies that the student is using in the computational procedures, it is frequently necessary to engage the student in an oral interview, or a "clinical math-

Table 6–4. Sample Analytical Inventory: Subtraction

Problem Type	Exercises for Child to Complete			
Basic subtraction facts without zero	1. $\begin{array}{r} 4 \\ -2 \\ \hline \end{array}$	2. $\begin{array}{r} 8 \\ -1 \\ \hline \end{array}$	3. $\begin{array}{r} 17 \\ -\ 3 \\ \hline \end{array}$	4. $\begin{array}{r} 15 \\ -\ 6 \\ \hline \end{array}$
Basic subtraction facts involving zero		5. $\begin{array}{r} 7 \\ -7 \\ \hline \end{array}$	6. $\begin{array}{r} 9 \\ -0 \\ \hline \end{array}$	
Higher-decade subtraction fact requiring no regrouping		7. $\begin{array}{r} 79 \\ -\ 6 \\ \hline \end{array}$		
Higher-decade subtraction fact requiring regrouping		8. $\begin{array}{r} 75 \\ -\ 9 \\ \hline \end{array}$		
Higher-decade subtraction fact, with difference in ones' place		9. $\begin{array}{r} 25 \\ -23 \\ \hline \end{array}$		
Higher-decade subtraction fact; zero in ones' place in minuend		10. $\begin{array}{r} 20 \\ -\ 3 \\ \hline \end{array}$		
Subtraction of ones and tens with no regrouping required		11. $\begin{array}{r} 47 \\ -24 \\ \hline \end{array}$		
Three-digit minuend minus two-digit subtrahend; no regrouping		12. $\begin{array}{r} 169 \\ -\ 45 \\ \hline \end{array}$		
Subtraction of ones, tens, hundreds; no regrouping		13. $\begin{array}{r} 436 \\ -215 \\ \hline \end{array}$		
Two-digit minuend minus two-digit subtrahend; regrouping tens and ones in minuend required		14. $\begin{array}{r} 46 \\ -38 \\ \hline \end{array}$	15. $\begin{array}{r} 72 \\ -34 \\ \hline \end{array}$	
Three-digit minuend minus two-digit subtrahend; regrouping tens and ones in minuend required (zero in difference)		16. $\begin{array}{r} 272 \\ -\ 64 \\ \hline \end{array}$		
Three-digit minuend minus two-digit subtrahend; regrouping hundreds and tens of minuend required		17. $\begin{array}{r} 528 \\ -\ 54 \\ \hline \end{array}$		
Subtraction of ones, tens, hundreds; regrouping tens and ones in minuend required		18. $\begin{array}{r} 742 \\ -208 \\ \hline \end{array}$	19. $\begin{array}{r} 750 \\ -374 \\ \hline \end{array}$	
Subtraction of ones, tens, hundreds; regrouping hundreds and tens in minuend required		20. $\begin{array}{r} 724 \\ -183 \\ \hline \end{array}$	21. $\begin{array}{r} 307 \\ -121 \\ \hline \end{array}$	
Subtraction of ones, tens, hundreds; regrouping entire minuend required		22. $\begin{array}{r} 531 \\ -173 \\ \hline \end{array}$		
Four-digit minuend minus three-digit subtrahend; regrouping entire minuend required		23. $\begin{array}{r} 1076 \\ -\ 247 \\ \hline \end{array}$	24. $\begin{array}{r} 5254 \\ -\ 968 \\ \hline \end{array}$	25. $\begin{array}{r} 5805 \\ -\ 978 \\ \hline \end{array}$
Subtraction of ones, tens, hundreds, thousands; regrouping hundreds, tens, and ones of minuend required		26. $\begin{array}{r} 4553 \\ -1258 \\ \hline \end{array}$		

(continued)

Table 6–4 *Continued*

Problem Type	Exercises for Child to Complete
Subtraction of ones, tens, hundreds, thousands; regrouping entire minuend required	27. 9563 − 2687
Five-digit minuend minus four-digit subtrahend; regrouping entire minuend required	28. 23238 − 3879
Five-digit minuend minus four-digit subtrahend; regrouping entire minuend (involving zeros) required	29. 10000 − 7192
Five-digit minuend minus five-digit subtrahend; regrouping entire minuend required	30. 30503 − 19765

Figure 6–4.   Follow-Up Exercises for the Analytical Test of Subtraction

1. Make a dot drawing to represent the fact that 17 take away 8 leaves 9.
2. What subtraction fact does this drawing illustrate?

12 cookies in all

OOOOOOOOOOOO

left   eaten

3. Show on the number line how the answer to 31 minus 12 might be found.
4. Start at 57 and count down by 5's to the first number in the thirties. To do this, say, "57, 52, 47," and so on.
5. Write three different ways to read the number statement $24 - 8 = 16$ (as "8 from 24 leaves 16").
6. What is the result when zero is subtracted from a number?
7. What is the result when a number is subtracted from itself?
8. What pairs of one-digit numbers would make each a true sentence?
    $\Box + \Box = 9$ $\quad \Box + \Box = 11 \quad$ $\Box + \Box = 13$
9. What basic subtraction fact helps you to subtract 6 from 53?
10. Start with 13, subtract 6, add 3, subtract 4, subtract 3. Where are you?
11. There is a two-digit minuend and a one-digit subtrahend whose difference is 9. What might they be?
12. Think the answers to the following questions. Then write the answers.
    a. 7 from 18 leaves how many?
    b. 68 and how many more equals 72?
    c. The difference bewteen 77 and 24 equals what number?
    d. Is 19 minus 12 equal to 7?
    e. When 203 is taken from 526, what is left?

Figure 6–4   *Continued*

    f. Is 60 from 388 equal to 328?
    g. Does 65 minus 9 equal 56?
    h. If you think 36 from 64, what do you get?
    i. How many are left if 19 is subtracted from 52?
    j. 525 is how much less than 3478?

13. In subtracting 1 ft 3 in. from 3 ft 1 in., to what name would you change one of the measures?

14. When 16 is subtracted from 51, to what number name is the 51 changed?

15. Do the following subtractions, using numerals and words.

    a. $20 = 2$ tens 0 ones $=$ b. $31 = 3$ tens 1 one $=$
         $- \ 3 =$ _____ 3 ones$=$ $- 17 = 1$ ten 7 ones $=$

    c. $500 = 5$ hundreds 0 tens 0 ones $=$
        $- 125 = 1$ hundred 2 tens 5 ones $=$

16. Use the words hundreds, tens, and ones to show the renaming of 413 in subtracting 187 from 413.

17. What do the digits at the top of the work mean?

                               9 1̶0̶
       3 13   6 12   4 10
    a.   4̶3̶   b.   7̶2̶4   c.   5̶0̶0̶
       $- 18$ $- 183$ $- 125$
        25

18. Write the number sentence for this word problem. There are 527 pupils in the Madison School, of whom 283 are boys. How many girls are there?

19. How can an equivalent addition question be written for the subtraction question $42 - 26 = n$?

20. Does $n + 17 = 42$ represent an addition or a subtraction situation?
    Does $n - 17 = 25$ represent a subtraction situation?

21. For each addition statement, write the subtraction statement that "undoes" it. The first one is done for you.
    $6 + 4 =$ $36 + 7 =$ $58 + 17 =$
    $10 - 6 = 4$
       or
    $10 - 4 = 6$

22. Write the missing numeral for each of the following statements:
    $19 - \square = 7$ $\square - 47 = 24$ $36 - 28 = \square$

23. Subtract $6.98 from $10.00.

24. Subtract. Check your answers by subtracting the difference from the minuend. Check again by adding the difference and the subtrahend.

                      162   806   1422   8461
                       75   436   766   7298

Source: P. C. Burns, Analytical testing and follow-up exercises in elementary school mathematics, *School Science and Mathematics*, 65 (1965), 34–38. Reprinted with permission.

ematics interview." The oral interview may be used to search for the student's error strategies, or it may be used to confirm (or disconfirm) "hunches" that the teacher has derived from an examination of the student's written work. Because of the time-consuming nature of the oral interview, the teacher will want to confine its use to "hard-core" problems. The procedures described below have been adapted from Cawley (1978) and Lankford (1974), as well as from the authors' experience.

1. *One problem area should be considered at a time.* Problems should be dealt with in the order in which they appear in a task analysis or in Figure 6–3. For example, if a student is having difficulty in both addition and multiplication, addition problems should be cleared up first. Once this has been accomplished, the student will need to be retested on written multiplication before oral probing in that area. It may be that correction of the faulty addition strategy will modify the difficulty in multiplication.
2. *The easiest problems should be presented first.* To help give the student a sense of confidence, the teacher should first present the student with a problem that he or she probably can perform correctly. Then problems of increasing difficulty (for the child) can be provided.
3. *A written record or tape should be made of the interview.* The student should be told whether his or her explanations are being recorded on tape or in writing.
4. *The student should simultaneously solve the problem in written form and "explain" what he or she is doing orally.* The teacher must remember that the oral interview is a diagnostic exercise, not an instructional lesson.
5. *The student must be left free to solve the problem in his or her own way without any hint that he or she is doing something wrong.* The teacher should avoid giving clues or asking leading questions. If the student directly asks whether the answers are correct, the teacher should tell the student to concentrate on "telling in his or her own words" how he or she is solving the problem.
6. *The student should not be hurried.* Depending on the complexity of the operations being diagnosed, the oral interview can take from 15 to 45 minutes.

Analysis of Errors

The identification and interpretation of a student's errors, whether evidenced in written work or in the oral interview, provide the basis on which the teacher develops an appropriate instructional program. It is important, therefore, for the teacher to be proficient in the analysis of pupil errors. This section identifies some of the common types of errors made by pupils (see Table 6–5) and provides

Table 6–5. Types of Arithmetic Habits and Errors Observed in Elementary School Pupils

Addition

Errors in combinations
Counting
Added carried number last
Forgot to add carried number
Repeated work after partly done
Wrote number to be carried
Irregular procedure in column
Carried wrong number
Grouped two or more numbers
Split numbers into parts
Used wrong fundamental operation
Lost place in column
Depended on visualization
Disregarded column position
Omitted one or more digits

Errors in reading numbers
Dropped back one or more tens
Derived unknown combination from familiar
  one
Disregarded one column
Error in writing answer
Skipped one or more decades
Carried when there was nothing to carry
Used scratch paper
Added in pairs, giving last sum as answer
Added same digit in two columns
Wrote carried number in answer
Added same number twice

Subtraction

Errors in combinations
Did not allow for having borrowed
Counting
Errors due to zero in minuend
Said example backwards
Subtracted minuend from subtrahend
Failed to borrow; gave zero as answer
Added instead of subtracted
Error in reading
Used same digit in two columns
Derived unknown from known combination
Omitted a column
Used trial-and-error addition
Split numbers

Deducted from minuend when borrowing was
  not necessary
Ignored a digit
Deducted 2 from minuend after borrowing
Error due to minuend and subtrahend digits
  being same
Used minuend or subtrahend as remainder
Reversed digits in remainder
Confused process with division or
  multiplication
Skipped one or more decades
Increased minuend digit after borrowing
Based subtraction on multiplication
  combination

Multiplication

Errors in combinations
Error in adding the carried number
Wrote rows of zeros
Carried a wrong number
Errors in addition
Forgot to carry
Used multiplicand as multiplier
Error in single zero combinations, zero as
  multiplier
Errors due to zero in multiplier

Confused products when multiplier had two
  or more digits
Repeated part of table
Multiplied by adding
Did not multiply a digit in multiplicand
Based unknown combination on another
Errors in reading
Omitted digit in writing product
Errors in carrying into zero
Counted to carry

(continued)

Table 6–5 *Continued*

Multiplication, continued	
Used wrong process—added	Omitted digit in multiplier
Error in single zero combinations, zero as multiplicand	Split multiplier
	Wrote wrong digit of product
Errors due to zero in multiplicand	Multiplied by same digit twice
Error in position of partial products	Reversed digits in product
Counted to get multiplication combinations	Wrote tables
Illegible figures	
Forgot to add partial products	

Division	
Errors in division combinations	Used remainder without new dividend figure
Errors in subtraction	Derived unknown combinations from known
Errors in multiplication	one
Used remainder larger than divisor	Had right answer, used wrong one
Found quotient by trial multiplication	Grouped too many digits in dividend
Neglected to use remainder within problem	Errors in reading
Omitted zero resulting from another digit	Used dividend or divisor as quotient
Counted to get quotient	Found quotient by adding
Repeated part of multiplication table	Reversed dividend and divisor
Used short division form for long division	Used digits of divisor separately
Wrote remainders within problem	Wrote all remainders at end of problem
Omitted zero resulting from zero in dividend	Misinterpreted table
Omitted final remainder	Used digit in dividend twice
Used long division form for short division	Used second digit or divisor to find quotient
Said example backwards	Began dividing at units digit of dividend
	Split dividend
	Counted in subtracting
	Used too large a product
	Used endings to find quotient

Source: G. T. Buswell and Leonore John, *Diagnostic Studies in Arithmetic* (Chicago: University of Chicago Press, 1926). Used with the permission of the publisher.

some examples of error analyses. Errors made in verbal problem solving are dealt with in the next section.

A systematic analysis of error types, easily adapted for classroom use, was reported by Roberts (1962). The failure strategies employed by children usually fall into one of the categories outlined in Table 6–6.

Roberts found in his group of third-graders that the most common type of error was use of a defective algorithm. Only the lowest-functioning children made errors of another type—and these were random responses.

The utilization in the diagnostic-instructional sequence of the student's written work and his or her statements during an oral interview is illustrated in

Table 6–6. Failure Strategies Employed by Elementary Pupils

	Example	
Strategy	Problem	Pupil Response
Wrong operation (the pupil performs an operation that leads to an incorrect result)	38 − 11	38 −11 ̄ ̄ 49
Obvious computational error (the pupil makes an obvious error in basic number facts)	42 × 3	42 ×3 ̄ ̄ 146
Defective algorithm (the pupil makes procedural errors as he or she tries to apply the correct process)	562 − 387	562 −387 ̄ ̄ ̄ 225
Random response (the pupil's response does not relate in any discernible way to the problem)	742 × 59	742 ×59 ̄ ̄ 123

Source: Adapted from Roberts (1962).

Figure 6–5. In each case, what the child does and what the child says lead the teacher to a tentative hypothesis concerning the source of difficulty. After identifying the problem, the teacher can make a good guess as to what instructional procedures will be effective with the child. Possible teaching strategies for each instance are exemplified in the column "What the teacher does next."

TEACHING MATHEMATICS

Once the student's performance has been analyzed in detail, instruction can begin. The teacher's attention shifts now to considerations of materials, methodologies, and approaches. This section begins with a discussion of a few principles that will assist the teacher in making sound instructional decisions. This discussion is followed by descriptions of several instructional approaches that lend themselves to use with students having particular difficulty in mathematics. Because of the particular difficulty experienced by many students with verbal (story) problem solving, this aspect of instruction has been singled out for special attention.

Important Principles Involved in Instruction

Before actually implementing an intervention in math, the teacher should be familiar with three of the more important principles associated with teaching material in this subject area: (1) the place of the discovery method, (2) the use of flexibility in programming, and (3) the role of strategy training.

Figure 6–5. Sample Inventory of Subtraction of Whole Numbers: Error Analysis*

Problem Presented	What the Child Writes	What the Child Says (Oral Interview)	Error Analysis— Teacher's Hypotheses	What the Teacher Does Next
7 −3	7 −3 / 2	7 take away 3 = 2.	Doesn't know number fact.	Presents same problem in another form (to rule out random error). Checks other subtraction facts. Provides practice with physical objects, worksheets, number line, flashcards, games, etc. Retests before going to more difficult subtraction.
15 − 6	15 −6 / 11	6 take away 5 is 1; 1 stays the same.	Faulty algorithm; doesn't understand integrity of minuend and subtrahend; doesn't know number fact.	Checks further to see if child always subtracts smaller number from larger. Reviews addition and subtraction at enactive and iconic level (Brunner) with one-digit numbers, then two-digit. Has child respond orally before returning to written form.
85 − 3	85 −3 / 52	3 from 8 is 5; 3 from 5 is 2.	Subtraction problem worked left to right; problem with place value (subtracting ones from tens).	Reviews place value at the enactive, iconic, and symbolic levels; provides practice with subtraction algorithm in simpler two-digit problems.
85 − 9	8⁵5 −9 / 86	The 8 goes down here; then you have to change the 5 to 15, then subtract 9 from 15.	Subtraction problem worked left to right; doesn't understand effect on tens of regrouping ones.	Provides experience with place value—manipulating bundles of straws (1's, 10's, 100's), pocket chart, or Stern materials; then provides workbook pictorial practice. Finally, reworks symbolic problem.

Problem	Child's explanation	Diagnosis	Teaching suggestion
$\begin{array}{r} 91 \\ -83 \\ \hline \end{array}$ (answer: 1)	Since you can't take 3 from 1, the answer is 1; also because 8 from 9 is 1.	Problem in regrouping; possible problem in number fact.	Reviews place value (tens and ones); performs several problems of this type on the pocket chart, or with Cuisenaire rods. Provides successful experience on problems of this type before returning to numerical form.
$\begin{array}{r} 523 \\ -284 \\ \hline 249 \end{array}$	This 2 (in tens place) should be 12, that makes this 5 a 4. Now $12 - 8 = 4$ and $4 - 2 = 2$. To take 4 away over here (ones column) you make the 3 to a 13; $13 - 4 = 9$; change 12 to 11.	Sequence is the problem here. The child performed all the steps correctly but in the wrong order.	Provides practice with right-to-left sequence in problems not involving regrouping. Uses place value box or chart to show why sequence affects results.
$\begin{array}{r} 300 \\ -157 \\ \hline 653 \end{array}$	You have to get ones from the three because there aren't any here (pointing to 0's); 3 take away 2 makes the 3 a 1. Now we have 10 ones, and 10 tens, and we can subtract.	Relationship of empty sets of ones to tens to hundreds a problem. Child doesn't understand conversion from one unity to another.	Provides child with experience in converting tens to ones and hundreds to ones. (It might be very effective to use dollars, dimes, and pennies first, and then the paper-and-pencil mode.) First provides practice using only tens and ones together, then hundreds and tens together, then hundreds and ones together, finally conversions involving all three units in one problem.

*For an excellent discussion and numerous examples of error analysis, the reader is referred to R. B. Ashlock, *Error Patterns in Computation: A Semiprogrammed Approach* (Columbus, Ohio: Charles E. Merrill, 1982).

The Place of the Discovery Method

The most widely discussed issue in the field of mathematics education has been the extent to which teachers should use a "discovery approach" in teaching. The widespread adoption of this style of teaching is based on the belief that children learn more thoroughly and better retain principles and concepts that were acquired through a "discovery" process rather than through didactic instruction on the part of a teacher. In using the discovery method, the teacher limits the number of cues that are given to assist the student in solving a particular problem. The cues that are withheld might be process cues, e.g., telling the child to do such-and-such, or product cues, e.g., giving "hints" as to where to look for the answer.

The debate over the discovery method takes on particular significance when one is talking about the instruction of students who have problems in mathematics performance. One could define such students as those for whom cues that were sufficient for their peer group were insufficient. That is, the quantity and types of cues that made it possible for their classmates to learn did not work for this group. To advise further cue reduction for these students seems almost irresponsible. Should students with mathematics problems be presented only with expository type teaching? Although there is no research evidence one way or the other, we believe such a course to be equally unwise. *All* children, including those with learning difficulties, should be exposed to a variety of teaching styles and instructional approaches. Naturally, we do not advocate persisting with an approach that has been manifestly ineffective. What we are asserting is that there is more than one way to teach mathematics to children, and discovery learning should not be ruled out for any child. Similarly, to rely exclusively on the discovery method seems to us to be foolhardy. Optimum learning appears to take place when teacher behavior is indirect but supportive, and when the student is in an active as opposed to a passive learning mode (Becher, 1980). This appears to be the case particularly in the development of the cognitive prerequisites to formal mathematics learning.

Flexibility in Using Instructional Approaches

As stated in the preceding section, the effective teacher utilizes more than one approach, depending on the child, the task, and the situation. Olson (1972), noting that children can acquire the same knowledge when instructed in different modes, has presented a model that relates mode of experience to the acquisition of an underlying system of knowledge and skills (see Table 6–7). Note that a child may acquire the concept of the diagonal, for example, by direct or directed reinforced experience; by observing someone demonstrate the concept; or by verbal instruction through a symbol system (in this case, the English language).

Table 6–7. Proposal for Relating Three Modes of Experience to the Acquisition of an Underlying System of Knowledge and Skills

Cognitive Development		Categories of Behavior (Modes) From Which Information May Be Extracted		Informational Coding (Alternatives Specified by:)
Knowledge	Skills			
Diagonal	Checkerboard Drawing Speaking	Contingent experience	{ Direct Directed (instructional)	Reinforcement consequent upon one's acts (learning theory)
Chair	Sitting Drawing Describing	Observational learning	{ Observation Modeling (instruction)	Modeled alternatives (social learning theory)
Objects	Locomotive			
Events Space Time	Prehensive Linguistic Mathematical Iconological	Symbolic Systems	{ Communication Instruction	Coded alternatives (cognitive theory)

Information extraction processes ⬇

Olson's proposal has enormous implications for the teacher of mathematics (and all other teachers). If he is correct, teachers have considerably more choice than they may have thought they had in selecting an instructional mode. Thus, at times they may select procedures derived from learning theory (reinforcement consequent upon one's acts), at other times procedures derived from social learning theory (modeled alternatives) or from cognitive theory (coded alternatives).

The same general thinking underlies a series of research studies conducted at the University of Connecticut. Cawley and his coworkers (Cawley, Fitzmaurice-Hayes, Shaw, & Bloomers, 1980) have postulated an *interactive unit model* (see Table 6–8) to describe the interaction of teacher and pupil in the mathematics teaching-learning situation. The instructional requirements for the teacher vary from manipulating something to displaying something, saying something, or writing something. The child, when interacting with the teacher, can manipulate something, identify something, say something, or write something. The possible combinations of teacher input and student output are sixteen in number. This flexibility permits maximum discretion on the part of the teacher in planning for individuals or groups of children. Thus, if a child is a nonreader, for example, there are still twelve other ways that he or she and the teacher can interact in the instructional setting.

The teacher can evidence flexibility in mathematics instruction in other ways, such as by permitting pupils to select the materials with which they wish to work or encouraging pupils to use unusual or alternative algorithms in working mathematical problems. Most textbook-prescribed algorithms are based on convention and on "efficiency," but there are other equally acceptable ways of performing the same operation. For example, students who are having an inordinate amount of difficulty with subtraction involving borrowing may wish to use the alternative algorithm known as the "equal addition method" (Ashlock, 1982). For the problem

$$773$$
$$-\ 254$$

the solution by this method is

$$77\overset{1}{3}$$
$$-\ 2\underset{6}{5}4$$
$$\overline{5\ 1\ 9}$$

The rationale for this approach is the principle of compensation: whatever is added to the minuend must be added to the subtrahend. Since 10 ones are added to the minuend, 1 ten is added to the subtrahend to compensate. Then subtraction proceeds normally.

Table 6–8. The Interactive Unit (Example Selected: Teaching the Concept of "Open" and "Closed")

| | | INPUT, usually by Teacher (T) | | |
	Manipulates	Displays	States	Writes
Manipulates	T demonstrates "open" and "closed" with containers; P models with containers.	T displays containers to P; P opens or closes items as requested.	T states "open" or "closed"; P forms open or closed figure with yarn.	T writes "open" or "closed" on chalkboard; P closes or opens containers.
Identifies	T constructs examples of open and closed containers; P points to his or her own sample that matches T's.	T presents containers or pictures to P; P selects open or closed as requested.	T states "open" or "closed"; P points to appropriate picture.	P circles workbook picture that has "open" printed at top of page.
States	T constructs examples of open and closed containers; P correctly says "open" or "closed," as required.	T presents open and closed items to P; P states whether they are open or closed.	T asks P to name open and closed objects in the room.	P reads word from board, then states which items correspond.
Writes	T constructs examples of open and closed containers; P correctly writes "open" or "closed," as required.	T presents pictures of open and closed items to P; P writes "open" or "closed."	T describes items; P writes "open" or "closed."	T writes "open" or "closed" at top of page; P writes word under pictures.

OUTPUT, usually by Pupil (P)

Definitions	
Manipulate (do)	To pile, build, arrange two- or three-dimensional objects or materials.
Display (see)	To show in fixed representations either two- or three-dimensional stimuli.
Identify (see)	To point to or otherwise mark nonsymbolic options in a multiple-choice task.
State (say)	To orally state.
Write (say)	To write with symbols (letters/numerals) or to draw.

Source: Adapted from J. F. Cawley, *Learning Disabilities in Mathematics: A Curriculum Design for Upper Grades* (unpublished manuscript, University of Connecticut, Storrs, Conn., 1976).

Strategy Training in Mathematics

In order to implement strategy training with an individual student, the teacher must identify the areas in which the student is experiencing difficulty and the levels at which he or she is functioning in those areas. Intervention commences with the area in which the student has the greatest degree of difficulty. For example, if the student's greatest problem is in multiplication, additional informal assessment is undertaken to pinpoint precisely the student's instructional level in multiplication so that intervention can begin there. This procedure is somewhat similar to what Cullinan, Lloyd, and Epstein (1981) call "task class analysis."

The next step is to devise a strategy for attacking the particular problem on the basis of how a competent performer would go about solving this class of tasks. This attack strategy is then subjected to a task analysis for the purpose of identifying the entry skills that the student needs in order to use the attack strategy. Examples of an attack strategy for multiplication computation and of a task analysis of entry or preskills required for that particular strategy are provided in Figures 6–6 and 6–7.

The actual teaching of the task strategy incorporates the self-instructional procedures developed by Leon and Pepe (1983). Their procedure includes the following five stages: modeling, self-administration of reinforcement, feedback, coping instructions, and self-instructional dialogue. An example, applied to the multiplication strategy, is delineated below:

> Stage 1—The teacher computes the problem using overt self-instruction. Both the computation strategy and the self-instructional technique are modeled.

Figure 6–6. Attack Strategy for Multiplication Facts

Attack Strategy: Count by one number the number of times indicated by the other number.

Steps in Attack Strategy	*Example:*
1. Read the problem.	2 × 5 = ____
2. Point to a number that you know how to count by.	student points to 2
3. Make the number of marks indicated by the other number.	////
4. Begin counting by the number you know how to count by and count up once for each mark, touching each mark.	"2, 4 . . ."
5. Stop counting when you've touched the last mark.	". . . 6, 8, 10"
6. Write the last number you said in the answer space.	2 × 5 = <u>10</u>

Source: D. Cullinan, J. Lloyd, and M. H. Epstein, Strategy training: A structured approach to arithmetic instruction, *Exceptional Education Quarterly*, 2, 1 (1981), 41–49.

Figure 6–7. Task Analysis Showing Preskills for Multiplication Attack Strategy

1. Say the numbers 0 to 100.
2. Write the numbers 0 to 100.
3. Name × and = signs.
4. Make the number of marks indicated by numerals 0 to 10.
5. Count by numbers 1 to 10.
6. End counting-by sequences in various positions.
7. Coordinate counting-by and touching-marks actions.

Source: D. Cullinan, J. Lloyd, and M. H. Epstein, Strategy training: A structured approach to arithmetic instruction, *Exceptional Education Quarterly,* 2, 1 (1981), 41–49.

Stage 2—The teacher and the student together work through a computation problem, using the multiplication strategy and verbalizing the self-instruction strategy.

Stage 3—The student computes the problem, verbalizing the self-instruction strategy as he or she does so.

Stage 4—The student computes the problem, whispering the self-instruction strategy as he or she does so.

Stage 5—The student computes the problem covertly using the self-instruction strategy.

Once students have correctly demonstrated the use of the strategy for several consecutive problems, they are allowed to work independently to consolidate the strategy. Increasingly more difficult examples of the multiplication computation paradigm (using the same strategy) are employed until the students regularly achieve mastery at at least 90 percent of the criterion level. They are then ready to acquire a new strategy for a new task.

Approaches to Teaching Mathematics

As stated in the introductory section to this chapter, there has been a great increase recently in the number of instructional mathematics materials available to teachers. This section briefly describes some of the approaches that might be used with students with problems in mathematics achievement.

Basal Math Texts

For many years, the use of basal texts has been the most common way of teaching mathematics. Generally the materials consist of student texts, student workbooks, and teacher's manuals. Sometimes additional supplementary materials are available, such as spirit duplicator masters, charts for recording pupil progress, or quizzes or tests to establish whether a child is ready to begin a new section. Among the best of the elementary basal math series are

> Essentials of Math (Ginn)
> Harper and Row Mathematics
> Holt Math 1000 (Holt, Rinehart & Winston)
> Holt School Mathematics (Holt, Rinehart & Winston)
> Individualized Mathematics Improvement Series (Bobbs-Merrill)
> McGraw-Hill Mathematics
> Math for Individual Achievement (Houghton Mifflin)
> Scott, Foresman Mathematics
> Skillseekers (Addison-Wesley)
> SRA Mathematics Program (Science Research Associates)

Math Kits

Increasing numbers of publishers are producing mathematics instructional programs in the form of kits or packages with various components. Usually these consist of activity cards for daily lessons, teacher's guides, and materials for student activities. A summary of such kits is presented in Table 6–9. (All of these kits were developed in the latter 1970s or early 1980s.)

Special Approaches

A few educational approaches have been developed for children who require a more concrete, less abstract approach to mathematics—the Cuisenaire-Gattegno approach, Stern's *Structural Arithmetic* approach, the *Direct Instruction Mathematics* program, and the *Key Math Early Steps Program*. Each of these is described briefly.

Cuisenaire-Gattegno Rods.   Invented by George Cuisenaire in 1953, and further developed by Caleb Gattegno, the Cuisenaire rods are instructional aids that seem particularly relevant to a modern mathematics curriculum (Davidson, 1969). They are capable of generating pupil interest and enthusiasm while promoting a dialogue between learner and teacher. The rods are based on a definition of mathematics as a process of observation and discovery of relationships. They were designed for the purpose of teaching conceptual knowledge of the basic structure of mathematics, rather than simply the manipulative skills. The teacher's role in the setting provided by the rods is to observe and ask questions about what the children are discovering for themselves, rather than to instruct or explain. It would appear that a child who works out facts and ideas for

Table 6–9. Summary Descriptions of Instructional Math Kits

Title and Grade Level (Publisher)	Comments
Basic Computation Skills Series 1,2,3 (Holt, Rinehart)	Self-administered diagnostic tests prescribing work on Study-Do sheets. Record sheets, teacher's guide.
Diagnosis: An Instructional Aid (Science Research Associates)	Survey and diagnostic tests (probes), prescription guides, remediation activities. Management system for teaching pupil progress.
DISTAR: Arithmetic I, Arithmetic II (K–2) (Science Research Associates)	Direct instructional method. Teacher's and pupils' books. Take-home workbooks.
Foundations for Math: Basic Math Skill Development (Teaching Resources)	Skill development emphasized.
Fundamentals Underlying Numbers (Teaching Resources)	
Individualized Math System (Rev.) (1–8) (Ginn)	"Program" consists of reusable laminated pages. Pre- and post-tests, prescriptive tests.
Math: An Activity Approach (6–9) (Science Research Associates)	Individualized. 188 games and activities from whole numbers through statistics. New skills, review of old skills. Application.
Math—Series 300 to 800 (3–8) (Educational Progress)	Individuals work at own rate and level. Concepts and skill sequence based on most widely used texts. Activity cards. Audio tapes. Student record-keeping.
Project MATH (K–6) (Educational Development Corp.)	Multiple-option curriculum. Interactive units based on teacher/learner: input/output.
Skill Modes in Math (4–Adult) (Science Research Associates)	Self-diagnosis. Self-teaching. Student activity and practice cards, record books.

himself or herself will learn and retain them better. Through the use of rods, a kindergartener is introduced to algebraic equations and a basic appreciation of place value and the number system.

Training Techniques.   There are 291 wooden Cuisenaire rods, varying in length and color. The rods use both color and length to embody algebraic principles and number relationships. They are 1 centimeter square in cross section and from 1 to 10 centimeters long. There are five color families. The red rods represent the quantities of 2, 4, and 8; the blue-green rods, 3, 6, and 9; the yellow rods, 5 and 10; the black rod, 7; and the white cube, 1.

Since the rods have no numerals on them, children who have not yet developed an adequate number background can use the materials to explore logic as well as relationships between quantities. Children who possess basic number awareness can work with the rods in terms of the principles identified with particular operations.

Introduction of the rods at any given grade level is done in the following four stages:

1. Independent exploration, in which the child is permitted to "play" with the rods.
2. Independent exploration and hands-on activities with the rods, in which relationships are observed and discussed without the use of mathematical notation. The following aspects of mathematics are explored at this point: equivalence, trains (sequences), patterns, greater than and less than, staircase (seriation), complements, trains of one color, transformations, and odds and evens.
3. Directed activities in which mathematical notation is introduced and used without assigning number value to the rods. Opportunities for independent exploration are still needed.
4. Directed activities in which the use of mathematical notation is extended and number values are assigned to the rods. Independent exploration will go beyond the directed activities.

Care should be taken to ensure that rods are used for proper purposes, that is, discovery and verification. The method is valueless if students are unable to do sums without the help of the rods. As soon as the student understands the process, he or she must be encouraged to work it out mentally.

Four booklets that accompany the rods treat such topics as cardinality, ordinality, factors, equivalence, permutations, transformations, complements, various forms of measurement, inequalities, proportions, basic whole numbers and rational number operations, and number properties. The booklets are concerned with various aspects of basic mathematics; however, they cannot be considered a complete program.

Although these materials can be used in grades kindergarten through six, they are usually emphasized through grade three. They may be used with an entire class, a small group, or an individual child. They have been successfully utilized with children possessing a varied range of abilities—the deaf, mentally retarded, gifted, and emotionally disturbed—as well as with other children who need visual and tactile reinforcement for effective learning.

Program Evaluation.   Research on the Cuisenaire-Gattegno materials has not been conclusive, but it has indicated that the rods are at least as effective as more traditional approaches. In addition, these materials minimize drill and rote learning and promote discovery and understanding by the individual child according to his or her own developmental level. Student interest and enthusiasm is usually high. The concreteness of the materials and their suitability for manipulation by a tactile modality make them particularly useful for children with whom a traditional mathematics program has been unsuccessful.

The Cuisenaire rods have been criticized on the grounds that children become too dependent on them and are unable to function at a symbolic, abstract level without them. However, used judiciously in conjunction with other models and approaches, the Cuisenaire rods have a place as supplemental materials in a modern mathematics curriculum for children with learning problems.

Structural Arithmetic. The *Structural Arithmetic* (Stern, 1965) system is based on the assumption that arithmetic is the basis for the further study of mathematics and science; it presumes that mathematical concepts can and must be developed at the beginning of school life. Furthermore, the program ensures mastery in computation by having the student experiment with concrete materials that reveal the structure of the number system. Through this experimentation the student develops insight into number relationships.

The goals of this approach are to develop mathematical thinking and nurture an appreciation for its exactness and clarity. Mathematical thinking can develop only if the student has obtained insight into the characteristic structure of the entire set of concepts to which specific addition or subtraction facts belong, or if the student has developed insight into structural relationships that make transfer of learning possible. All experiments in *Structural Arithmetic* are designed to develop concepts that lead the child to arrive at generalizations essential to the understanding and mastery of arithmetic.

Structural Arithmetic hopes to achieve its goals through the following approaches:

1. By using concrete materials that allow the student to discover a number fact.
2. By following a carefully arranged sequence of experiments through which the student advances step by step from simple number concepts to the mastery of arithmetical computation and problem solving.
3. By presenting in the workbooks functional illustrations that help the student reconstruct any forgotten number fact.

It is hoped that the child will experience the following achievements as a result of the use of structural materials:

1. Immediate success in arithmetic. (There will be a carryover from work with concrete materials to ability to do abstract figuring.)

2. Development of self-reliance. (The student can check answers and make corrections; the student will become accustomed to always checking for correctness.)

3. Preparation for the mathematical thinking necessary in the later development of mathematics.

Training Techniques.   The materials for *Structural Arithmetic* (SA) are packaged in four kits, appropriate for kindergarten level and grades one through three. Materials for each grade include a teacher's manual, pupils' workbooks, and manipulatable materials (number markers, number guide, number track, number stand and accompanying slides, pattern board, unit box with unit blocks, subtraction shield, number cases, and a box of 100 cubes).

The approach in SA is based on measuring. The numbers are represented by blocks that measure 1 unit, 2 units, 3 units, and so on. With these devices the student can discover all existing number relations by himself or herself. He or she not only finds out relations by measuring what block combinations yield 10, but also discovers processes of carrying and borrowing, multiplying and dividing. The blocks are suitable for both group and individual instruction.

Problem solving is an important part of SA. Pupils are prepared step by step for solving problems. They begin by listening carefully to oral problems and then demonstrating the problems with the manipulative materials. In SA 1, problems are presented through pictures without any printed words, so that a child's lack of reading ability will not hold him or her back. Word problems are introduced in SA 2 and used in SA 3. The vocabulary is kept simple throughout. In addition to providing work with structural materials, most of the lessons contain suggestions that teachers may use to provide an opportunity for pupils to do oral computation. Mastery tests appear at the end of each workbook and are also used throughout the SA program.

The teacher's guide helps the teacher set up experiments that guide pupils to make appropriate discoveries and generalizations. From each experiment the pupils are to gain insight into an arithmetical procedure. To check whether the demonstration was successful, the teacher should present examples that the students can solve without the structural materials or pencil and paper. Following the experiment, the students continue using the topic of the day's experiment in the workbooks. There are provisions for additional experiments for the student who is having difficulty, and enrichment activities for the student who wishes to work independently.

Program Evaluation.   *Structural Arithmetic* is a complete mathematics program that is flexible, well organized, and concrete. The teacher's guide is very thorough and includes detailed teaching suggestions. The program has been successful with mildly retarded and learning disabled children, as well as in regular classes. The materials are nonconsumable.

Direct Instruction Mathematics. The *Direct Instruction Mathematics* (Silbert, Carnine, & Stein, 1981) approach is based on the belief that teachers are responsible for a number of the variables that affect mathematics learning, including program design, presentation techniques, and organization of instruction. The explicit purpose of *Direct Instruction* is to provide the teacher with a set of direct prescriptions to bring about student acquisition, retention, and generalization in mathematics.

Training Techniques and Program Organization. Direct Instruction Mathematics comes in book form. It can be thought of as a comprehensive outline of a mathematics program with numerous examples and models. It offers suggestions in eight areas of teacher instruction—specifying objectives, devising problem-solving strategies, determining necessary preskills, sequencing preskills and skills, selecting a teaching procedure, designing formats (such as criteria for acceptable student responses or procedures for correction of errors), selecting specific examples, and providing for practice and review.

Presentation techniques are provided as well, to ensure student attention and encourage teachers to teach to a criterion of mastery rather than to just the end of the lesson.

The program also deals with considerations involved in selecting materials, modifying commercial programs, and placing and grouping students. Finally, it provides a coherent plan to assist the teacher through a unit of instruction.

Evaluation. Direct Instruction Mathematics has its own criterion-referenced evaluation procedures which facilitate evaluation. The program has a great deal of structure and teacher control and requires specific responses from students, in contrast to other approaches, which allow greater teacher and student variation. Its emphasis on public, observable teacher behavior makes this program more easily supervised and evaluated than some others.

The design of the program provides a framework for analyzing a student's performance in order to separate student problems due to faulty teaching from student problems arising from deficiencies within the student. This latter feature makes the program especially useful in remedial settings. A more detailed evaluation of this program is provided by V. L. Brown (1985).

Key Math Early Steps Program. The *Key Math* (Connolly, 1982) mathematics program for kindergarten, first grade, and handicapped students is designed to combine the advantages of both textbook-oriented and activity-oriented methods. It is presented as a systematic, consistent program that fosters the development of cognitive skills and promotes content application. Provisions are made for differentiating among average, slow, and fast learners.

Organization, Materials, and Techniques. *Early Steps* is organized into stages that address fifty-five broad instructional objectives. Each stage is an extended lesson that includes, in order: (1) presentation activities, (2) small-group exploration, (3) teacher-led integration, (4) seatwork, and (5) optional practice and enrichment activities.

Program materials consist of a variety of concrete, pictorial, and symbolic materials, including the following: teacher's guide, instructional manual, 300 Key Math cubes, 60 attribute blocks, 180 math chips, 12 tumblers, 4 deck cards, 28 numeral cards, 2 math boards, 5 math trays, 8 meter ropes, 20 activity cards, 10 resource folders, 200 blackline masters, and a scope-and-sequence chart.

At the end of each stage, one or more worksheets are used to evaluate each student's understanding of that stage. Criteria for rating students at the mastery, partial mastery, and awareness levels are included.

Evaluation. The teacher's guide notes that the program was field tested in twenty-six schools, but the results of the field test are not presented. Other research on the program has not yet appeared.

Verbal Problem Solving

In 1980, the National Council of Teachers of Mathematics (NCTM) stated that "Problem solving must be the focus of school mathematics in the 1980s" (p. 2). Since that time, the NCTM Yearbook, *Problem Solving in School Mathematics*, and numerous articles have tried to strengthen instruction in problem solving. However, the most recent National Mathematics Assessment (Lindquist et al., 1983) does not reveal any significant increases in student performance.

Several authors have noted that there is much more to verbal problem solving than merely deciding on the correct computational procedure and performing the computation. Solving problems potentially involves questions of judgments concerning reasonableness and practicality, as well as other considerations. McGinty and Meyerson (1980) have schematically portrayed the way in which solving problems in mathematics is related to problem solving in everyday life (see Figure 6–8). Cawley, Fitzmaurice, Shaw, Kahn, and Bates (1979) make much the same point when they note that many problems appropriately posed in the mathematics program involve no computation at all. They also point out that some students are able to "solve" the rather contrived typical mathematics problems, but are not able to solve real-life problems. Such problems, they observe, entail an integration of computational skill, concept analy-

Figure 6–8. Aspects of Problem Solving

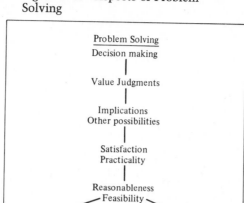

sis, selection and derivation of relevant information, and decision making (p. 37). An adequate problem-solving program in mathematics prepares students for real-life problem solving, which often involves numbers. Some of these numbers (such as Social Security numbers, telephone numbers, or utility readings) may not require computation, but problem-solving skills are required for their successful use in day-to-day living. Living skills include map-reading, writing and keeping track of checks, indexing and cross-referencing, comparison shopping, measuring in standard and metric measures, computing interest, and understanding such things as rental agreements requiring different kinds of deposits.

Probably no area of mathematics performance causes students more difficulty than verbal problem solving. Although all the causes of poor problem-solving ability are not known, they almost certainly include the following:

1. *Lack of practice.* Some teachers do not fully recognize the complexity of problem solving and fail to teach it in a systematic way. Considerable time must be allotted for the successful development of problem-solving skills.

2. *Inadequate development of underlying capabilities.* Task and analysis and research have indicated that the following are related to ability to solve mathematical problems:

   a. *Ability to perform required computations.* An understanding of the four fundamental operations (addition, subtraction, multiplication, division) is vital for problem solving.

Table 6–10. Suggested Steps in Verbal Problem Solving

	Problem A	*Problem B*
	Mary has 3 apples. Betty has 2 oranges. Peter has 4 apples. How many pieces of fruit do the girls have?	Bill has 7 quarters, 3 dimes, and 4 pennies. How much money will he have left if he spends 45 cents for candy?
A. Preview: read the problem		
1. Identify unknown words	None	None
2. Identify words with unusual usages	None	None
3. Identify any "cue" words, e.g., "total," "in all," "how many were left"	None	"How much . . . have left"
B. Re-reading: information processing		
1. Identify what is given		
a. Is renaming required?		
i. unit conversion	No	Quarters and dimes to cents
ii. categorization (superordinate, subordinate categories)	Apples and oranges to fruit	No
b. Is sufficient information given?	Yes	Yes
c. Is irrelevant or distracting information given?	"Peter has 4 apples."	
2. Identify what is asked for; formulate hypothesis		
a. What process is required? (comparing, combining, etc.)	Combining	Converting, combining, separating
b. What unit or category is required? (minutes, inches, apples, dollars, etc.)	Fruit	Dollars and cents
C. Refine hypothesis: operations analysis		
Decide what operations need to be performed; possible strategies:	Combining: addition	Combining: addition, then separation: subtraction
1. Substitute easier numbers in the problem	Not applicable	Bill has (10 cents). How much money will he have left if he spends 5 cents for candy? Solution pattern: subtract money spent from original amount of money, or original money − money spent = *required answer.* Now substitute numbers from Problem B.
2. Use manipulative objects, number line, or doodles drawn on paper to help "visualize" the problem.		

Table 6–10 *Continued*

	Problem A	Problem B
	Mary has 3 apples. Betty has 2 oranges. Peter has 4 apples. How many pieces of fruit do the girls have?	Bill has 7 quarters, 3 dimes, and 4 pennies. How much money will he have left if he spends 45 cents for candy?
D. Write the mathematical sentences	$3 + 2 = $ *required answer*	$7 \times .25 = a$ $3 \times .10 = b$ $4 \times .01 = c$ $a + b + c = d$ $d - .45 = $ *required answer*
E. Perform the operation	$3 + 2 = 5$	$7 \times .25 = 1.75$ $3 \times .10 = .30$ $4 \times .01 = .04$ $1.75 + .30 + .04 = 2.09$ $2.09 - .45 = 1.64$
F. Check the answer 1. Recheck reason and computation	Repeat steps A–E	Repeat steps A–E
2. Estimate the answer and compare estimate to obtained answer	Will vary	Will vary
G. State the result in terms of E and B.2.b (above)	The girls now have 5 pieces of fruit.	Bill will have $1.64 left.

Source: Adapted from K. Kramer, *The Teaching of Elementary School Mathematics* (Boston: Allyn and Bacon, 1970); J. F. Cawley, *Learning Disabilities in Mathematics: A Curriculum Design for Upper Grades* (unpublished manuscript, University of Connecticut, Storrs, Conn., 1976); and from author's experience.

b. *Ability to read with understanding.* It is apparent that students with reading problems are at a disadvantage in mathematics. Such students will have difficulty reading and understanding directions and explanations in the mathematics book. They will have particular trouble with story problems, even if they know the required computations and procedures. Reading mathematical problems is further complicated by the fact that many words have a different meaning in mathematical context than in everyday life, for example, "set," "order," "power," or "root."

c. *Ability to estimate answers.* Checking the "reasonableness" of an obtained answer requires the ability to estimate. Poor problem solvers tend not to be proficient in the skill of estimating.

d. *Acquisition of prerequisite concepts and cognitive structures.* There is reason to believe that the capacities described in the section on "Readiness" are necessary for children to solve mathematical problems. For example, Steffe (1968) reported that ability to conserve was related to problem-solving performance.

e. *Ability to organize required problem-solving steps in sequence.* Although the evidence is mixed as to the necessity for teaching specific problem-solving steps to most children, we advocate the use of such procedures for children who are having inordinate difficulty. The problem-solving procedure followed is outlined in Table 6–10.

How does a teacher find appropriate verbal problems for students who have difficulty with mathematics? Some children have reading problems; some have computational difficulties; others are unable to deal with extraneous information or are unable to discern whether they have sufficient information to solve a given problem. Cawley et al. (1979) have suggested that teachers develop a matrix that incorporates those dimensions of problem solving that seem to be problematic for the students in question. For example, if the teacher has students who have poor reading ability and variable computational skills, a matrix such as Figure 6–9 can be constructed, with separate matrices for problems in addition, subtraction, and so on.

Figure 6–9. Sample Problem-Solving Matrix

Level of Computational Difficulty	←————————————Reading Level————————————→			
	2nd Grade	3rd Grade	4th Grade	5th Grade
1 digit	A	B	C	D
2 digit No regrouping	E	F	G	H
2 digit Regrouping	I	J	K	L
etc.	M	N	O	P

A student who has a second-grade reading level but computational mastery with two-digit numbers (no regrouping) would be given problems from cell E. If the student's reading level improved, but computational skills stayed constant, verbal problems at a higher reading level but constant comprehension level (cells F, G, H) would be given to the student. If the student's computational level improved, but reading level did not, problems written for cells I and M would be given to the student. Use of a matrix such as this one permits teachers to make verbal problems individualized and relevant to the needs of specific children.

chapter 7

Evaluating and Managing Classroom Behavior

by Linda Brown

Teachers are expected to manage most of the behavior problems that arise in their classrooms. Of these problems, aggressive behaviors, such as fighting, stealing, or destroying property, are the most apparent. They are obviously harmful to the children involved, and they certainly disrupt the ongoing educational program. Passive behaviors, such as withdrawing, refusing to begin or complete work, or crying, are less obvious; but they, too, prevent the affected child from participating fully in the academic and social activities of the classroom. Dealing with both passive and aggressive behaviors consumes a great deal of the teacher's time and attention. Time is also devoted to managing numerous less serious but not necessarily less aggravating problems, such as students' throwing spitwads, swearing, poking classmates, or running noisily through the corridors. We are confident that teachers can evaluate and manage the vast majority of these problems.

This chapter presents a variety of strategies that teachers can use to handle the problem behaviors, large and small, that occur every day in their classrooms. The assessment techniques described in the first section emphasize an ecological model that encourages teachers to approach a problem behavior directly and to pay special attention to situational and environmental influences that may contribute to the difficulty or aggravate it. The eclectic selection of management techniques presented in the second section will help the teacher manage or change problematic behavior patterns observed in the class or alter ecological variables determined to be important aspects of such behaviors.

ASSESSING PROBLEM BEHAVIORS

The evaluation of school-based problems is a responsibility that usually is shared by classroom teachers and school psychology personnel. In some instances such evaluations are the sole responsibility of teachers, especially during the initial stages. The assessment unit of this chapter has been designed to assist classroom teachers in the evaluation process. In the first part of this section, we describe and present a rationale for ecological assessment, a model that we believe is well suited to behavioral evaluations. In the second part, we describe eight specific assessment strategies for teachers to use in measuring problem behaviors.

An Ecological Framework for Assessing Problem Behaviors

Teachers often observe behaviors that interfere with a student's school learning or that are symptomatic of emotional distress. For example, Jim cries every morning while on the school bus, unusual behavior for a fourth-grade student; Mary cuts high school English repeatedly but attends her other classes regularly; Willie is given to spitting on other people and pulling out patches of his hair; Nellie is friendless, is frequently involved in fighting and teasing episodes, and is verbally abusive to her classmates; Sarah constantly talks out in class and almost never is in her seat; and David is abnormally reticent and withdrawn.

In any instances in which a student is suspected of being emotionally or behaviorally disordered or of exhibiting behavioral problems related to a learning difficulty, school personnel will need considerable information about the problem before they can make placement, diagnostic, or educational decisions. When the situation is thought to be serious, the teacher will want to prepare a written description detailing the precise behaviors that are of concern and the situations in which these behaviors occur. The teacher will need to document through objective means the presence and severity of the difficulty and to probe the areas of perceived difficulty fully and systematically. Such documentation may be necessary to qualify a youngster for special services, to help the teacher set priorities for those behaviors requiring immediate attention, or to demonstrate that behavioral change has occurred as a result of treatment.

It is important that this information be gathered within an ecological frame of reference. Ecological assessment allows an examiner to evaluate a student's status in the various ecologies or environments in which the student functions. This type of evaluation is rapidly gaining popularity in the public schools, and many states now require that students identified as emotionally disturbed be evaluated in an ecological manner.

We advocate ecological assessment because it avoids at least two of the problems inherent in more traditional evaluations. First, ecological assessment obviously provides a much broader and more natural picture of the target child than do conventional evaluations that typically remove the child from the classroom and that are conducted in an isolated, sterile environment such as a testing room or the school psychologist's office. Ecological assessment also differs radically in its assumptions about the nature of behavioral difficulties. Whereas traditional evaluations assume that the child is or has the problem, ecological assessment assumes that many factors other than student-centered ones may cause or aggravate behavioral problems.

No behavior occurs in a vacuum. It is possible that a so-called problem behavior is, in fact, "normal," but that a particular perception of that behavior is deviant. For instance, a teacher who is unfamiliar with six-year-olds may perceive normally busy first-graders as hyperactive and make referrals on that basis. We know that teachers' evaluations of behavior can affect their subsequent academic evaluations and that estimates of academic competence can affect behavioral evaluations (L. Brown & Sherbenou, 1981). Students of average or above-average academic ability seem to be given greater behavioral latitude than their less academically competent peers. It also is possible for elements of an environment to exacerbate problem behaviors. A classic example is provided by the student (or teacher!) who becomes restless and troublesome in a hot, noisy classroom. It should be apparent that the source of the problem may lie within the environment and not within the child. Only through ecological assessment can any of these suppositions be validated. "Ecological assessment can be very versatile; it can permit the exploration of positive, as well as negative, elements of the classroom or school" (Wallace & Larsen, 1978, p. 141).

Several environments may be tapped during ecological assessment. Among these are the school, the home, and the community, as well as the student's interpersonal environment and his or her internal ecology. Within the school setting, which is the environment we are most concerned with in this chapter, a teacher can assume that students change ecologies each time they change classes, teachers, or academic content or format within the same classroom. An example of the latter might be moving from a supervised reading group to an art interest center or even to independent reading activities. Presumably the requirements for success vary in each of these ecologies. One environment may require a great deal of verbalization (a language-experience reading group) whereas another requires silence (the library); one may require independence and creativity (an exploratory interest center) whereas another requires strict conformity and adherence to established rules and regulations (a chemistry lab or woodworking shop). It would not be unusual for a student to function in all of these very different environments during a typical school day.

Ecologies also may be discerned on the basis of the perceptions being recorded. The activities taking place in a reading group no doubt look very different through the teacher's eyes than through the students' eyes. Most teachers

Table 7–1. Relationship of BRP Components to Type of Respondent and Ecology

BRP Component	Respondent				Ecology		
	Student	Teacher(s)	Parent(s)	Peers	Home	School	Social-life
Student Rating Scale: Home	X				X		
Student Rating Scale: School	X					X	
Student Rating Scale: Peer	X						X
Teacher Rating Scale		X				X	
Parent Rating Scale			X		X		
Sociogram				X			X

Source: Reprinted with permission of the authors and publisher of L. L. Brown and D. D. Hammill, *The Behavior Rating Profile* (Austin, TX: Pro-Ed, 1983).

involved in ecological assessment will want to seek the perceptions of the target student and that student's teacher(s), parent(s), and peers. If the student in question is participating in a work-study program, the teacher may want to gather information from supervisors or co-workers in that environment.

In the Behavior Rating Profile (BRP), an ecological assessment battery which will be described in detail later, L. Brown and Hammill (1983) propose a two-dimensional model that includes a variety of perceptions that are evaluated within several environments or ecologies. Using this model, which is presented graphically in Table 7–1, the teacher would decide which ecologies should be assessed and whose perceptions should be sought. Data then would be gathered from these sources and assembled into an ecological profile.

Laten and Katz (1975) have defined the five phases in conducting an ecological assessment.

1. *Assimilating referral data.* The first phase involves gathering broad intake data from each of the ecologies in which the student functions. Of particular interest at this time is the degree of success that the student enjoys in each ecology.

2. *Identifying ecological expectations.* The expectations or requirements that each ecology demands of the student are identified in the second phase. What level of academic proficiency is expected? What social behaviors are required? Are there any special demands? In general, the teacher attempts to learn what things the student must do in each ecology in order to succeed and meet the requirements.

3. *Organizing behavioral descriptions.* What does the student do? How does he or she behave? What skills does he or she possess and use? Par-

ticular attention is given to determining the student's behaviors with regard to the expectations that were identified in the preceding phase. Descriptions of the professional skills and support services that each ecology can provide are included.

4. *Summarizing data.*
5. *Establishing goals.* Goals are established for the student and for the professionals within each ecology. Reasonable goals for improvement are defined for the student, and guidelines for the material and personnel support that will be provided in each category are established.

In each of these phases, data are gathered from all relevant ecologies. The instances in which the student experiences success are scrutinized as carefully as those in which the pupil is experiencing difficulty. Interested readers are referred to Laten and Katz (1975); to Wiederholt, Hammill, and Brown (1983), and to Wallace and Larsen (1978) for more detailed descriptions of the ecological assessment process.

Eight General Techniques for Assessing Problem Behaviors

Eight general techniques that classroom teachers can use to evaluate problem behaviors are described in this section. These include (1) direct observation, (2) behavioral checklists and inventories, (3) Q-sorts, (4) interviews, (5) analysis of the physical environment, (6) examination of teacher-pupil interaction in the classroom, (7) peer-nominating techniques, and (8) standardized tests of personality. By taking care to note the people from whom information is gathered and the environments that they seem to evaluate, teachers can tailor ecological assessment plans to satisfy their particular assessment needs.

Direct Observation

The most convenient method for measuring problem behavior is to observe it directly in the classroom. Cartwright and Cartwright (1974) provide an excellent discussion of classroom observation skills; interested readers are encouraged to consult their text. R. V. Hall (1983) presents three direct observation techniques that will be described here. They are (1) automatic recording, (2) analysis of permanent products, and (3) observational recording.

Automatic Recording. Automatic recording involves the measurement of behavior by machines. For instance, in biofeedback such behaviors as pulse, heart rate, blood pressure, and galvanic skin response are measured by sensitive mechanical devices. In laboratories where animal research is conducted, such machines are used frequently to record the movements or responses of the laboratory animals. These machines are costly to purchase and to repair, and they are rigid in their functioning, usually incapable of being adapted to measure more than a single behavior or set of behaviors. For these reasons, automatic recording devices are rarely used in school settings. They are mentioned here only to familiarize teachers with their existence.

Analysis of Permanent Products.   The product-analysis technique is infinitely more useful to teachers. In using this approach, the teacher evaluates the product of a behavior rather than the behavior itself. For example, a student's spelling paper is the "permanent product" of taking a spelling test. The number of correctly spelled words (or correctly worked algebra problems, complete sentences, etc.) can be counted and verified easily. Although it is often used by teachers to measure pupil status or progress in academics, the technique is seldom employed to assess affective behaviors because they do not usually have permanent products associated with them.

Observational Recording.   Observational recording of classroom behavior problems can be accomplished in one of six ways: (1) maintaining anecdotal records, (2) event recording, (3) duration recording, (4) interval recording, (5) time sampling, or (6) planned activity check. Data obtained from these observational techniques should be recorded in a systematic way so that they can be interpreted quickly and easily. Anecdotal records, of course, must be presented in narrative form. The most common way of recording data gathered through the other five techniques is by graphing, as in Figure 7–1. The teacher can easily glance at a graph to note trends or to see when the rate or duration of a behavior begins to increase or decrease.

1. *Anecdotal records* provide an account of everything that is done to, with, for, by, or around the target student. Obviously, no individual teacher can take the time to gather all the anecdotal data that are required for a comprehensive record. Occasionally, other personnel such as trained volunteers, aides, or student teachers can be assigned some responsibility for gathering these data. Ideally, a videotape recording of the student's entire school day should be available for analysis, but, of course, this is not practical in most situations. A coding system or some form of shorthand may be devised to permit the observer to record as much information as possible in a short amount of time and space. The shorthand is transcribed later into narrative form that can be understood by individuals who are unfamiliar with the coding system. A coded entry in an anecdotal record might look like this: "1025—sci ctr—X pokes SL—SL cries, X pokes more—M, SR, PR also in ctr—M calls △, others tell X to quit—△ comes to ctr." Translated, this means that at 10:25 in the science interest center, the target child (X) poked at Susan Lily (SL) until

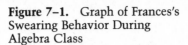

Figure 7–1. Graph of Frances's Swearing Behavior During Algebra Class

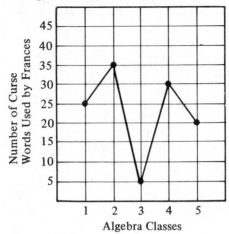

she cried, after which he continued poking her. The other children in the science center (M, SR, and PR) told the target child to quit poking, and M called the teacher (△), who then came to the science center. Anecdotal records are especially useful when a teacher is unable to identify the pattern of the student's problem. By analyzing a continuous recording of the student's behavior over a period of time, the teacher may learn that the behavior occurs only in certain situations or at certain time periods in the day or that every occurrence of the problem behavior is followed by a positive reward, perhaps by increased teacher attention and interest. In most instances, however, the classroom teacher can identify these variables using continuous recording, a more time-efficient measurement device.

2. *Event recording* is a frequently used observational recording technique. It is simply a record of the number of times a defined behavior occurs, or a behavioral frequency count. Using this technique, a teacher learns that Frances used 27 curse words during the 30-minute algebra class on Monday, 33 on Tuesday, 8 on Wednesday, 28 on Thursday, and 19 on Friday. These data are recorded in the form of a conventional graph in Figure 7–1.

3. *Duration recording* is used when a teacher is more concerned with how long a behavior lasts than with the frequency of occurrence. A record of the duration of a child's temper tantrum, for instance, may occasionally

be more important than a record of the number of outbursts occurring during a given time period. Consider the case of Linda, who has difficulty attending to the task at hand. She exhibited only one instance of offtask behavior during the independent work period; regrettably, that one instance lasted for twenty minutes.

4. *Interval recording* combines the two previously described techniques, giving the teacher a measure of both the frequency and the duration of a behavior. An observation period is divided into equal, usually short, time periods. For instance, the 5 minutes after recess may be divided into thirty 10-second intervals. The teacher observes continuously during the 5-minute session and notes whether or not the defined behavior occurs during each of the shorter intervals. For instance, if Pat talked without permission during twenty-five of the thirty 10-second intervals, the results would be reported as 83 percent of the time spent talking out. The record of Pat's talking (T) would probably look something like the following:

T 1	T 2	T 3	T 4	T 5	T 6
T 7	T 8	T 9	T 10	11	12
13	T 14	T 15	T 16	T 17	T 18
T 19	T 20	T 21	T 22	T 23	T 24
T 25	T 26	T 27	T 28	29	30

The duration of the talking can be calculated easily: Pat was talking during twenty-five 10-second intervals, or for 4 minutes and 10 seconds. Event data also can be extracted: Pat talked out twice, from the first through the tenth 10-second interval and from the fourteenth through the twenty-eighth interval. Data for a period of days could be graphed in any of the three ways shown in Figure 7–2.

5. *Time sampling* is very similar to interval recording, but it is more useful because it does not require the teacher to observe continuously. The observation period again is divided into equal, but usually longer, time periods. For instance, Mr. Nixon, the world history teacher, may divide his 50-minute class period into five 10-minute intervals. He then conducts a time sampling of Henry's behavior while Henry is supposed to be answering the questions at the end of Chapter 14 in the world history text-

Figure 7–2. Methods of Graphing Data

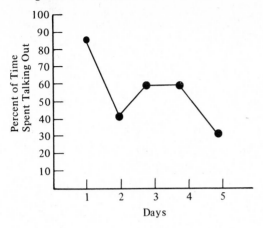

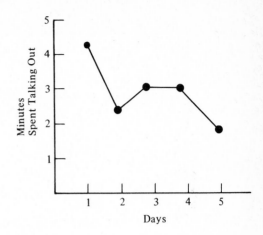

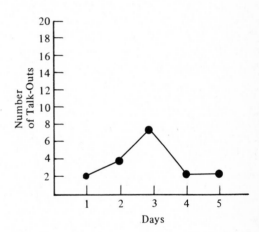

book. At the end of (not throughout) each 10-minute interval, Mr. Nixon observes to see if Henry is answering the questions. If Henry were working (W) four of the five times that Mr. Nixon observed him, he would be recorded as working 80 percent of the time. Mr. Nixon's time sampling record might look like the following:

W	W	W	W	

6. *Planned activity check,* sometimes called "placheck," is used to measure the behaviors of groups of children. Teachers using this technique would be interested in the percentage of students engaged in a defined behavior. Perhaps a teacher would want to do a placheck of the children working on an assignment in an interest center. The teacher first would count the number of students working and then would count the number of students actually in the interest center. If ten students were in the center and only four were engaged in the assignment, the placheck record would be 40 percent. Placheck records often are taken on a time sampling basis. For example, Mr. Nixon, the world history teacher, might do placheck every 10 minutes during his fifty-minute class period. If twenty-five students were in the class and twenty-four were working at the first check, twenty at the second check, twenty-five at the third and fourth checks, and five at the final check, the placheck records would be 96, 80, 100, 100, and 20 percent, respectively. Mr. Nixon might conclude that studying behavior dropped off during the final 10 minutes of his class, particularly if this pattern continued over a period of time. He might adjust his planning to make better use of the final 10 minutes.

Behavioral Checklists and Inventories

On some occasions, the teacher may find it helpful to assess problem behaviors by using checklists and inventories. Checklist items typically relate to a variety of both normal and problem behaviors. They do not concentrate solely on behaviors that are disturbing and disruptive. In addition, checklists are intended for use with several children, not for a single student, and they derive some objectivity from this characteristic. Teachers may find checklists particularly useful in identifying students who are passive or withdrawn or engage in behaviors that might go unnoticed in a busy classroom. Many teachers use checklists to narrow their target behaviors or to find precise descriptions of target behaviors. Some published checklists also give teachers guidelines for determining the seriousness or severity of particular behavior problems. In this section we will describe some published checklists and inventories and present criteria for the development of informal behavioral checklists.

Published Checklists. A few published checklists are norm referenced and yield standardized results. Most provide only rough criteria for interpretation and do not have adequate reliability or demonstrated validity (Spivak & Swift, 1973). Care should be taken to limit the use of such instruments to general observation and assessment where they can be of some value despite these shortcomings. We will describe three specific batteries of scales in detail: the Behavior Rating Profile (L. Brown and Hammill, 1983), the Test of Early Socio-emotional Development (Hresko & Brown, 1984), and the Behavior Evaluation

Scale (McCarney, Leigh, & Cornbleet, 1983). Other behavioral checklists and inventories will be described briefly, and their age/grade ranges, reliability, and ecological characteristics will be summarized. Some of these instruments, and others not mentioned here, are reviewed in Buros's (1978) *Eighth Mental Measurements Yearbook.* Teachers are encouraged to consult Buros before selecting a published checklist or inventory. Borich and Madden (1977) also describe and evaluate hundreds of published and unpublished measures that teachers may find helpful. They include instruments in nine classifications: about the teacher from the teacher, from the pupil, and from an observer; about the pupil from the teacher, from the pupil, and from an observer; and about the classroom from the teacher, from the pupil, and from an observer.

Behavior Rating Profile (BRP).   The BRP is an ecological assessment battery that includes five norm-referenced scales and a sociogram. The six components of the BRP are independent and individually normed measures that can be used separately or in conjunction with the other components.

The BRP was standardized on a large, national population. It is appropriate for use with students ages six to eighteen years and with their parents and teachers. The BRP has high internal consistency reliability with both normal and deviant populations, and test-retest reliability is acceptable. Reliability coefficients consistently exceed .80. Concurrent validity of the instrument was established by research studies. In a study of the BRP's diagnostic validity, the six components accurately discriminated among groups of emotionally disturbed, learning disabled, and normal children. The constructs of the BRP have been empirically validated, and content validity has been established.

The BRP examines the home, school, and interpersonal environments of a target student from the perspectives of that student and his or her parents, teachers, and peers. (Table 7–1 depicted the relationship of the various BRP components to type of respondent and ecology.) Because of its unique construction, the BRP permits a user to identify children suspected of being emotionally disturbed or behaviorally disordered, to document the degree of perceived deviance, to identify settings in which problem behaviors seem to be most prominent, and to identify individuals who have varying perceptions of a student's behavior.

There are three Student Rating Scales on the BRP—Home, School, and Peer—each containing twenty items. The items have been combined into a single sixty-item response sheet. Students completing these scales are asked to classify each item as True or False.

Items on the Student Rating Scale (Home) describe behaviors or situations that are found primarily at home. Examples of these items include:

1. My parents "bug" me a lot.
33. I have lots of nightmares and bad dreams.
47. I often break rules set by my parents.

Items on the Student Rating Scale (School) relate to the school and classroom environment. Examples of these items include:

14. I sometimes stammer or stutter when the teacher calls on me.
29. My teachers give me work that I cannot do.
59. The things I learn in school are not as important or helpful as the things I learn outside of school.

Items on the Student Rating Scale (Peer) describe behaviors involving interpersonal relationships or skills. Examples of these items include:

6. Some of my friends think it is fun to cheat, skip school, etc.
10. Other kids don't seem to like me very much.
31. I seem to get into a lot of fights.

The Teacher Rating Scale assesses the perceptions of the student's teacher(s) concerning that student's classroom behavior. The scale contains thirty items which teachers classify into four categories: Very Much Like The Student, Like The Student, Not Much Like The Student, and Not At All Like The Student. Examples of these items include:

4. Tattles on classmates
17. Is an academic underachiever
30. Doesn't follow class rules

The Parent Rating Scale is completed by either or both of the target student's parents. Parent surrogates (foster parents, houseparents) are also appropriate respondents for this instrument. Respondents are asked to classify each of the thirty items into one of four categories: Very Much Like My Child, Like My Child, Not Much Like My Child, or Not At All Like My Child. Examples of these items include:

1. Is verbally aggressive to parents
10. Is shy; clings to parents
27. Won't share belongings willingly

The sociogram is not a checklist. It is a peer-nominating technique that has been adapted to provide peer input into the BRP. It is described here to give readers a picture of the entire BRP profile. To administer the sociogram, the teacher selects one or more pairs of questions; e.g., "Which of the girls and boys in your class would you most like to have in your class at school next year?" and "Which of the girls and boys in your class would you least like to have in your class at school next year?" Students are asked to nominate three classmates in response to each question. A unique scoring system allows the examiner to derive the same type of standard, scaled score for the sociogram as for the five BRP scales.

The examiner may administer any one or all of the BRP components. When several are administered, the resulting scaled scores can be recorded on a profile sheet. The examiner then can review the various possible relationships inherent in the profile, such as particular ecologies or respondents characterized by unusually high or low scores.

Test of Early Socioemotional Development (TOESD). TOESD is a downward extension of the BRP. Its four components may be used with children from 3-0 to 7-11 years. The TOESD includes a thirty-item Student Rating Scale, a thirty-four-item Parent Rating Scale, a thirty-six-item Teacher Rating Scale, and a Sociogram, all of which are similar to their BRP counterparts in both format and content. The scale items were constructed to tap (1) a student's personal behavior, (2) a student's behavior with peers, and (3) a student's behavior with authority figures.

TOESD was normed on a large sample of 1006 children, 1773 parents, and 1006 teachers. The normative sample was demonstrated to be nationally representative in terms of geographic location and domicile, sex, racial and ethnic groups, and socioeconomic status as indicated by parental education and occupation. Both internal consistency and test-retest coefficients associated with the TOESD components are in the .80s and .90s. Concurrent validity studies using the BRP, the Behavior Evaluation Scale, and the Classroom Behavior Scale of the Basic School Skills Inventory—Diagnostic are reported in the test manual, along with a study of the TOESD's utility in discriminating among normal, behaviorally disordered, learning disabled, and mentally retarded youngsters.

Like the BRP, the TOESD scales are normed independently and so can be administered individually or as an ecological battery. A sample TOESD profile is reproduced in Figure 7–3.

Behavior Evaluation Scale (BES). The BES is a unique behavioral checklist in that its five subscales deal with behaviors that are indicative of the five components of the federal definition of severe emotional disturbance: (1) Learning Problems, (2) Interpersonal Difficulties, (3) Inappropriate Behavior, (4) Unhappiness/Depression, and (5) Physical Symptoms/Fears. Raw scores are weighted according to the severity of the behavior and the frequency with which it is observed; standard scores are generated for each subscale and for the total test.

The BES was normed on 1018 school-aged children. The normative sample was representative of the national population in terms of sex, race, parental occupation, and geographic region and domicile. Internal consistency coefficients range from .77 to .96, and test-retest coefficients all exceed .97; unfortunately, since the effects of age were not controlled in either instance, the reported coefficients probably are somewhat inflated. The validity of the BES is supported by empirical evidence of its concurrent relationship to the BRP, of appropriate in-

Figure 7–3. TOESD Profile Sheet

TOESD

Student Rating Scale
and
Profile

Wayne P. Hresko
Linda Brown

Child _Christopher Whiting_
Parent(s) _Bobby and Pam Whiting_
Address _115 Simon Way #26A_
Teacher _Mr. Paul_
School _John Ross Elementary_
Examiner/Title _E. Wentworth / Ed. Diag._

Date tested	84	2
	year	month
Date of birth	78	6
	year	month
Child's age	5	8
	years	months

TEST CONDITIONS

	Interfering	Not Interfering
Ability to understand test format		✔
Ability to understand test content		✔
Noise level		✔
Lighting, temperature, etc.		✔
Motivation		✔
Other:		

TOESD PROFILE

TOESD Component	Raw Score	Standard Score	Percentile Rank
Student Rating Scale	18	4	2
Teacher Rating Scale #1	56	4	2
Teacher Rating Scale #2	77	8	25
Parent Rating Scale #1	47	5	4
Parent Rating Scale #2	40	3	1
Sociogram	11.5	10	50

Profile grid columns: Student Rating Scale, Teacher Rating Scale #1, Teacher Rating Scale #2, Parent Rating Scale #1, Parent Rating Scale #2, Sociogram, OTHER MEASURES OF: Behavior/Personality (BSSI), Conceptual Ability (WPPSI FS), Achievement (TERA). Standard Scores 1–20.

Plotted points (Standard Score): Sociogram = 10; Behavior/Personality (BSSI) = 7; Achievement (TERA) = 7; Conceptual Ability (WPPSI FS) = 6; Teacher Rating Scale #2 = 5; Student Rating Scale = 4; Teacher Rating Scale #1 = 4; Parent Rating Scale #1 = 4; Parent Rating Scale #2 = 3.

COMMENTS

Christopher seems to have a lot of friends despite very immature behavior. He was referred to determine readiness for 1st grade.

Additional copies of this form #0533 are available from PRO-ED, 5341 Industrial Oaks Blvd., Austin, Texas 78735

Reprinted by permission.

tercorrelations among the subscales, and of its ability to discriminate between normal and behaviorally disordered students. The BES profile and student record form are reproduced in Figure 7–4.

Other Behavior Checklists. Some other popular behavior checklists and inventories are summarized in Table 7–2. Most of these instruments are administered to the target pupil, to the referring teacher(s), or to the student's parent(s). Administering the school-related instruments to classmates of the target student and to several teachers may provide a broader picture of the problem behavior. Let's take the example of James, a student whose behavior is viewed as deviant by his fifth-grade teacher. Do his other teachers—the art teacher, the physical education instructor, the band director, the special education teacher—view him similarly or do their responses on a behavioral checklist reveal markedly different perceptions? If the latter, is this because his behavior is different in each of these settings (something that could be determined through direct observation) or is it because the teachers' requirements and expectations differ (something that could be determined through an interview)? Likewise, if James views his class as a negative experience, is this perception shared by his classmates? Do they also find the class to be negative or is his perception unique?

Similarly, the examiner may find it helpful to ask a student's parents to complete behavioral checklists on all of their children rather than just on the target child. Do the parents view their children similarly? Do mother and father express similar feelings or does each parent express different perceptions? The same axiom may be applied to inventories completed by the target student: do brothers and sisters concur with that child's perceptions of the home ecology?

We emphasize that even though investigations of this scope are consistent with the principles of ecological assessment, they should be undertaken only when the need is warranted. The process can be quite time consuming, and there is no reason to lengthen it unnecessarily. We suggest these variations as a means of stimulating the formation of alternative hypotheses regarding problem behaviors. L. Brown and Hammill (1983) warn that "a low score [on a behavioral measure] . . . should not be interpreted flatly as a sign of deviance on the part of the child" (p. 32). It is the profile or pattern of scores that is important.

Informal Behavioral Checklists. Instead of using published checklists, teachers will find that in some instances—perhaps most—an informal behavioral checklist based on a particular classroom checklist or student is most helpful. Bower and Lambert (1971) discussed teacher-made behavioral checklists and concluded that items should describe behaviors seen specifically (1) in the target student, (2) in the target student's interaction with other students in the class, and (3) in the teacher's interaction with the target student. More recently,

Figure 7–4. BES Profile

Behavior Evaluation Scale

Stephen B. McCarney, Ed.D.

James E. Leigh, Ph.D.

Jane Cornbleet, M.Ed.

STUDENT RECORD FORM

Name of Student: _____ Ethnic Origin: _____ Sex: _____

Class: _____ School: _____ Grade: _____

City: _____ State: _____ Rated by (Observer's name): _____

Date of Rating _____ _____ _____
                  (year) (month) (day)

Date of Birth _____ _____ _____
              (year) (month) (day)

Age at Rating _____ _____
              (years) (months)

Dates during which student participated in your class: From _____ To _____

Length of time spent with student: Per day _____ Per week _____

BES PROFILE

Quotients	Behavior Quotient	Standard Scores	Subscale 1 Learning Problems	Subscale 2 Interpersonal Difficulties	Subscale 3 Inappropriate Behavior	Subscale 4 Unhappiness/ Depression	Subscale 5 Physical Symptoms/Fears	Standard Scores
150	•	20	•	•	•	•	•	20
145	•	19	•	•	•	•	•	19
140	•	18	•	•	•	•	•	18
135	•	17	•	•	•	•	•	17
130	•	16	•	•	•	•	•	16
125	•	15	•	•	•	•	•	15
120	•	14	•	•	•	•	•	14
115	•	13	•	•	•	•	•	13
110	•	12	•	•	•	•	•	12
105	•	11	•	•	•	•	•	11
100	—•—	10	—•—	—•—	—•—	—•—	—•—	10
95	•	9	•	•	•	•	•	9
90	•	8	•	•	•	•	•	8
85	•	7	•	•	•	•	•	7
80	•	6	•	•	•	•	•	6
75	•	5	•	•	•	•	•	5
70	•	4	•	•	•	•	•	4
65	•	3	•	•	•	•	•	3
60	•	2	•	•	•	•	•	2
55	•	1	•	•	•	•	•	1
50	•	0	•	•	•	○	•	0

Reprinted by permission.

Table 7-2. Checklists and Inventories That Assess Aspects of School, Home, and Internal Ecologies

Ecology Measured	Tests	Age/Grade*	Intended Population	Respondent	Reliability*
School	AAMD Adaptive Behavior Scale, Public School Version (Nihira, Foster, Shellhaas, & Leland, 1975)	7–13 yrs.	Mentally retarded and emotionally maladjusted	Teacher	Interscorer, $\bar{X}$ = .67
School	Barclay Classroom Climate Inventory (Barclay, 1971)	Grades 3–6	Normal	Student and teacher	Split-Half, .58–.90 Test-Retest, .34–.77
School	Devereux Adolescent Behavior Rating Scale (Spivak, Spotts, & Haimes, 1967)	13–18 yrs.	Normal and emotionally disturbed	Teacher	Interscorer, Median = .82
School	Devereux Elementary School Behavior Rating Scale (Spivak & Swift, 1967)	Grades K–6	Normal	Teacher	Test-Retest, Median = .87
School	Learning Environment Inventory (Anderson, 1973)	Grades 7–12	Normal	Student	Alpha Coefficients, .54–.85 Test-Retest, .43–.73
School	Pupil Behavior Rating Scale (Lambert, Hartsbough, & Bower, 1979)	Grades K–7	Normal	Teacher, student, and peers	None Reported
School	Behavior Problem Checklist (Quay & Peterson, 1979)	Grades 1–6	Normal and emotionally disturbed	Teacher	None Reported

(continued)

241

Table 7-2 *Continued*

Ecology Measured	Tests	Age/Grade*	Intended Population	Respondent	Reliability*
School	Walker Problem Behavior Identification Checklist (Walker, 1970)	Grades 4–6	Normal and emotionally disturbed	Teacher	Split-Half, .98
Home	Devereux Child Behavior Rating Scale (Spivak & Spotts, 1966)	8–12 yrs.	Emotionally disturbed and emotionally retarded	Person with "intimate living arrangement"	Test-Retest, .83
Home	Family Relations Test (Bene & Anthony, 1977)	Preschool–grade 6	Normal and emotionally disturbed	Student	Split-Half, .68–.90 Internal Consistency, $\underline{X} = .83$
Home	Vineland Adaptive Behavior Scales (Sparrow, Balla, & Cicchetti, 1984)	Birth–18-11	Normal and mentally retarded	Parent, Teacher	Test-Retest, $\underline{.97}$ Interscorer, $\overline{X} = .96$
Internal (Self-Concept)	Animal Crackers (D. C. Adkins & Balliff, 1973)	Preschool–grade 1	Normal	Student	Kuder-Richardson, .90
Internal (Self-Concept)	Coopersmith Self-Esteem Inventory (Coopersmith, 1968)	8–10 yrs.	Normal	Student	Test-Retest, .78–.88
Internal (Self-Concept)	Piers-Harris Children's Self-Concept Scale (Piers and Harris, 1969)	Grades 3–12	Normal	Student	Kuder-Richardson, .78–.93 Test-Retest, .72

242

Wiederholt, Hammill, and Brown (1983) have suggested that these same three categories of behavior should be sampled by checklist items. These authors go on to recommend that a teacher-made checklist include no more than thirty items. They provide a sample teacher-made checklist, which is reproduced in Figure 7–5.

Q-Sorts

Q-sorting is uniquely suited to ecological assessment because it is a technique that can be used by teachers to compare two interpretations of a single set of behaviors. For example, a teacher might describe behaviors associated with reading (e.g., reads well, doesn't like to read, reads at home) or even social attributes (e.g., dates a lot, can't dance, has friends). The teacher then would compare how a child or teenager viewed the various items from both realistic and idealistic points of view. Commercial Q-sorts are available, or teachers can easily devise Q-sorts of their own to match the classroom situations and behaviors of particular interest to them. Directions for constructing a Q-sort and suggestions for its use will be presented in this section.

The first step in using the Q-sort technique is to devise a list of descriptor statements such as the following:

Parent Q-Sort Items[1]
1. Does assigned chores.
2. Does homework on time.
3. Goes to bed without problems.
4. Comes home when he should.
5. Argues with parents.
6. Has friends.
7. Likes school.
8. Cries or sulks when he doesn't get his own way.
9. Throws temper tantrums.
10. Likes to watch TV.
11. Likes to read.
12. Plays alone.
13. Eats between meals.
14. Is overweight.

[1]Reprinted with permission of the author and publisher of R. Kroth, The behavioral Q-sort as a diagnostic tool, *Academic Therapy*, 8 (1973), 327 (Academic Therapy Publications, San Rafael, California).

Figure 7–5. Teacher-Made Checklist for Measuring Problems in Social and Emotional Development

---

Teacher Checklist: This measure was designed to be used by teachers in any classroom to make them more aware of their students' behavior. This list might help identify behavior that otherwise might be overlooked or misunderstood. From here the teacher might want to take frequency counts of identified behavior, or in some other way further analyze the situation.

	Frequently	*Not Frequently*

1. Self-Image
   A. Makes I can't statements
   B. Reacts negatively to correction
   C. Gets frustrated easily
   D. Makes self-critical statements
   E. Integrity:
      Cheats
      tattles
      steals
      destroys property
   F. Makes excessive physical complaints
   G. Takes responsibility for actions
   H. Reacts appropriately to praise

2. Social Interaction
   A. Seeks attention by acting immaturely:
      thumbsucking, babytalking, etc.
   B. Interacts negatively
   C. Fails to interact
   D. Initiates positive interaction
   E. Initiates negative interaction
   F. Reacts with anger, verbally
   G. Reacts with anger, physically

3. Adult/Teacher Relationships
   A. Seeks attention by acting immaturely
   B. Excessively demands attention
   C. Reacts appropriately to teacher requests
   D. Inappropriately reacts to authority figures

4. School-Related Activities
   A. Attends to task
   B. Exhibits offtask behavior
   C. Interferes with the other students' learning
   D. Shows flexibility to routine changes

Date the checklist and complete one for each child. Once the checklist has been completed and reviewed a narrative report can be written with explanations and suggestions for the future. For the list to be effective, the teacher must use the results to actually make changes in the classroom.

Source: Developed by the following teachers and used with their permission: Lee Person, Becky Beck Browning, Margaret Hughes Hiatt, and Margaret Morey-Brown. Reprinted with permission of the authors and publisher of J. L. Wiederholt, D. D. Hammill, and V. L. Brown, *The Resource Teacher* (Austin, Tex.: Pro-Ed, 1983).

15. Is destructive of property.
16. Gets ready for school on time.
17. Makes own decisions.
18. Chooses own clothes.
19. Is unhealthy.
20. Fights with brothers and sisters.
21. Has a messy room.
22. Responds to rewards.
23. Does acceptable schoolwork.
24. Is a restless sleeper.
25. Stretches the truth.

The items can be drawn from any setting deemed to be important or of interest: home, school, nonacademic classroom activities, interpersonal relationships, and so on. A different set of descriptions should be developed for each ecology. Although most Q-sorts have twenty-five or thirty-six items, any number of descriptor statements may be included as long as the items can be sorted into a perfect pyramid, as in Figure 7–6. The descriptor statements are written on small cards, one item per card, to be read to or by the students who are responding.

After reading through the items, students sort them onto a formboard such as the one in Figure 7–6. All the squares on the pyramidlike form must be used: none may be left blank and none may be used twice, although students may rearrange the items until they are satisfied with their responses. Students sort the items twice. On the first sort they place the items into categories that reflect how they believe they really are; this is called the *real sort.* The second time, the students sort the items into the categories as they wish they were; this is called the *ideal sort.*

Students' responses are recorded on the form shown in Figure 7–7, and a simple correlation is calculated between the two sorts. For example, if a student sorted item 1 as "A Little Like Me" on the real sort, a 4 would be recorded in the first column (S-1). If the student rated the same item as "Unlike Me" on the ideal sort, a 7 would be recorded in the second column (S-2). The difference between the sorts is 3, and this value is recorded in the D column. The difference squared (D^2) is 9. The D^2 column is summed, and the total (ΣD^2) is substituted into the formula beside the chart. This formula will yield a correlation coefficient; it will not be larger than $+1.00$ or smaller than -1.00. The further the correlation is from $r = .00$, the greater the agreement between the real and ideal sorts.

In most instances, the teacher will be less interested in the correlation between the two sorts than in those individual items that have large discrepancies between them. Items with great discrepancies between the sorts probably de-

Figure 7-6. Q-Sort Formboard

1	2	3	4	5	6	7	8	9
Most Like Me (or Most Like My Child)	Very Much Like Me (or Very Much Like My Child)	Like Me (or Like My Child)	A Little Like Me (or A Little Like My Child)	Undecided	A Little Unlike Me (or a Little Unlike My Child)	Unlike Me (or Unlike My Child)	Very Much Unlike Me (or Very Much Unlike My Child)	Most Unlike Me (or Most Unlike My Child)

Source: Reprinted with permission of the author and publisher of R. Kroth, The behavioral Q-sort as a diagnostic tool, *Academic Therapy,* 8 (1973), 327 (Academic Therapy Publications, San Rafael, California).

Figure 7–7. Q-Sort Record Form

Name of Subject _____ Sex _____ Date Tested _____

Address _____ Phone _____ Date of Birth _____

School _____ Teacher _____ Grade _____ Age _____

Name of Examinee _____ Relationship to Child _____

Card No.	Column S-1	Column S-2	D	D^2
1				
2				
3				
4				
5				
6				
7				
8				
9				
10				
11				
12				
13				
14				
15				
16				
17				
18				
19				
20				
21				
22				
23				
24				
25				
			$\Sigma =$	

$$n = 1 - \frac{\Sigma D^2}{200}$$

Source: Reprinted with permission of the author and publisher of R. Kroth, The behavioral Q-sort as a diagnostic tool, *Academic Therapy,* 1973, 8, 327 (Academic Therapy Publications, San Rafael, California).

scribe target behaviors for intervention. If the student rates an item such as "Likes to read" as "Like Me" on the ideal sort but as "Very Unlike Me" on the real sort, the teacher may have identified an area in which the student is ready to begin work for improvement.

Kroth (1973a) has an excellent article on the uses of the behavioral Q-sort, and interested teachers are advised to read it. He suggests that Q-sorts could be administered to children's parents and teachers, with the real sort representing the way they believe their children behave and the ideal sort representing the way they wished their children would behave. This use of the technique would permit analysis of various combinations of Q-sort responses: e.g., the child's ideal sort compared with the parent's ideal sort, the regular classroom teacher's real sort compared with the resource teacher's real sort, the child's real sort compared with the teacher's real sort, and so on. Again, particular discrepancies may be more important than the actual correlation between the sorts. If the child's regular class teacher rates "Likes to read" as "A Little Unlike My Child" and the special education teacher rates this same item as "Like My Child," a source of conflict *may* have been identified.

Q-sort items can be read to nonreaders, although this approach has not been particularly successful. Children who cannot read the items have great difficulty in manipulating the cards, especially when only a few slots are left on the formboard and some switching is necessary. Students who are easily frustrated also have difficulty with the Q-sort because they are forced to limit each category to a specific number of items. Most students, however, enjoy the activity and can complete it independently after brief instructions have been given.

Target Behavior (Kroth, 1973b) is a commercially packaged Q-sort that includes a formboard, item cards, record sheets, and instructions for administration and interpretation. In other variations of the Q-technique, Riley (1971) devised a pictorial Q-sort using animal Lotto cards; Baumrind (1971) used a similar method for the Preschool Behavior Q-Sort. By using devices that already are prepared, teachers can avoid the tedious task of building their own instruments, but they do lose the specificity of having items that relate to a particular student or classroom situation.

Interviews

Interviewing is a versatile and useful technique in ecological assessment. It can be used to gather a great deal of information from students, parents, and other teachers. Interviews are certainly subjective in nature, and they are quite informal. Despite the informality, however, specific goals should be established before an interview is scheduled, and the interviewer should consider several possible approaches to conducting the interview.

In general, interviewers will want to begin by stating the purpose of the interview, establishing the time parameters of the conversation, and briefly introducing themselves, describing their role or position in the school. McCallon and McCray (1975) provide the following tips on conducting an interview:

1. Open the interview by asking factual, nonthreatening questions.
2. Locate major pieces of information through unstructured lead questions.
3. Make use of guide questions.
4. Make an effort to locate fruitful areas of conversation.
5. Use probes to obtain specific information.
6. Pursue fruitful areas once they are found.
7. Clarify unclear responses through further questioning.
8. Follow up areas where the respondent shows emotional involvement.
9. Redirect the interview to different topics when useful data are not emerging.
10. Be alert to sensitive subjects and handle them diplomatically.
11. Answer any direct questions posed by the respondent.
12. Complete the interview before the respondent becomes tired or bored.
13. Evaluate the general climate of the interview before deciding whether to take notes or otherwise record the interview.

It is possible to gather several types of information during an interview. If the current status of the target student is not known—age, grade, general background, and health information—it should be established early in the interview. The student's educational situation may be explored: academic and social competence, relationships with peers or school personnel, any evaluation data that may be available from school or private sources, and unique perceptions or expectations of particular teachers. It may be helpful to gather personal information during the interview, such as the student's attitudes toward the settings in which he or she functions and the various people encountered in those environments, any hobbies or special interests, goals and aspirations, particular likes or dislikes. It also may be possible to learn more about a student's home life from an interview, particularly the attitudes and values that are present at home and the extent of cooperation that can be expected from that quarter. With adolescents, it may be fruitful to interview employers or co-workers. In all cases, it is important for the interviewer to establish a clear need for any information requested during an interview. An interview is not a fishing expedition. It is easy to become a professional voyeur, asking questions out of curiosity rather than need.

Both McCallon and McCray (1975) and Stewart and Cash (1976) emphasize the need to maintain a friendly, nondefensive atmosphere throughout the interview. They suggest the use of probe questions or remarks such as "Can you give me an example of what you mean?" "What did you have in mind?" "You feel that . . .?" or "That's a really good idea. How do you think we can implement it?" Such remarks facilitate the gathering of information without jeopardizing an open atmosphere that may have been established. They also lay a base for future cooperative efforts that may grow out of the interview.

Interested readers are referred to Losen and Diament (1978), McCallon and McCray (1975), and Stewart and Cash (1976) for more detailed information on the interviewing process. The discussion on life-space interviewing presented later in this chapter may be helpful, too.

Analysis of the Physical Environment

Not all of the behavior problems that occur in school can be understood fully if analysis is limited to the behaviors of individual students. Many of the difficulties experienced by students are caused by elements of the physical environment of the classroom and the school. For this reason, teachers will want to examine the classroom environment for physical variables that may be stimulating or maintaining problem behaviors. Lighting, temperature, and noise level in a classroom are obvious examples. Redl (1959) identified four variables relating to aspects of the school's physical environment that can be manipulated to prevent or ameliorate behavior problems. These variables are space, equipment, time, and props. Careful examination of each of these variables may be indicated when teachers are assessing student behavior problems.

The teacher first must be aware that these variables can cause or contribute to classroom behavior problems. The teacher will want to ask such questions as "Does the student need more space for a particular activity?" "Does the student need to move around the class more?" "Does the student need to work within precise boundaries?" "Could the problem be avoided by using (or discarding) certain pieces of equipment?" "If the activity were rescheduled for a different time, would the behavior problems associated with it decrease?" "Is attention being drawn away from a lesson or activity and focused on a nonrelevant but highly seductive item such as a noisy pencil sharpener, other classes going out to recess, or the smell of food from the cafeteria?" If the answer to any of these questions is yes, the teacher will want to document the existence and severity of the problem by using one of the measurement techniques described earlier (event recording, time sampling, and so on). For instance, if the teacher believes that Jenny's problems are aggravated by having too much work space, the following sequence would be appropriate for both assessment and intervention. First, the teacher would define and measure the problem behavior(s). The teacher would then alter the troublesome variable. In this instance, excess space could be handled by providing Jenny with a study carrel or a small, well-defined study area. Using the same measurement technique as before, the teacher would note any changes in the target behavior after the study carrel was introduced. If no change is noted, the teacher can be relatively certain that space is not a relevant variable in Jenny's current problems or that the solution selected, in this instance the use of a carrel, was not effective. If changes are noted, the teacher has a ready-made prescription to relieve the behavior problem. Each of Redl's four variables (space, time, equipment, and props) is explained briefly below.

Space.   Space refers to the amount of physical area allotted to a particular activity and the ways in which that space affects students' behaviors. Redl notes that it is difficult to hold the attention of a small group of students located in the gymnasium. Similarly, disruptive behaviors may arise when too many students are crowded into a small area, as when all the fifth-hour social studies classes are sent into one classroom to view a film. The example above documents the difficulty that an individual student may have coping with personal space in the classroom.

Time.   The period of the day when an activity is scheduled is important. Most elementary school teachers intuitively utilize this element in their planning: the bulk of the basic academic work is scheduled for the early morning, and "winding-down" activities are employed after recesses and lunch periods. A hot, sweaty student who has just returned from a stimulating game of kickball can hardly be expected to buckle down immediately to a sheet of long-division problems. Unfortunately, teachers in secondary schools have little control over scheduling. They work in a system that assumes, probably fallaciously, that these same considerations need not be applied to high school students. Woe to the English teacher who must present the delights of Chaucer to a class in which many of the students have just returned from band practice, physical education, or lunch!

Equipment.   Materials and equipment that are required for each activity should be identified and acquired before the activity is initiated. Is the necessary equipment available, is it in working order, can the students or teacher operate it? In individualized instruction, a student's ability to use equipment is an important factor in his or her ability and willingness to continue working without disruption. Equipment can be highly motivating or highly frustrating and disruptive. In group instruction, the teacher's attention may be divided as a consequence of preoccupation with arranging or setting up materials and equipment. Students who are wondering just how much they can get by with when the teacher isn't looking are likely to begin testing classroom rules. The flow of activity is again disrupted when the teacher is forced to stop arranging equipment to manage the problem behaviors. It may be difficult to resume a steady pace. Equipment also can assume the alluring characteristics attributed below to props.

Props.   Most classrooms are filled with "props" that teachers use to set the classroom stage. Unfortunately, items that hold students' attention during a mathematics lesson do not suddenly lose their charms when instruction is switched to social studies. If these items are more attention holding and alluring than either the teacher or the lesson at hand, disruptive behaviors are sure to ensue. By the same token, disinterested behaviors will be elicited when the props supporting a lesson are *not* interesting and seductive. The teacher's job is to determine which props contribute to the program, which detract from the program, and which should be present occasionally and absent at all other times.

Examination of Teacher-Pupil Interaction in the Classroom

By now it should be apparent that many of the problems in classrooms do not spring from a single cause. Rather, they are products of the interaction of two or more variables. This section examines techniques used to measure the type and quality of teacher-child interaction. There are a number of interaction analysis instruments on the market. Four of the more prominent ones include Flanders Interaction Analysis System, the Observation System for Instructional Analysis, Dyadic Interaction Analysis, and the Florida Climate and Control System.

The Flanders Interaction Analysis System (Flanders, 1970) does not focus on any one student's interactions with the teacher. Instead, it codes and analyzes the verbal interactions between the teacher and all the students in the class. It is more valuable for teachers who wish to modify their own behavior in the classroom than for teachers who are interested in those few students who are exhibiting behavior problems. Flanders identifies ten behaviors, which are recorded in 4-second intervals. The ten behaviors include seven teacher responses and initiations, two student behaviors, and a no-behavior or silence category. The teacher responses are (1) accepting students' feelings, (2) praising or encouraging students, and (3) accepting/using students' ideas. Teacher initiations are (4) asking questions, (5) lecturing, (6) giving directions, and (7) criticizing. The two student behaviors are (8) responding to the teacher and (9) initiating talk or conversation. The final category is (10) silence or confusion. Observational periods should be short, perhaps a maximum of 30 minutes at a time, and data should be taken for several days.

The Observation System for Instructional Analysis (OSIA) (Hough, 1967) was developed from the original Flanders system. In OSIA the number of student behavior categories was increased so that it would equal the number of teacher behavior categories; the instrument codes a total of 16 behavior types. OSIA was "designed to enable investigators to test hypotheses from learning (reinforcement) theory [and] . . . to distinguish between teachers who reinforce different kinds of student responses" (Gauthier, 1980, pp. 20–21). A particularly helpful aspect of OSIA is the revisions devised for use during specific types of classroom instruction, such as reading, mathematics, and physical education.

Dyadic Interaction Analysis (Brophy & Good, 1969) is similar to the Flanders system in the types of behavioral contacts that are coded. However, Brophy and Good devised their instrument to identify and measure interactions between the classroom teacher and one particular student. The five sets of behaviors analyzed by the Brophy and Good system are (1) pupil responses to teacher questions, or Response Opportunities; (2) students' oral presentations, or Recitation; (3) general classroom management, or Procedural Contacts; (4) interaction concerning a student's written work, or Work-Related Contacts; and (5) discipline and individual remarks about student behavior, or Behavioral Contacts.

The Florida Climate and Control System (Soar, Soar, & Ragosta, 1971) is widely used in research, but it is quite elaborate. A teacher probably would not use this system for personal purposes. In addition to coding more than fifty incidences of student and teacher interaction, the Florida system also codes variables related to the physical environment of the classroom, including the size and type of class, the nature of the classroom activity at the time of the observation, student and teacher tasks, classroom structure, seating arrangements, and the use and type of various displays in the classroom.

These and other interaction analysis instruments are described and evaluated by Borich and Madden (1977).

Peer-Nominating Techniques

Peer-nominating techniques are the traditional means for gathering information about the way a student is perceived by classmates or age-mates. Sociometrics and other peer-nominating techniques are discussed in this section.

Sociometrics. The sociometric nominating technique was originally developed by Moreno (1953). Sociometrics may be used to determine each student's position within the class by analyzing peer choices made by each student in the group. R. L. Thorndike and Hagen (1977) have stressed that in order to understand the individual student and the climate of the class, it is important to appraise the role of the student within that group.

In applying this technique to the classroom situation, the teacher asks each student to choose one, two, or three students with whom he or she would like to engage in the activity specified in the stimulus question; e.g. inviting to a party, bringing home after school, doing homework. This information can aid the teacher in understanding the social structure within the group. Nominations on a sociogram may be mapped as illustrated in Figure 7–8. In this example, ten students were asked to choose two classmates with whom they would like to work on an art project.

Examination of the diagram shows that Grace was most highly desired as a partner, whereas Lee was an "isolate," neither making nor receiving any nominations. Wayne was an unchosen member of the group; although he did choose two students, he was not selected by any member of the group.

After the teacher has determined which student is isolated or without friends, he or she can begin to seek out the causes. Frequently, the explanations are quite simple, such as being new to the class, living outside the community, being older than the other children, or having poor personal hygiene. The teacher can then be sensitive to structuring situations in which the isolate can interact with others. Sometimes the causes are more complicated, but only if they are understood can the teacher help the student develop the social, athletic, or academic skills necessary to enter into the mainstream of the group's social system. Isolation also may be the result of attitudes toward minority-group members. In that case, the teacher should focus on *group* attitudinal and behavioral changes instead of changes within the isolated member.

Figure 7–8. Example of a Sociogram

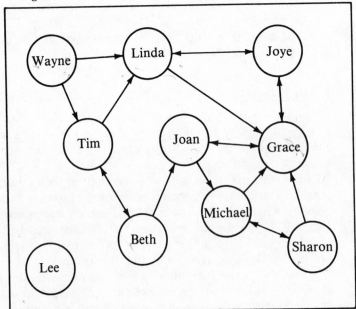

Another use of sociometrics, infrequently practiced, is to provide feedback on the teacher's behavior. Often the teacher consciously or unconsciously praises or rebukes the same student. This habit could be corroborated or disproved by asking the class to "Write the name of the class member whom Ms. Jones likes best" or "Write the name of the class member whom Ms. Jones does not like." If the teacher receives a variety of names in response to these questions, she is not isolating the same children. If only one or two names are reported by the class, the teacher actually may be betraying personal preferences, causing the certain class members to feel rejected or anonymous.

L. Brown and Hammill (1983) suggest that sociograms are most efficient with classes of at least twenty students. They also emphasize that students participating in the sociogram should have been in the class for at least six weeks, in order to permit the formation of the relationships measured by the sociogram.

There has been a general feeling (e.g., Gronlund, 1981) that responses to one pair of stimulus questions should not be generalized to anticipated responses from another pair of questions. For instance, a set of questions related to cooperating on schoolwork presumably would attract different responses than a set of questions related to playing together on a kickball team. Preliminary evidence (L. Brown, 1981) suggests that the distinction may not be necessary with elementary students. This research indicates that popular, rejected, and ignored children tended to maintain their relative status across several stimulus questions, although children with middle status ranks seemed to be differentially chosen. In addition, this research indicates that the reliability of sociometric responses seems to be both age and sex related. Young children in kindergarten and grade one and girls in grades five and six were less reliable respondents than other children. Fiske and Cox (1960), Hollander (1965), Lindzey and Borgatta (1954), and Reynolds (1966) have offered evidence suggesting that sociometric peer rating is one of the most dependable rating techniques. It not only assesses the present status of the group but also acts as a valuable tool for measuring the effectiveness of teacher intervention.

Most sociograms are informal measures, and evaluations of them are subjective. Their value, therefore, is directly related to the skill and experience of the person conducting the sociogram or interpreting its results. An exception is the sociogram of the Behavior Rating Profile (L. Brown & Hammill, 1983), which was described earlier in this chapter. Unlike other sociograms, this instrument is standardized and yields a scaled score.

Other Peer-Nominating Techniques.   Good examples of nonsociometric peer-nominating techniques are found in three of Bower and Lambert's (1971) screening instruments: Class Pictures, Class Play, and Student Survey. These instruments were developed for use with students in kindergarten through grade three, grades three through seven, and junior and senior high school, respectively. No normative data or information concerning reliability and validity is available for these instruments, but the reader may find their indirect formats to be useful and interesting.

Class Pictures is individually administered. Twelve pictures containing twenty items are shown to students. Ten items depict students engaging in "maladjusted" behaviors (five with boys and five with girls), and the remaining ten items depict positive or neutral behaviors (again, five with boys and five with girls). Students are asked which of their classmates is like the subject in each of the twenty situations. A score is derived by comparing the student's negative perceptions to the total number of peer selections for any role.

Class Play describes twenty hypothetical roles. Students are asked to nominate classmates for each role. Another form of the instrument, used to judge students' self-perceptions, asks them to select roles for themselves and to identify roles they think others would select for them.

In the Student Survey, students are asked to name a classmate who is best characterized by the description in each of twenty items, ten presumably describing "emotionally disturbed" behaviors and ten describing positive or neutral behaviors. This instrument also could be adapted to a self-report measure in the manner described for the Class Play.

Standardized Tests of Personality

Occasionally a teacher will be provided with the results of standardized tests of personality or character that have been administered to a student. These are usually found in cumulative folders of students who have been referred to another professional in the school or to an agency specializing in disturbed or disruptive students. In assessing a referral, school counselors, psychologists, and other mental health specialists often use standardized personality measures as well as many of the observational techniques and checklists already described in this chapter. Personality tests are rarely, if ever, given by classroom teachers. However, since the results of such tests are frequently shared with them, teachers should have some basic information about commonly used personality measures.

One broad category of personality testing involves the use of self-report devices, e.g., sentence-completion tests or checklists completed by the child. There are several weaknesses inherent in any self-report device. Predominant among these is the ease with which the individual completing the instrument can hide or disguise feelings. Some instruments have built in "lie scales" to help offset such effects. Other instruments have adopted a projective format to elicit responses indirectly, thereby reducing any apparent need for deception that the respondent may feel.

Sentence-completion tests contain sentence stems that the student is asked to complete. Typical sentence stems might be:

The thing I like most about school is _____

My mother _____

I am afraid when _____

Personality inventories also might be included in an assessment of a problem area. These tests present the student with (1) a series of statements ("I am happy," "People usually like me.") to which the child responds with "True," "False," or some noncommital response ("Not sure," "Cannot say"); (2) a series of questions ("Are you frequently ill?" "Do you like to attend parties?") to which the child responds "Yes" or "No"; or (3) pairs of statements between which the student must choose ("I like to play team sports," "I like to play games by myself"). Tests of this type include the Minnesota Multiphasic Personality Inventory (MMPI) (Hathaway & McKinley, 1967), the California Test of Personality (Thorpe, Clark, & Tiegs, 1953), the Bell Adjustment Inventory (Bell, 1961), the Junior Eysenck Personality Inventory (Eysenck, 1965), and IPAT's Children's Personality Questionnaire (Porter & Cattell, 1975) and Sixteen Personality Factor Questionnaire (Cattell, 1967).

Locus-of-control tests, such as the Bialer Children's Locus of Control Scale (Bialer, 1961) or the Children's Intellectual Achievement Responsibility Questionnaire (Crandall, Kathovsky, & Crandall, 1965), are also classified in this category. Tests of this type are administered to determine whether students accept responsibility for their own behavior (internal locus of control) or assign responsibility for their behavior to other people, to circumstance, or to fate (external locus of control).

Projective instruments constitute another major type of standardized personality measure. Cronbach (1970) asserts that these instruments are of two types—tests in which the type of problem solving is important (stylistic tests) and tests in which the content of the solution is important (thematic tests). The Rorschach Inkblot Test (Rorschach, 1966) and the Bender Visual-Motor Gestalt Tests (Bender, 1938) are stylistic. The Thematic Apperception Test (TAT) (Murray, 1943) and the Children's Apperception Test (Bellak & Bellak, 1961) are thematic in nature. In projective testing the student is presented with a stimulus such as an inkblot, a drawing, or a picture and is then asked to describe what is seen or to tell a story about the picture. Two instruments used with students, the Blacky Tests (Blum, 1958) and Buttons (Rothman & Berkowitz, 1963), use a dog and a rabbit, respectively, to present stories or situations that the responding student is asked to complete or resolve.

Analyses of students' drawings are also frequently included in these assessments. The Draw-A-Person (Urban, 1963) and House-Tree-Person (Buck & Jolles, 1966) Tests are popular examples. Drawings from the Bender may also be used. Rough standards for interpretation are usually included in the manuals accompanying these measures. Yet even when these are available, the results of projective testing are quite subjective. They are, therefore, highly dependent on the competence and experience of the examiner.

After studying the extent to which the use of these projective tests yielded valuable information, Kessler (1966) concluded that the derived information can usually be obtained from other sources, notably from teacher assessment. Salvia and Ysseldyke (1985) note, "Psychologists have been called on repeatedly to defend their activities and have had considerable difficulty defending the practice of personality assessment, both in terms of the psychometric adequacy of the devices and the educational relevance of the information provided by those devices" (pp. 447–448). For other detailed discussions of personality testing, the reader is referred to Anastasi (1982), Kessler (1966), Thorndike and Hagen (1977), and Ullmann and Krasner (1975).

MANAGING PROBLEM BEHAVIORS

The intervention strategies about to be presented have become strongly associated with specific schools of thought. For instance, the various behavior modification strategies were developed and are used primarily by individuals holding a behavioral point of view, and techniques such as life-space interviewing evolved from the work of analytically oriented professionals. Analytic professionals often scoff at the uses of behavior modification, and the behaviorists almost invariably advise against the use of analytic techniques.

To us, the division of management techniques according to discrete philosophical categories is a useless activity that only reduces the number of tools available to today's teachers. We believe that each of the techniques described in this section has value in some situations and that use of all of them is well within the professional educator's ability.

The first important aspect of an intervention plan—establishing a goal for behavioral improvement and assessing the current level of the behavior problem—has already been discussed. In this section eight methods for managing behavior are described: behavior modification; behavioral self-control; contracting; Long and Newman's techniques for managing surface behaviors; Trieschman's strategies for managing temper tantrums; life-space interviewing; projective techniques such as role playing, puppetry, play therapy, and art and music therapy; and cognitive therapies. Commercially available programs that purport to assist in the development of students' affective domains also will be reviewed.

Behavior Modification

Rationale

Classroom management, consequence management, or behavior modification has its roots with the behavioral learning theorists such as Thorndike, Pavlov, Watson, and Jones. Ayllon (1965), Skinner (1953), and Ferster and Skinner (1957) expanded and refined the theory and popularized its clinical use, enabling the behavioral specialist to use it in modifying deviant behavior. Clinical experimentation with individual children and adults brought this approach into the foreground in the 1960s, with the renewed interest in the interaction between people and their environment. In short, behavior modification is a systematic, highly structured approach to altering behavior. Its use will have the effect of strengthening, weakening, or maintaining target behaviors. For a more detailed description of the specific techniques involved, the reader is referred to several excellent instructional texts, including Alberto and Troutman's (1982) *Applied Behavior Analysis for Teachers*, Axelrod's (1977) *Behavior Modification for the Classroom Teacher*, Buckley and Walker's (1970) *Modifying Classroom Behavior*, R. V. Hall's (1971, 1974, 1983) series of *Managing Behavior* monographs, L. K. Miller's (1975) *Principles of Everyday Behavior Analysis*, and Sulzer-Azaroff and Mayer's (1977) *Applying Behavior Analysis Procedures with Children and Youth*.

Procedures

A plan to modify a target behavior comprises four phases: (1) obtaining baseline data, (2) selecting and implementing a particular modification technique, (3) verifying results, and (4) applying the program in the classroom.

Taking Baseline Data. The selection of any intervention technique is predicated upon the assumption that the teacher has defined the target behavior and has taken baseline data regarding its frequency or duration. R. V. Hall's (1983) direct observation techniques, described earlier in this chapter, are employed often in gathering baseline information. To ensure a representative sample of a student's behavior, five measurement periods usually are devoted to collecting baseline data. The effects of intervention strategies can then be determined objectively by comparing the baseline with subsequent increases or decreases in the targeted behaviors. The data graphed earlier in this chapter represent baseline data.

Selecting a Treatment. Reinforcement and punishment are the two basic treatments in behavior modification. Extinction, differential reinforcement, shaping, discrimination training, generalization, modeling, and token economies are other popular techniques.

Reinforcement.   A reinforcer is any event that occurs after a behavior and that increases the frequency or duration of the behavior and/or increases the likelihood that the behavior will reoccur (R. V. Hall, 1971). A graph depicting the frequency of a behavior that is being reinforced will show an upward trend. Teachers may assume that being smiled at, receiving an A grade, or being given five minutes of free time is a reinforcing event, at least to most students; but this conclusion is only justified when there is an observed increase in the behaviors that these events follow. In fact, the teacher will quickly discover that many students who exhibit problem behaviors are not reinforced by the "usual" things.

Some behaviorists refine this definition of reinforcement by describing its negative and positive instances. For instance, the reader may have encountered the terms "negative reinforcement" (a reinforcement procedure in which something aversive or negative is removed from the environment) and "positive reinforcement" (a reinforcement procedure in which something pleasant or positive is added to the environment). These refined definitions can be quite confusing. We have elected to use Hall's definition cited above because it is simple, practical, and straightforward.

Observation of students will generally give the teacher ample ideas of things that are likely to be rewarding for them. Additional information can be obtained by asking individual students to complete an interest inventory or by directly asking students what they like to do. The teacher can select a potential reinforcer from the lists that have been developed. If the event proves to be reinforcing, that is, if the target behavior increases, the teacher will continue to use the reinforcer, alternating it occasionally with other reinforcers to prevent the pupil from becoming tired of "the same old thing." Overuse of a reinforcer eventually will result in satiation and in the loss of reinforcement power. If the event does not prove to be reinforcing (i.e., if the target behavior does not increase), the teacher must select another potential reinforcer from the student's reinforcement menu. See Hall and Hall (1980a) for other means of selecting reinforcers.

Reinforcers may be primary or secondary. Examples of primary reinforcers are the following:

food
money
a drink of water
lavatory privileges
playing ball in the gym

    drawing paper

    crayons

    chewing gum

Secondary reinforcers usually are social rather than tangible or physical, and often gain their power from being associated with a primary reinforcer. Following are several examples:

    receiving a star or an A

    moving one's seat close to the teacher

    verbal praise

    sending a praising note home to parents

    a pat on the shoulder

    a hug

It should be reemphasized that one of the goals of behavior modification is to encourage a student or class of students to work for social reinforcement. Thus, whenever food or toys are given as a consequence, they must be accompanied by social reinforcement—verbal praise, a smile, or a hug—so that the primary reinforcement becomes associated with social approval. Eventually, the social reinforcement will have the same effect as a tangible item.

    Reinforcement can be delivered on either a ratio or an interval schedule, and in either case the arrangement or reinforcement can be fixed or variable. With *ratio* schedules, the number of responses a student makes is important. The rate of reinforcement on ratio schedules is largely self-controlled, because the more behaviors the students emit, the more reinforcement they will receive. For this reason, ratio schedules usually yield fairly high rates of responding. *Interval* schedules deliver reinforcement after a specified amount of time has elapsed, rather than after a particular number of behaviors. Reinforcement on interval schedules is controlled by the teacher, not by the student; a set amount of time must pass before reinforcement can be delivered, regardless of the number of behaviors students have emitted. Consequently, interval schedules tend to yield low rates of responding. On a *fixed* schedule, reinforcement occurs at a regular interval or after a set number of responses. Fixed schedules are characterized by pauses in responding after reinforcement, because the students know when reinforcement will occur again. Reinforcement in *variable* schedules occurs at irregular intervals or after varying numbers of responses. Variable schedules therefore are characterized by fairly steady rates of responding, because the students are not certain just when reinforcement will be delivered.

    Thus, reinforcement can be of four varieties: fixed ratio, variable ratio, fixed interval, and variable interval. *Fixed ratio* schedules result in high rates of behavior with pauses. *Variable ratio* schedules produce high steady rates of responding. *Fixed interval* schedules yield low rates of responding with pauses. *Variable interval* schedules result in low steady rates of responding. Cumulative graphs of typical behavior patterns on each of these schedules are shown in Figure 7–9.

On a continuous fixed ratio schedule (CFR), every behavior or response is reinforced. This schedule is valuable for stimulating behaviors that may not occur frequently. On the other hand, it is an inefficient means of maintaining behaviors, because the acquired behavior disappears rapidly if reinforcement ever is withdrawn. The behaviors that we exhibit in using vending machines are frequently cited as examples of those maintained on a CFR schedule. The insertion of a quarter into a pop machine almost always is rewarded with a can of

Figure 7–9. Cumulative Graphs of Behaviors Maintained on Different Schedules of Reinforcement

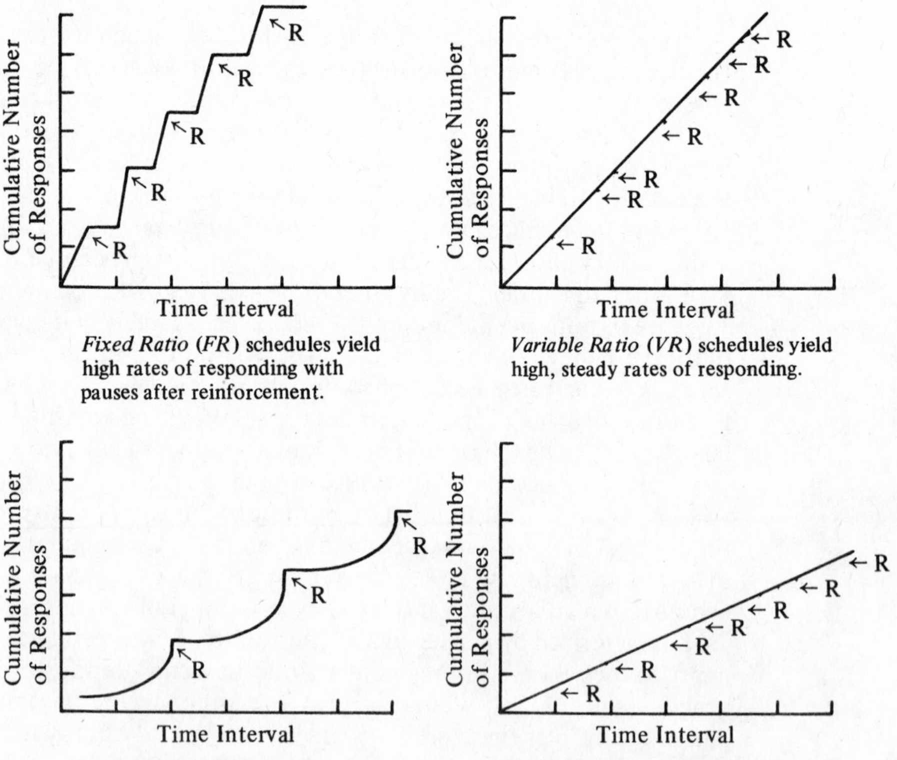

Fixed Ratio (FR) schedules yield high rates of responding with pauses after reinforcement.

Variable Ratio (VR) schedules yield high, steady rates of responding.

Fixed Interval (FI) schedules yield low rates of responding with pauses after reinforcement.

Variable Interval (VI) schedules yield low, steady rates of responding.

Note: R ↑ indicates when reinforcement was delivered.

soda. This is a CFR schedule: every behavior is reinforced. If the machine is broken, however, the insertion of a quarter will not be reinforced by the appearance of a can of soda. One might insert a second quarter, but it is unlikely that an individual would continue to put money into the machine. Therefore, one of the intermittent schedules described below is preferred for maintaining a behavior after it has been acquired on a CFR schedule.

On a fixed ratio schedule (FR), reinforcement follows a fixed number of responses. For example, a behavior that is reinforced on an FR-3 schedule would be reinforced after every third response (i.e., after the third, sixth, ninth, twelfth, etc., behaviors). In fact, CFR could be called an FR-1 schedule. Piecework is an example of behavior that is maintained on an FR schedule. Fruit pickers who are paid by the basket are reinforced on an FR schedule, as are students who receive free time after completing a set amount of work. An FR schedule results in high rates of behavior with pauses after reinforcement has been delivered. For instance, a student who completes three pages of problems in a math workbook and then is reinforced (by receiving a star, a smile, or an "attaboy" from the teacher) is likely to rest or take a breather before beginning the next task.

On a variable ratio schedule (VR), reinforcement follows an average number of responses. On a VR-3 schedule, reinforcement might follow any number of behaviors, as long as the average number of responses per reinforcement is 3. Gambling on slot machines is an example of behavior that is maintained on a VR schedule. The machines are calibrated to provide reinforcement (a jackpot) after an average number of coins has been inserted. A VR schedule results in a high, steady rate of responding. Such response patterns might be seen in classes where the teacher moves around the room reinforcing the students after they have completed varying amounts of work.

On a fixed interval schedule (FI), reinforcement follows the first behavior to occur after a fixed period of time has elapsed. FI-2 minutes means that reinforcement will follow the first behavior to occur after 2 minutes, 4 minutes, 6 minutes, and so on. It does not matter whether the student emits 1 behavior or 100 behaviors during the 2-minute interval; reinforcement will occur only after the allotted time has passed. The FI schedule yields a low response rate with pauses after reinforcement. Students who know that their math workbooks will be checked every morning at 11:00 (FI-24 hours) are likely to work with increasing speed until that time and to stop working until the interval is about to close the next morning, again working at faster rates as 11:00 approaches. On a variable interval schedule (VI), reinforcement follows the first behavior to occur after an average amount of time has passed. This schedule yields low steady rates of behavior.

Take, for example, David, who has fifteen math problems to complete during the twenty-minute math period. On an FR-5 schedule, David would receive reinforcement after completing each group of five problems, e.g., after the fifth, tenth, and fifteenth problems were completed. The teacher would expect David to work fairly quickly in order to receive his reinforcement faster, but also would expect him to take a break after receiving each reinforcement and before starting the next block of five problems. If David were receiving reinforcement on a VR-5 schedule, he would be reinforced after an average of every five problems completed, e.g., after the second, ninth, and fifteenth problems. On this schedule, the teacher again would expect David to work relatively quickly, since he controls his own rate of reinforcement, and to work without pauses or breaks, since he doesn't know exactly when reinforcement will be forthcoming. On an FI-5 minute schedule, the teacher would reinforce David for the first problem completed after every 5-minute interval, e.g., at 5-, 10-, 15-, and 20-minute intervals during the math period. The teacher would expect David to work more slowly than he did under ratio reinforcement, since his work rate won't affect the amount of reinforcement; David also would be expected to pause after each reinforcement was delivered. Finally, on a VI-5 minute reinforcement schedule, David would be reinforced for the first problem completed after an average of 5 minutes had passed, e.g., after 4, 11, 14, and 20 minutes. The teacher would expect the same lower rate of responding, but would also expect steady work, since David cannot anticipate when reinforcement will occur.

Regardless of the reinforcement schedule that a teacher elects to employ, it is imperative that the teacher deliver reinforcement as quickly as possible to avoid reinforcing the wrong behavior. The student should know why reinforcement is delivered. It helps if the teacher verbalizes the reason as the points, tokens, or praise are delivered: "Good, Billie! You worked quietly for two minutes." It also is important to remember that the reinforcement is delivered *only* as a consequence of the desired behavior. If free time is the reinforcer that is being used, then free time should not be available to the target student at any other time in the regular daily schedule.

Reinforcing incompatible responses involves rewarding action that is incompatible with the bothersome behavior. For example, suppose a pupil talks out loud most of the morning. Instead of punishing the student for talking without permission, the teacher decides to reward the child for completing ten arithmetic problems. In order to accomplish this task and obtain the reward, the child works hard, becoming too busy to talk. The desired behavior is incompatible with talking aloud. Not only does this approach reduce disturbing behavior, but it also increases desirable academic performance (see Table 7–3). Although reinforcing incompatible responses has not received as much emphasis as other behavior-modification techniques, it appears to be an easily applied and effective procedure for classroom use.

Punishment.   A *punisher* is any event that follows a behavior and that decreases the frequency or duration of the behavior and/or decreases the likeli-

Table 7–3. Simultaneous Effects of Reinforcing Incompatible Responses

Target Behavior	Behavioral Results
Disturbing, annoying	Decrease
Desirable academic performance	Increase

hood that the behavior will reoccur (R. V. Hall, 1971). The frequency graph of a behavior that is being punished will show a downward trend. Again, the assumption that such things as expulsion from school, low grades, or standing in the hall are punishing must be proved. Let's look at a brief example. Brett swears in class and his teacher decides to punish this behavior by sending him to the principal's office. If Brett's swearing increases, the teacher must assume that going to the principal's office, is, in fact, reinforcing for Brett, not punishing. Expulsion and suspension are classic examples of presumed punishers that usually aren't punishing, which is why we frequently see "repeat offenders" in detention hall or on suspension.

Negative and positive reinforcement were discussed earlier. The reader also may encounter descriptions of two punishment procedures; punishment can be achieved by adding something aversive to the environment or by removing some pleasurable consequence. The important thing for the teacher to note is whether the target behavior decreases.

The teacher will select a punishment procedure if the goal is to decrease a behavior and if this goal cannot be achieved by reinforcing an incompatible behavior. Obviously, precise definition of the target behavior is crucial. For instance, a teacher could elect to reinforce a student for talking only with permission, to punish the same student for talking without permission, or to do both. In the vast majority of instances, it is more desirable to reinforce than to punish. Whenever punishment is used, it should be accompanied by reinforcement if at all possible. Punishing a behavior only tells the student that the behavior is unacceptable; it does not in any way indicate alternative behaviors that are considered appropriate.

Punishment has the effect of arresting or suppressing behavior without eliminating or extinguishing it. It is beneficial only when applied to specific acts (running out into the street) rather than to generalized situations (being naughty). Momentarily stopping an undesirable behavior has positive effects when it is accompanied by the demonstration and reinforcement of alternative responses.

The effectiveness of a punisher is governed by many of the same variables that affect reinforcers. Punishers will be more powerful if they are delivered immediately, if the student knows why they are delivered, and if delivery of pun-ishment is contingent upon a specific behavior. In addition, punishers and rein-forcers are most effective when they are not overused (e.g., when the student is not satiated).

The teacher must be aware of the possible negative effects of using punish-ment. The emotional side effects, such as guilt, fear, withdrawal, and frustra-tion, may lead to other maladaptive behaviors. In addition, the punishing teacher may serve as a negative, aggressive model for other students or may become a conditioned punisher.

Extinction.   Extinction occurs when a reinforcing event is withdrawn and the behavior that it followed decreases. For example, Carolee had a tendency to talk without permission. After she was corrected by the teacher Carolee's talk-ing without permission increased, so we can assume that the teacher's correc-tions reinforced the unwanted behavior. Extinction has occurred if Carolee's talking out behavior decreases after the teacher withdraws the apparent rein-forcement (the corrections) and ignores the talking out. As teachers, we often unwittingly reinforce undesirable behaviors, as Carolee's teacher did. Extinc-tion, then, is a tool that can be invaluable. Unfortunately, extinction is difficult to implement because many troublesome behaviors cannot be ignored or extin-guished. Violent or destructive behaviors obviously cannot be ignored. Similarly, behaviors that continually disrupt the educational program are not good candi-dates for extinction; sanctions from the teacher or from classmates usually must be applied. Contagious behaviors, such as false hiccoughing or perhaps swearing, also do not lend themselves well to extinction. Finally, teachers shouldn't attempt to ignore or extinguish behaviors that are outside their own personal tolerance levels. Some teachers, for instance, can ignore swearing, thereby robbing it of its shock or annoyance value and extinguishing it. However, teachers who find that they cannot tolerate swearing (or other behaviors) should not attempt to extinguish the behaviors but should look instead for alternative management techniques. We all have behaviors that "pull our chains"; having recognized what they are, we should not expect ourselves to exhibit the super-human effort needed to ignore or extinguish them! Hall and Hall (1980b) offer guidelines for the effective use of planned ignoring and extinction.

Differential Reinforcement.   Differential reinforcement involves two or more different responses: one response is reinforced and the other(s) is/are extin-guished. For example, Marty frequently made self-depracatory remarks (one re-sponse), only rarely noting something that he did well (a second, different re-sponse). His teacher ignored the negative remarks (extinction) and reinforced the positive remarks (by attending to them). Eventually, Marty spoke more highly of himself as a result of differential reinforcement. Differential reinforcement is valuable because its use reduces or eliminates undesirable behaviors while simultaneously encouraging behaviors considered to be appropriate.

Shaping. Shaping is the differential reinforcement of successive approximations of a behavior. Let's consider the example of Karen, a first-grader who is out of her seat 60 percent of the time in the reading period. Using differential reinforcement, the teacher extinguished Karen's out-of-seat behavior (by ignoring it) and reinforced her in-seat behavior (by praising it). The goal for Karen is to be in her seat throughout the reading period. Successive approximations of this goal would be increasing percentages of time she spent in her seat before she received reinforcement, perhaps 50 percent, then 55 percent, and so on. The final goal (i.e., for her to be in seat during the entire reading period) would be achieved through a shaping process. In fact, education itself is primarily a process of shaping. Panyan's (1980) monograph discusses the use of shaping procedures with children.

Discrimination Training. Discrimination training involves a single behavior that is reinforced in the presence of one stimulus and is extinguished in the presence of other stimuli. For instance, Matt is reinforced for responding "two" when he is asked to supply the answer to "1 + 1 = _____." However, that same response ("two") is extinguished when Matt is asked to supply the answer to other questions, such as "2 + 3 = _____" and "1 + 2 = _____." Discrimination training has also occurred with the students who learn that they can be late for Mr. Penny's English I class but that they must be on time for Ms. Schroeder's algebra class. Discrimination training also might be used to teach a retarded adolescent that kissing is acceptable with some people (e.g., with relatives) but that it is not acceptable with strangers or on the job.

Generalization. Generalization is the occurrence of a response learned through discrimination training in the presence of a novel or unknown stimulus. For example, Matt has learned through discrimination training to respond "red" when he sees red circles and squares and to refrain from making that response when he sees circles and squares of other colors. Generalization has occurred if Matt responds "red" when presented with novel stimuli such as red triangles and does not respond "red" when presented with blue, green, or yellow triangles. Generalization is the desired outcome of any intervention plan, regardless of the methodology employed. Students must be able to generalize what is learned, or else they will have to treat every situation they encounter as a new one. The following steps will facilitate the generalization of a student's behavior from one school situation to another or from school to home.

1. Place the behavior on intermittent reinforcement (every behavior is *not* reinforced).

2. Fade the reinforcer from primary to social.

3. Have another adult (parent or student volunteer) participate in the treatment.

4. Have an extinction period, gradually withdrawing reinforcement and returning to no treatment.

5. Contract with the student to monitor his or her own behavior by keeping a record and turning it in at the end of the week for reinforcement, thinning the reinforcement schedule.

6. Use tokens to bridge the gap between primary and social reinforcement and to encourage delay in gratification. Delay in gratification should occur under natural circumstances and should not become an exercise to its own end. It is doubtful that any teacher reading this book would wait a week to pick up a paycheck, just to demonstrate the self-discipline to delay gratification!

The time requirements for this technique are great. The steps are essential, however, for successful application. Once this procedure has been practiced, its time efficiency increases markedly. Interested readers are encouraged to consult Baer (1981) for additional information on planning for generalization.

Modeling.   In modeling, verbal instructions or imitation is used to teach a student a new behavior. According to L. K. Miller (1975), instructional training, a form of modeling, involves three steps: a verbal description of the desired behavior, a demonstration by the learner of the described behavior, and reinforcement following the demonstration of the behavior. Imitation training, another form of modeling, also consists of three stages: demonstration by the teacher of the target behavior, an imitation by the learner of the demonstrated behavior, and reinforcement of the imitation. Instructional training is said to take place when, for instance, the teacher says, "Please sit at your desk," the student complies, and the teacher smiles and says, "Thank you." Imitation training occurs when the teacher makes the short *s* sound, the student imitates it, and the teacher says, "Good."

Modeling also occurs when the student observes that another student who is engaging in instructional or imitation learning is being reinforced (or punished) for complying (or not complying). The student who observes that Mark is permitted to go to recess as soon as he has complied with the teacher's instructions to clear off his desk is quite likely to follow suit and clear off her desk, too (if recess is reinforcing). Likewise, the same behavior will result if she sees that the recess privilege is withdrawn from a student who failed to comply with this request. Striefel's (1981) book is an excellent source for information on teaching through the use of modeling and imitation.

Token Economies.   Reinforcers may be delivered in *token economies,* settings in which the students receive tokens with which they can later buy tangible items or privileges. Kazdin (1977) and Walker and Buckley (1974) describe the construction and use of token economies; interested readers are referred to their texts for more detailed information. In a token economy, the student has a task (his or her "job"), such as correctly working five arithmetic problems or sitting quietly in the reading circle, and is paid with a token upon completion of the job. Poker chips, pieces of paper, and stars are examples of items that can be used as tokens. Tokens (like money) are then exchanged in the economy for things the student wants: 5 tokens may buy a piece of gum, 10 may buy a luncheon date with the teacher or some free time, 50 may buy a field trip, and 500 may buy a day off from school. Frederickson and Frederickson (1975) support the use of both teacher-determined and self-determined reinforcement in a classroom token economy.

There are a number of advantages to a token economy system. The problem of satiation is avoided because the "store" where tokens are exchanged provides a wide variety of reinforcers on the "menu." The system also eases the problem of thinning the reinforcement schedule, because a student eventually must do more work for each token; e.g., inflation occurs! Whereas 5 minutes of independent work may be needed to earn one token today, a month later it may take 6 or 7 minutes of independent work to earn a token. Token systems demand that the students exercise some delay of gratification while providing immediate, tangible reinforcement. They are also very natural. Students can see a variety of token systems functioning in the "real world" around them. Additional advantages and disadvantages are discussed by Ayllon and McKittrick (1982) and Iwata and Bailey (1974).

Verifying Results.   Most teachers will readily recognize the effects of an intervention and will not see the need to verify the results experimentally. In some instances, however, it is important to demonstrate formally that the changes achieved through a behavior modification plan are not the result of other happenings. For instance, Sandy's teacher may have instigated a behavior modification program to reduce the girl's aggressive behavior and the behavior may have disappeared, but there is no proof that the change in behavior was a result of the program that the teacher instigated rather than a visit by Sandy's grandmother or some other variables at home. A reversal or return to baseline is one form of verification. This involves a brief interruption of the intervention program to see if the target behavior begins to approximate its previous baseline level. The program is then reinstituted, and the results are verified if the behavior again changes. Many teachers object to using the reversal procedure because they believe they are "pulling the rug out from under" a pupil by reinforcing a particular behavior and then momentarily withdrawing the reinforcement. Multiple baseline is a verification procedure that avoids this problem. This procedure involves the use of the same intervention program for several students exhibiting similar behavior problems or for one student exhibiting a variety of behavior problems; e.g., cursing for Sally, Susie, and Sara, or cursing, spitting, and fighting for Sally. If similar results are achieved on each of the multiple baselines after the same intervention has been initiated, verification has taken place. Although the classroom teacher may find these procedures to be too cumbersome and time consuming to implement on a regular basis, certainly behavior modification results of an experimental or research nature should be verified through these or other means. R. V. Hall (1983) offers guidelines for verifying results using applied behavior analysis research designs.

Applying Programs in the Classroom.	There is an abundance of research reporting the significant effects of behavior modification with different populations of students. Since it is impossible to describe all the research here, we cite several studies that have particular relevance to problem students. In most of these studies token economies were set up, where students received points, poker chips, etc., to be traded in at a specified time for desirable reinforcers.

Wadsworth (1971) investigated the efficacy of two different types of instructional approaches to increase motivation in reading for learning-disabled boys. He found that the reinforcement technique was significantly more effective than clinical tutoring in facilitating increased reading motivation and achievement. In another study (Glavin, Quay, & Werry, 1971), a token economy was established in a classroom of poorly disciplined children. It was successful in decreasing deviant behavior (such as jumping out of the seat), while simultaneously increasing attention and academic performance. Perline and Levinsky (1968) and Sulzbacker and Hauser (1968) reported similar results with mentally retarded children.

In a class of seventeen emotionally disturbed nine-year-olds, O'Leary and Becker (1967) attempted to use a token reinforcement system to eliminate deviant behaviors. They were successful in decreasing these behaviors from a range of 66 to 91 percent to a range of 3 to 32 percent. Preschool problem children were involved in a study by Allen, Turner, and Everett (1970). Through the use of contingency reinforcement, disruptive behaviors (hitting, kicking, spitting) were significantly reduced while appropriate behaviors, such as play and motor skills, were increased. Additional classroom applications may be found in R. V. Hall's (1974) *Behavior Modification: Applications in School and Home*, Kazdin's (1975) *Behavior Modification in Applied Settings*, O'Leary and O'Leary's (1977) *Classroom Management*, and Wolpe's (1976) *Theme and Variations: A Behavior Therapy Casebook*.

Behavioral Self-Control

Rationale

This self-control technique is one in which students themselves implement programs to change their own behaviors. Self-control can be implemented as a first effort to change behavior, or it can be used to maintain behaviors when externally implemented behavior modification programs are phased out. Behavioral self-control programs are helpful in getting students to assume responsibility for their own behavior and in relieving school personnel or parents of the time requirements associated with more traditional behavior modification methods. For more detailed information than we are able to provide in this space, readers are referred to four excellent sources, Esveldt-Dawson and Kazdin's (1982) programmed monograph, *How to Use Self-Control*; Fagen and Long's (1979) article "A Psychoeducational Curriculum Approach to Teaching Self-Control" and text *Teaching Children Self-Control* (Fagen, Long, & Stevens, 1975); and Workman's (1982) text, *Teaching Behavioral Self-Control to Students*. In addition, Workman and Hector (1978) provide a thorough review of the self-control literature.

Procedures

Self-control techniques can be taught to most school-aged children. In this section we describe four specific techniques: self-assessment, self-observation, self-reinforcement, and self-punishment.

Self-assessment, or self-evaluation, techniques require students to appraise their behavior. Teachers can help students assess their behavior by having them (1) complete a rating scale or checklist, (2) prompt or cue appropriate behaviors verbally (e.g., "Now I am going to . . .,"), or (3) discuss orally or in writing a specific rule infraction or disruptive behavior they have committed. Obviously this technique requires some verbal competence and is not appropriate for language-disordered students or particularly concrete thinkers.

Self-observation, or self-monitoring, is simply observing and recording one's own behavior in a consistent, systematic way. Awareness of one's behavior frequently is sufficient impetus to improve or change it. For instance, keeping a calorie count or a weight chart is often helpful in maintaining desired weight. In the classroom, students can be taught to record such behaviors as talking without permission or completing assigned work; teachers can record the number of positive (or negative) comments they make in the course of a school day. A simple recording technique, such as a tally sheet or graph, will be easy to use and will provide a visual indication of behavioral improvement (or deterioration). Self-observations can be made on a frequency or duration basis.

Self-reinforcement occurs when individuals reward themselves for good or appropriate behaviors. Students decide what the reinforcer will be as well as establish the reinforcement/behavior ratio. Self-reinforcement is often implemented as a token economy where students reward themselves initially with stars, checkmarks, or tokens that are later exchanged for tangible rewards or privileges at school and home. Workman (1982) even describes the use of fantasies as self-reinforcers. Obviously, self-reinforcement must be preceded by self-observation.

Self-punishment is used less frequently than the other techniques for the same reasons that punishment is used less frequently than reinforcement in traditional behavior modification programs. In addition, it requires great fortitude to consciously inflict punishment on oneself! People who are trying to quit smoking and burn a dollar bill for each cigarette they smoke are practicing self-punishment. In school, students may be trained to remove points from their total for such infractions as being tardy or failing to complete assignments. Self-punishment works most effectively when combined with self-reinforcement of competing or alternative behaviors.

Other self-control techniques the reader may encounter include self-instruction (which involves rehearsal, prompting, and verbal mediation strategies), alternative response training (which involves learning to substitute a new behavior for a less appropriate one), and stimulus control (which involves arranging the environment to avoid stimuli that are known to elicit inappropriate or unwanted behaviors). All of these techniques, though, involve some form of self-assessment, self-observation, self-reinforcement, or self-punishment.

Contracting

Contracting for behavioral change is a popular and effective method for giving students some responsibility for changing their own behavior. A contract is a *two-way* agreement. The child agrees to behave in a certain fashion or to do a certain task at or within a given period of time. The teacher (or parent or other school personnel) agrees to deliver specific kinds of support during the contract and a particular payoff when the contract has been fulfilled. Sample behavioral contracts are shown in Figures 7–10 and 7–11. For additional sample contracts, the reader is referred to Kohfeldt's (1974) excellent little book, *Contracts,* and to Thompson and Quinby's (1981) *Individualized Interest Area Contracts.* In addition, R. V. Hall and Hall (1982) outline the process for negotiating a behavioral contract.

Long and Newman's Techniques for Managing Surface Behaviors

Rationale

Perhaps the most succinct discussion of the management of surface behaviors is offered by Long and Newman (1980). Their techniques are intended for use as

Figure 7–10. Formal Contract

Date: SEPT. 5, 1977

STUDENT: I agree to follow these rules to student behavior: 1) *when my teacher is giving instructions, I will look at her and listen* 2) *I will complete my workbook assignments in reading*

Signed: Albert Johnson

TEACHER: I agree to help Albert by: 1) *calling him by name when I am giving instructions* 2) *Giving him short workbook assignments he will be able to finish. I will give him a check at the end of each hour for following each rule and I will send his checklist home every Friday*

Signed: Mrs J. Rhoads

PRINCIPAL: I agree to help Albert by: *Having a 10 minute conference with him every Friday to discuss his progress*

Signed: Pete Principle

PARENTS: I/We agree to help Albert by: *Purchasing Sullivan workbooks for him. 2) He will earn 2¢ of his allowance for each check he brings home on Friday*

Signed: Albert Johnson, Sr.
Mary G. Johnson

Source: Reprinted with the permission of the author and publisher of P. Hawisher, *The Resource Room: Access to Excellence* (Lancaster, S.C.: S.C. Region V Educational Service Center, 1975).

Figure 7–11.   Informal Contracts

Date: *October 12, 1974*

STUDENT: *I agree to use only good student language today. When I talk I will speak quietly.*

Signed: *Phillip Carson*

TEACHER: *Phillip* will earn the following reward: *to wear the Good Citizenship Button tomorrow*

Signed: *Mr. Stanley*

Date: *November 13, 1975*

I will *not hit Susie this week*

I will *say "darn it" when I am angry*

I will _____

Signed: *Jim*

I will arrange for: *Jim to see a movie on Friday if he has 19 teacher signatures by that time.*

Signed: *Mrs. Reagan, Counselor*

Monday	Tuesday	Wednesday	Thursday	Friday
JRB	JRB	JRB	JRB	JRB
LM	LM	LM	LM	LM
R Trayer	R Trayer	R Trayer	R Trayer	R Trayer
VFT	VFT	VFT	VFT	VFT

Source: Reprinted with the permission of the author and publisher of P. Hawisher, *The Resource Room: Access to Excellence* (Lancaster, S.C.: S.C. Region V Educational Service Center, 1975).

"stop-gap" devices to prevent escalation of behavior problems or to avoid negative contagion. If necessary, the behaviors may be explored in depth (clinical exploitation) at a later time.

Procedures

Twelve interference techniques are described: planned ignoring, signal interference, proximity control, interest boosting, hurdle lessons, restructuring of the classroom program, support from routine, direct appeal to value areas, removal of seductive objects, antiseptic bouncing, tension decontamination through humor, and physical restraint. *Planned ignoring* closely resembles the extinction procedure described in the previous section. The basic assumption is that many behaviors will disappear more quickly if they are ignored than if the teacher attempts to intervene in some way. *Signal interference* involves the use of some cue, usually a nonverbal one, which lets the student(s) know that particular behaviors should be abandoned. The "school marm" look which most teachers develop is an example of signal interference. *Proximity control* is a device that teachers have often used. The teacher's presence in a potential trouble spot is usually sufficient to stop many disruptive surface behaviors (such as whispering and note passing) and to prevent the spread of these behaviors. *Interest boosting* and *hurdle lessons* are very similar techniques. In the former, the teacher makes an attempt to demonstrate interest in the student as an individual. The latter involves individual attention, too, although it usually centers around providing academic assistance or on-the-spot tutoring to alleviate frustration. *Restructuring of the classroom program* and *support from routine* are opposite techniques. Both require that the teacher be sensitive to needs within the classroom: Do the students require a fresh outlook or will a familiar, no-surprises approach be more supportive? *Direct appeal to value areas* can be effective only when the teacher and the students share the same values or when the teacher is aware of those values that the students have internalized. *Removal of seductive objects* has a direct relationship to the props discussed by Redl (1959), which were presented earlier in this chapter. It is frequently easier to remove tempting objects than to manage the behaviors that they may elicit from students. *Antiseptic bouncing* is used to remove a student from the classroom without any punitive overtones. It is useful to prevent the spread of contagious behaviors such as giggling or false hiccoughing or to give an embarrassed or angry student an opportunity to regain control. Usually the student is asked to run an errand or to perform some other chore outside the class. *Tension decontamination through humor* reflects the power of a sense of humor. Many tense situations can be defused by a single good-natured or humorous remark from the teacher. The final management technique, *physical restraint*, is used on those rare occasions when a student has lost control completely. Physical restraint is intended to prevent the student from injuring himself or herself or others and to communicate the teacher's willingness to provide external control. Most teachers already use many, if not all, of these management techniques. Their power as intervention strategies will be increased if teachers use them consciously and on a planned basis.

Trieschman's Strategy for Managing Temper Tantrums

Rationale

Trieschman (1969) hypothesizes that a temper tantrum is not a single behavior but a series of events with definite stages. He identified six stages, which were given descriptive names: the Rumbling and Grumbling stage, the Help-Help stage, the Either-Or stage, the No-No stage, the Leave Me Alone stage, and the Hangover stage. Tantrums are managed by dealing with the behaviors in each stage. If the early stages are managed appropriately, the author asserts, tantrums may occur less frequently or may possibly be prevented from occurring at all.

Procedures

During the Rumbling and Grumbling stage, the student is generally grumpy. He or she appears to be "dribbling (as opposed to gushing) hostility" (Trieschman, 1969, p. 176). The student is seeking an issue over which to throw the tantrum he or she has already decided to have. In many instances, the issue that the student selects is one that lacks a satisfactory solution. For instance, a child may demand that an irreparably broken toy be mended immediately. Management is aided by identifying the pattern of Rumbling and Grumbling. Frequently, tantrums will have a similar time and place (e.g., right before lunch or only in the physical education class). The teacher who recognizes the pattern sometimes can help the student to verbalize the problem rather than to act out the "front issue" for the problem. This is usually accomplished through life-space interviewing, a technique that will be discussed later.

The Help-Help stage is the first really loud, noisy stage of the tantrum. The student "has found his issue and is now signaling his need for help. The signal he uses is usually a very visible and deliberate rule-breaking act" (p. 179), which is designed to attract adult attention. The child senses that he or she is losing internal control and is demanding that an authority figure intervene and impose external control. Management primarily involves teaching the student to signal a need for help in a more appropriate manner by substituting an appropriate signal for the inappropriate rule-breaking signal. It may be necessary at this point for the teacher to utilize the physical restraint technique described by Long and

Newman while verbalizing to the student a desire to help the student control his or her behavior. It is best, according to Trieschman, to avoid pointing out that the student broke a rule: the student knows he or she broke the rule, for it was done deliberately.

The Either-Or stage represents the student's attempt to show that he or she still can control the situation by setting out alternatives. The student often tries to insult the adult or authority figure who is attempting to help by making fun of the adult's personal or sexual characteristics. The most important part of the management at this stage is to model appropriate anger for the student. "Helpfully modeling reasonable anger is something a child could imitate more easily than boundless patience and complete passivity in the face of fury" (p. 186). Any either-or proposition that can be accepted should be promoted by the adult, and additional alternatives also may be proposed.

The No-No stage is the one in which the student will respond negatively to any suggestion or statement by the adult. It is frequently impossible to manage a tantrum that has reached this stage, although sometimes the tantrum can be pushed back to the previous, Either-Or stage. If good rapport exists between the student and the teacher, it may even be possible to point out the foolishness of the No-No stage by stating questions in such a way that the student actually complies with the teacher's wishes by saying "No." This technique can certainly backfire, however, and should be used with extreme caution so that the student does not come to believe that the teacher is making fun of him or her or that he or she is once again "the goat." The noisy part of the tantrum usually dies down at the end of this stage.

The Leave Me Alone stage is relatively quiet and is often mistaken for a return to normal behavior. It is not. The noise is gone and the student may be more amenable to assistance from the adult, but the student is not ready to resume interaction with the world and should not be expected to do so. The student's desire to be left alone should be respected, although the adult should remain within eyeshot or earshot to assure the student that external control is still available if it is necessary. As little conversation as possible is advisable at this stage.

During the Hangover stage, two states of affairs may arise. Some students experience a "clean drunk" after their tantrums. They have no painful memories of the tantrum and appear to have returned to normal. Other students experience a hangover and feel quite guilty and embarrassed about the incident. The memory is painful. The latter condition is more desirable. If a student experiences a clean drunk, it may be possible to induce a hangover that can be exploited, probably through life-space interviewing. Signal words can be devised, as can other alternative behaviors that are more acceptable than tantruming. "Reviewing the sequence of events . . . and learning alternative coping skills is constructive" (p. 192) use of the student's hangover.

Life-Space Interviewing

Rationale

Life-space interviewing (LSI) is a psychoeducationally oriented technique aimed at dealing with the everyday interactional problems that occur in the classroom. Originally designed for use by teachers assigned to cope with crisis situations, LSI can be used effectively within the classroom. Rational and semi-directional in its approach, LSI attempts to structure a situation so that students can work out their own problems. The teacher's role is one of listener and facilitator in the decision making enacted by the students involved. The technique is nonjudgmental and presents immediate concrete consequences to the students without the typical value appeals that adults frequently make in reaction to behavioral outbursts.

Procedure

Describing the way LSI might be used to deal with an actual incident is perhaps the most effective way of explaining the approach. Consider the following incident: In the middle of a handwriting lesson, Johnny and David suddenly broke out into a violent fight—cursing, yelling, and hitting each other; the teacher told the rest of the class to continue working and asked the two boys involved in the fight to come up and talk about what just happened.

The LSI approach would proceed in the following manner.

Step 1. The teacher asks Johnny what happened, telling David that he will have equal time to explain as soon as Johnny finishes. The aim of this step is to determine each child's *perception* of what happened. The facts are not important, but rather each child's understanding of the incident. At this point the teacher simply listens.

Step 2. Through objective questioning, the teacher tries to determine if the boys' explanations for fighting really constitute the crux of the problem. Are they fighting over the ownership of a pencil, or is this the manifestation of a deeper worry? Frequently, students bring to school arguments or hostilities that have developed at home or at recess. Questioning by the teacher is an attempt to discover how extensive the problem is, without making any interpretations.

Step 3. After the boys have had a chance to express thoroughly their feelings about the fight and why they think it happened, they are asked what they feel they *can* (not *should*) do about it. By asking this, the teacher brings the values of the children to the surface. If their suggestions for remedy are acceptable to all three involved, the interview is terminated here. A note of caution to the teacher: do not ententeverbalize. Given a structured and guided opportunity to deal with their problems, students often can reach an acceptable solution, without extensive suggestions by the teacher.

Step 4. If the problem is not resolved at this point, the teacher takes a more direct role, pointing out the reality factors of the situation and the consequences of the behavior if it occurs again. Once more, value judgments are minimized. The teacher should not moralize about the impropriety of cursing and fighting, but simply say that the rules of the school prohibit fighting in class and explain the consequences.

Step 5. By talking with the boys, the teacher can explore their motivation for change. If there is no discernible remedy for the situation, the teacher can make suggestions, such as breaking the pencil in half or flipping a coin.

Step 6. The final step is to develop a follow-through plan with the boys that includes discussing alternative procedures should the problem arise in the future. Consequences are once again clearly described by the teacher.

Redl and Wineman (1957) list two components of life-space interviewing: emotional first aid on the spot and clinical exploitation of life events. In differentiating these two, Coleman (1986) offers the following example:

> The teacher realizes that Suellen is having a particularly bad day, which began with an argument with her mother before she left home this morning. Suellen has a long-standing habit of rationalizing or making elaborate excuses for her obnoxious behavior. When she begins to taunt a classmate, the classmate blows up and a near-scuffle ensues. Arriving at the scene, the teacher may choose simply to break up the argument and talk to Suellen about her difficult day (emotional first aid) or may decide to use the event to illustrate to Suellen her habit of taking out her frustration on others and then excusing it (clinical exploitation).

Emotional first aid has five subcategories.

1. *Drainoff of frustration acidity* is an attempt to remove the "sting" from unexpected disappointment or frustration.
2. *Support for the management of panic, fury, and guilt* is a means of providing temporary support for a student who is unable to deal effectively with feelings of hate, guilt, anxiety, or anger.
3. *Communication maintenance in moments of relationship decay* is an attempt to maintain a thread of communication and to prevent the student from totally withdrawing.
4. *Regulation of behavioral and social traffic* is the consistent application of rules and/or guidelines for appropriate behavior.

5. *Umpire services,* the final category, is an attempt by an impartial adult to referee difficulties between two students or within a single student.

Redl and Wineman also identified five techniques of clinical exploitation, the in-depth analysis of situations in which problem behaviors occur.

1. *Reality rub-in* is an attempt to make the student aware of what really happened in a crisis situation.
2. *Symptom estrangement* helps the student let go of inappropriate behaviors.
3. *Massaging numb value areas* is a technique to stimulate dormant values that are appropriate to a student's particular situation.
4. *New tool salesmanship* is an attempt to "sell" a student on alternative forms of behavior that are more appropriate and/or socially acceptable.
5. *Manipulation of the boundaries of the self* is an attempt to make the student aware of himself or herself as an individual so that he or she will not be "sucked" unawares into roles or actions defined by others.

Any one or all of these techniques may be used in LSI.

The effectiveness of the LSI approach is dependent on the attitudes and behavior of the teacher. Consciously structuring responses will facilitate positive outcomes. During the interview, a casual and polite atmosphere should be maintained, for this reduces the defensive and hostile feelings of the students. The teacher should sit close to the students and avoid towering above them, appearing as much as possible to be neutral and approachable.

If the teacher knows something about the incident, he or she should confront the students with this knowledge. This frequently places the problem in its proper perspective and saves time by eliminating the need for each student to give a detailed description of the event. They will readily add their own perceptions of what occurred. The teacher should avoid asking "why" questions, because many young or disturbed students lack the insight or verbal ability to explain their actions. By calmly stating that situations like this sometimes do occur, or that no real harm has been done, the teacher reassures the student that the teacher is not such a terrible person, enabling the student to "open up" to the teacher. Most important, the students should be listened to, helped to plan for future incidents, and given a chance to ask questions.

The advantages of this approach have been summarized by Redl and Wattenberg (1959). LSI demonstrates to students that they have alternative ways of dealing with their problems. At the same time, they are encouraged to see the consequences of their behavior in an actual life experience without being subjected to moralizing and punishment. Through neutral and supportive communication between student and teacher, hostilities, frustrations, and guilt are relieved. This can help to avoid explosive outbursts later that same day. Because the intervention is immediate, the student's desire for help and motivation for change are greatly increased. Life-space interviewing frequently leads to as much growth in the teacher as in the pupils. This is particularly true when teachers and pupils come from different cultural backgrounds. Careful listening on the part of the teacher can lead to insights into the reasons underlying students' behavior.

There are, however, several limitations to this approach that must be described. First, in a class of perhaps twenty to thirty students, the immediate, time-consuming interview may not be feasible. However, if the teacher has confidence in the rationale of LSI, there is no reason why the teacher-pupil interaction cannot be delayed until recess or after school.

Second, LSI requires expert emotional control and sensitivity on the part of the teacher. If the teacher becomes involved in the emotionalism of the problem, effectiveness if sacrificed and the technique becomes useless.

LSI should not be attempted without supervised training and practice in the use of the technique. There is a third, more subtle limitation to LSI: by removing the student from a 30-to-1 classroom situation to a 2-to-1 personal interaction, the teacher may be reinforcing the negative behavior instead of changing it.

Projective Techniques

Rationale

Projective techniques frequently utilize supportive media such as puppets, dramatic plays, toys, books, art materials, and music as stimuli to encourage students to express ("project") feelings that they might not reveal in conversation or interviews. Therapies based on projective theory have been developed largely in clinical practice and are used primarily by specially trained professionals. Most have a decided neo-Freudian orientation. However, some of these techniques may be used by classroom teachers to highlight a specific problem area or to explore it in depth. In particular, role playing and puppetry are used by classroom teachers, as well as some aspects of art and music therapy. Some projective techniques will be used by members of the professional support team working with seriously disturbed children who are receiving help or therapy outside the classroom.

Role Playing

Role playing is a form of "let's pretend." The children act out situations that involve problems of getting along together. A distinctive version of role playing, called psychodrama, has been developed by Moreno (1946). Psychodrama is usually employed with a severely disturbed individual, who is required to come up on a stage and express real or fantasized feelings and problems. There is no criticism in psychodrama, only "controlled confrontation." Participation is voluntary. Some of Moreno's psychodramatic techniques include role reversal, soliloquy, double (where a "helper" participates in the play), mirror (where one participant "apes" the actions of another), behind the back (where other participants talk about the target individual), high chair, empty chair, magic shop (where goals and aspirations are expressed), and ideal other. Psychodrama requires the presence of a trained therapist because of its explosive nature; therefore, it is not recommended for use in the classroom. However, role playing as a technique for learning new behaviors and skills can be appropriately adapted to the classroom.

Interpersonal problems often find solution through acceptance of criticism or other forms of perceived punishment or rejection. Students can learn how to cope with these experiences by exploring various responses and reactions. One student might portray the role of an angry member of the class, and another student might play himself or herself entering into a potential fight with that student. Through suggestions from the teacher and class members, the student can learn to respond to anger more skillfully and without losing face. This technique can also help physically or mentally handicapped students face real or imagined social reactions without reverting to excessive emotional outbursts.

Harth (1966) applied role playing to a classroom of ten emotionally disturbed children from two public schools in a low socioeconomic area of a southern city. He studied the effects of the therapy on the children's attitudes toward school, their classroom behavior, and their reaction to frustration. During a five-week period, the experimental group engaged in two role-playing sessions weekly. During this time they portrayed school personnel in various problem situations centered around school. After the experimental period, Harth found no change in either the children's attitudes toward school or their reaction to frustration. However, classroom behavior of the experimental group did change from baseline information.

Although the results of this study indicate a cautious optimism, further studies are needed to demonstrate the effectiveness of this approach with various types and sizes of classes. This is not to imply that the teacher need wait for such substantiation before using role playing within the school setting. Wood (1981b) suggests useful and creative activities involving role playing, puppetry, and other "fantasy" activities.

Puppetry

Theories that utilize the construct of the "unconscious" as a potent motivator in human behavior recognize the need for bringing unconscious feelings to the level of consciousness. An effective way of doing this is through the use of puppetry (Woltmann, 1971), another form of psychodrama. The puppets have specific meaning to each student, who is able to project hate, anger, fears, and desires onto them in a neutral, fantasylike manner. Many of these feelings ordinarily remain suppressed because expression of them in actual life situations is often too threatening to the student or is socially unacceptable. But as Woltmann states: "Puppetry carries with it the reassurance that everything on the stage is only a make-believe affair" (p. 226). To kill the bad guy is acceptable. Not only does he always come to life during the next show, but with each "killing" comes the release of suppressed rage, which otherwise is often inappropriately released during instructional time.

All that puppetry requires is commercial or homemade puppets and a structure that can serve as a stage. Often the students themselves can create the needed equipment. The puppet characters should combine both fantastic and realistic factors, so that the student can enter easily into the activity and identify with the characters and their problems. Woltmann suggests the use of the following types of puppet actors: (1) the hero; (2) a bad mother, often appearing as a witch; (3) a bad father, appearing as a giant; (4) a boy or girl representing the student's idealized self; and (5) an animal. Other personalities can be added as the students begin to interact in this problem-solving world of fantasy.

Initially, it is best for an adult to act as the puppeteer, following the commands of the audience. Some students may yell out "Kill the witch! Kill her!" while others shrink away in fear. It frequently is helpful to bring a fearful student behind the stage while the acting is going to assure him or her that it is only make-believe. During the show all pupil commands should be accepted, but afterward alternative solutions to the problems revealed in the fantasy play can be discussed and acted out. Puppetry can dispel intense feelings and contribute to learning alternatives to stereotypic behaviors. The teacher should be careful to resolve any problems broached in the play so that the students have a "clean slate" and are relaxed for the next activity.

Play Therapy

The use of play therapy in school differs in some ways from play as a psychotherapeutic technique. A primary goal in school is to increase the individual's understanding of himself or herself by relating a free situation (play) in which the student is given the opportunity to self-actualize (Alexander, 1971). According to Axline (1947, 1964), an acknowledged authority on the technique of play therapy, "the child must first learn self-respect and a sense of dignity that grows out of his increasing self-understanding before he can learn to respect the personalities and rights and differences of others" (1964, p. 67). In psychotherapy the aim is to discover unconscious motivations by interpretative techniques. Both educational and psychotherapeutic play share several views: (1) the relationship between therapist (or teacher) and the student is the key to emotional growth, and (2) the selection and use of various play activities aids in expressing personal and social needs. The play situation is provided because it is usually the most comfortable one for the student and the most conducive to self-expression.

Play materials are provided for the student, but their use should not be contrived by the therapist. Recommended materials are

sandbox	basin filled with water
doll house	toy dishes
toy soldiers	toy police and fire trucks
crayons	toy animals
scissors	hammer

Ginott (1961), another early proponent of play therapy, suggests that young children who are "socially hungry" are the best candidates for play therapy. The technique seems to lose its effectiveness after about age eight, he says, pointing out that play therapy probably is counterindicated for children who are aggressive or have deviant sexual drives, children who suffer from intense sibling rivalries or extreme hostility, children who tend to steal, children who are prone to have unusually strong stress reactions, and children who engage in sociopathic behaviors.

Although there are no clear-cut procedures for play therapy, Kessler (1966, pp. 376–377) restates Axline's eight basic principles[2]:

1. The therapist must develop a warm, friendly relationship with the child.
2. The therapist accepts the child exactly as he is.
3. The therapist establishes a feeling of permissiveness in the relationship.
4. The therapist is alert to recognize the feelings [of the child] and to reflect the feelings back to the child so that she gains insight into her behavior.
5. The therapist maintains a deep respect for the child's ability to solve his own problems.
6. The child leads the way; the therapist follows.
7. The therapist does not attempt to hurry the therapy along.
8. The therapist establishes only those limitations that are necessary to anchor the therapy to the world of reality and to make the child aware of his responsibility in the relationship.

[2]From Jane W. Kessler, *Psychopathology of Childhood*, © 1966. By permission of Prentice-Hall, Inc.

The effects of play therapy have been equivocal. According to Pumerey and Elliott (1970) and Schiedlinger and Rauch (1972), the efficacy of play therapy is still doubtful. Axline (1947), Bills (1950), Fisher (1953), Fleming and Snyder (1947), and Ginott (1961) report favorable results from play therapy in relationship to personality adjustment and reading achievement with emotionally disturbed children. In a survey of thirty-seven investigations of the efficacy of psychotherapy with children (many using play therapy), Levitt (1957) noted the absence of differences between treated children and controls. Two-thirds of the children evaluated immediately after treatment and three-fourths evaluated at follow-up showed improvement. Since the statistics were approximately the same for control groups, Levitt concluded that this study fails to support the efficacy of this approach with children. The decision to use or not to use play therapy depends on more than reports of efficacy studies, however; the time required for the process and the size of the class are practical determinants. As Newcomer said in her book *Understanding and Teaching Emotionally Disturbed Children* (1980),

> . . . it seems most likely that play therapy is not the panacea that advocates like Axline think it is. It certainly is not the best means of remediating serious reading or spelling problems, as she has indicated. However, if the teacher's goals . . . pertain to helping children develop increasingly mature and adaptive social skills, establishing a nonthreatening relationship . . ., and/or providing opportunities . . . to model better adjusted peers, it may prove a helpful technique. (p. 365)

Art and Music Therapy

The goals of art and music therapy parallel those previously expressed for play therapy, puppetry, and role playing: encouraging students to express themselves freely and without fear. Music and various art media such as paint and clay may elicit expressions of feelings that would not surface otherwise. Art and music therapy provide nonthreatening situations in which students can share their feelings and release inner tensions.

For art therapy, a wide variety of media should be available in the classroom or therapy room. Freestyle activities such as finger painting, clay sculpting, and drawing will provide unstructured avenues for expression. Denny (1977) suggests a number of goals for art therapy in the schools. Among these are encouraging spontaneous expression, building rapport by encouraging interaction with other participants, facilitating the expression of inner feelings, and exploring self-perceptions. It is not unusual for teachers to detect some of the problems that students are experiencing by examining their art work. Usually, though, this will only confirm problems that already have been identified. Teachers are cautioned *not* to use art therapy as a diagnostic tool unless they have had specific training in this area. Readers who are interested in learning more about art therapy are referred to E. Kramer (1971), Naumberg (1973), Ulman and Dachinger (1977), and G. H. Williams and Wood (1981).

Music is often cited as a universal language, and it certainly plays an especially important role in the social life of many adolescents. Music can have a quieting effect on unusually active students and can promote concentration, since it helps to shut out noises that might otherwise be distracting (Reinert, 1980). Aggressive behaviors can be vented through such music activities as dancing; playing drums, rhythm sticks, or sandpaper blocks; and singing action songs. In addition to engaging in traditional therapeutic activities of singing, dancing, or playing musical instruments, students can talk or write about the feelings elicited by certain types of music or about musical content, such as historical information on certain pieces of music, composers' biographies, and so on. Readers interested in music therapy are referred to Michel (1971) and to Nordoff and Robbins (1971).

Cognitive Interventions

Cognitive behavior modification and other so-called rational approaches to behavior management have gained recognition in recent years. Prominent among these approaches are Glasser's (1965, 1969) work with reality therapy, Ellis's (1962, 1970, 1974; Ellis, Wolfe, & Moseley, 1974) work with rational-emotive therapy, and Meichenbaum's (1975, 1983) work with cognitive behavior management.

Rationale

Each of these approaches requires that the clients, patients, or students assume responsibility not only for their own behavior, but also for the therapy programs. For instance, in reality therapy students are asked to select a better course of behavior than the ones they have been following. Throughout the process, students make value judgments regarding their own behavior and commit themselves to change. Several "better courses" may be attempted before the student falls into a comfortable and acceptable behavioral pattern. The premise is that "all patients have a common characteristic: they all deny the reality of the world around them" (Glasser, 1965, p. 6). Similar views are expressed by Ellis (1962) when he describes the "irrational" beliefs that clients hold on to, such as the "idea that it is a dire necessity for an adult human to be loved or approved by virtually every significant other person in his life" (p. 153).

Procedures

Each of these approaches sports a full-blown therapy program to which we cannot do justice in the space allowed. Interested readers should consult the authors' original work before attempting to establish such programs in their schools. We will attempt here to summarize the basic tenets of these three cognitively based therapies.

Ellis (1974) discusses several premises that he believes are basic to his rational-emotive therapy (RET). Probably the most important tenet is that change must be effected in the inner language that people use to talk to themselves about their behavior, their values, and their reasons for acting in a particular way. Ellis believes that such a language change will facilitate behavior change by allowing clients to clarify their reasoning through the formation and use of hypotheses. Ellis emphasizes that the burden for the success of any intervention must be assumed by the client, although he stresses that no blame should be attached to failure and that the therapist can "sell" or market behavioral change in much the same way that one might sell an actual product. Ellis stresses that the causes of one's problems are found only in the present. He insists on practice and "homework" for clients. In general, this therapy is highly verbal and thus may not be appropriate for students who have language or general reasoning difficulties. Zionts (1985) devotes two chapters of his text to practical ways of implementing RET in a school.

According to Coleman (1986), reality therapy "consists of three general stages: establishing an involvement, forcing a value judgment, and finding alternative ways of behaving." Within this framework, the "3Rs" are emphasized: responsibility, reality, and right and wrong. Responsibility is required for people to meet their own personal needs without infringing on the rights of others in the process; irresponsibility, in Glasser's (1969) view, leads to disturbance. Reality requires that people accept the world around them, including societal canon law and, most important, the true relationship between their behavior and its consequences. Right-wrong requires a value judgment whereby people recognize that deviant behavior is wrong because it is harmful to self and others.

Glasser discusses ways that teachers can implement reality therapy in the classroom. He says that the teacher should continually ask three questions of the student: "What are you doing?" "Is your behavior helping you or those around you?" "What could you do differently?" He advocates a more behavioristic approach than does Ellis, and for this reason Newcomer (1980) suggests that reality therapy may be more useful with young children or with students whose verbal reasoning powers are limited or impaired.

Meichenbaum (1975) is even more behavioral. His methods are essentially values clarification combined with social skills training. He suggests the use of basic modeling principles to help students acquire self-control over their behaviors. In general, he suggests the need to identify problem areas through discussion or role playing. Skills to be acquired are broken down into subcomponents, and their verbal aspects are studied carefully. The teaching process begins after a concise explanation of why a particular skill needs to be learned. The steps of the skill are defined; modeled by the teacher, therapist, or a peer; practiced by the target student through role playing and real life situations; and altered or reinforced through feedback and praise. Meichenbaum believes that many of these steps can be accomplished in group sessions, because many students lack the same (or similar) basic social skills.

In reviewing cognitive behavior management strategies, Lloyd (1980) identified several characteristics that most approaches have in common.

1. Cognitive behavior modification is a self-imposed treatment, similar to the self-control strategies presented earlier in this chapter.
2. Self-talk or other verbalization strategies are taught, principally through modeling or imitation.
3. Problem solving is the primary goal, and a basic strategy is to help children consider several possible alternative behaviors before acting or responding.

Commercially Available Programs

Rationale

Until recently there was a noticeable paucity of materials designed to teach affective skills; several commercial programs are now available. Most of these programs are designed to teach students such skills as how to be open to new experiences, how to cope, how to label and appropriately express feelings, and how to identify and clarify values. For instruction, they depend heavily on the use of puppetry, role playing, sociodrama, and discussion. Although most of the materials were designed with "normal" students in mind, their use need not be limited solely to this population. Teachers can use those portions of the programs that seem appropriate and can integrate them with materials of their own design.

There is little empirical evidence to support the efficacy of commercially available affective programs. L. Brown (1980) studied the effectiveness of two commercial programs, Toward Affective Development (TAD) and Developing Understanding of Self and Others (DUSO), with groups of third-graders who were followed through the sixth grade. Triads of students, matched on the basis of sex, intelligence, and homeroom teacher, were randomly assigned to TAD, DUSO, or a control program of supervised free play. Several measures of behavioral and self-concept change were administered at the end of the one-year program and during each of the three following years. No significant group differences were detected on any measure, although more students who participated in the two commercial programs reported that they had fun.

Programs

Sixteen programs will be discussed briefly in this section: Human Development, DUSO-I and II, TAD, Lollipop Dragon, First Things, Dimensions of Personality, Child's Series on Psychologically Relevant Themes, Transition, Coping With, Contact Maturity, the Walker Social Skills Curriculum, Social Skills and Me, TLL, values clarification, and *The Sourcebook.*

My Friends and Me (Davis, 1977) was written for a preschool audience. Through the use of discussion, puppetry, role playing, and drawing, students go through the process of self-identification and recognition of group rights and responsibilities. There are eight units: Social Identity, Emotional Identity, Physical Identity, Intellectual and Creative Identity, Cooperation, Consideration for Others, Ownership and Sharing, and Dependence and Help.

The Human Development Program (Palomares & Ball, 1974), popularly known as Magic Circle, is one of the more widely used commercial programs for teaching affective skills. The basic premise of the program is that teacher-led discussions that take place in a structured setting (e.g., in the Magic Circle) will help students to develop richer, more meaningful interrelationships with each other. Manuals and materials are provided for students from age four to age eleven (preschool through sixth grade). Objectives of the Human Development Program include improving self-control, listening skills, and expression; learning the meaning of responsibility, fantasy, and role expectations; and developing a positive self-concept, trust, and satisfactory interpersonal relationships.

The Developing Understanding of Self and Others–Revised (DUSO-R) (Dinkmeyer, 1982) kits are designed for use from kindergarten through second grade (D-I) and for third and fourth grades (D-II). DUSO-I stresses the inquiry method of learning. Stories, puppetry, music, and discussion are used to promote the eight unit themes: (1) Understanding and Accepting Self; (2) Understanding Feelings; (3) Understanding Others; (4) Understanding Independence; (5) Understanding Goals and Purposeful Behavior; (6) Understanding Mastery, Competence, and Resourcefulness; (7) Understanding Emotional Maturity; and (8) Understanding Choices and Consequences. Daily lesson plans for DUSO activities are presented in the manual. Role playing, puppetry, and listening are the primary activities used to develop the eight themes in DUSO-II. Stimulus posters and situation cards are provided to assist the teacher in initiating discussion around these themes: (1) Towards Self-Identity: Developing Self-Awareness and a Positive Self-Concept; (2) Towards Friendship: Understanding Peers; (3) Towards Responsible Interdependence: Understanding Growth from Self-Centeredness to Social Interest; (4) Towards Self-Reliance: Understanding Personal Responsibility; (5) Towards Resourcefulness and Purposefulness: Understanding Personal Motivation; (6) Towards Competence: Understanding Accomplishments; (7) Towards Emotional Stability: Understanding Stress; and (8) Towards Responsible Choice Making: Understanding Values.

Toward Affective Development (TAD) (DuPont, Gardner, & Brody, 1974) is a popular, widely used affective curriculum. It was designed for "normal" children in grades three through six, but is appropriate for guidance or remedial work as well as for gifted populations. Lessons are organized into five major units that use a student's real or vicarious experiences as the basis for growing and learning. These units include Reaching In and Reaching Out; Your Feelings and Mine; Working Together; Me: Today and Tomorrow; and Feeling, Thinking, Doing. Most of the activities are verbal: brainstorming, role playing, and discussion groups. TAD's 190 activities are accompanied by manuals; shapes, pictures, print blocks, and pens to create stories and scenes; "alter ego" dolls named Willdoo and Candoo; records and cassettes; and spirit masters describing family activities that support the TAD program.

The Adventures of the Lollipop Dragon (1970) was designed for students in the primary grades. Six filmstrips are included in the kit. They depict stories that emphasize personal relationships and interdependency (e.g., taking turns, sharing with others, and working in groups). The "hero" of the series is the Lollipop Dragon, who inhabits a small kingdom where the economy is based on the production of lollipops. The filmstrips are accompanied by records and cassettes of the stories and by a coloring book, "How the Lollipop Dragon Got His Name."

First Things (Grannis & Schone, 1970) was designed for first-, second-, and third-graders. Five themes are developed through the use of videotapes, sociodramatics, and role playing. Group interaction and the classification and expression of feelings are stressed. The themes are (1) Who do you think you are? (2) Guess who's in a group! (3) What happens between people? (4) You got mad: are you glad? (5) What do you expect of others?

Dimensions of Personality (Limbacher, 1969) was written for students in the upper elementary grades (four through six). According to the manual, portions of the program may be suitable for use with low-reading junior and senior high school students as well. It purports to maintain a holistic approach to affective education through which "children will come to understand their physical, intellectual, and emotional growth better" (Reinert, 1980, p. 147). Provocative questions, posters, pictures, and cartoons are used to stimulate discussion activities.

The Child's Series on Psychologically Relevant Themes (Fasler, 1971) was designed for preschool and primary grade students. The themes are "relevant" within a psychoanalytic orientation. The kit contains six videotapes, each of which tells a story and promotes a major psychodynamic theme. The videotapes are (1) "The Man of the House," in which a young boy is the man of the house in his father's absence and must then relinquish the role when his father returns from a business trip; (2) "All Alone with Daddy," in which a young girl develops a close relationship with her father while her mother is away and then becomes jealous when the mother returns; (3) "Grandpa Died Today," in which a boy's reaction to the death of his grandfather is chronicled; (4) "Don't Worry Dear," in which a young girl is teased about stuttering and develops some immature habits such as bedwetting and thumbsucking; (5) "Boy with a Problem," in which a young boy develops a variety of hypochondriacal symptoms because he is keeping a problem inside himself; and (6) "One Little Girl," in which a little girl learns to compensate for her weaknesses by promoting her strengths.

Transition (DuPont & DuPont, 1979) is intended for students from ages twelve to fifteen (grades six to nine). It uses posters and pictures, eight cassette tapes with printed scripts, ditto sheets, discussion cards, a gavel, and feeling word cards in a program of activities that are primarily verbal in nature and are discussion oriented. Activities are incorporated into five units: Transition 1—Communication and Problem-Solving Skills; Transition 2—Encouraging Openness and Trust; Transition 3—Verbal and Nonverbal Communication of Feelings; Transition 4—Needs, Goals, and Expectations; and Transition 5—Increasing Awareness of Values.

The Coping With Series (Wrenn & Schwarzrock, 1984) was developed for students from upper elementary through early senior high school grades. It contains four sets of five books each. The books are arranged around the themes Coping with Personal Identification, Coping with Human Relationships, Coping with Facts and Fantasies, and Coping with Teenage Problems.

Contact Maturity: Growing Up Strong (1972) was designed for junior and senior high school students with low reading abilities. It stresses a language arts approach, and one of the major goals of the program is to encourage an interest in reading. Poetry, short stories, open-ended stories, posters, and pictures are used to stimulate discussion and values clarification. Students are also encouraged to keep diaries of their daily activities and of their feelings in specific situations.

The Walker Social Skills Curriculum (Walker, McConnell, Holmes, Todis, Walker, & Golden, 1983) is a complete social skills curriculum for use with handicapped and nonhandicapped students from kindergarten to sixth grade. It utilizes direct instruction principles to teach specific social skills in the areas of Classroom Skills (Listening to the Teacher; When the Teacher Asks You to Do Something; Doing Your Best Work; Following Classroom Rules), Basic Interaction Skills (Eye Contact; Using the Right Voice; Starting, Listening, Answering; Making Sense; Taking Turns Talking; Questions; Continuing), Getting Along Skills (Using Polite Words; Sharing; Following Rules; Assisting Others; Touching the Right Way), Making Friends Skills (Good Grooming; Smiling; Complimenting and Friendship Making), and Coping Skills (When Someone Says "No"; When You Express Anger; When Someone Teases You; When Someone Tries to Hurt You; When Someone Asks You to Do Something You Can't Do; When Things Don't Go Right). The kit includes scripts for teaching these skills, suggested behavior management techniques, a screening device and suggestions for selecting children for the program, sample forms, and guidelines for training teachers to use the curriculum. Two optional videotapes are available, one that demonstrates appropriate and inappropriate examples of the skills being taught and another that demonstrates the program's application for parent and teacher groups.

Social Skills and Me (Crane & Reynolds, 1983) is a social/behavioral curriculum intended for use with disturbed students in the first through sixth grades. The curriculum's 100 lessons, to be used for one hour each day, focus on the skill areas of Communication (the messages one sends to other people with one's voice and body), Responsibility (acting appropriately and accepting responsibility for one's own behavior), Assertiveness (polite ways of expressing opinions and standing up for one's rights), and Problem Solving (solving problems in ways that please oneself without hurting others). Group and individual activities include relaxation exercises, keeping a scrapbook, individual student conferences, reinforcement time, and I Like Me activities, in addition to specific lesson activities. Although the authors recommend supervised training in the use of the curriculum, the materials are detailed enough for most teachers to self-instruct.

TLC is an acronym for Talking, Listening, Communicating (Bormaster & Treat, 1982), a curriculum guide that outlines 156 activities to help students build interpersonal relationships. The activities require thirty minutes or less and include paper-and-pencil as well as interactive activities. The book is sequenced around the following topics: Preparing Yourself, Understanding Yourself, Communication, Building Groups, Relating to Others, Developing Creativity, Making Decisions, Solving Problems, and Ending a Group in a Positive Manner.

Values clarification is an affective program, although it is not packaged as a kit. Several authors (such as Fine, 1973, and Weinstein & Fantini, 1970) discuss the uses of a values clarification program in the classroom. The reader is referred to an excellent book, *Values Clarification* by Simon, Howe, and Kirschenbaum (1978), which describes the technique of values clarification and provides activities for the teacher to use. In essence, values clarification is a questioning procedure that "should serve to generate thought regarding what values the student holds to, how the value was acquired, what the pragmatic implications are of the value and what complementary or competing values might exist on the part of the classmates" (Fine, 1973, p. 68). Values clarification is usually most successful with older elementary students and with adolescents because the technique requires participants to be able to identify and talk about abstract concepts such as values, emotions, and feelings.

The Sourcebook (Crane, Reynolds, & Sparks, 1983) is not a curriculum, strictly speaking. However, teachers who are planning to use commercial cur-

ricula in addition to other intervention techniques may find it a helpful resource. In the introductory sections of *The Sourcebook*, the authors provide
guidance for teachers who are attempting to write behavioral IEPs to outline appropriate short-term behavioral goals and objectives for behavior disordered and
disturbed students, or to devise a discipline contingency hierarchy. The appen-
dix, which constitutes the majority of the book, includes annual goals for both
teaching and counseling; the goals are crossreferenced with the federal guidelines for severe emotional disturbance.

chapter 8

Preparing Problem Learners for Independent Living

by Jim L. Daniels and J. Lee Wiederholt

Up to this point the chapters in this book have focused on areas of formal education that are familiar to most professionals, i.e., the "3 Rs" and "Deportment/ Conduct." This chapter deals with another important area of education that is less familiar to many but that is employed frequently with students who have learning and/or behavior problems. Specifically, this chapter focuses on educational endeavors that develop students' independent living skills. In the first section, the nature of independent living is described. The second section provides an overview of commonly used assessment techniques, and the third section discusses teaching programs and activities used to foster independent living.

THE NATURE OF INDEPENDENT LIVING

A significant number of students leave school without sufficient skills to handle everyday living (see, e.g., Bowe, 1978; National Commission on Excellence in Education, 1983; Northcutt, 1975). In attempting to remedy this situation, school personnel over the years have established several different types of programs to prepare students for adult life. The hope has been that participation in these programs will help students to function independently upon leaving school. This section provides a history of the changes in the concept of independent living as well as a current definition.

History of Independent Living Concept

Over the years several terms and definitions have been used to describe the concept of independent living. These terms include "literacy," "basic literacy," "survival skills," "basic skills," "competence," "communicative competence," and "functional competence." Wiederholt, Cronin, and Stubbs (1980) have noted an ever increasing expansion of what is included in definitions of independent living. For example, prior to the 1870s, one who could leave his or her "mark" (signature) on stone, wood, or paper was considered to be a literate person. During the 1870s and 1880s, the ability to write one's name became the indicator of a literate person. By 1890, additional writing, such as personal correspondence and record-keeping, was required.

World War I recruits were considered literate by the federal government if they could read, write, and comprehend a 2800+ word vocabulary. In addition, a reading speed of 150 words per minute was necessary. After World War II, the United Nations Educational, Scientific, and Cultural Organization (UNESCO) developed a definition of literacy to be used worldwide. The official UNESCO definition stated that literacy was the ability to read and write a short simple statement about everyday life with understanding. In 1965 the U.S. Office of Education (USOE) established a national norm for literacy. The USOE norm coupled satisfactory achievement of four years of elementary school with the ability to function in society. Functional literacy included math, reading, and writing ability as well as a general understanding of everyday life, e.g., banking, working, maintaining a home, etc.

In 1975 the Adult Performance Level (APL) study funded at The University of Texas by the U.S. Office of Education further expanded the understanding of the nature of independent living. Northcutt (1975) described the APL study and outlined four critical aspects of adult functional competencies. First, functional competency was seen as a concept that is meaningful only in a specific societal context. A person who is functionally competent in one environment may be incompetent in another. For example, an individual may do quite well in a rural low-income area but may be functionally incompetent in an urban "million-aire's row." Also, as the technology of a society changes, the requirements for competency change. A recent example here would be the strong emphasis on high school students' becoming "computer literate." Second, functional competency was seen as two dimensional and was described as a set of skills (e.g., reading and writing) applied to a set of general knowledge areas (e.g., Occupational, Health, and Government). Third, persons were viewed as functionally competent only to the extent that they could meet the requirements extant at a given time. Specifically, functional competency was seen as a dynamic rather than a static state. For example, as people get older they may become less functionally competent. Fourth, functional competency was viewed as directly related to success in adult life. More competent adults would be more successful.

Wiederholt and Larsen (1983), although in basic agreement with this model of functional competency, added a third dimension to the two-dimensional (skills and knowledge) model proposed by the APL group. The third dimension they proposed was that of *application*, which refers to the day-to-day use of skills and knowledge. Wiederholt and Larsen noted that a person could be knowledgeable about a subject and possess an adequate level of required skills but still not use them effectively. They further stated:

> The application of specific knowledge and skills relates significantly to the motivation and interest a person has in using them in real life situations. They also relate to a great extent to the values in which they are held. A case in point would be persons on the welfare rolls. Some individuals are on welfare because they have no other choices. Others, however, are able to work but view welfare as an acceptable alternative to gainful employment. The use of birth control methods, alcohol, and drugs, as well as others, are additional areas in which the "values/motivations" change from individual to individual. (1983, p. 4)

Current Independent Living Concept

Daniels (1984) expanded the APL model and the Wiederholt and Larsen (1983) recommendations by delineating (1) additional specific skills needed by people, (2) additional knowledge areas he believed important, and (3) intervention levels for aiding people who were partially or totally incompetent. Daniels's recommendations are discussed next.

Specific Skills Needed by People

Daniels describes eleven skill areas needed by people to function independently in life. These areas and their definitions follow:

1. Speaking—production of oral language appropriate to situational communication needs.

2. Listening—derivation of meaning from auditory stimulus.
3. Viewing—derivation of meaning from nonverbal visual stimulus.
4. Reading—derivation of meaning from printed material (verbal, mathematical).
5. Writing—production of written language or visual images appropriate to situational communication needs.
6. Calculating—application of mathematical concepts to solve life situations.
7. Relating—application of interpersonal communication skills to develop and maintain relationships.
8. Moving—using physical/motor skills to locomote between or within environments.
9. Problem solving—application of decision-making skills in order to develop and/or implement plans of action.
10. Recreating—development of activity patterns that result in personal relaxation or enjoyment.
11. Feeling—derivation of emotion from experience that is either expressed, controlled, or denied.

Ackland (1976) noted that not all of these skills are absolutely necessary for surviving independently. Persons who are deaf, nonreaders, or in other ways skill deficient are often able to survive and do quite well in daily life. This is because in real life people employ different skills to solve the same problem. For example, a person who is a nonreader would not have the reading skills to fill out a federal income tax form and might, as a result, seek help from another person who possesses this skill. Also, as noted by the APL study, the level of skill required is based on the specific societal context in which a person functions. For example, the level of writing skill needed by a cashier in a drugstore would be much lower than that needed by a college professor.

Knowledge Areas Needed by People

Daniels noted seven types of areas in which people need knowledge in order to function independently. These areas and their definitions are as follows:

1. Self—awareness, attitudes, values, interests, abilities, changing, health, grooming, feelings
2. Others—friends, family, relationships, neighbors, co-workers, cultural diversity, global thinking
3. Career—vocational selection, job seeking, job holding, awareness, job-specific skills

4. Community—resources (use of, location of, types of)
5. Government and law—rights, law, voting, world awareness, issues and trends
6. Humanities—art, music, history, literature, drama
7. Economics—budgets, shopping, selling, contracts, markets

Several attempts have been made to specify in more detail the knowledge needed by individuals to function independently. Some of these attempts include the Utah study (Alfaro & Gillpatrick, 1978), the Adkins-Connecticut reconnaissance study (Adkins, 1977), the California adult competencies study (NOMOS Institute, 1978), the New York external state high school diploma program (Nickse, 1977), the National Center for Research in Vocational Education study (Selg & Jones, 1980), the Northwest Regional Educational Laboratory functional literacy project (Reder, 1978), as well as the APL study mentioned previously. J. K. Fisher (1980) has noted that although great progress has been made, much still needs to be investigated. The cumulative findings of these studies are presented in the following list. Under each of the seven knowledge areas appears a list of subjects on which specific information is believed to be important for independent living.

Self
Applying the decision-making process
Identifying one's own values, goals, roles and needs
Employing safety measures, prevention of injury or accident
Health needs and concerns of the adolescent and ways to ease transition to adulthood
Maintaining good mental and physical health
Understanding self and interpersonal relationships
Proper nutrition
First aid for emergencies
Health and medical insurance
Use of drugs and federal control of drugs
Effect of life-cycle positions on problems individuals face
Communicating with physicians

Others
Interpreting the facial expressions of others
Functioning within a group
The effects of one group upon another
The relationship between the individual and the environment

Communicating in a socially acceptable manner

Diseases and other health problems associated with one's family

Making family decisions with family members

Recognizing social norms in a variety of situations and exhibiting cooperative skills for participating in social life

Difficulties in meeting someone of the opposite sex

Pregnancy and prenatal care

Family planning and birth control

Money problems as a major source of argument between husband and wife

Difficulties of separation, divorce, or desertion

Conflicts over raising children from a previous marriage

Dealing with children's wishes because of peer pressure

Child-rearing practices and procedures for guarding health and safety of a child

Helping children with handicaps or special problems

Finding day care facilities or responsible people to care for children

Problems of child abuse

Dealing with lying, stealing, and sneaky behavior

Dealing with neighbors' children and neighbors

Feelings that there are few places one can admit one's ignorance

Difficulties in balancing home and family responsibilities and responsibilities to self

Dealing with discrimination because of being too short, fat, or a minority

Career

Sources of employment

Requirements of different occupations

Occupational interests

Private and other employment agencies

Job applications and interviews

Standards of behavior for types of employment

Attitudes and skills that may lead to promotion

Financial and legal aspects of employment

Aspects of employment other than financial that affect job

Discrimination against women, minorities, and others in employment

Availability of on-the-job training programs, summer employment, etc.

Managing one's own time and activities

Using reading and math skills on the job

Community

Types of community resources

How and when to apply for community services, such as Social Security and Medicare

Recreational services

Informational services (e.g., media, telephone, library)

Resources for acting on citizens' complaints

Recognizing traffic signs, driving regulations, safety

Transportation schedules, fares, informational services

Time zones, daylight savings time

Making travel plans and arrangements

Relationship between transportation and public problems (traffic problems, energy)

Influence of mass media

Dealing with school, medical, and health services

Government and Law

Structure and function of the federal government and state and local governments (Constitution, branches, etc.)

Participation in government process

Relationship between individual and the government

Relationship between individual and the legal system

Legal documents, contracts

Relationship between government services and taxes

Humanities

Art in everyday life

Reacting to or creating an exhibit

Reacting to a live performance

Identifying music that manipulates emotions

Using history in making decisions or plans

Contributions of different cultures to American life

Fundamental assumptions and world views about concepts such as fairness, truth (philosophy, science, history)

Individual responsibility for consumption of world resources

Economics

Counting and converting coins and currency, weights and measures

Income tax

Managing money (budgeting) and consumerism
Using catalogs
Using consumer guides
Factors that affect costs of goods and services
Comparison shopping: price versus quality
Packaging of goods: cost-effectiveness for quality and storage
Sales (understanding and making decisions to buy)
Advertising techniques
Ordering food and tipping in a restaurant
Obtaining housing, utilities (telephone, gas, electricity, etc.)
Purchasing home furnishings
Buying and maintaining a car
Caring for personal possessions (cleaning, having things fixed, using warranties)
Banking services
Obtaining mortgages
Determining the most profitable way to save money
Credit systems
Establishing a credit rating
Bank loans
Financing through a store
Understanding and selecting insurance
Fraudulent practices: resources for protection

Attempts at defining information that adults must know have centered upon those bits of knowledge that are believed to be common to all members of society. For example, everyone should know that ingesting poison can be fatal or that showing up for work is critical if one wishes to retain a job. However, large amounts of needed information are idiosyncratic to groups or individuals. For example, a nurse's aide, a cook, and an engineer all need quite different information to perform their jobs.

Intervention Levels

Individuals with learning and behavior problems range from those with minor difficulties to those with major problems. Daniels specified three intervention levels that reflect the severity of problems:

1. Informational—Learners need minor intervention in one or more skill or knowledge areas necessary for eventual independent functioning.

2. Instructional—Learners need in-depth intervention in one or more skill or knowledge areas necessary for eventual independent functioning.

3. Advocacy—Learners need in-depth intervention in several or all skill/knowledge areas necessary for eventual independent functioning, but most will never achieve totally independent functioning in all areas.

The level of help needed ranges from minor to major intervention. Some of the assessments and interventions commonly employed with students who have learning and behavior problems are discussed in the remainder of this chapter.

In sum, historically the standard for individual competency has moved from the ability to sign one's name in the most rudimentary way to a much more complex standard that includes knowledge, skills, use, and level of intervention. Although some knowledge is common to almost all citizens, other knowledge is idiosyncratic to groups or individuals. The types and levels of skills needed by individuals also vary from person to person. Finally, even with adequate knowledge and skills, some individuals simply choose not to apply them appropriately in their daily lives for any number of reasons.

ASSESSING INDEPENDENT LIVING SKILLS

General assessment considerations are presented first in this section. Next, the major types of assessments usually performed relative to independent living skills are discussed. These include both standardized tests and other specific types of assessment procedures.

General Assessment Considerations

Two general factors need to be considered when a student's independent living skills are assessed: first, the student should be involved in the assessment process; second, assessments performed in academic and behavioral areas should be analyzed in relationship to independent living.

Student Involvement

The student who is being evaluated should understand the purpose and results of the evaluation to the largest extent possible. Independence in a changing world requires the ability to continually self-evaluate and modify behavior based on the evaluation. Ultimately the individuals must accept responsibility for the types of jobs they do, the people they associate with, how they spend their time, how they feel about themselves, etc. Involvement at every step of the evaluation process allows the student the optimal learning opportunity, i.e., the experience of making life-relevant decisions.

Evaluation of independent living skills requires that the student consider his or her life goals. This point is particularly important in regard to students' self-understanding. Poor math skills is a more critical deficit in a student who is intent on being an engineer than in a student who wants to be a musician. Poor self-care skills are less of a concern if the student plans on living in a group home than if the student plans to live independently. The key point is *congruence* between student characteristics and the most likely post-school environment. When incongruence is found, it serves as the point of intervention for either remediating the incongruence (i.e., improving the skill level) or modifying the student's plan.

Table 8–1 presents some of the important areas that may foster or hinder independence. Within each area an example is given. Many important areas of independent living assessment are areas in which students must continually and realistically evaluate themselves. Students who cannot realistically self-evaluate will likely encounter problems in daily living.

Students must understand the purposes of the assessments and actively participate in them, and they must understand that self-evaluation is a continual process throughout life. The life-skills assessment activities undertaken

Table 8–1. Important Areas of Independent Living Assessment

Areas	*Example*
1. Interpersonal skills	How you relate to others
2. Values	What you believe in or desire
3. Aptitudes/abilities/achievement	What you can do
4. Attitudes	How you feel about self, things, others
5. Appearance	How you look
6. Mobility	How well you move
7. Work history	What you have done, how well, and how long
8. Daily living skills	How well you manage activities of daily living
9. Interests	What you like
10. Expectations	How much power you feel you have; what goals you have
11. Health	What limitations you have
12. Job-seeking skills	How successful you are at identifying and getting appropriate jobs

during the elementary and secondary years provide an excellent opportunity for teaching students how to self-evaluate.

Assessment in Other Areas

The results of assessments used to determine a student's capability in academic or behavioral areas can also be used in independent living assessment. Results from techniques discussed throughout this book such as standardized tests, teacher-made tests, checklists, Q-sorts, direct observation, role playing, and interviews can provide information about a student's occupational or daily living capabilities.

Table 8–2 relates the skill areas of reading, writing, spelling, handwriting, mathematics, behavior, perceptual/motor, speaking, and listening to both independent living areas usually assessed in adults and possible results of the skill deficits to daily living.

Table 8–2.   Skills and Their Relationship to Independent Living

Skill Area	Independent Living Assessment Area	Possible Result of Deficit
Behavior	Ability Daily living skills Job-seeking skills Mobility Interpersonal skills Appearance Health Values Attitudes	Restricted job choice Daily living difficulty Communication problems Difficulty in relationships—job or personal Mobility problems Problems finding a job
Handwriting	Ability Job-seeking skills Daily living skills Interpersonal skills Appearance	Restricted job choice Daily living difficulty Communication problems Difficulty in relationships—job or personal
Listening	Interpersonal skills Ability Daily living skills Job-seeking skills Values Attitudes	Restricted job choice Daily living difficulty Communication problems Difficulty in relationships—job or personal Problems finding a job
Mathematics	Ability Daily living skills Job-seeking skills	Restricted job choice Daily living difficulty Mobility problems Problems finding a job

(continued)

Table 8–2 *Continued*

Skill Area	Independent Living Assessment Area	Possible Result of Deficit
Perceptual/ Motor	Ability Interpersonal skills Mobility Health Job-seeking skills Appearance Daily living skills	Restricted job choice Daily living difficulty Communication problems Mobility problems Problems finding a job
Reading	Ability Daily living skills Job-seeking skills Mobility	Restricted job choice Daily living difficulty Communication problems Difficulty in relationships—job or personal Mobility problems
Speaking	Interpersonal skills Ability Daily living skills Job-seeking skills Values Attitudes Appearance	Restricted job choice Daily living difficulty Communication problems Difficulty in relationships—job or personal Problems finding a job
Spelling	Job-seeking skills Daily living skills Ability Appearance	Restricted job choice Daily living difficulty Communication problems
Writing	Interpersonal skills Job-seeking skills Ability Daily living skills	Restricted job choice Daily living difficulty Communication problems Problems finding a job

Those who assess independent living skills will want to use information already available about a student's abilities in academic and behavioral areas. The overall assessment process entails:

1. compiling, summarizing, and integrating existing assessment information,

2. identifying problem areas or areas where more evaluation is necessary,

3. performing the required assessments,

4. assisting the student in understanding the meaning of the assessment, and

5. analyzing, with the student, the implications of assessment information.

Standardized Tests of Independent Living

The types and formats of standardized procedures used to assess independent living skills are as varied as those used to assess academic and behavioral areas. Some tests are used to measure occupationally relevant areas, whereas others are used to measure daily living skills. Some are traditional paper-and-pencil tasks, others require extensive apparatus, and still others are behavior recording formats. Some have "right" answers and no time limits; others have no "right" answers and time limits. The general types of standardized procedures available and some representative examples are discussed in this section.

Occupations

Holland (1973), Roe (1956), and Super (1957) have developed theories to explain how individuals arrive at an occupational choice. These theories, and others, range in orientation from developmental to trait analysis to behavioral, but all attempt to explain the process of *match* between individuals and job characteristics. Several terms are used to describe this match. For example, *selective placement* is believed to exist when individuals perform in an occupation in which their abilities are maximized and disabilities minimized. When individuals are able to perform a job well, they are said to be *job satisfactory. Job satisfaction* is said to exist when individuals enjoy their jobs.

Many constructs have been postulated as important to occupational choice, e.g., self-concept, genetic predisposition, needs, achievement orientation, personality, locus of control. Many of these are difficult to operationalize in standardized test formats. Therefore, the standardized measures that exist serve only as screening instruments and as general indicators of occupations that should be included or excluded from consideration.

There are three major ways in which individuals are matched to an occupation. These include (1) occupational aptitudes, (2) occupational interests, and (3) work evaluation systems.

Aptitudes. Aptitudes are specific capacities required for an individual to perform or learn to perform a task (Isaacson, 1978). Each job can be analyzed to identify the major job elements and to specify the corresponding skills, knowledge, and traits necessary for successful performance (Anastasi, 1982). Aptitude tests are designed to measure either multiple or specific abilities. Table 8–3 describes common subtests of multiple aptitude test batteries. Specific aptitude tests also are available to measure sensory, motor, mechanical, clerical, artistic, musical, and creative abilities.

From the beginning, aptitude tests have been plagued by low correlations between test performance and actual job performance. High coefficients are

Table 8–3.   Common Subtests of Multiple Aptitude Test Batteries

Aptitude Name	Subtest Name	Brief Description
Verbal	Vocabulary	Several variants: Select correct meaning, find synonyms or antonyms
Numerical	Arithmetic	Addition, subtraction, multiplication, division
	Word Problems	Situational arithmetic
Clerical	Name or Word Comparison	Recognizing whether or not two names or words are exactly alike
Spatial Perception	Spatial Relations	Recognizing the same form in two and three dimensions
Form	Tool Matching	Given one graphic detail tool, recognizing another from a set of four or five
	Form Matching	Given one form, finding another exactly like it from a set of X
Dexterity		
Overall	Mark Making	Making a prescribed mark in prescribed ways; generally a timed task
Finger	Finger Dexterity	Usually some small nut-and-bolt assemble/disassemble task
Manual	Manual Dexterity	Usually timed tasks testing both bilateral and dominant hand/arm movement

generally in the .40s, meaning that there is only a 16 percent chance that a person's performance on the test predicts whether he or she could (or could not) do a given job. However, results from such tests can be useful to:

1. identify relatively strong and weak areas within an individual's abilities,
2. assist individuals to more realistically appraise their abilities, and
3. broadly screen individuals into programs for which there are limited numbers of positions.

Table 8–4 lists commonly used aptitude tests. One test, the Occupational Aptitude Survey (Parker, 1982), measures the aptitude of students in grades eight to twelve. The test, normed on a national sample of 1398 students from eleven states, can be administered to individuals, small groups, or complete classes in thirty to forty minutes. The Aptitude Survey measures general ability, verbal aptitude, numerical aptitude, spatial aptitude, perceptual aptitude, and manual dexterity. Validity and reliability coefficients are acceptable. The numerical, spatial, and manual dexterity subtests are nonverbal. The verbal and perceptual subtests require the matching of words and phrases. Minimum aptitude scores for 120 occupations are presented in the test manuals, and scores are

Table 8–4. Commonly Used Aptitude Tests

Test Name (Publisher, Publication Date)	Target Population
Aptitude Tests for Occupations (ATO) (Pro-Ed, 1977)	High school students, college students, adults
Career Ability Placement Survey (CAPS) (Educational and Industrial Testing Service, 1981)	Junior high students, high school students, college students, adults
Differential Aptitude Tests (DAT) (The Psychological Corporation, 1982)	High school students
General Aptitude Test Battery (GATB) (United States Employment Service, 1982)	High school students, college students, adults
Non-Verbal Aptitude Test Battery (NATB) (United States Employment Service, 1982)	High school students, college students, adults
Occupational Aptitude Survey and Interest Schedule (OASIS) (Pro-Ed, 1982)	Junior high students, high school students

directly keyed to the *Dictionary of Occupational Titles* (1977), *Guide for Occupational Exploration* (1979), and the *Worker Trait Group Guide* (Winefordner, 1978).

Interests.   Occupational interests refer to an individual's preference for certain occupational fields. The matching of personal interests with job characteristics is considered an important element in job success. For instance, a person who has a high aptitude in math but dislikes it is not likely to succeed in an engineering job; nor is a person who is interested in engineering but lacks the basic math skills to complete preparatory math courses.

Interest tests generally present the test-takers with a series of items in which they must choose among several activities; for example,

> Would you rather
>   Read a book
>   Read a book to someone else
>   Write a book

Most tests have an extensive number of items covering broad areas of human activity. Scoring criteria for the items are developed by administering the item pool to groups of people with known interests (e.g., plumbers, people in business careers). Scores are then reported for general interest areas and/or specific occupational interests. A score showing a high interest in social work can be interpreted to mean that the person's responses to test items are similar to those of social workers, but not that the person necessarily likes the occupation of social worker.

Interest tests that report general interest scores are considered more suitable for junior high and high school students. Tests that report occupationally specific scores are generally considered more suitable for adults. Some recent tests report both general and specific occupational interests. Table 8–5 presents a list of some of the more commonly used instruments. Most general interest tests list nine to twelve areas of interest. Although there are slight variations in categories, the classification system of the U.S. Employment Service (USES) presented here is representative of general interest areas.

1. Artistic	7. Business Detail
2. Scientific	8. Selling
3. Nature	9. Accommodating
4. Protective	10. Humanitarian
5. Mechanical	11. Leading-Influencing
6. Industrial	12. Physical Performing

Table 8–5. Commonly Used Occupational Interest Tests

Test Name (Publisher, Publication Date)	Type of Interest Reported
AAMD-Becker Reading-Free Interest Inventory (Elbern Publications, 1981)	General
California Occupational Preference System (Educational and Industrial Testing Service, 1981)	General
Career Assessment Inventory (National Computer Systems, 1978)	General and specific
The Geist Picture Interest Inventory—Revised (Western Psychological Services, 1978)	General
The Jackson Vocational Interest Survey (Research Psychologists Press, 1978)	General
Kuder Interest Survey—Form E, Form DD (Science Research Associates, 1976)	General and specific
OASIS—Interest Schedule (Pro-Ed, 1982)	General
Ohio Vocational Interest Survey (2nd Edition) (The Psychology Corporation, 1981)	General
Planning Career Goals—Interest Inventory (CTB/ McGraw-Hill, American Institute for Research, 1977)	General
Strong-Campbell Interest Inventory (Stanford University Press, 1981)	General and specific

The Occupational Interest Schedule (Parker, 1982) was normed on the same population as the Occupational Aptitude Survey discussed in the previous section. It also measures each of the USES classification systems cited above. The Interest Schedule contains 240 items scored as "Like," "Neutral," or "Dislike." Reliabilities range from .86 to .94; construct validity has been determined. The test meets guidelines for sex fairness within validity constraints. Scores are directly related to the *Guide for Occupational Exploration* (1979) and the *Worker Trait Group Guide* (Winefordner, 1978).

Work Evaluation Systems.   Work evaluation systems are designed to provide more specific information regarding work abilities than that obtained through general aptitude tests. General aptitude tests may only test a person's speed, whereas work evaluation systems may examine speed, stamina, persistence, improvement, adaptability, and cooperation. Many work evaluation systems employ extensive apparatus in order to simulate common work stations and tasks found in business and industry.

Work evaluation systems vary greatly in the number of work samples included and the types of information derived from student performance. Much of the diversity results from the fact that many available systems were developed to serve specific purposes with specific populations. Table 8–6 lists eight of the most commonly used work evaluation systems, their respective number of subtests, and the target population for whom the system was originally designed. Because many of these systems require large expenditures of money and time, they are most often found in sheltered workshops or rehabilitation facilities and not in public schools.

The Wide Range Employability Sample Test (WREST) (Jastak, 1980) contains many features standard to work evaluation systems. It was initially designed as a screening device for use in a sheltered workshop and consists of a timed performance on the following ten work samples: folding, stapling, packaging, measuring, stringing, gluing, collating, color matching, pattern matching, and assembly. Work samples can be administered separately or as a group, using standard materials provided by the publisher. Administration time for individual students is about one and a half hours; small groups of three to five persons may take two hours. Learning and performance are separated in measurement, as each client is allowed to reach minimum criteria on each task before being tested in a timed situation. Student behavior with respect to both work performance (e.g., ability, stamina) and work habits (e.g., attitudes, safety) is reported. Time and quality norms are given for sheltered employees, competitively employed workers, and the general population. Sample size ranges from 200 to 4000 on the various work samples, with all subjects coming from the state of Delaware. Reported test-retest reliabilities over a three-month period are in the .90s. Correlations between supervisor ratings and time and error standard scores on the WREST for 428 employed workers in the .80s were cited by au-

Table 8–6.   Commonly Used Work Evaluation Systems

System Name (Publisher, Publication Date)	Number of Subtests	Target Population
Comprehensive Occupational Assessment and Training System (Prep, 1981)	26	Secondary students and rehabilitation prospects
Hester Evaluation System (Evaluation Systems, 1981)	28	Mentally and physically disabled
McCarron-Dial Work Evaluation System (McCarron-Dial Systems, 1981)	17	Mentally retarded, learning disabled, emotionally disturbed
Philadelphia Jewish Employment and Vocational Service (Vocational Research Institute, 1977)	28	Mentally retarded
Pre-Vocational Readiness Battery (Valpar Corporation, 1977)	11	Mentally retarded
Talent Assessment Programs (Talent Assessment, 1981)	10	Age fourteen and up, IQ score of 60 or above
The Tower System (IC Rehabilitation and Research Center, 1974)	93	Physically and emotionally disabled
Valpar Component Work Sample Series (Valpar Corporation, 1981)	16	General populations, industrially injured worker
Wide Range Employability Sample Test (Jastak Associates, 1980)	10	Mentally and physically handicapped adolescents and adults

thors as proof of test validity. The WREST is more restricted than other systems in types of work samples and consequently is limited as a tool for use in occupational exploration. Other systems such as the Tower System or the Comprehensive Occupational Assessment and Training System provide a broader exposure to various work activities but have less established reliability and validity than the WREST.

Daily Living Skills

Occupational competence is only one aspect of the total constellation of abilities necessary for independent living success. Almost everyone knows someone who can maintain a job but cannot seem to keep the remainder of his or her life in order—the person may feel lonely all the time, spend money foolishly, break the law, or have trouble maintaining good health. The cumulative effects of any one deficit over a period of time or of simultaneous multiple deficits can be chronic dependence. In recent years there has been an increase in the development of instruments for assessing independent living skills, but the usefulness of many of these has yet to be validated. The instruments presented in Table 8–7

Table 8–7. Representative Standardized Measures of Daily Living Skills Appropriate for School-Aged Populations

Skill	Test Name (Publisher, Publication Date)
Self-Care	Adaptive Behavior Scale (American Association on Mental Deficiency, 1975)
	Social and Prevocational Information Battery (CTB/McGraw-Hill, 1975)
	Vineland Adaptive Behavior (American Guidance Service, 1984)
Practical Knowledge	Adult Performance Level Program (American College Testing Program, 1976)
	Career Awareness Inventory—Elementary (Scholastic Testing Service, 1974)
	Career Development Inventory (American Personnel and Guidance Association, 1979)
	Career Maturity Inventory (CTB/McGraw-Hill, 1978)
	Knowledge of Occupations Test (Psychologists and Educators, 1974)
	Social and Prevocational Information Battery (CTB/McGraw-Hill, 1975)
	Tests for Everyday Living (Slosson Educational Publications, 1980)
	Test of Practical Knowledge (Pro-Ed, 1982)
Personal/Social Skills	Adaptive Behavior Scale (American Association on Mental Deficiency, 1975)
	Behavior Rating Profile (Pro-Ed, 1983)
	Career Adaptive Behavior Inventory (Slosson Educational Publications, 1981)
	Coopersmith Self-Esteem Inventories (Consulting Psychologists Press, 1981)
	Culture-Free Self-Esteem Inventory (Slosson Educational Publications, 1981)
	Piers-Harris Children's Self-Concept Scale (Counselor Recordings and Tests, 1984)
	Temperament and Values Inventory (Interpretive Scoring Systems, 1976)
	Vineland Adaptive Behavior (American Guidance Service, 1984)
	Vocational Preferences Inventory (Consulting Psychologists Press, 1978)

are categorized by their emphasis on self-care, practical knowledge, or personal/social skills. Self-care covers health, appearance, grooming, household maintenance, cooking, money management, and recreation. Practical knowledge relates to government and law, consumer economics, transportation, functional academics, community resources, first aid, occupational knowledge, and problem solving. Personal/social skills encompass friendship, dating, sexuality, family, parenting, feelings, communication, self-awareness, co-worker relationships, and adjustment to change.

Many of these standardized instruments are based on behavior observation formats relying on information about student behavior from family, teachers, counselors, peers, caretakers, or the student. The multiple observer approach is necessary because many of the competencies required in independent adult living are not observable within the school environment. Also, students may display different abilities or problems in different environments. Like standardized instruments in the occupational area, these tests may be useful as screening devices to identify potential problem students among larger groups or to identify deficits within the total group.

One of the tests listed in Table 8–7, the Test of Practical Knowledge (TPK) (Wiederholt & Larsen, 1982), has been normed on the same population as the Occupational Aptitude Survey and Interest Schedule (Parker, 1982) discussed previously. The TPK consists of three subtests: Personal Knowledge, Social Knowledge, and Occupational Knowledge. The TPK reliabilities are in the .80s and .90s. It also correlates highly with tests of school achievement. It takes between thirty and forty minutes to administer the TPK to individuals, small groups, or complete classes.

Other Assessment Procedures[1]

Many times required information cannot be obtained through standardized formats. For example, standardized formats will not reveal that an individual is capable of tasks but will not attempt them for fear of failure. This response style is often called "learned helplessness." In other instances, areas of interest, such as values, feelings, or day-to-day behavior, may not be amenable to standardized testing or appropriate tests simply may not exist. In these cases the following assessment procedures may be considered: simulations, observation, and paper-and-pencil formats.

Simulation Formats

A simulation is an approach in which certain aspects of reality are artificially re-created. Simulations can permit assessment or intervention within classroom settings of situations that would be difficult to observe otherwise. Simulation techniques can be useful in assessing areas of feeling, relating, and problem

[1]Many of the techniques described in this section were developed and used by the University of Texas at Austin, Job Readiness Clinic, directed by Jim Daniels from 1975 to 1983 and by Karen Wolffe since 1983.

solving. For instance, classrooms generally simulate several important characteristics of work settings: meeting time schedules and production standards,
dealing with interpersonal relationships, and following directions. Attention to
student performance in these aspects of classroom behavior can provide useful
information regarding independent living functioning.

Two specific types of simulations are role playing and work samples. Role
playing can be designed to assess relating or problem solving within any content
area. Key elements to successful role playing are

1. An open and relaxed classroom atmosphere.
2. A description of the purpose of the activity.
3. A description of the circumstances before each role play.
4. Role play cards with instructions for each performer.
5. Sufficient time for the role play to develop.
6. Time spent discussing the role play after completion.

The situations and role play card content can be varied to suit the individual situation. Role reversal is a specific modification of the role play situation in
which the student is placed in a role opposite the one he or she normally plays
(e.g., parent, employer). This technique permits assessment of the student's understanding of the thoughts, feelings, and actions of others.

Work samples are another example of a simulation type of assessment.
Work samples have traditionally been associated with sheltered workshops
where students were asked to perform at a certain work station to determine (1)
their level of skill at the task, (2) their attitude toward the task, and/or (3) their
work habits within that setting. Some work samples can easily be set up within
a public school classroom, such as assembly, sorting, or clerical tasks, whereas
others require specialized space and equipment. Work samples sometimes seem
artificial, but they do permit the observation of job-related behavior in situations normally inaccessible within academic classroom settings.

Observation Strategies

Observation strategies are useful for developing information about student behavior within the regular classroom and within simulation activities. Devices
used include records of targeted behavior, nonstandardized checklists, and rating scales.

Recording targeted behavior involves making set time-interval (two-min-
ute; five-minute) observations of a student's behavior during instruction. This
technique is particularly useful in identifying visible deviancies in behavior
that detract from the student's ability to make a positive interpersonal impression. Deviancies might include hiding mouth behind hand when smiling, gig-

gling inappropriately, or other annoying mannerisms. Observation recording should include the stimulus and consequence of the response. Analysis of such records often reveals problems that are amenable to intervention.

Nonstandardized checklists may be used to give structure to observations. Many different types of commercial and teacher-made checklists are available. Some are designed for use by an observer; others are designed for self-evaluation. A sample checklist that may be used by the teacher, a peer, or the student to evaluate a student's performance within a job interview format is given in Figure 8–1.

Rating scales are similar to checklists but are designed to provide more qualitative information regarding a student's performance. A checklist only asks the rater to indicate that a behavior has been observed; a rating scale asks the rater to make a judgment about the behavior. Rating scales are more reliable if clear guidelines for each level of rating are given. For example, if the stimulus item is "Student initiates contact with peers," a rating scale that ranges from "never" to "always" is less precise than one that gives the following choices:

1. Never
2. Once a month
3. Once a week
4. Once a day
5. Once an hour

Paper-and-Pencil Assessment Formats

Intervention with certain groups of students may require that the teacher tailor assessment tools for a specific situation. Although many independent living assessment tools exist, it may be more time efficient for the teacher to design his or her own tools. In other circumstances, the teacher may want to modify some existing instrument to make it more suitable for his or her particular classroom. The information in this section should give the teacher a range of options in test design, because each type of format may be used in more than one assessment area. There are five types of paper-and-pencil formats that teachers may want to use in designing tools to assess independent living skills: incomplete sentence, forced choice, semantic differential, questionnaire, and discrepancy analysis.

Incomplete Sentence Format.   In the incomplete sentence format, the student is presented with a series of sentence beginnings to complete. The stimulus sentence stems are usually developed to elicit information concerning the student's feelings about school, self, family, jobs, friends, or other areas of interest.

Figure 8–1.   Sample Job Interview Checklist

	Yes	No
Appearance		
Dresses appropriately for job	—	—
Introduces self	—	—
Maintains eye contact	—	—
Seems alert and confident	—	—
Sits naturally (no distracting mannerisms)	—	—
Job Knowledge		
Knows about company	—	—
Describes which job is sought	—	—
Understands job duties	—	—
Describes past experience relevant to current job	—	—
Giving Information		
Can give a brief overview of self	—	—
Answers personal questions positively and briefly	—	—
Gives reason for seeking job	—	—
Answers questions about qualifications for job	—	—
Makes positive statements about self as a worker for this job (at least three)	—	—
Relates future goals to current job	—	—
Explains any negative aspects of work history in a positive way	—	—
Can explain why disability will not affect job performance	—	—
Gives positive information in response to employer objection to hiring	—	—
Getting Information		
Asks job-relevant questions (e.g., training, work setting)	—	—
Finds out when hiring decision will be made	—	—
Gets information about job duties	—	—
Gets information about work setting	—	—
Gets information about salary, benefits, schedule	—	—
Overall Impression		
Good voice tone	—	—
Courteous	—	—
Pays attention	—	—
Believable	—	—
Enthusiastic	—	—
Talkative	—	—
Hire	—	—

The biggest problems with the jobs I want are _____ .

If I could be anything, I would _____ .

The happiest times of my life are_____ .

I've always wanted to be _____ .

My friends_____ .

I really hate _____ .

Interpretation of these instruments is based on projective principles. That is, the content of the specific responses is not as important as the general tone of the responses or the themes that emerge. Is the person angry, happy, sad, or fearful? Do there seem to be specific areas of concern that consistently arise—family, friends, self? Is the person open or restricted in responses? Obviously, such interpretations are highly subjective, and any tentative assumptions must be verified through further interactions or assessments.

Forced Choice Formats.   Forced choice formats present the student with a choice between two items. Items are designed so that equally attractive or unattractive statements are paired. This feature allows some control over the social desirability factor.

 a. I would rather have a secure job.
 b. I would rather have a job with prestige.

 a. It is important to take care of oneself.
 b. You should always be willing to help others.

 a. I would like to have a lot of friends.
 b. I want to have as many good things as possible.

Such tests are generally designed to help clarify the relative importance of elements among a set of values, goals, or behaviors. This procedure can be used to reduce the complexity of a rank ordering task involving a large number of variables.

Semantic Differential Format.   Like rating scales, semantic differentials ask the student to assume a general response set to a stimulus concept and then rate the concept along several dimensions. For example, students may be asked to rate their feelings about "school" and then check the blanks below closest to their feelings.

```
       happy __:__:__:__:__:__:__ sad
   beautiful __:__:__:__:__:__:__ ugly
       dirty __:__:__:__:__:__:__ clean
      honest __:__:__:__:__:__:__ dishonest
        poor __:__:__:__:__:__:__ rich
        good __:__:__:__:__:__:__ bad
    pleasant __:__:__:__:__:__:__ unpleasant
        fair __:__:__:__:__:__:__ unfair
     healthy __:__:__:__:__:__:__ sick
unsuccessful __:__:__:__:__:__:__ successful
```

Various responses to a stimulus may be analyzed individually or as a group. However, a more useful approach is to provide the student with a set of stimuli similar to the following so that more intraindividual comparisons can be made.

People, Me, Family, Friends, Teachers
Home, School, Play, Work
Math, Science, Reading, Writing, Talking

This approach allows the teacher to understand each student's attitudes toward important aspects of his or her environment.

Questionnaire Format.   Questionnaires are simply questions to which students are asked to respond. They are useful for collecting basic information within specific areas of assessment interests. For instance, the teacher may want to know about the students' home environments, their hobbies and interests, their work experiences, their awareness of jobs, or their career planning. Questions are chosen that request the required information. A sample questionnaire used to assess the career planning of secondary students is given in Figure 8–2.

Discrepancy Analysis Formats.   In discrepancy analysis, students rate two separate aspects of themselves (e.g., jobs, friends) and then compare the two ratings in order to identify differences. Many times the ratings deal with the real versus the ideal. For instance, students might be asked to rate their current personality traits and what they consider to be perfect personality traits. They could then be asked to identify the difference between their personality and the perfect as a way to find areas in which they may want to change. This technique can also be applied to current versus desired behavior, current abilities versus those required in certain jobs, or current life style versus desired life style. The advantage of this approach is that it actively involves the student in a process that can be generalized to many real-life situations.

Both standardized and other assessment procedures provide useful information for teaching independent living skills. Of course, continual assessment is necessary throughout the teaching process for measuring growth, determining the efficacy of the instructional program, and specifying directions for modifying or changing the instructional approach.

TEACHING INDEPENDENT LIVING

Educators have attempted to teach independent living skills in three major ways: through school-based programs, community-based programs, and specific intervention strategies. Each of these approaches is described in this section.

Figure 8–2.   Sample Career Planning Questionnaire

What jobs can you do now? _____
_____ .

What jobs do you think you might like to do in two years? _____
_____ .

What jobs do you think you might like to do ten years from now? _____
_____ .

To do the jobs you want two years from now, what skills will you need to improve?
_____ .

To do the jobs you want ten years from now, what abilities will you need to improve? _____
_____ .

What are your biggest problems with the jobs you can do now? _____
_____ .

What problems do you have getting a job now? _____
_____ .

What can you do about these problems? _____
_____
_____ .

School-Based Programs

Career education and vocational education are examples of school-based programs. Both are found in almost every school district, although there are wide disparities from one district to another in the quantity of services provided. Some districts have implemented an extensive career education program, whereas others give only minimal attention to this type of program. Similarly, some districts have a wide variety of vocational education programs, whereas others have a very limited number of these programs.

Career Education

The concept of career education was formulated in the 1960s and early 1970s, in part because of the erosion of the work ethic. This erosion was reflected in high dropout rates from school as well as high unemployment. Schneider and Ferritor (1982) describe the decline of people's desire to work and note broad benefits that work provides for individuals.

> . . . work provides economic, social, and personal benefits. In addition to money for the necessities and luxuries of life, work provides a setting for individuals to develop new friends and to socialize with old ones. The work atmosphere is a focus for personal evaluation, a mechanism for shaping a sense of identity, and a way of bringing order into one's life. Although work is not the only source of economic survival, sociability, or self-esteem, it is an easily recognizable, often quantifiable, public indicator of the results of an individual's life. (p. 33)

In the early days of the career education movement, there was a widespread tendency for professionals to equate the words *career* and *occupation*. However, Super (1976), a recognized pioneer and leader in career development, pointed out that *career* is broader in meaning than *occupation*. Careers are the major positions occupied by a person throughout his or her preoccupational, occupational, and postoccupational life. Specifically, careers include work-related roles such as that of student, employee, and pensioner, as well as complementary avocational, familial, and civic roles.

In the context of career education, the word *career* is conceived of as referring to the various life roles that an individual plays. Career education is therefore designed to help students select roles for their lives as well as to teach them how to function in these various roles. Kokaska and Brolin (1985) define career education in the following manner.

> Career education is a life-centered approach focusing on the individual as a productive worker in many different jobs. Individuals perform both paid and unpaid work at home, in the community, and on a job. Productive work includes that of a homemaker and a family member, citizen and volunteer, student, retiree, employee, and participant in meaningful avocational pursuits. Thus the challenge of career education is to provide learners with opportunities that will help them function adequately in these various life roles. (p. 43)

Career education is viewed as beginning in kindergarten and continuing throughout life. The U.S. Office of Education's (1972) model of career education reflects this viewpoint (see Figure 8–3). It defines three different stages of career development: career awareness, career exploration, and adult and continuing education.

Stage I—Career Awareness. Attitudes, information, and self-understanding are three elements of career awareness. Attitudes are the foundation upon which the entire career education program is based. Beginning in kindergarten and continuing through sixth grade, students are taught that they must make

Figure 8–3.   U.S. Office of Education's Career Education Model

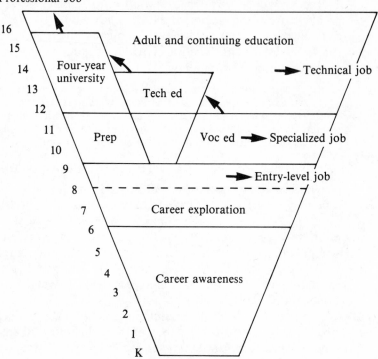

conscious efforts at producing some benefits for themselves and others. They are taught that people work for economic, psychological, and societal reasons. They learn that work produces a major source of personal identification and satisfaction. Information is provided about a variety of jobs as well as avocational, leisure, and other life pursuits. Kolstoe (1976) and Kokaska and Brolin (1985) have noted that understanding one's relationship to the community and possible choices for eventual adult roles is part of self-understanding.

Stage II—Career Exploration.   Career exploration begins in seventh grade. The major thrust at the middle school level is for students to explore various occupations as well as the preparation requirements, opportunities for obtaining training, and life-style implications of each occupation. The U.S. Office of Education has delineated fifteen job clusters that usually form the basis of exploration by students. These clusters are shown in Figure 8–4. Along with exploring various jobs, students are provided opportunities to examine their own abilities and goals, with the help of guidance counselors.

Figure 8–4. U.S. Office of Education's Job Clusters

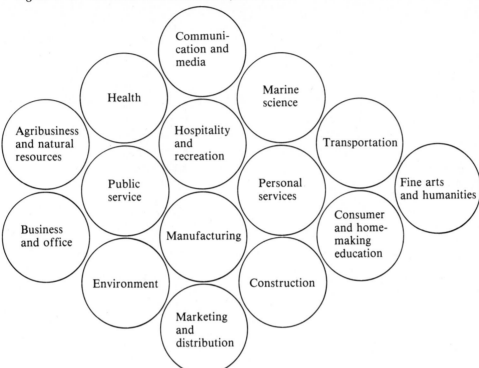

At the high school level students enter into a college preparatory program, a technical education program, or a vocational education program. In vocational programs emphasis is placed on specific occupational preparation within one of the occupational clusters.

Stage III—Adult and Continuing Education. Some occupations and life styles require university training. Others require post–secondary school technical training. Still other specialized positions require no additional training. Regardless of which option an individual takes, there should be opportunities throughout adult life for additional education. Individuals should view education as a lifelong process and feel comfortable in changing occupations and life styles if they have the desire and ability to do so.

In school districts with extensive career education programs, the concept of preparing students for adult independent living has been infused into day-to-day instruction. Sequential instruction with themes ranging from career awareness to career placement is conducted at various stages of the student's schooling. Many students with learning and behavior problems, handicaps, or economic disadvantage profit from this educational approach.

Vocational Education

Vocational education focuses on the occupational preparation of individuals. It is concerned with career exploration, vocational assessment, training, job tryouts, and job placement (Brolin & Brolin, 1979). As such, it is a part of career education but is not as broad in its focus; it is specific to paid employment. The Vocational Act of 1963 (P.L. 88–201) defines this educational endeavor as follows:

> Vocational education means vocational or technical training or retraining which is given in schools or classes (including field or laboratory work and remedial or related academic and technical instruction incident thereto) under public supervision and control or under contract with a state board or local education agency and is conducted as part of a program designed to prepare individuals for gainful employment as semiskilled or skilled workers or technicians or subprofessionals in recognized occupations and in new and emerging occupations or to prepare individuals for enrollment in advanced technical programs, but excluding any program to prepare individuals for employment in occupations which the Commissioner determines, and specifies by regulation, to be generally considered professional or which require a baccalaureate or higher degree. . . . (Sec. 108)

There are several different vocational education fields. These include agricultural education, business and office education, distributive education, health occupations education, home economics education, and trade and industrial education. The content of these programs has been classified by the U.S. Office of Education (1969) in Handbook VI, *Standard Terminology for Curriculum and Instruction in Local and State School Systems*. The content of the different vocational education programs is as follows:

Agricultural Education
Agricultural Mechanics
Agricultural Production
Agricultural Products (Processing, Inspection, Marketing)
Agricultural Resources (Conservation, Utilization, Services)
Agricultural Supplies and Services
Forestry
Ornamental Horticulture

Business and Office Education
Accounting and Computing Occupations
Business Data Processing Systems Occupations
Filing, Office Machines, and General Clerical Occupations
Information Communication Occupations
Materials Support Occupations
Personnel, Training, and Related Occupations
Stenographic, Secretarial, and Related Occupations
Supervisory and Administrative Management Occupations
Typing and Related Occupations

Distributive Education
Advertising Services
Apparel and Accessories
Automotive
Finance and Credit
Floristry
Food Services
General Merchandise
Hardware, Building Materials, Farm and Garden Supplies
Home Furnishings
Hotel and Lodging
Industrial Marketing
Insurance
International Trade
Personal Services
Petroleum
Real Estate
Recreation and Tourism
Transportation

Health Occupations Education
Dental
Environmental Health
Medical Laboratory Technology
Mental Health Technology
Miscellaneous Health Occupations Education

Nursing
Ophthalmic
Radiologic
Rehabilitation

Home Economics Education

Homemaking (Preparation for Personal, Home, and Family Living; these programs are not specifically directed toward preparation for gainful employment)

Occupational Preparation (Care and Guidance of Children; Clothing Management, Production, and Services; Food Management, Production, and Services; Home Furnishings, Equipment, and Services; and Institutional and Home Management and Supportive Services)

Trade and Industrial Education

Air Conditioning
Appliance Repair
Automotive Services
Aviation Occupations
Blueprint Reading
Business Machine Maintenance
Commercial Art Occupations
Commercial Fishery Occupations
Commercial Photography Occupations
Construction and Maintenance Trades
Custodial Services
Diesel Mechanics
Drafting
Electrical Occupations
Electronics Occupations
Fabric Maintenance Services
Foremanship, Supervision, and Management Development
General Continuation
Graphic Arts Occupations
Industrial Atomic Energy
Instrument Maintenance and Repair

Some of the occupations may not seem to be in keeping with the definition of vocational education, i.e., nonprofessional jobs. However, in each field there are varying levels of requirements for training. For example, under Health Occupations Education, consider Nursing. Although a nurse would be considered a professional, a nurse's aide would not. Obviously, there are support personnel in each of the occupation areas.

Vocational education programs become available to students in high school. School districts, of course, cannot usually afford to establish vocational preparation programs in each of the fields. Consequently, the characteristics of the student population as well as the community needs generally dictate which programs are established. For example, one would be more likely to find an extensive agricultural vocational education program in a rural area than in an urban one. Conversely, one would be more likely to find a strong distributive vocational education program in an urban area than in a rural one.

Both career education and vocational education are school-based programs that have as their specific focus the training of students for independent living. Career education begins in kindergarten and continues throughout life. It helps students to become aware of various life roles, to explore some of the career roles, and to clarify for themselves which careers they intend to incorporate into their life style. Vocational education, while part of career education, focuses on training students for semiskilled, skilled, technical, or subprofessional jobs.

Students with learning or behavior problems can profit from career education in that it helps them develop a better understanding of themselves and their responsibilities to themselves and others. For those who have no wish or ability to pursue higher education, vocational education offers an opportunity to prepare for post–high school employment.

Community-Based Organizations

Although schools cannot bear total responsibility for the life development of students, teachers are in a good position to assess when certain critical needs are not being met. Many community-based organizations provide services related to independent living skills; the teacher who is knowledgeable about such services is able to refer students in need to the appropriate support services. All of the services and organizations presented in the following glossary of services and organizations may not be available in a specific community, and names and functions of organizations may differ from state to state. Consequently, the information presented in this section is intended to help identify the types of services and agencies that may be available in a specific community. Teachers will want to determine which agencies and services exist within their local community in order to make the appropriate referral for specific students.

Glossary of Services

Employment

Career counseling helps individuals set career goals and make career plans.

Employment counseling helps individuals find a job that best matches their abilities and interests.

Job placement helps the person find a job.

On-the-job training allows someone to learn how to do a job while being paid a salary.

Sheltered employment provides noncompetitive employment to handicapped workers and pays wages on the basis of job performance.

Work evaluation provides an assessment of a person's skill level compared to that of others.

Housing

Group homes provide supervised housing.

Halfway houses provide supervised housing.

Independent living centers provide supported housing with control in the hands of residents.

Residential facilities offer supervised housing and educational or rehabilitation programming.

Interpersonal

Drug and alcohol abuse (chemical dependency) counseling helps individuals recognize and resolve drug abuse problems.

Family counseling helps family members work individually or together on family issues.

Genetic counseling provides individuals with information on the chances that they might pass on a condition to any children they might have.

Personal adjustment counseling helps individuals identify and solve personal problems.

Personal/social adjustment training helps people to improve feelings about themselves or their interactions with others.

Recreation

Adaptive recreation provides accessible and appropriate recreation activities for persons with handicaps.

Day activity centers provide daytime programming geared toward improving independent living abilities.

Support

Advocacy programs take many forms. Some provide legal assistance; others provide peer tutoring or mentor programs (e.g., Association for Retarded Citizens, Big Brother/Big Sister).

Services for disabled student offices, available at many community colleges, colleges, and universities, assist disabled students in enrolling in and attending school.

Social Security disability income program provides income support in the form of monthly checks and medical support in the form of Medicare.

Supplemental Security income program provides income support in the form of welfare checks, food stamps, and Medicaid.

Training

Job-seeking skills training trains the person to look for a job effectively.

Personal adjustment training helps individuals develop self-care skills.

Rehabilitation centers provide temporary housing coupled with extensive rehabilitation programming.

Vocational training teaches skills for a specific job.

Work adjustment training trains the person in good work habits.

Glossary of Organizations

Community colleges provide academic college courses and vocational training. Many have a special office to provide help to disabled students.

Community schools provide an assortment of non–college credit courses ranging from human growth and development through avocational training.

Planned parenthood provides information on sex education, birth control, and genetic counseling, as well as referrals to other agencies.

Residential facilities provide supervised housing for persons who cannot live at home or on their own. Most states have special schools for children with disabilities like deafness, blindness, and mental retardation. Many communities also have private full-care facilities, halfway houses, and group homes. Some facilities offer many rehabilitation services besides housing.

Specific disability organizations provide and promote services to persons with certain types of disability. Examples are The Association for Retarded Citizens, United Cerebral Palsy Associations, Easter Seal Society for Crippled Children and Adults, and the Association for Children and Adults with Learning Disabilities. Services provided vary with the organization. In addition to national organizations and their affiliates, many independent agencies exist in local communities.

State departments of human resources help with social problems such as hunger, child abuse, housing, and medical care for dependent children, the disabled, and the aged. Services may include financial assistance such as food stamps, medical assistance such as Medicaid, personal and family counseling, or assistance in finding housing, training, etc.

State employment agencies help employers and job applicants find each other. Free services include vocational interest and aptitude assessments, job counseling, and information about job openings.

State or local mental health agencies provide counseling assistance to people who are having personal problems. Services provided may include individual, group, and family counseling and drug abuse counseling.

State rehabilitation agencies provide a variety of services designed to help disabled individuals over age sixteen go to work. Rehabilitation counselors may provide vocational interest and aptitude assessments, personal and vocational counseling, assistance to find and pay for adaptive equipment, medical procedures, etc., and job placement assistance. Some services are based on economic need.

Vocational rehabilitation facilities serve a particular need or a special population. Examples are Goodwill Industries and Lighthouse for the Blind. Depending on the facility, services may include work evaluation, adjustment to work training, sheltered employment, on-the-job training, personal adjustment training/counseling, and vocational training.

Specific Intervention Strategies

Various methods and materials are available for teaching independent living skills. In this section a discussion of some general intervention issues is followed by overviews of commercially available materials and teacher-directed activities.

General Intervention Issues

Intervention in independent living skills teaching is not radically different from intervention in academic or behavioral areas. However, three issues need special consideration. These are ways of individualizing instruction, ways of augmenting the traditional school curriculum with independent living skills content, and ways of teaching problem solving and other skills.

Individualizing Instruction. Individualization of instruction is critical to good teaching, particularly when one is working with special needs learners. Individual characteristics to be accommodated in the instructional process include learning rate, learning preference, instructional content, and learning environment (Dollar & Dollar, 1976). Rate refers to the student's speed of acquisition of new knowledge or behavior. Preference refers to the student's preference for a specific mode of instruction (e.g., visual, auditory, interactive). Content considerations are the student's preference with respect to content (interest) and the effectiveness of particular types of concept presentation. Learning environment must be accommodative of individuals with differences in sensory, mobility, or affective areas. Assessment should help identify the student's preferences or needs in each of these areas in addition to identifying the student's specific content and skill deficits.

Instruction in independent living skills can be individualized through the use of Daniels's (1984) three levels of intervention, described earlier. It was noted previously that basically all students can be viewed as occupying some point on a continuum between no need for assistance and massive need for assistance. Figure 8–5 depicts three general categories that represent school-aged students' needs in areas of development important to success in independent living. More students will be at the informational level than at the instructional level, etc. Holland (1974) has noted that most students progress through these levels of need without assistance, given normal socialization and school experiences. Other students require specialized assistance in order to achieve their maximum potential for independent living. The teacher must seek a balance between providing the required intervention and providing interventions that contribute to dependency (Carkhuff, 1969; Glasser, 1965; Lazarus, 1971).

Table 8–8 presents an example of how these levels of needs can dictate different types of intervention within a job-seeking training program. By recognizing the levels of student needs, the teacher can more clearly identify which specific methods or materials are appropriate in a specific setting. For instance, in a class of students homogeneous in regard to most characteristics, including poor reading ability, the teacher will provide primarily informational level interven-

Figure 8–5. Continuum of Student's Needs for Independent Living Interventions

Total Needs   No Needs

Advocacy:	Instructional:	Informational:
Needs help in most skills and content areas and assistance to perform daily living tasks.	Needs help mastering certain content or skills.	Needs help applying content or skills.

Table 8–8. Interventions Categorized by Job-Seeking Skills Areas and Levels of Student Capability

| Job-Seeking Skills | Levels of Intervention | | |
	Informational	Instructional	Advocacy
Selecting an appropriate job goal	Give information about jobs Help student to analyze information about self Monitor selection process	Educate about jobs Educate about self Educate about selection process	Select job goal for student
Looking for the selected jobs in an effective way	Provide information about where to find job leads Monitor job search	Educate about job leads Educate about job search process Select job leads Structure job search	Select jobs for student to pursue Arrange interviews
Writing job applications/resumés	Provide minimal assistance with applications Monitor applications Review resumé	Educate about job applications Practice filling out job applications Structure writing of resumés	Complete job applications for student
Presenting best qualities within job interviews	Provide interviewing information Give information about company	Educate about job interviews Practice interviewing Help set up interviews	Accompany student to interviews Assist during interviews
Following up on job leads until job is found	Monitor follow-up efforts	Educate about follow-up Structure follow-up	Perform or help student to perform follow-up

tions and adapt the manner in which material is presented (e.g., lower reading level, use more audiovisual presentations). In a classroom situation involving students who vary greatly in many abilities, the teacher will have to possess a larger number of methods and materials across a greater range of instructional interventions in order to accommodate individual student differences.

Construction of a materials/activities correlation chart such as Figure 8–6 can facilitate accommodation of learner differences. Correlation charts provide the teacher with a synopsis of an instructional area and types of instructionally relevant materials. In Figure 8–6, the first column lists the instructional objectives and the subsequent columns list classroom instructional activities for that objective in reading, audiovisual, game, and other formats. The objectives

Figure 8–6. Example of a Correlated Resources Chart

Objectives	Reading	A-V	Game Sim.	Other
6.I$_1$	2:1–5 6:3–4 10:1–5	Tape 6.1		P.S. 2
6.I$_2$	5:7–14	FS: "World of Work"	"Job Match"	
6.I$_3$	4:3–6 2:6–7	FS: "How to Use Leisure . . ."		P.S. 4
6.I$_4$	8:7–8		"Play Match"	
6.C$_1$	3:2	Tape 6.2	"Concentration"	W.S. 5–8
6.A$_1$	5:6–7 7:8–12 9:138–39	TR 8–13	Role play codes 6, 12	P.S. 9–12

Source: Jim Daniels and Susan Dollar, *Career Planning Model* (Austin: University of Texas Department of Education). Copyright 1978.

in this chart relate to step 6 of the Career Planning Model (Daniels & Dollar, 1978), identification of future job goals. Specific instructional objectives are listed as either introductory (I), contrast (C), or applications (A) objectives. Objective 6.I$_1$ (students will identify the difference between work and play) can be taught by having students read selected pages from reading resources 2, 6, or 10, listen to tape 6.1, or complete problem-solving activity number 2. Audiovisual activities include audio tapes, filmstrips (FS), films, and transparencies (TR). Games activities include teacher-designed games ("Job Match") and role-play cards. In this example "Other" activities include both problem-solving cards (P.S.) and work simulation situations (W.S.). This structure helps the teacher to provide different learning activities based on learner characteristics and to provide different methods when reteaching a concept.

Augmenting the School Curriculum.   School curriculums are very disparate in the amount of attention given to students' independent living abilities. Some have integrated career education concepts throughout the entire curriculum, whereas others use the "Back to Basics" approach.

Independent living abilities are developmental in nature. First individuals develop an awareness of themselves in the world and basic self-care skills; next they develop an awareness of occupations and work habits; then they match self to occupation and life styles; and finally they prepare for placement within the adult world. Table 8–9 presents a normal sequence of independent living devel-

Table 8–9.   Normal Sequence of Independent Living Related Developments

Preschool	Learns to listen, cooperate, do for self, show initiative, be honest, etc.
	Differentiates work from other activities
	Understands different types of work and associated roles
	Develops feelings toward work
Elementary	Fantasizes different roles
	Understands parents' work
	Has continued and more complex career fantasies
	Is exposed to and develops understanding of wide variety of work roles
	Develops understanding of good work qualities
	Continues to develop and implement communication skills
	Learns to interact appropriately with peers and authority
Junior High	Has part-time or summer job
	Does chores at home
	Develops hobbies or special interests
	Begins to understand personal strengths and weaknesses
	Understands relative rewards, demands, and requirements of major categories of work
	Accepts responsibility for career decisions
	Begins to crystallize personal values and self-concept
High School +	Continues exploration of various career possibilities
	Prepares for career or initial employment
	Crystallizes interests
	Changes plans or jobs
	Understands and acts upon personal strengths and weaknesses
	Develops skills
	Crystallizes personal values and self-concept
	Independent living
	Establishes intimate relationships
	Refines hobbies or special interests
	Learns how to get jobs and holds several different jobs
	Learns and displays appropriate work behavior

opments. Many times learners with problems have missed certain experiences critical to development in independence. The teacher must identify these deficits and either provide in-school remediation or refer the student/family to a community-based organization that can provide the appropriate intervention.

If in-school remediation is chosen, developmental information can help the teacher identify the best approach to augmenting the school curriculum. One possibility at the elementary level is an infusion approach in which independent living skills and content are integrated with traditional elementary curriculum. For instance, money management concepts can be taught through math instruction, sexuality concepts can be taught through health instruction, and communication concepts can be taught through language arts instruction.

Other concepts important to independent living (problem solving, relationships, careers) can be taught through instruction in virtually any area. With the infusion approach, standard elementary subjects are still taught, but both the interest level of activities and the relevance of traditional academic instruction to the real world are increased.

At the secondary level a separate programming approach is possible. Independent living skills content can be offered in units of instruction designed to meet the individual needs of students. This approach allows the teacher to

1. provide a block of instruction to a whole class of students who are deficient in some area,
2. design learning centers to meet instructional needs of a few students, and/or
3. utilize curriculum and materials specifically designed for independent living skills instruction.

In some instances, a mixed model in which some topics are infused and others are presented as separate units may be appropriate.

Teaching Problem Solving and Other Skills.   Some attention should be directed toward teaching students to solve problems and take more responsibility for their own learning. Some approaches include the decisioning process, the behavioral change model, the learning strategies approach, and the relating skills model.

Many approaches to problem solving are based on decision-making models. Essentially all such programs incorporate or modify the decisioning process as described by John Dewey in 1910. Dewey's six steps in decision making are as follows:

1. Define the problem.
2. Generate a list of alternative solutions to the problem.
3. Develop criteria for a minimally acceptable solution.
4. Gather information necessary to compare the list of possible solutions to the criteria established in no. 3.
5. Select preferred solution.
6. Implement and reevaluate.

When the problems students exhibit in decision-making situations are analyzed on the basis of these steps, specific interventions can be designed to stimulate abilities that need development. A student who has difficulty defining the problem may be helped by communication-based group interaction, individual counseling, or provision of relevant examples. The student who has difficulty in generating alternatives may benefit from group brainstorming activities.

Somewhat related to the decision-making model is the behavior change model of Carkhuff (1969), which integrates cognitive and behavioral therapy approaches. Simply presented, the Carkhuff model is based on the following sequence.

1. Exploration of thoughts and feelings leads to goal setting.
2. Understanding problems and goals leads to plan development.
3. Acting on goals and plans helps to resolve problems.

The process is considered sequential and cyclical—i.e., one has to explore self in order to understand the problem, one has to understand the problem in order to act appropriately, and if action does not remedy the problem one has to return to exploration. Students with no goals need exploratory activities such as exercises involving valuing, giving and receiving feedback from other people, and sharing personal thoughts and feelings. Students with goals but no plan may need information about possible plans of action and support resources.

The learning strategies approach (Alley & Deshler, 1979) is based on the assumption that learning disabled secondary students require instructional approaches focused on improving their "acquisition, manipulation, integration, storage, and retrieval of information across situations and settings" (p. 13). Employing this approach, the teacher uses content as an opportunity to teach a skill. For example, instead of having content-specific objectives in math, science, or English, the teacher may focus on teaching organizational skills (that is, how to perceive organization and how to organize information to facilitate learning) in all these areas. Learning strategies approaches have been identified in reading, writing, mathematics, thinking, social interaction, speaking, and listening. There are specified subskills within each skill area, and instructional objectives within those subskills. For example, thinking skills are subdivided into the subskills of time management, organizing, and problem solving, and the time management category consists of the instructional goals of setting priorities, goal setting, awareness of time traps, planning, time recording, and evaluating and modifying plans.

Another approach, the interpersonal skill model, focuses on the skills involved in the three areas of self-awareness, behavior analysis, and communication. These are often called "relating" skills.

Self-awareness training develops students' understanding of their own identity. How learners feel about themselves is a key variable in determining how they will relate to others. In activities in this area, students examine their feelings, their attitudes, their values, their perceptions of others, and others' perceptions of them. It is axiomatic that students must gain an awareness of their behavior before they can change it.

Behavior analysis training is designed to teach students to analyze their own behavior and the behavior of other people. Students are taught to view interactions as consisting of chains of stimuli and responses. They are further taught that their responses may either "signal" subsequent response from the other person or "consequate" a previous response. Students learn to use this schema to first analyze and then understand problem situations that they encounter.

Communication skills training attempts to help students overcome problems they have in giving or receiving messages about their wants, needs, or feelings. At certain points in language and social development, certain deviant behaviors generally occur naturally within most individuals (e.g., stuttering, shyness, name calling, self-doubt). If the behaviors do not disappear as expected, they may cause the individual problems in interpersonal relationships. Many interpersonal problems can be traced to common communication deficits such as problems in expressing feelings, asserting opinions, accepting criticism, and beginning or maintaining conversations. Communication training helps students develop general strategies to overcome their specific personal and interpersonal problems. It requires an interactive environment where the teacher assumes a role as a communication facilitator. To master communication skills, students need general relating information, a good model, ample practice opportunities, and a "safe" environment in which to try out new behaviors.

Commercially Available Materials

The broad nature of the skills and content necessary for independent living has resulted in a proliferation of instructional materials. A computer-generated bibliography of independent living skills materials compiled in 1975 identified over 1500 different materials (University of Texas, Special Education Instructional Materials Center). In the last ten years many more materials have come onto the market. Consequently, a comprehensive review would be a book in itself.

Commercial materials vary in quality of design and in breadth of coverage. Some present only curriculum outlines; others present only learning activities; still others include instructional objectives, curriculum outlines, learning activities, and pre- and post-assessment devices. Some materials are targeted toward specific concepts (e.g., functional mathematics); others address all areas (e.g., independent living curriculum). Each teacher has to consider learner characteristics and the academic curriculum in order to decide upon the appropriate materials to use.

Teachers usually can find many relevant materials in their school district's materials collection or in regional education resource centers. Tables 8–10 and 8–11 are presented to help in identification and access of appropriate independent living instructional materials. Table 8–10 lists representative titles of materials that are relevant to daily living and occupations. These titles will assist teachers in doing library searches or in requesting materials from material col-

Table 8–10. Representative Titles of Materials Relevant to Independent Living

Daily Living	Occupations
Active Listening	Career Awareness
Adaptive Physical Education	Career Clusters
Attitudes	Career (Job) Exploration
Budgeting	Career Goals
Citizenship	Career Guidance
Communication Skills	Career Planning
Community Resources	Form Preparation
Decision Making	Job Readiness
Functional Academics	Job Seeking
Functional Signs	Job Skills
Grooming	Occupational (Job) Descriptions
Health	Occupational Orientation
Interpersonal Skills	Pre-employment Preparation
Life Skills in Reading, Math, etc.	Pre-vocational Skills
Marriage and Family	Work Habits
Money Concepts	
Nutrition	
Parenting	
Problem Solving	
Self-Awareness	
Self-Care Skills	
Shopping	
Social Skills	
Survival Skills	
Values	

lections. Table 8–11 presents a selected list of publishers who have a substantial number of independent living materials in their inventory. Information is provided about content areas and age levels covered. Most publishers will send a catalog of their materials upon request.

For illustrative purposes, let us look at two specific materials—*Teaching Interpersonal and Community Living Skills* (Valletutti & Bender, 1982) and *Planning for Your Own Apartment* (Belina, 1975). *Teaching Interpersonal and Community Living Skills* is more of a curriculum outline than an actual instructional material. The authors first give a general overview of curriculum development considerations for independent living instruction and then present chapters on the individual as (1) a responsible person, (2) a member of a household, (3) a traveler, (4) a learner, (5) a worker, (6) a participant in leisure activities, (7) a consumer of goods and services, and (8) a responsible citizen. In each of these chapters, learning objectives are identified and the functional contexts, cognitive dimensions, psychomotor aspects, and health-safety factors related to

Table 8–11. Selected Publishers of Independent Living Training Material

Selected Publishers (City)	Content Areas							Target Populations			
	Self	Others	Career	Community	Government and Law	Humanities	Economics	Elementary	Junior High	High School	Adults
American Guidance Service (Circle Pines, Minnesota)	X	X	X					X	X	X	
Career Aids, Inc. (Centswealth, California)	X	X	X		X		X		X	X	X
C. C. Publications, Inc. (Tigard, Oregon)	X	X			X		X	X	X		
Edits (San Diego, California)			X						X	X	
Frank E. Richards Publishing Co., Inc. (Phoenix, New York)	X				X		X		X	X	
Hubbard (Northbrook, Illinois)	X						X	X	X	X	
Materials Development Center (Menomonie, Wisconsin)	X	X	X							X	X
Ponorama (Washington, D.C.)	X	X	X			X	X	X	X	X	
Pro-Ed (Austin, Texas)	X	X	X	X			X	X	X	X	X
Science Research Associates (Chicago, Illinois)	X	X	X					X	X	X	
Steck-Vaughn (Austin, Texas)				X	X	X	X	X	X	X	

the objective are described. At the conclusion of each chapter, the authors present a sample lesson plan based on one objective from that chapter; the lesson plan specifies materials/equipment required, reinforcement schedules, motivating activities, and instructional resources. The text does not provide immediately usable materials but may help teachers identify objectives and approaches to instruction.

Planning for Your Own Apartment is an example of a highly specific material based on one objective. This illustrated text-workbook, designed for special needs students, covers apartment hunting, leases, rental agreements, furnished and unfurnished apartments, budget considerations, and decorating. Several learning activities are presented for each topic, and all learner material is written on approximately the third-grade level. This material can be used either as a separate instructional unit or to infuse life-relevant content into instruction in math, health, or social studies.

Teacher-Directed Activities

When commercial materials are unavailable, either because fiscal restraints prevent acquisition of new materials or because the teacher is trying to meet an instructional need specific to a class or to one student, the teacher must develop instructional materials. Following are several general guidelines for creating instructional materials.

1. Use real-life materials whenever possible. If teaching banking, use real bank books; if teaching job applications, use real job applications.

2. Provide real-life experiences whenever possible. Allow students to learn by doing. Rather than talking about jobs, go see them. Rather than talking about calling for a job, let students make real calls. In order to develop independence, students must be encouraged to make decisions and enjoy (suffer) the consequences of those decisions.

3. Use both interactive and individual activities. Some skills and content can only be mastered by working with others (e.g., relating, feeling, self, others). Students' needs in other skill and content areas will be so specific and varied that individual activities will be required (e.g., job selection, leisure interests).

4. Design materials that allow you to interact with students or model behavior. Interaction allows you to develop a more trusting relationship with students and also facilitates assessment; modeling allows you to demonstrate behaviors that are hard to describe (making an assertive statement, acting on values, listening to constructive criticism).

5. Use as many community resources and resource people as possible. Many agencies and organizations have excellent community education programs that will provide speakers or equipment, arrange tours, and/or provide instructional material. By using these resources, you can broaden student experiences and acquaint them with the local community.

6. Use techniques that have been successful in other content areas for teaching independent living. For example, assigning writing may be a good method of instruction. Topics such as "What I want out of life," "My perfect job," "How I want to live in ten years," or "The car I want" require students to do research into independent living and give them a chance to think about their goals or plans.

7. Organize curriculum presentations around concepts.[2] Concepts are de-

[2]This discussion is taken from the ideas and research of Bruner et al. (1956); Dollar and Dollar (1976); and Engelmann (1969).

fined by specific characteristics. Each example or instance has certain observable characteristics. Therefore, any given concept is defined by referring to the observable, common characteristics of the examples collected to represent the concept. This unique group of common characteristics defines the concept and is not shared by any other concept. It follows that when presenting examples to the learner one must never vary or change the determined essential or defining characteristics, but must always vary the unimportant characteristics of the instances. For example, in teaching the concept of "job," certain characteristics are important to remember. Outdoor location, physical activity, routine duties, close supervision, output of a product, and receipt of a weekly salary may all be characteristics of one example of "job." As other examples of "job" are presented, salary and product will emerge as the only characteristics that are essential to "job" (see Figure 8–7). If outdoor location, physical activity, routine duties, close supervision, or other characteristics are not varied within the concept set of examples, these characteristics will be learned as being essential to the concept.

In fostering independent living skills, the teacher may want to make use of free materials and speakers, classroom discussions, simulations, occupational information, goal setting and plan development, support groups, and learning centers.

Free Materials and Speakers.   Daily living skills and occupational knowledge involve many content-based competencies. Knowing how to care for oneself and how to manage the details of daily living relates directly to the amount of

Figure 8–7.   Concept of "Job"

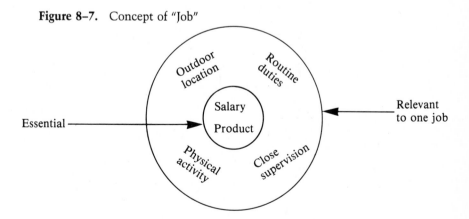

independence one has. Table 8–12 presents methods, materials, and resources that can aid independence-oriented instruction of special needs learners. Resources are categorized by area and rated according to the most appropriate instructional arrangements. The chart is intended to stimulate thinking about sources of free instructional support within a specific community.

Classroom Discussions.   Before classroom discussions start, the group should agree upon a set of ground rules about acceptable behaviors (e.g., Everyone has a right to his or her opinion, Everyone shares in group decisions), which will serve as a contract among members of the group. The teacher then structures group activities to stimulate communication among group members. Discussion may be organized around topics selected by students or around the giving and receiving of feedback about the students themselves.

Simulations.   The classroom is in many ways a simulation of a work place, and students can learn to relate classroom expectations to work expectations. Teachers may design role play situations to teach interpersonal skills or develop work activity simulations to provide students experience in the demands of work not normally encountered in the classroom. A good approach when using simulations is to videotape them and then allow the simulators to view the videotape prior to debriefing. The learning attained from simulations is based on the quality of the experience as well as the discussion after the simulation.

Occupational Information.   An important development during the school years is the attainment of information about occupations, first in a general sense and then in an individual sense. Materials descriptive of occupations, field trips to representative local businesses, and guest speakers from different occupational groups can all contribute to a student's broad understanding of occupations. At the secondary level, each student will need to research his or her specific choice through reading and relating to other people. Two specific approaches that are helpful are information interviewing and job analysis. Information interviewing is a technique in which the student sets up and carries out an interview with a worker in a given occupation and then prepares a job analysis based on interview information. Job analysis is a technique that involves describing jobs in a standard way so that they can be compared. A very basic outline for a job analysis is included below.

1. *Job purpose*—a general statement about the overall purpose of the job.
2. *Job duties*—a list of the major tasks that the worker must perform.

monitor, a disk drive or tape drive, or a *mouse,* which is a hand-held controller that can be used to direct the CPU to do certain things.

When the CPU performs an operation in response to instructions received through an input device, there must be a way to show the user the result of the operation. Accordingly, every CPU needs a display or output device to show the results of the operations it has performed. Typically the display is in the form of configurations on a monitor (or a television screen hooked up to the computer). If a permanent copy of the display is required, the computer is hooked up to a printer which produces permanent, or "hard," copy of the display.

Any displays or results of computer operations can also be saved on disk or tape for later retrieval, review, or modification. A disk drive or a tape or cassette player thus serves not only as an input device, but also as a storage medium through which files, either text or graphic, can be saved for subsequent use.

Although disk drives are now preferred, some schools still rely on cassette tape recorders for program input and storage. Tape systems are much cheaper than disk drives, but they are ten to sixty times slower, are less reliable, and store much less information. In addition, many educational programs are unavailable in cassette form.

Most microcomputer systems with disk drives use 5¼-inch disks, and most educational programs are marketed in this format. However, the Apple MacIntosh requires 3½-inch disks, and larger computer systems may use 8-inch Winchester drives. Larger disk systems are much faster and even more reliable than the more typical 5¼-inch drives; they are also much more expensive. As yet, few educational programs have been designed for them.

Central processing units come in many different sizes. Many CPUs found in classrooms today have 48K or 64K bytes of random access memory (RAM). Random access memory refers to the part of a CPU's capacity that is available for user use, as opposed to read only memory (ROM), which is the set of permanent instructions within the CPU. The size and complexity of a computer program are limited by the amount of available RAM—most educational programs require a minimum of 48K RAM to execute.

Printers for school use come in two basic forms—dot matrix and letter-quality. Most classroom teachers prefer dot matrix printers because (1) they are generally capable of printing graphics as well as text and (2) they are usually faster than letter-quality printers. Speed and clarity of type are major issues to consider when one is pricing printers for classroom use.

Peripherals and Other Computer Adaptations for the Handicapped

The promise of computers and related technologies for handicapped persons is enormous. Many kinds of equipment have been designed to enable handicapped students to perform tasks or to gain access to materials ordinarily beyond their capabilities. For example, sensory enhancement or translation equipment can either clarify an audio or video signal or translate from one to the other so that the signal can be received by a hearing-impaired or visually impaired student. Other adaptations can make it possible to "train" a computer to recognize a discrete vocabulary or set of phrases.

For deaf persons, communication via telephone is now possible through special teletypewriter or telecommunication devices for the deaf. The availability of the latter in many libraries is enabling deaf students to obtain full information and reference services.

Many types of sophisticated equipment are available for visually impaired students. The Kurzweil Reading Machine converts printed materials in approximately 300 type styles and sizes into synthetic English speech, at a rate that can be variably controlled. The Optacon Print Reading System is a portable device that allows blind and deaf-blind students to have immediate independent access to printed materials of all kinds through translation of a visual signal (letter) into an enlarged vibrating tactile form. To assist blind students in writing, reading, note-taking, and storing braille text, the VersaBraille System is available in portable form. This device may be attached to a computer modem or teletypewriter for communication with remote sources. Both VersaBraille and the Optacon were developed by Telesensory Systems.

A variety of electronic visual aids for partially sighted students have been developed. Visualtek's products have variable print size (allowing magnification of print up to sixty times), image contrast enhancement (making images sharper), and built-in lighting (to provide appropriate illumination), as well as other features. Viewscan, another computer-controlled device for the partially sighted, is a portable device for magnifying and clarifying visual images.

Various devices aid those with motor impairments. Computer-based devices allow even quadriplegics to operate their own wheelchairs or classroom "desks." Electronic page-turners permit severely physically handicapped students to have independent access to books. Students who lack the motor coordination required for a standard keyboard can access standard computer programs using a keyboard emulator. The emulator may be in the form of an enlarged keyboard or may consist of a matrix of large squares which accept the touch of a headstick or a light-beam headpointer. An adaptive-firmware card developed for the Apple computer allows disabled students to run standard, unmodified software (such as games or educational programs) using any of ten input routines, some of which require the use of only a single switch (Schwejda & Vanderheiden, 1982). All of these devices permit students to have access to programs they would otherwise not be able to use.

Using Computers in the Classroom

The preceding section has provided an overview of basic computer hardware and some of the adaptations and peripherals that make it possible for students with particular cognitive, sensory, or motor problems to benefit from classroom instruction. We now consider in more explicit form the actual use of computers in a classroom.

Much has been written about how computers will revolutionize what happens in the classroom. Our position is that classroom teachers will continue to be central in the instructional process, and that computers provide but one more resource, in some cases a unique resource, for enabling learning to take place.

In considering the ways in which computers can be used in a classroom, it is useful to distinguish between computer use that is directly instructional in nature (computer-assisted instruction, or CAI), computer use for the management of instructional activities (computer-managed instruction, or CMI), and computer use for testing and record-keeping. We will look at each of these in turn.

Computer-Assisted Instruction (CAI)

CAI takes a number of different forms, depending on the purpose that a teacher has in mind. This purpose in turn depends on the kind of learning that the teacher is promoting, the student's stage of learning (acquisition, consolidation, retention, or generalization of skills), and the kind of software that is available. The following are the types of CAI that are currently in widest use.

Tutorial Programs.   Tutorial programs are a mode of computer-assisted instruction in which the program does actual teaching—it assumes the role of the teacher in presenting material for the student to learn. At intervals, questions are asked of the student to assess whether the material has been mastered. If the student's responses are acceptable, new material is presented; if not, the program usually makes provisions for review or remediation of the faulty learning. This kind of program is best suited to students with good independent work habits and good reading comprehension skills.

Simulations.   Simulations are designed to re-create some aspect of reality or a situation analogous to a reality that is relevant to an instructional curriculum. Simulations are especially appropriate in cases where it would not be feasible or safe to undertake the learning in the real-life situation, e.g., initial driver education training or training in first-aid techniques. The greater the similarity between the simulation and the real phenomenon that is being modeled, the more likely it is that appropriate generalization will occur. To date, only a few high-quality educational simulation programs are available.

Problem Solving.   Relatively few good problem-solving programs are available at the present time, but the potential for this kind of instruction is enormous. Currently the most widely used problem-solving applications in CAI are in the computer language LOGO. The LOGO approach allows the student not only to solve problems but also to generate and define problems to be solved (Papert, 1980). It is particularly useful for students who are disorganized in their approach to solving problems, because it creates a set of highly motivating circumstances in which students must organize themselves in a precise manner. The skill of defining and resolving problems in a coherent manner is one that many students with learning and behavioral problems need to develop.

Educational Games.   Educational games are designed to be fun as well as to encourage appropriate learning. Frequently the game strategy is similar to that of the popular commercial computer games, with an educational component built in. In general, educational games rely heavily on dazzling graphic effects; the educational aspect is not always an integral part of the game and may appear contrived. Educational games have great potential for students of low motivation, or for students who are "turned off" by traditional academic formats. In some instances, computer games can be used effectively as reinforcers for other instructional tasks successfully completed by a student.

Drill and Practice.   By far the most common use of CAI is for drill and practice. Used properly, computer-assisted drill and practice can provide an interesting and novel way for students to consolidate and integrate previously learned material. At worst, drill and practice can be "computer seatwork," with little advantage over the paper-and-pencil variety. Drill and practice programs are most effective with students who require immediate feedback on their responses, and with students who benefit from repeatedly going over previously learned material.

Computer-Managed Instruction (CMI)

A fully developed computer-managed instructional program allows a teacher to assess entry skills of a pupil, to prescribe appropriate learning experiences (both print and nonprint), to reassess progress, to assign additional learning exercises if warranted or to "promote" a student to the next module, and to keep complete dated records on each pupil including a record of particular areas of difficulty. Of course, not all CMI programs have all of these features, but their basic purpose is the same—to diagnose student strengths and weaknesses in a particular content area and then to prescribe instructional activities (e.g., "Read pages 22–26 of your text," or "View the videotape 'Christopher Columbus' ") based on the student's correct and incorrect responses.

CMI programs are not difficult for teachers to develop themselves. To be effective, they should be correlated directly to the student's curriculum and should reflect precisely the learning resources and activities that are available for students (for example, it doesn't make sense to have a program that prescribes reading material that isn't in the local library). Used appropriately, CMI is a wonderful teaching approach for individualizing instruction, because students can proceed at their own pace and learning activities can be tailored to the particular learning needs of each student.

Using Computers for Testing

The assessment of students through teacher-made tests in a CMI format was described briefly above. Computers can also be of assistance in more direct testing of pupils. Computers can help teachers with item banking, test assembly, test administration, test scoring, and record-keeping.

Item Banking.   Item banking refers to a procedure by which test items are saved and "pooled" so that they can be used in more than one test period, sometimes by more than one teacher. When a test item proves confusing to students, or obsolete, or otherwise unsatisfactory, a simple stroke of the keyboard eliminates the item from the item bank. Over time, a teacher can develop a comprehensive collection of test items from which to choose when designing a test. When item banking is combined with item performance data (e.g., proportion correct, number of examinees selecting a given item, reliability estimates, and test summary statistics), the quality of the tests that a teacher prepares can be improved greatly. Item banking also reduces the amount of time needed to prepare a test.

Test Assembly.   If items are banked in a computer, the actual assembly of a test is very simple. Using a word processing and/or an editing program, the teacher simply identifies test items and adds instructions. This feature reduces the chances that errors will be introduced through faulty typing or proofreading.

Test Administration.   A number of commercially produced tests (e.g., Kottmeyer Diagnostic Spelling Test, Sequential Assessment of Mathematics Inventory) are available for administration via a computer format. However, the administration of tests by computer is not limited to standardized tests; in fact, some of the greatest advantages of computer test administration become most obvious with teacher-generated tests. The format of a teacher-made test, including its spatial organization, time allowed for each item, and the use of color and graphics to highlight important information, can be easily modified when the test is administered by computer.

Modifications are particularly appropriate for many students with learning disabilities (Salend & Salend, 1985). Alterations of the presentation mode (e.g., by using a speech synthesizer) and/or the response mode (e.g., by accepting input from a joystick, switch, or keyboard emulator as well as a regular keyboard) can be made to accommodate students with particular difficulties or handicaps. Since the computer presents items in sequence, poorly organized students will not miss items. Furthermore, the motivational aspect of computers can help to keep certain students on task; the teacher can build feedback or reinforcement into the test by interspersing encouraging phrases such as "Keep trying" or "You're doing a good job" in flashing letters or graphics. A well-constructed computer-administered test can appear more like a game than a test to students who are afraid of tests.

Test Scoring and Record-Keeping.   Commercially prepared tests have been scored and profiled by computer for many years. However, even teacher-made tests can be computer scored and individual and group records kept, with only a minimum amount of expertise on the part of the teacher. For teachers without programming ability, the utilization of an authoring language such as Pilot or SuperPilot can greatly facilitate test scoring and record-keeping (as well as test development). An alternative is to hire a professional programmer to develop a model skeleton test into which test items and pupil names can be inserted in each new testing situation.

Using Computers for Record-Keeping and in the IEP Process

Computers have wide applicability in managing virtually any kind of data or records. In fact, one of the major commercial uses of computers is in data base management or management information systems. A survey of special education administrators (Burrello, Tracy, & Glassman, 1983) showed that the most popular use of computer technology in schools was for student-data management, including student enrollment and rosters, student tracking, student program management, and assessment. Business-data management, such as handling budgets, personnel files, inventories of books and supplies, and transportation, was also frequently done by computer. And finally, word processing and information retrieval were also popular.

Although few classroom teachers would need to use computers for the scope of activities described above, computers can be helpful in record-keeping and aspects of managing Individual Educational Plans at the classroom level. The previous section described how teachers can develop test item banks. Inventories of pupil activity sheets, picture files, or any other instructional files also can be organized, stored, and kept up to date by computer. IEP objectives for a given child and a record of his or her progress toward meeting those objectives can be conveniently tracked using a number of IEP programs that are now available for computers. Each child can be assigned a file using any one of a number of available data base management programs. All test results are entered into the student's file as they occur, and at the touch of a keystroke a printer will print out a formatted summary of the student's progress. This procedure can save a teacher much time and effort and produce attractive and accurate pupil reports. If desired, such pupil reports can be directly conveyed to the school's central office mainframe or minicomputer through a networking arrangement in which all computers in a school are interconnected.

Selecting Software for Classroom Use

A pervasive and persistent difficulty encountered by teachers who want to use computers in their classrooms is the generally low quality of educational programs that are available to run on the computers once these have been purchased. These programs, called software (as opposed to hardware, the actual physical equipment), are available in disk form, on cassette tapes, or on cartridges. Although there has been some improvement in the past few years, it is still true that educational software is technically less sophisticated and educationally less sound than it could be. For this reason, teachers themselves must develop some degree of sophistication in selecting software that is appropriate for their particular classroom situation. A number of software evaluation formats have been developed to assist teachers in this task; one that we believe is both comprehensive and realistic is reproduced in Figure 9–1.

Responsible Use of Computers

Computers have moved onto the educational scene with such rapidity that many educators are left poorly prepared for the new professional skills and attitudes that their use requires. Accordingly, a number of professional organizations have established committees to draft guidelines for teachers and others who use computers and other new technologies in the schools. These guidelines typically address professional skill areas and touch on pertinent legal and ethical considerations. On pages 359–361 is one such set of guidelines developed by the International Reading Association.[1]

[1] Prepared by the 1983–1984 Computer Technology and Reading Committee: Alan E. Farstrup, Chair, Ossi Ahvenainen, Isabel Beck, Darlene Bolig, Jayne DeLawter, Shirley Feldmann, Peter Joyce, Michael Kamil, Gerald J. Kochinski, George E. Mason, Harry B. Miller, Jane D. Smith, Art Willer, Carmelita K. Williams, Linda Roberts, Consultant. Reprinted with permission of the International Reading Association.

Figure 9–1. Modified MCE Program Evaluation Form

Directions: This evaluation form is designed to evaluate four software programs. Answer each of the questions about each program you evaluate. Use the following rating scale:

> 3 = EXCELLENT
> 2 = ABOVE AVERAGE
> 1 = AVERAGE
> −1 = BELOW AVERAGE
> −5 = POOR

After rating programs in each area, add up the total scores and place them in the appropriate spaces. Let this rating help you in your decision making in the purchase of microcomputer software.

Names of Programs Evaluated: *Type of Program Evaluated (i.e., tutorial, etc.)*

1. _____   _____

2. _____   _____

3. _____   _____

4. _____   _____

Comments on Each Program:

1. _____

   _____

2. _____

   _____

3. _____

   _____

4. _____

   _____

Program Choice (if applicable):

_____

_____

_____

Figure 9–1 *Continued*

	Program Names			
	1	*2*	*3*	*4*

I. Instructional Content

1. Is the content consistent with the goals and objectives of the program?
2. Is the program one of a series in which carefully planned learning objectives have been followed?
3. Does the Instructional Guide provide information, suggestions, and materials to assist the teacher in successfully implementing the program?
4. Are program goals provided that are usable for individualized education programs?
5. Are evaluation materials and/or criteria provided that are usable for individualized education programs?
6. Are prerequisite skills, vocabulary, and concepts determined and presented?
7. Is vocabulary defined or paraphrased in text or in the prerequisite skills portion of the Program Principles Section of the Instruction?
8. Are diagnostic or prescriptive procedures built into the program?
9. Does the text follow established rules for punctuation, capitalization, grammar, and usage?
10. Are supplemental materials provided for learner and teacher?
11. Is the product designed for appropriate age and ability groups?
12. Is the program compatible with the curriculum?
13. Is the program compatible with the needs of the teacher?
14. Is the content accurate and complete?
15. Are examples provided with directions when appropriate?
16. Are redundancy and drill used effectively?
17. Is language appropriate in tone and selection?
18. Are concrete applications for concepts provided?
19. Is feedback immediate?

(continued)

Figure 9–1 *Continued*

	Program Names			
	1	*2*	*3*	*4*

II. Educational Adequacy

1. Is instructional design of high quality using accepted learning theory?
2. Are learners always the target of interaction with the computer—a personalized element?
3. Are positive responses reinforced?
4. Are frames that follow incorrect responses nonpunishing?
5. Is reinforcement variable and random in context and established by behavior management principles?
6. Is branching used where the learner demonstrates need for further concept development before proceeding?
7. Are avenues of communication from the learner to the computer logical and at comprehensible levels?
8. Is evaluation of each concept appropriate and sufficient?
9. Are concepts and skills task analyzed into appropriate steps?
10. Are color, graphics, and animation used effectively to enhance the lesson?
11. Are sound, inverse print, etc., employed for attention and reinforcement purposes and not distracting?
12. Is syllabification provided for new and/or unfamiliar words?
13. Is sentence length dependent on need and learner levels?
14. Is the learner always provided with frames that allow for progression through the program?
15. Does the program provide suitable directions for the learner?

III. Technical Adequacy

1. Will the program run to completion without being "hung up" because of unexpected responses?
2. Are the programs difficult or impossible to be inadvertently disrupted by the learner?

Figure 9–1 *Continued*

	Program Names			
	1	*2*	*3*	*4*
3. Can learners operate the programs independently?				
4. Is the amount on each frame appropriate?				
5. Is the length of each section appropriate?				
6. Are words and lines spaced for ease of reading?				
7. Is variation of type and organization of textual materials appropriate for a clear presentation?				
8. Are inappropriate responses considered and handled appropriately?				
9. Is the educational technology (i.e., microcomputer) the best available for presenting this subject matter?				
10. Are backups available?				
IV. Overall Evaluation Rating of Program in Its Entirety				
Total for each program				

Source: MCE Inc., 157 S. Kalamazoo Mall, Suite 250, Kalamazoo, MI 49007.

Guidelines for Educators on Using Computers in the Schools

The Computer Technology and Reading Committee of the International Reading Association has compiled the following guidelines in an effort to encourage the effective use of technology in reading classrooms. The guidelines are designed to highlight important issues and provide guidance to educators as they work to make the best possible use of the many new technologies which are rapidly finding their way into schools and classrooms everywhere.

1. About Software Curricular needs should be primary in the selection of reading instructional software. Above all, software designed for use in the reading classroom must be consistent with what research and practice have shown to be important in the process of learning to read or of reading to learn. The IRA believes that high quality instructional software should incorporate the following elements:

- clearly stated and implemented instructional objectives.
- learning to read and reading to learn activities which are consistent with established reading theory and practice.
- lesson activities which are most effectively and efficiently done through the application of computer technology and are not merely replications of activities which could be better done with traditional means.

- prompts and screen instructions to the student which are simple, direct and easier than the learning activity to be done.
- prompts, screen instructions and reading texts which are at a readability level appropriate to the needs of the learner.
- documentation and instructions which are clear and unambiguous, assuming a minimum of prior knowledge about computers for use.
- screen displays which have clear and legible print with appropriate margins and between-line spacing.
- documentation and screen displays which are grammatically correct, factually correct, and which have been thoroughly proofed for spelling errors.
- a record keeping or information management element for the benefit of both the teacher and the learner, where appropriate.
- provisions for effective involvement and participation by the learner, coupled with rapid and extensive feedback, where appropriate.
- wherever appropriate, a learning pace which is modified by the actions of the learner or which can be adjusted by the teacher based on diagnosed needs.
- a fair, reasonable and clearly stated publisher's policy governing the replacement of defective or damaged program media such as tapes, diskettes, ROM cartridges and the like.
- a publisher's preview policy which provides pre-purchase samples or copies for review and which encourages a well-informed software acquisition process by reading educators.

2. About Hardware   Hardware should be durable, capable of producing highly legible text displays, and safe for use in a classroom situation. Hardware should be chosen that conforms to established classroom needs. Some characteristics to be aware of include, but are not limited to, the following:

- compatibility with classroom software appropriate to the curriculum.
- proven durability in classroom situations.
- clear, unambiguous instruction manuals appropriate for use by persons having a minimum of technical experience with computers.
- sufficient memory (RAM) capability to satisfy anticipated instructional software applications.
- availability of disk, tape, ROM cartridge or other efficient and reliable data storage devices.
- screen displays which produce legible print, minimize glare, and which have the lowest possible screen radiation levels.
- a functional keyboard and the availability of other appropriate types of input devices.
- proven, accessible and reasonably priced technical support from the manufacturer or distributor.

3. About Staff Development and Training   Staff development programs should be available which encourage teachers to become intelligent users of technology in the reading classroom. Factors to consider include, but are not limited to, the following:

- study and practice with various applications of computer technology in the reading and language arts classroom.
- training which encourages thoughtful and informed evaluation, selection and integration of effective and appropriate teaching software into the reading and language arts classroom.

4. *About Equity*   All persons, regardless of sex, ethnic group, socioeconomic status, or ability, must have equality of access to the challenges and benefits of computer technology. Computer technology should be integrated into all classrooms and not be limited to scientific or mathematical applications.

5. *About Research*   Research which assesses the impact of computer technology on all aspects of learning to read and reading to learn is essential. Public and private funding should be made available in support of such research. Issues which need to be part of national and international research agendas include, but are not limited to:

- the educational efficacy of computer technology in the reading and language arts classroom.
- the affective dimensions of introducing computer technology into the schools.
- the cognitive dimensions of introducing computer technology into the reading classroom.
- the application of concepts of artificial intelligence to computer software which address issues of reading diagnosis, developmental reading, remedial reading, and instructional management.
- the impact of new technology on students, reading teachers, schools, curricula, parents, and the community.

6. *About Networking and Sharing Information*   Local area and national networks or information services should be established and supported which can be accessed through the use of computers. Such services should be designed to provide an information resource on reading related topics. Such services could also be used to provide linkage and information exchange among many institutions, including professional associations such as the IRA.

7. *About Inappropriate Uses of Technology*   Computers should be used in meaningful and productive ways which relate clearly to instructional needs of students in the reading classroom. Educators must capitalize on the potential of this technology by insisting on its appropriate and meaningful use.

8. *About Legal Issues*   Unauthorized duplication and use of copyrighted computer software must not be allowed. Developers and publishers of educational software have a right to be protected from financial losses due to the unauthorized use of their products. Consumers of educational software have a concomitant right to expect fair prices, quality products and reasonable publishers' policies regarding licensing for multiple copies, replacement of damaged program media, network applications and the like. Without mutual trust and cooperation on this important issue both parties will suffer and, ultimately, so will the learner.

TUTORING INDIVIDUAL STUDENTS

Today, adults, high school students, and even elementary pupils are often employed effectively as tutors in the schools. Even though these paraprofessionals may instruct students in basic school subjects, the primary qualifications for a tutor are not necessarily academic, a fact that is reflected in the following guidelines for selecting individuals to serve as tutors.

The tutor must:

1. Be dependable, for missing only one or two sessions will destroy the tutoring relationship and allow the student to regress.
2. Be patient and ready to go over material a number of times before the student has finally learned it.
3. Have an understanding of the student's problems and feelings.
4. Have integrity; for example, the tutor must be truthful and never leave the student with the impression that he or she is doing much better than actually is the case.
5. Be capable of handling interpersonal relations well.

Beyond these qualifications, the tutor must be interested in helping students, accept responsibility readily, and follow directions.

Several elements must be considered before an effective tutorial program can be initiated. First, the student's problems must be assessed carefully. Second, those areas in which the tutor will work must be chosen. Third, the approach and materials to be used should be selected. Fourth, the period of time to be spent on any activity should be estimated. It is very important that the tutor know exactly what is expected, what is to be done, and how to do it. Therefore, some training should be conducted before the tutor begins the program. Left to his or her own devices without proper training and supervision, the tutor may unwittingly create problems and end up being "more trouble than he or she is worth."

Record-Keeping

Each tutor should be given a notebook (preferably looseleaf) in which there are three distinct kinds of pages. The first should be the Tutor's Lesson Plan. On this page, the activities, the procedures, and the amount of time to be devoted to each student can be listed. If special materials are required, they should be mentioned, along with an indication of where they may be obtained. A sample lesson plan is shown in Figure 9–2.

The second kind of page that should be included in the Tutor's Notebook is a Tutor's Log Sheet. On this page, the tutor may record any observations about the progress of the child on a particular day that seem pertinent. The availability of this sheet will foster ongoing communications between the tutor and the busy classroom teacher. An example is given in Figure 9–3.

The third kind of sheet is the Teacher's Note. On this page, the teacher can make comments, suggestions, and/or recommendations for changes in the Tutor's Lesson Plan. For an example, see Figure 9–4.

Figure 9–2. Tutor's Lesson Plan

Name _Stanley Miller_   Date Started _10/7/85_

School _West Elementary_   Tutor _Mrs. Clark_

Grade _4_   Reading Level _Preprimer_

Description of the Problem

Stanley has a limited sight vocabulary, poor attention and concentration, and has had almost no success in school.

9:00 – 9:10 Ask ~~what~~ Stanley what he thinks will happen to the Chinese brothers. Then finish the 5 Chinese Brothers.

9:10 – 9:20 Review the Dolch Sight Vocabulary Words that he missed yesterday. Have him put those that he still doesn't know on 3" x 5" cards.

9:20 – 9:30 Use SRA Lab II Rate Builder, Red 3, as a listening exercise. Help him to set a purpose for listening. Remember to keep a record of the number of answers that he gets correct.

Figure 9–3. Tutor's Log Sheet

Tutor _Mrs. Clark_   Student _Stanley Miller_

Date _10/7/85_   Grade _4_ School _West Elementary_

Stanley couldn't think what might happen but he listened and said, "Now I know!" when we came to it. We reviewed the Dolch Words and he missed 6 of them. He asked me if he could take them home. I told him I'd check with you. He answered all the questions on the rate builder correctly. This is 4 in row — he may be ready for the next color.

Figure 9–4.   Teacher's Note

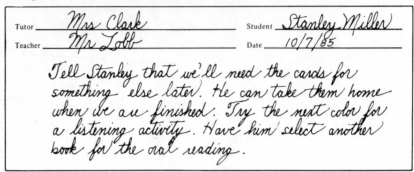

Tutor _Mrs Clark_   Student _Stanley Miller_
Teacher _Mr Lobb_   Date _10/7/85_

Tell Stanley that we'll need the cards for something else later. He can take them home when we are finished. Try the next color for a listening activity. Have him select another book for the oral reading.

Tutor Training

The teacher must not only assess, prescribe, and gather materials, but also make sure that the tutor can and does carry out the program as specified. The teacher will usually have to provide the tutor with at least some minimal training (the tutor will have to be taught to complete the forms described in the previous section, familiarized with the basic methods and strategies used by the teacher, etc.). Of course, it is not possible for the experienced teacher to transfer to the tutor all of the skills and expertise that he or she has acquired as a result of completing a four-year college program and several years of teaching, but the teacher can make sure that the tutor knows what to do and has the materials to do it.

Whenever possible, the tutor's training should be by example. Working with a student, the teacher should demonstrate items of importance in a tutorial lesson. For example, demonstrations for reading tutors might cover:

1. Qualities of good oral reading (creating interest in a story, setting purposes, anticipating outcomes, etc.).
2. Various ways to use flashcards for drill.
3. Teaching the student to trace words correctly, if this technique is used.
4. Selecting, or helping the student to select, an appropriate book.
5. Using a positive (reinforcing) attitude in all activities.
6. Keeping comprehensive records.
7. Various materials; their location and use.
8. Physical surroundings (e.g., adequate lighting).
9. Use of a dictionary when necessary.

During the training period, rapport between the tutor and the teacher must be established. If rapport is properly fostered, the tutor will feel free to ask the teacher any question about the program. Rapport can be enhanced and maintained if, when asked a question, the teacher carefully considers a response before answering. For example, it is far better for the teacher to say, "I'm sorry; I should have told you that," than to say, "I thought that you'd use your common sense." Negative criticism can shut off communication quickly.

Problems in Tutoring

Even when tutors have received a great deal of training, problems will still arise, because a tutor cannot be expected to learn everything that he or she needs to know all at once. As a result, a tutor may make gross mistakes occasionally. For example, the tutor may try to get the student to "sound out" words that are not phonetic; or to make sure that a pupil is reading, the tutor may encourage the student to whisper or to move his or her lips when reading silently. From time to time, a tutor may inadvertently threaten a student with such statements as "If you don't do this, I won't like you" or "I can't understand why you don't know this; I've told you a hundred times!" The tutor may not recognize when a student is frustrated. There are many things, some great, some small, that can go wrong in a tutoring program, so the importance of adequate preparation, planning, tutor training, and supervision cannot be stressed too often.

If possible, tutors should be paid. Although adult volunteers can fill a gap, they often leave for a paying job, especially after they get some experience and can qualify for employment in a day care center, nursery school, or private preschool. Also, they are often undependable. On the other hand, there is a wealth of untapped student talent in the school district. Students can make excellent volunteer tutors. For example, older students can work with younger pupils ("cross-age tutoring"), and students of the same age can, and often do, tutor each other ("peer tutoring").

There exists a fairly impressive body of research that testifies to the merits of student tutoring (e.g., Chiang, Thorpe, & Darch, 1980; Cloward, 1967; Erickson, 1971; Lane, Pollack, & Sher, 1972; Thomas, 1972). Teachers who want to know the particulars involved in implementing and maintaining peer tutoring programs will find most useful the recent books by Ehly and Larsen (1980), *Peer Tutoring for Individualized Instruction*, and by Pierce, Stahlbrand, and Armstrong (1984), *Increasing Student Productivity Through Peer Tutoring*.

INVOLVING PARENTS IN SCHOOL PROGRAMS

Many teachers would like to see the parents of their classroom pupils involved in school programs. Properly motivated and informed, parents can be strong partners with schools in helping students learn. Why then are parents so rarely involved?

Part of the difficulty seems to be due to fears on the part of teachers and principals. Some of these fears are that the parents are basically not interested in their children's education; that they wouldn't come to school if invited, especially the parents who need to come; that they wouldn't understand the volunteer program; and that if they did understand, they would want to control the program (Granowsky, Middleton, & Mumford, 1979).

Yet it has been found that parents are, in fact, interested in their children's education; that they know whether or not their children are having problems; and that they help their children to the best of their knowledge (Nicholson, 1980).

Several schools have successfully involved parents in programs (Granowsky et al., 1979; Criscuolo, 1979, 1980). The success of such programs seems to be due to the following factors:

1. *Making parents feel welcome at school.* This may take the form of scheduling parent conferences to accommodate parents' work responsibilities, providing a resource room where parents may browse or borrow materials, or arranging for parent observation and participation in programs.

2. *Keeping parents informed about the school's programs.* Many parents may be confused about the purpose and approach of some of the school's programs. They may wonder why particular material is or is not being taught or why their child does or does not have homework. A newsletter, parent brochure, bulletin board, or Parent Information Night can help keep parents informed, as well as informal means of communication.

3. *Keeping parents informed about their children's progress.* Keeping parents informed means more than sending home grades or report cards three or four times a year. Most parents want to know where their child is in learning essential skills (descriptive, criterion-referenced information). Such information can be conveyed through regular progress reports, informal notes, and parent conferences, as well as the typical report card. Information about a student's progress can profitably be accompanied by specific ideas about how parents can help their children improve.

SELECTING EDUCATIONAL MATERIALS AND RESOURCES[2]

In any teaching situation, much time is usually devoted to selecting the content of the curriculum that will be used, assessing the individual needs of the stu-

[2]This section was written by Judy Wilson and was a chapter in earlier editions of this book.

dents involved, and choosing the specific teaching methods that will be employed. Comparatively little time is spent on the selection or alteration of the instructional materials, in spite of the fact that at least 75 percent, and as much as 99 percent, of the students' instructional time is arranged around the materials used in the classroom. Given that teaching is the interaction among the curriculum, the student, and the teacher, materials must be chosen carefully to ensure that they are compatible with all three elements in the triad and in fact serve to draw them together.

Most instructional materials are designed to meet the needs of groups of students, not one specific student. Therefore, teachers have always had to make certain accommodations in the materials used in order to meet individual differences (e.g., having a student use chapters out of sequence or complete only the even-numbered questions). The further the student's needs and abilities deviate from those of the group for whom the material was originally designed, the greater this need for accommodation becomes.

For the student with learning and/or behavior problems, the variance may necessitate the use of completely different materials, a need that is often overlooked or inappropriately met by many teachers, owing to their training and orientation. Most teachers have been trained to teach a prescribed curriculum that is usually dictated by the school, to use the materials that have been selected for them by the textbook committee, and to move students through the same set of learning experiences. To satisfy the special, and often unique, requirements of the student with problems, the teacher must exchange this group orientation for an individual one in which the curricular requirements are identified in terms of the exact skills to be taught to a particular student and instructional materials are selected on the basis of curricular, student, and teacher variables.

To aid in the selection of appropriate materials, this section includes a discussion of the variables related to the curricular-student-teacher triad, an application of this information to the retrieval of materials information, and a system for the analysis of materials. The purpose of this section is to provide teachers with a frame of reference for selecting those materials that are appropriate to their own curricula, students, and teaching methods.

Variables Related to the Curriculum-Student-Teacher Triad

The effect of the curriculum-student-teacher triad upon selection of material is analogous to that of the building-occupant-builder triad. The specifications for the building most certainly affect the types of materials to be used, but the selection of materials is also affected by the needs of the occupants, the desires of the builder, and what he or she knows to be effective and available.

Curricular Variables

In elementary and secondary schools, teachers often are expected to use a curriculum in which educational goals are vague, global, and/or much too general. Sometimes the curriculum is dictated by a specific text. Thus it is difficult for a teacher to specify what precise skills the student must learn at any given point. Yet, for the student with problems, it is this precise identification of targeted skills that may be most conducive to proper instruction. To aid the teacher in this identification, we have devoted much of the preceding chapters to presenting the skill sequences and needs related to successful performance in learning. Such information must be used by teachers to determine exactly what it is that they will include in a curriculum for the student with problems and how they will present it in order to relate the teaching as nearly as possible to the components of the regular curriculum. If the information to be taught is stated in terms of the expected learning outcomes, the teacher will be better able to decide which instructional materials are required for carrying out the teaching of the curricula.

In the delineation of curricular variables the teacher should consider items such as the following:

1. *Content area.* Is the information usually associated closely with one area or does it cut across several content areas? (For example, initial consonants may be associated with reading alone or with reading, oral language, and spelling.)
2. *Specific skills.* Are there specific skills that can be identified as components of the concepts? (For example, addition with sums greater than nine is part of the broad concept of addition.)
3. *Theories and techniques associated with the concepts.* Are there specific theories of curriculum development for the concepts? (For example, the spiral curriculum is associated with the social sciences.)
4. *Methodology.* Does the curriculum require certain types of methods? (For example, oral language development would require materials allowing dialogue, discussion, etc.)
5. *Modification.* Can the order of the curricula be modified or is it developmental? (For example, in mathematics, skills are developmental and multiplication builds upon concepts developed in addition.)

Knowledge about these items may help the teacher to evaluate an existing curriculum and to alter and/or develop one to suit the needs of an individual student.

Student Variables

The two variables that are most critical from the standpoint of the student are current level of functioning and the most immediate educational needs. Although consideration of individual variables will obviously be influenced by the specific nature of each student, there are some common areas that should be examined. These areas include:

1. *Needs of the student.* What skills and concepts are required of the student for immediate success?
2. *Current level of functioning.* What is the student's level of performance within the sequence of skills? What is the student's current reading level for instructional purposes?
3. *Grouping.* How well does the student work in groups of varying size (e.g., in small groups, in large groups, individually)?
4. *Programming.* What is the best arrangement for presentation to the student? Can the student work independently? Is the student self-directed and motivated? Does the student require direct teaching and/or frequent reinforcement?
5. *Methods.* Is there a history of success or failure with any particular methods? Does the student react positively or negatively to particular modes of instruction (e.g., multimedia versus print only)?
6. *Physical, social, and psychological characteristics.* Are there characteristics that imply unique needs (e.g., orthopedic restrictions, family problems, ethnic or cultural diversity, etc.)?

This list could also include such factors as ability to follow directions, both written and oral; ability to deal with material on a grade level different from the student's placement; and others.

Teacher Variables

The authors of most of the literature relating to materials state that teachers need only know what and who is to be taught in order to select materials. This point of view neglects one third of the triad, the teachers. It is the teacher who must act as the catalyst to ensure interaction between the other two components. Since the teacher must make decisions about curricular and student variables, the teacher's desires, knowledge, and competence must be considered. Teacher variables, like those for the student, will no doubt be affected by the nature of the individual, but, again, certain common areas exist:

1. *Method.* What method does the teacher want to employ? What is the teacher's philosophy toward the teaching of particular content?
2. *Approach.* What approach is required by the teacher and the teacher's organization (e.g., group instruction or individual instruction, a phonetic approach, etc.)?
3. *Time.* Does the teacher have specific and required time constraints for delivery of instruction? Does the teacher have someone else who can deliver the instruction?
4. *Training.* Has the teacher been trained to use certain materials?
5. *Education.* Has the teacher been trained to be competent in the content area, or will the teacher require that the material be all-inclusive?

None of these lists of variables is intended to be exhaustive in nature. Rather, they are intended to serve as guidelines for identification of relevant variables that will aid in the selection and use of materials and to ensure that the materials indeed meet the specified needs of the curriculum, student, and teacher.

Retrieval of Materials Information

Once the critical variables involved in selecting materials have been identified, the teacher is ready to secure information on the specific materials that are being considered for use. The teacher may need to use a variety of available resources to secure information on materials. The following list of resources will serve as a guideline for this process.

1. *Colleagues.* The most immediate source of information is other teachers. Not only are they within easy access; they may have students with similar needs and therefore be able to share information on their experience with specific materials.
2. *Special resource personnel.* This category includes such people as the media/materials coordinator, librarian, and curriculum coordinator. These individuals have information on a wide variety of materials and often know or have access to information on specific aspects of the material. This information may include availability, names of others who are using the materials, evaluations of past effectiveness of the materials, and personal appraisal of the material. Resource personnel can also supply names of companies that usually publish the type of material under consideration.
3. *Publisher information.* The information available from publishers usually comes in at least three forms: catalogs, other sales material, and representatives or consultants. Publisher information includes bibliographic information, a physical description, and price information.

Publishers also may describe correlated and adjunct materials. It is important to keep in mind that the information provided by publishers is slanted toward the sale of the item.

4. *Media/materials resource centers.* Many school districts and/or regional centers have central collections of instructional resources. These centers may house general collections or may be directly related to special education. Such centers may have a broad array of information including media/materials for examination and use, publishers' catalogs, retrieval systems for materials information, evaluation data on materials, facilities for adaptation and production of materials, and knowledgeable materials resource personnel. Thus, the teacher may locate information on specific products and types of products, examine actual products, use the materials with students, find out about new products, determine what others may know about the products, and gain a great deal of first-hand information about the products.

5. *College/university resources.* Most special education training programs have specific courses offered by faculty involved in media/materials and collections of instructional media/materials. Information is generally also available from the departments of curriculum and instruction, elementary education, and secondary education. Such information will often be slanted more toward the availability of, research on, and physical features of media/material than toward actual classroom application.

6. *Prepared materials lists.* Lists of materials provide good resources for identifying specific information about materials. These lists may be derived from a variety of sources. In some states or school districts, approved lists of materials are identified each year. Frequently, curriculum guides will include lists of materials correlated to the content of the guides. In some of the professional texts, materials lists accompany the discussions of teaching methods and strategies. Also, in in-service and professional development workshops, lists of materials are frequently disseminated and exchanged among teachers. Materials lists may be organized in a variety of ways, such as by handicapping conditions, by difficulty or grade level, or by curriculum area. When using lists, the teacher should consider the source of the list, the organization of the list, and the fact that in most cases the list provides primarily bibliographic information about the materials, not efficacy information.

7. *Conferences.* Most conferences and conventions provide exhibits by publishers, presentations about materials by authors and/or publishers, presentations of research studies in which specific materials were used, and opportunities to discuss materials with others who have common needs. One of the more valuable types of conferences for the purpose of learning about materials is the type usually referred to as a "publisher's

conference." In such a meeting, specific publishers are invited to make formal presentations about particular programs that are new to the market. Such presentations allow the teacher to gain comprehensive information about a specific material, the author, the development process, and research data.

8. *Retrieval systems.* A number of instructional materials retrieval systems have been developed by commercial companies, through federal funding, and by school systems at the local, regional, and occasionally building level. If such a system is available, the teacher should become familiar with the capabilities of the system, the techniques or procedures for use, and the data base of the system. Retrieval systems can provide a good deal of information about the physical characteristics of materials available to meet a specific need. With some systems it is also possible to secure information on evaluation and availability of the material. Once materials have been located, they should be carefully examined prior to final selection. This step is usually considered to be one of analysis. It may best be described as a static evaluation, since it is based on the physical characteristics of the material rather than on the experimental data derived from the use of the material. This physical examination should be carried out in a systematic manner to ensure that the materials are all evaluated on an equal basis.

9. *Other fields.*

Materials Analysis

Many articles (Armstrong, 1971; Junkala, 1970; McIntyre, 1970) have addressed the issues involved in materials analysis and have suggested various ways to conduct such evaluations. For a more comprehensive discussion of materials analysis and experimental evaluation, the reader is referred to Bleil (1975), V. L. Brown (1975), and Watson and Van Etten (1976). Each of these articles suggests approaches and criteria for the examination of materials. In a comprehensive review of the literature on selection and evaluation of materials, Ventura (1980) notes that evaluation processes range from responding to five questions to completing a six-page evaluation form. Since so much variety exists with respect to criteria, the teacher must choose the number and type of critical items. Ward (1968) states that teachers must systematically examine materials and "be the competent professional who selects and uses instructional materials in order to increase the learning of children" (p. 23).

The following ten categories represent the variables found in many of the articles. Each of these categories has subcomponents and may be expanded to the extent the teacher feels is necessary. The process should, however, be kept short and simple enough to be a help and not a hindrance. Closer examination of the categories may help clarify the type of information that can be useful.

1. *Bibliographic and price information.* This information is necessary for future reference or purchase, as well as to make determinations that may assist in analysis. The teacher may consider such items as:
   Title—The name of the product may help identify the content area and whether the product is part of a set or series.
   Author—Is it someone known for his or her work in a specific area or someone associated with a particular approach?
   Copyright—Is it current? Will the work reflect new trends and facts?
   Price—Is it within the budget limitations? Is it in keeping with other materials prices and does it appear reasonable for the work's teaching value?
   Publisher—Does the company have a reputation for producing a certain kind or quality of material? Does the company support its products through staff development and services for purchasers?

2. *Instructional area and skills, scope and sequence.* Does the material cover the content area or specific components of the area? Does it address the specific skills needed? Does the material present initial instruction, remediation, and practice and/or reinforcement activities for the skills? Are the skills presented in the appropriate sequence? Is each skill given an equal amount of coverage?

3. *Component parts of the material.* Are there multiple pieces to the material? Can the pieces be used independently? Can the pieces be used for other purposes? Are there consumable pieces? Can the pieces be purchased independently? Will it be a problem to keep track of all components?

4. *Level of the material.* Does the publisher state the readability level of the material? Is it consistent throughout the material? Is there more than one book for each level? Is there an attempt to control the use of content-specific vocabulary? Is the interest level appropriate to the content, pictures, and publisher's statements?

5. *Quality.* Is the material (e.g., paper, tape, acetate, film, etc.) of good and durable quality? Is the print clear and of appropriate size and contrast with the background color? Are the illustrations clear and relevant to content? Do they add to rather than detract from the instruction?

6. *Format.* Is the form appropriate (e.g., workbook, slide, tape, etc.)? Does it utilize the appropriate receptive and expressive modes for the content? Is the material clear and easy to follow? Is special equipment required (e.g., projector, recorder, etc.)?

7. *Support materials.* Are there additional components besides the instructional items used by the child (e.g., placement tests, check-tests, resource files, objective clusters)? Are there teacher's guides and/or teacher's editions? Are there teacher-training materials?

8. *Time requirements.* Are the tasks of an appropriate length? Does the material allow flexibility for scheduling? Does it allow flexibility in instructional procedures?

9. *Field test and research data.* Does the publisher offer any research that would support the validity or reliability of the material? Are there any data to support either process or product studies? In essence, do the data support the contention that the material will do what the publisher says it will do for the type of student indicated?

10. *Method, approach, or theoretical bases.* Does the material utilize a specific approach or method, or is it based on a specific theoretical concept? Is it one that meets the needs of the triad? Is it compatible with other ongoing instruction? Is the method, approach, or basic theory substantiated by any published research?

As in the case of the curriculum-student-teacher triad, these variables may change with needs; however, they should serve as basic criteria for the selection process. Selection of materials cannot be viewed as a simple process; it requires a great deal of effort and knowledge on the part of the trained professional responsible for the design and delivery of instruction for students with learning and behavior problems.

USING DIRECT OR INDIRECT INSTRUCTION

Our book concludes with a brief discussion of current methodologies used in the schools. Specifically, this section discusses direct and indirect instructional practices and their influence within a remedial and special education perspective.

For convenience, the concepts of direct and indirect instruction are discussed in terms of reading, but they can be easily generalized to math, writing, and other school subjects.

Indirect Instruction

In indirect instruction, X activities are engaged in to produce Y results. For example, one might teach students to recall strings of digits, to walk a balance beam, or to crawl and creep properly, because such activities are thought to be in some way a part of, related to, or prerequisites for reading. A characteristic of this kind of training is that the prescribed activities don't look at all like reading and can be related to reading only in terms of highly abstract constructs.

The goal of indirect instruction is to develop hypothetical psychological processes, basic abilities, or faculties in the brain (mind) that are supposedly related theoretically to reading. For example, advocates of indirect instruction argue that since reading is believed to involve sequencing, visual discrimination, and memory, instruction in these abilities will strengthen the student's capacity for reading. Therefore, they often recommend activities that have little apparent relationship to reading, e.g., bead stringing (to teach sequencing), geometric form differentiation (visual discrimination), and recalling strings of visual patterns (memory). These activities may be part of a readiness, developmental, or remedial program.

Direct Instruction

In direct instruction, *X* activities are engaged in to produce *X* results. For example, one might teach a student to name letters of the alphabet, to recognize when a book is upside down, to see the main themes of paragraphs, and to comprehend the thematic as well as the phonic nature of written language, because such activities are thought to constitute important aspects of reading. The relevance that an individual attaches to any one or on any set of activities depends, of course, on how he or she conceptualizes reading. Regardless, everyone would agree that the activities just mentioned are all closely associated with reading.

Advocates of direct (on-task) teaching are frequently heard to say, "If one wants to teach Johnny to read, expose him to reading," or "One learns to read as a consequence of reading." Professionals who espouse direct instruction can be separated readily into two different (and often contending) camps—the atomistic and the holistic orientations.

Atomistic Orientation

To atomistically inclined individuals, the whole (reading) is the sum of its parts (skills). For example, the word cat is believed to be composed of three separate graphemes, c-a-t. Teaching students the sounds that go with the letters and having them say them fast is considered the heart and soul of atomistic education. Some atomistically inclined professionals do teach reading comprehension, but even here they tend to think of comprehension in terms of sequenced skills and conceive of it as being merely one of the many reading subskills. Sometimes this type of instruction is called "skill-centered" or "bottom-up."

Rather than relying on the student's natural language and interests, atomistically inclined teachers use scope-and-sequence charts composed of phonemically regular words and arbitrarily sequenced skills as guides for selecting material to be taught. Since contrived vocabularies must be used, the interest level of the reading material is usually low. Therefore one often finds that behavior modification and management programs are used in conjunction with atomistic instruction. Invariably, atomistic instruction is curriculum- or program-centered even when individuals are being taught. Oral reading is emphasized.

Holistic Orientation

To holistically inclined individuals, the whole (reading) is never the sum of its parts (skills). These people would not break a word into its phonemic or graphemic parts for fear of destroying its meaning. The more dogmatic holistic educators would probably not even teach words in isolation, only in context. In choosing strategies, activities, and content for instruction, holistically oriented teachers rely heavily on their knowledge of the student's home environment, desires, and natural language. The approach is decidedly student-centered. Silent reading for comprehension and retelling are mainstays in instruction. This type of instruction is frequently called "meaning-centered" or "top-down."

Interactional Orientation

Of course, in practice, most professionals find themselves positioned somewhere between polar opposites; i.e., no one is completely atomistic or holistic in his or her instructional efforts. This has led some individuals, e.g., S. Jay Samuels, to postulate a third approach to instruction, the interactional. In this approach, professionals incorporate both atomistic and holistic principles into their instructional and diagnostic attempts.

Still, individuals do tend to gravitate toward one focus or the other, as can be seen when professionals talk about why they teach in this way or that way or discuss their educational philosophies.

A Special/Remedial Education Perspective

Both the direct and the indirect approach have at one time or another been pervasive in special and remedial education in the United States. The indirect approach was paramount from around 1930 to 1975. This was the heyday of "process" and "aptitude-treatment interaction" training. In special education, the movement began with the perceptual hypotheses of Strauss and Werner, among others, and was operationalized in the programs of Frostig and Horne, William Cruickshank, Ray Barsch, Gerald Getman, and Newell Kephart. This trend continued with renewed vigor when Samuel Kirk incorporated these concepts into his idea about "psycholinguistic" training (à la 1957 Osgood).

Indirect instruction never received the same degree of acceptance in the fields of speech or reading as it did in special education, where for years it was dominant. Since the early 1970s, however, this approach has come under increasing attack from special education researchers (see the work of Stephen Larsen, J. Lee Wiederholt, Joe Jenkins, Thomas Lovitt, Frank Velluntino, Thomas Stephens, Lester Mann, Michael Epstein, James Kauffman, Douglas Cullinan, James Ysseldyke, Douglas Carnine, and Donald Hammill). Today few articles supporting the benefits of indirect instruction are published in peer-reviewed journals.

Since 1975, the mainstream of special education has turned to the use of direct instruction methodologies. The proponents of atomistic instruction are pervasive today. The theories and programs of Siegfried Engelmann, Douglas Carnine, Thomas Stephens, James Kauffman, Tom Lovitt, Joe Jenkins, Anna Gillingham, among many others, have a practical, heady appeal. Only recently, since the start of the 1980s, have the holistic ideas of Jean Piaget, Frank Smith, Jerome Bruner, and Ken and Yetta Goodman begun to seep into the special education current, to join there those long advocated by Grace Fernald.

A special issue in the *Learning Disability Quarterly* (1984, 7:4) is devoted to holism as the concept pertains to remedial instruction. Reading this issue will provide readers with a basic understanding of the fundamental ideas underlying the approach. It is hoped that before long these ideas will stimulate the development of programs, strategies, and research. Holistic education is now the frontier of special and remedial education. Though we find this approach philosophically pleasing, it remains to be seen whether holism, either alone or as a part of interactional efforts, will prove to be preferable to purely atomistic approaches.

References

Ackland, H. (1976). If reading scores are irrelevant, do we have anything better? *Education Technology, 16,* 25–29.

Adkins, D. C., & Balliff, B. L. (1973). *Animal crackers: A test of motivation to achieve.* Monterey, CA: CTB/McGraw-Hill.

Adkins, W. R. (1977). *Where they hurt: A study of the life coping problems of unemployed adults.* New York: Teachers College, Columbia University.

Adventures of the lollipop dragon. (1970). Chicago: Society for Visual Education.

Aho, M. S. (1967). Teaching spelling to children with specific language disability. *Academic Therapy, 3*(1), 45–50.

Alberto, P. A., & Troutman, A. C. (1982). *Applied behavioral analysis for teachers.* Columbus, OH: Charles E. Merrill.

Alexander, E. D. (1971). School centered play-therapy program. In N. J. Long, W. C. Morse, & R. G. Newman (Eds.), *Conflict in the classroom* (pp. 251–257). Belmont, CA: Wadsworth.

Alfaro, J., & Gillpatrick, T. (1978). *Functional consumer education competencies for adults living in Utah.* Logan: Utah State University, Consumer Research Center.

Allen, K. E., Turner, K. D., & Everett, P. M. A. (1970). A behavior modification classroom for Head Start children with problem behaviors. *Exceptional Children, 37,* 119–127.

Alley, G., & Deshler, D. (1979). *Teaching the learning disabled adolescent: Strategies and methods.* Denver: Love Publishing.

Anastasi, A. (1982). *Psychological testing* (5th ed.). New York: Macmillan.

Anderson, G. J. (1973). *The assessment of learning environments: A manual for the Learning Environment Inventory and the My Class Inventory.* Halifax, Nova Scotia: Atlantic Institute of Education.

André, M. E. D. A., & Anderson, T. H. (1978–1979). The development and evaluation of a self-questioning study technique. *Reading Research Quarterly, 14,* 606–623.

Archer, C. P. (1930). Transfer of training in spelling. In *University of Iowa studies in education.* Iowa City: University of Iowa Press.

Armstrong, J. R. (1971). A model for materials development and evaluation. *Exceptional Children, 38,* 327–334.

Ashlock, R. B. (1970). *Current research in elementary school mathematics.* New York: Macmillan.

Ashlock, R. B. (1982). *Error patterns in computation: A semi-programmed approach* (2nd ed.). Columbus, OH: Charles E. Merrill.

Axelrod, S. (1977). *Behavior modification for the classroom teacher.* New York: McGraw-Hill.

Axline, V. M. (1947). Non-directive therapy for poor readers. *Journal of Consulting Psychology, 11,* 61–69.

Axline, V. M. (1964). *Dibs: In search of self.* New York: Ballantine Books.

Ayllon, T. (1965). Intensive treatment of psychotic behavior by stimulus satiation and food reinforcement. In L. Krasner and L. P. Ullmann (Eds.), *Case studies in behavior modification.* New York: Holt, Rinehart and Winston.

Ayllon, T., & McKittrick, S. M. (1982). *How to set up a token economy.* Austin, TX: Pro-Ed.

Baer, D. M. (1981). *How to plan for generalization.* Austin, TX: Pro-Ed.

Barclay J. R. (1971). *Barclay Classroom Climate Inventory.* Lexington, KY: Educational Skills Development.

Barenbaum, E. M. (1983). Writing in the special class. *Topics in Learning and Learning Disabilities, 3(3),* 12–20.

Barksdale, M. W., & Atkinson, A. P. (1971). A resource room approach to instruction for the educable mentally retarded. *Focus on Exceptional Children, 3,* 12–15.

Basic Educational Skills Inventory in Math. Olathe, KS: Select-Ed, 1972.

Baumann, J. F. (1984). The effectiveness of a direct instruction paradigm for teaching main idea comprehension. *Reading Research Quarterly, 20,* 93–115.

Baumrind, D. (1971). *Preschool Behavior Q-Sort.* Berkeley: University of California Press.

Becher, R. M. (1980). Teacher behaviors related to the mathematical achievement of young children. *Journal of Educational Research, 73,* 336–340.

Belina, V. (1975). *Planning for your own apartment.* Belmont, CA: Fearon-Pitman.

Bell, S. (1961). *Bell Adjustment Inventory.* Monterey, CA: Consulting Psychologists Press.

Bellak, L., & Bellak, S. S. (1961). *Children's Apperception Test.* Monterey, CA: Consulting Psychologists Press.

Bender, L. (1938). *A Visual Motor Gestalt Test and Its Clinical Use.* New York: American Orthopsychiatric Association.

Bene, E., & Anthony, J. (1977). *The Family Relations Test.* Windsor, England: NFER.

Betts, E. A. (1956). *Foundations of reading instruction.* New York: American Book Co.

Bialer, I. (1961). Conceptualization of success and failure in mentally retarded and normal children. *Journal of Personality, 29,* 303–320.

Bijou, S. W. (1977). *The Edmark Reading Program.* Bellevue, WA: Edmark Corporation.

Bills, R. E. (1950). Non-directive play-therapy with retarded readers. *Journal of Psychology, 14,* 246–249.

Bleil, G. (1975). Evaluating educational materials. *Journal of Learning Disabilities, 8,* 19–26.

Bloom, B. S., Englehart, M. D., Furst, E. J., Hill, W. H., & Krathwohl, D. R. (1956). *Taxonomy of educational objectives, Handbook I: Cognitive domain.* New York: David McKay.

Blum, G. (1958). *The Blacky Pictures: Manual of instructions.* New York: Psychological Corporation.

Bolterbush, K. (1980). *A comparison of commercial vocational evaluation systems.* Stout, WI: Materials Development Center.

Bond, G. L., & Dykstra, R. (Eds.). (1967). First grade reading studies: Findings of individual investigation. Newark, DE: International Reading Association.

Borich, G. D., & Madden, S. K. (1977). *Evaluating classroom instruction: A sourcebook of instruments.* Reading, MA: Addison-Wesley.

Bormaster, J. S., & Treat, C. L. (1982). *Talking, listening, communicating: Building interpersonal relationships.* Austin, TX: Pro-Ed.

Bos, C. S. (1982). Getting past decoding: Assisted and repeated readings as remedial methods for learning disabled students. *Topics in Learning and Learning Disabilities, 1*(4), 51–57.

Botel, M. (1966). *Botel Reading Inventory.* Chicago: Follett.

Bourque, M. L. (1980). Specification and validation of reading skills hierarchies. *Reading Research Quarterly, 15,* 237–267.

Bowe, F. (1978). *Handicapping America.* New York: Harper and Row.

Bower, E. M., & Lambert, N. M. (1971). In-school screening of children with emotional handicaps. In N. J. Long, W. C. Morse, & R. G. Newman (Eds.), *Conflict in the classroom.* Belmont, CA: Wadsworth.

Brailsford, A., Lloyd, J., & Epstein, M. H. (1984). Strategy training and reading comprehension. *Journal of Learning Disabilities, 17,* 287–290.

Britton, J. (1978). The composing process and the functions of writing. In C. Copper and L. Odell (Eds.), *Research on composing points of departure.* Urbana, IL: National Council of Teachers of English.

Brolin, J. C., & Brolin, D. E. (1979). Vocational education for special students. In P. Cullinan & M. H. Epstein (Eds.), *Special education for adolescents.* Columbus, OH: Charles E. Merrill.

Brophy, J., & Good, T. (1969). *Teacher-child dyadic interaction: A manual for coding classroom behavior.* Austin, TX: Research and Development Center, University of Texas.

Brown, L. (1980, April). *A four year study of the efficacy of the TAD and DUSO curricula.* Paper presented at the annual meeting of the Council for Exceptional Children, Philadelphia.

Brown, L. (1981, April). *The reliability of sociometric measures with elementary, junior high, and senior high school students.* Paper presented at the annual meeting of the Council for Exceptional Children, New York.

Brown, L., & Hammill, D. D. (1983). *Behavior Rating Profile: An ecological approach to behavioral assessment.* Austin, TX: Pro-Ed.

Brown, L., & Sherbenou, R. J. (1981). A comparison of teacher perceptions of student reading ability, reading performance, and classroom behavior. *Reading Teacher, 34,* 557–560.

Brown, V. L. (1975). A basic Q-sheet for analyzing and comparing curriculum materials and proposals. *Journal of Learning Disabilities, 8,* 409–416.

Brown, V. L. (1984a). A comparison of two sight word reading programs designed for use with remedial or handicapped learners. *Remedial and Special Education, 5*(1), 46–54.

Brown, V. L. (1984b). D'Nealian Handwriting: What it is and how to teach it. *Remedial and Special Education, 5*(5), 48–52.

Brown, V. L. (1985). Direct Instruction Mathematics: A framework for instructional accountability. *Remedial and Special Education, 6*(2), 53–58.

Brown, V. L., & McEntire, B. (1984). *Test of Mathematics Abilities.* Austin, TX: Pro-Ed.

Brownell, W. A. (1951). Arithmetic readiness as a practical classroom concept. *The Elementary School Journal, 52,* 15–22.

Brueckner, L. J. (1955). *Diagnostic tests and self-helps in arithmetic.* Los Angeles: California Test Bureau.

Brueckner, L. J., & Bond, G. L. (1967). The diagnosis and treatment of learning difficulties. In E. C. Frierson & W. B. Barbe (Eds.), *Educating children with learning disabilities* (pp. 442–447). New York: Appleton-Century-Crofts.

Bruner, J., Goodnow, J., & Austin, G. (1956). *A study of thinking.* New York: Wiley.

Buchanan, C. D. (1968). *Programmed reading book 4.* New York: McGraw-Hill/Webster Division.

Buck, N. J., & Jolles, I. (1966). *The House-Tree-Person Test.* Los Angeles: Western Psychological Corporation.

Buckley, N. K., & Walker, H. M. (1970). *Modifying classroom behavior.* Champaign, IL: Research Press.

Buffie, E. G., Welch, R. C., & Paige, D. D. (1968). *Mathematics: Strategies of teaching.* Englewood Cliffs, NJ: Prentice-Hall.

Burns, H. L. (1984). Computer-assisted prewriting activities: Harmonics for invention. In R. Shostak (Ed.), *Computer in composition instruction.* Eugene, OR: International Council for Computers in Education.

Burns, P. C. (1962). Arithmetic fundamentals for the educable mentally retarded. *American Journal of Mental Deficiency, 66,* 57–61.

Burns, P. C. (1965). Analytical testing and follow-up exercises in elementary school mathematics. *School Science and Mathematics, 65,* 34–38.

Burns, P. C., and Broman, B. L. (1983). *The language arts in childhood education* (5th ed.). Boston: Houghton Mifflin.

Burns, P. C., Broman, B. L., & Wantling, A. L. L. (1971). *The language arts in childhood education.* Chicago: Rand McNally.

Buros, O. K. (1978). *Eighth mental measurements yearbook.* Highland Park, NJ: Gryphon.

Burrello, L. C., Tracy, M. L., & Glassman, E. J. (1983). A national status report on use of electronic technology in special education management. *Journal of Special Education, 17,* 342–353.

Burton, W. H., Kemp, G. K., Baker, C. B., Craig, I., & Moore, V. (1975). *The developmental reading text workbook series.* Indianapolis: Bobbs-Merrill.

Carkhuff, R. R. (1969). *Helping and human relationships* (Vol. 2, Chapters 3, 4, 5). New York: Holt, Rinehart and Winston.

Carlson, R. K. (1979). *Sparkling words: Two hundred practical and creative writing ideas.* Geneva, IL: Paladin House Publishers.

Carroll, J. B. (1978). Psycholinguistics and the study and teaching of reading. In S. Phlaum-Connor (Ed.), *Aspects of reading education* (pp. 11–43) (National Society for the Study of Education Series on Contemporary Educational Issues). Berkeley, CA: McCutcheon.

Cartwright, C. A., & Cartwright, G. P. (1974). *Developing observational skills.* New York: McGraw-Hill.

Cattell, R. G. (1967). *The Sixteen Personality Factor Questionnaire.* Champaign, IL: Institute for Personality and Ability Testing.

Cawley, J. F. (1976). Learning disabilities in mathematics: A curriculum design for upper grades. Unpublished manuscript, University of Connecticut, Storrs, CT.

Cawley, J. F. (1984). *Developmental teaching of mathematics for the learning disabled.* Rockville, MD: Aspen Systems.

Cawley, J. F., Fitzmaurice-Hayes, A. M., Shaw, R., & Bloomers, K. (1980). *Multi-model mathematics.* Storrs, CT: The University of Connecticut.

Cawley, J. F., Fitzmaurice, H. M., Shaw, R. A., Kahn, H., & Bates, H. (1979). Math word problems: Suggestions for LD students. *Learning Disability Quarterly, 2,* 25–41.

Chiang, B., Thorpe, H. W., & Darch, C. B. (1980). Effects of cross-age tutoring on word-recognition performance of learning disabled students. *Learning Disability Quarterly, 3,* 11–19.

Chomsky, C. (1971). Write first, read later. *Childhood Education, 47*(6), 296–299.

Christopolos, F., & Renz, P. (1969). A critical examination of special education programs. *Journal of Special Education, 3,* 371–379.

Clay, M. M. (1968). A syntactic analysis of reading errors. *Journal of Verbal Learning and Verbal Behavior, 1*, 434–438.

Cline, R. K. J., & Kretke, G. L. (1980). An evaluation of long-term SSR in the junior high school. *Journal of Reading, 23*, 503–506.

Cloward, R. D. (1967). Studies in tutoring. *Journal of Experimental Education, 36*, 25.

Clymer, T. (1968). What is "reading"? Some current concepts. In H. M. Robison (Ed.), *The sixty-seventh yearbook of the National Society for the Study of Education.* Chicago: University of Chicago Press.

Cohen, A. S. (1974–1975). Oral reading errors of first grade children taught by a code emphasis approach. *Reading Research Quarterly, 10*, 616–650.

Cohen, C. R., & Abrams, R. M. (1976a). *Spelling: Testing and evaluating. Book One.* Greenland, NH: Learnco.

Cohen, C. R., & Abrams, R. M. (1976b). *Spelling: Testing and evaluating. Book Two.* Greenland, NH: Learnco.

Coleman, J. H., & Jungeblut, A. (1965). *Reading for meaning.* Philadelphia: Lippincott.

Coleman, M. C. (1986). *Behavior disorders: Theory and practice.* Englewood Cliffs, NJ: Prentice-Hall.

Combs, W. E. (1977). Sentence-combining practice aids reading comprehension. *The Reading Teacher, 21*, 18–24.

Connolly, A. J. (1982). *Key Math Early Steps Program.* Circle Pines, MN: American Guidance Service.

Connolly, A. J., Nachtman, W., & Pritchett, E. M. (1976). *Key Math Diagnostic Arithmetic Test.* Circle Pines, MN: American Guidance Service.

Contact maturity: Growing up strong. (1972). Englewood Cliffs, NJ: Scholastic Book Service.

Coopersmith, R. (1968). *The antecedents of self-esteem.* San Francisco: W. H. Freeman.

Crandall, V. C., Kathovsky, W., & Crandall, V. J. (1965). Children's beliefs in their own control of reinforcement in intellectual-academic achievement situations. *Child Development, 36*, 91–109.

Crane, C., & Reynolds, J. (1983). *Social skills and me.* Houston: Crane/Reynolds.

Crane, C., Reynolds, J., & Sparks, J. (1983). *The sourcebook: Behavioral IEPs for the emotionally disturbed.* Houston: Crane/Reynolds.

Criscuolo, N. P. (1979). Activities that help involve parents in reading. *Reading Teacher, 32*, 417–419.

Criscuolo, N. P. (1980). Effective ways to communicate with parents about reading. *Reading Teacher, 34*, 164–166.

Cronbach, L. J. (1970). *Educational psychology.* New York: Harcourt, Brace and World.

Cullinan, D., Lloyd, J., & Epstein, M. H. (1981). Strategy training: A structured approach to arithmetic instruction. *Exceptional Education Quarterly, 2*(1),

41–49.

D'Angelo, K., & Wilson, R. M. (1979). How helpful is insertion and omission miscue analysis? *Reading Teacher, 32,* 519–520.

Daniels, J. (1984). *Model of functional literacy.* Austin, TX: University of Texas Transitional Leadership Training Program. (U.S. Department of Education Grant.)

Daniels, J., & Dollar, S. (1978). *Career planning model.* Austin, TX: University of Texas Department of Special Education.

Davidson, J. (1969). *Using the Cuisenaire rods.* New Rochelle, NY: Cuisenaire.

Davis, L. (1977). *My friends and me.* Circle Pines, MN: American Guidance Service.

Dechant, E. V. (1964). *Improving the teaching of reading.* Englewood Cliffs, NJ: Prentice-Hall.

Denny, J. M. (1977). Techniques for individual and group art therapy. In E. Ulman & P. Dachinger (Eds.), *Art therapy in theory and practice.* New York: Schocken.

Deshler, D. D., Warner, M. M., Schumaker, J. B., & Alley, J. R. (1983). The learning strategies intervention model: Key components and current status. In J. D. McKinney & F. Feagans (Eds.), *Current topics in learning disabilities* (Vol. 1). Norwood, NJ: Ablex.

Dewey, J. (1910). *How we think.* Boston: Heath.

Dictionary of Occupational Titles (4th ed.). (1977). Washington, DC: Superintendent of Documents, U.S. Government Printing Office.

Dinkmeyer, D. (1982). *Developing understanding of self and others—revised.* Circle Pines, MN: American Guidance Service.

Doehring, D. G., & Aulls, M. W. (1979). The interactive nature of reading acquisition. *Journal of Reading Behavior, 11,* 27–40.

Dolce, C. J. (1969, January). The inner city—a superintendent's view. *The Saturday Review,* p. 36.

Doll, E. A. (1965). *Measurement of social competence: A manual for the Vineland Social Maturity Scale.* Circle Pines, MN: American Guidance Service.

Dollar, B., & Dollar, S. (1976). *Learning opportunities for teachers.* Austin, TX: Accommodative Instructional Systems.

Duffy, G. G., & Roehler, L. F. (1982). Direct instruction of comprehension: What does it really mean? *Reading Horizon, 23,* 35–40.

Dunn, L. M. (1968). Special education for the mildly retarded—is much of it justifiable? *Exceptional Children, 35,* 5–22.

Dunn, L. M., & Markwardt, F. (1970). *Peabody Individual Achievement Test.* Circle Pines, MN: American Guidance Service.

DuPont, H., & DuPont, C. (1979). *Transition.* Circle Pines, MN: American Guidance Service.

DuPont, H., Gardner, O. S., & Brody, D. S. (1974). *Toward affective development.* Circle Pines, MN: American Guidance Service.

Durrell, D. D. (1940). *Improvement of basic reading abilities.* Yonkers, NY: World Book.

Dutton, W. H., & Adams, L. J. (1961). *Arithmetic for teachers.* Englewood Cliffs, NJ: Prentice-Hall.

Edgington, R. (1967). But he spelled them right this morning. *Academic Therapy Quarterly, 3,* 58–59.

Ehly, S. W., & Larsen, S. C. (1980). *Peer tutoring for individualized instruction.* Austin, TX: Pro-Ed.

Ellis, A. (1962). *Reason and emotion in psychotherapy.* New York: Lyle Stuart.

Ellis, A. (1970). Rational-emotive therapy. In L. Hershner (Ed.), *Four psychotherapies.* New York: Appleton-Century-Crofts.

Ellis, A. (1974). *Humanistic psychotherapy.* New York: McGraw-Hill.

Ellis, A., & Harper, R. (1977). *A new guide to rational living.* New York: Harper and Row.

Ellis, A., Wolfe, J. L., & Mosley, S. (1974). *How to raise an emotionally healthy, happy child.* Hollywood, CA: Wilshire.

Emig, J. (1977). Writing as a mode of learning. *College Composition and Communication, 28,* 122–128.

Engelmann, S. (1969). *Conceptual learning.* San Rafael, CA: Dimensions Publishing.

Engelmann, S., & Bruner, E. C. (1973). *DISTAR Reading I.* Chicago: Science Research Associates.

Engelmann, S., & Bruner, E. C. (1974). *DISTAR Reading II.* Chicago: Science Research Associates.

Engelmann, S., & Bruner, E. C. (1975). *DISTAR Reading III.* Chicago: Science Research Associates.

Engelmann, S., Haddox, P., Hammer, S., & Osborn, J. (1978). *Thinking basics: Corrective reading program comprehension.* Chicago: Science Research Associates.

Engelmann, S., & Silbert, J. (1983). *Expressive writing 1 & 2.* Tigard, OR: C. C. Publications.

Erickson, M. R. (1971). A study of a tutoring program to benefit tutors and tutees. Ann Arbor: University of Michigan. (University Microfilm No. 71–16914)

Estes, T. H., Estes, J. J., Richards, H. C., & Roettger, D. (1981). *Estes Attitude Scales.* Austin, TX: Pro-Ed.

Esveldt-Dawson, K., & Kazdin, A. E. (1982). *How to use self-control.* Austin, TX: Pro-Ed.

Eysenck, S. B. G. (1965). *Junior Eysenck Personality Inventory.* San Diego: Educational and Industrial Testing Service.

Fagen, S., & Long, N. J. (1979). A psychoeducational curriculum approach to teaching self-control. *Behavior Disorders, 4,* 68–82.

Fagen, S., Long, N. J., & Stevens, D. (1975). *Teaching children self-control.* Columbus, OH: Charles E. Merrill.

Fasler, J. (1971). *Child's series on psychologically relevant themes.* Westport, CT: Videorecord Corporation of America.

Fernald, G. (1943). *Remedial techniques in basic school subjects.* New York: McGraw-Hill.

Ferster, C. B., & Skinner, B. F. (1957). *Schedules of reinforcement.* New York: Appleton-Century-Crofts.

Fine, M. J. (1973). *The teacher's role in classroom management.* Lawrence, KS: Psych-Ed.

Fiscus, E. D., & Mandell, C. J. (1983). *Developing individualized education programs.* St. Paul, MN: West.

Fisher, B. (1953). Group therapy and retarded readers. *Journal of Educational Psychology, 44,* 354–360.

Fisher, J. K. (1980). Competencies for adult basic education and diploma programs: A summary for studies and cross-reference of results. In *APL revisited: Its adaptations in states.* Washington, DC: National Institute of Education.

Fiske, D. W., & Cox, J. A., Jr. (1960). The consistency of ratings by peers. *Journal of Applied Psychology, 44,* 11–17.

Flanders, N. (1970). *Analyzing teacher behavior.* Menlo Park, CA: Addison-Wesley.

Fleming, L., & Snyder, W. U. (1947). Social and personal changes following nondirective group therapy. *American Journal of Orthopsychiatry, 17,* 101–106.

Fountain Valley teacher support system in mathematics. (1976). Huntington Beach, CA: R. A. Zweig Associates.

Frederickson, L. W., & Frederickson, C. B. (1975). Teacher-determined and self-determined token reinforcement in a special education classroom. *Behavior Therapy, 6,* 310–314.

Fry, D. (1966). The development of the phonological system in the normal and the deaf child. In F. Smith and G. Miller (Eds.), *The genesis of speech* (pp. 187–206). Cambridge, MA: MIT Press.

Fry, E. (1977). Fry's readability graph: Clarification, validity and extension to level 17. *Journal of Reading, 21,* 242–252.

Gallup, G. H. (1982). Gallup poll of the public's attitude toward the public schools. *Phi Delta Kappan, 64*(1), 37–50.

Gambrell, L. B. (1978). Getting started with sustained silent reading and keeping it going. *Reading Teacher, 32,* 328–331.

Gambrell, L. B. (1980). Think-time: Implications for reading instruction. *Reading Teacher, 34,* 143–146.

Garrett, H. E. (1954). *Statistics in psychology and education.* New York: Longmans Green.

Garrett, H. E. (1965). *Testing for teachers.* New York: American Book.

Gates, A. I. (1947). *The improvement of reading.* New York: Macmillan.

Gates, A. I., & Peardon, C. C. (1963). *Reading exercises.* New York: Teachers College Press.

Gauthier, R. A. (1980). *A descriptive-analytic study of teacher-student interaction in mainstreamed physical education classes.* Unpublished doctoral dissertation, Purdue University, Indiana.

Gillingham, A. (1958). Correspondence. *Elementary English, 35,* 118–122.

Gillingham, A., & Stillman, B. (1970). *Remedial training for children with specific disability in reading, spelling, and penmanship.* Cambridge, MA: Educators Publishing Service.

Ginott, H. (1961). *Group psychotherapy with children.* New York: McGraw-Hill.

Ginsburg, H. (1986). *Assessing arithmetic.* Austin, TX: Pro-Ed.

Ginsburg, H., & Baroody, A. (1983). *Test of Early Mathematical Abilities.* Austin, TX: Pro-Ed.

Ginsburg, H., & Mathews, S. (1984). *Diagnostic Test of Arithmetic Strategies.* Austin, TX: Pro-Ed.

Glasser, W. (1965). *Reality therapy.* New York: Harper and Row.

Glasser, W. (1969). *Schools without failure.* New York: Harper and Row.

Glavin, J. N., Quay, H. C., Annesley, F. R., & Werry, J. S. (1971). An experimental resource room for behavior problem children. *Exceptional Children, 38,* 131–137.

Glavin, J. N., Quay, H. C., & Werry, J. S. (1971). Behavioral and academic gains of conduct problem children in different classroom settings. *Exceptional Children, 37,* 441–446.

Gleason, M., & Stults, C. (1983a). *Basic writing skills: Sentence development.* Tigard, OR: C. C. Publications.

Gleason, M., & Stults, C. (1983b). *Basic writing skills: Capitalization and punctuation.* Tigard, OR: C. C. Publications.

Goodman, K. S. (1965). A linguistic study of cues and miscues in reading. *Elementary English, 42,* 639–642.

Goodman, K. S. (Ed.). (1968). *The psycholinguistic nature of the reading process.* Detroit: Wayne State University Press.

Goodman, K. S. (1969). Analysis of oral reading miscues: Applied psycholinguistics. *Reading Research Quarterly, 5,* 9–30.

Goodman, K. S. (1976). Reading: A psycholinguistic guessing game. In M. Singer & R. Ruddell (Eds.), *Theoretical models and processes of reading.* Newark, DE: International Reading Association.

Goodman, Y. M. (1972). Reading diagnosis—qualitative or quantitative. *The Reading Teacher, 26,* 32–37.

Goodstein, H. A. (1985). Measurements and assessment. In J. F. Cawley (Ed.), *Secondary school mathematics for the learning disabled.* Rockville, MD: Aspen.

Graham, S., & Miller, L. (1980). Handwriting research and practice: A unified approach. *Focus on Exceptional Children, 13,* 1–16.

Grannis, J. C., & Schone, V. (1970). *First things.* Pleasantville, NY: Guidance Associates.

Granowsky, A., Middleton, F. R., & Mumford, J. H. (1979). Parents as partners in education. *Reading Teacher, 32,* 826–830.

Graves, D. (1978). *Balance the basics: Let them write.* New York: Ford Foundation.

Greene, H., & Petty, W. (1967). *Developing language skills in the elementary school.* Boston: Allyn and Bacon.

Gronlund, N. E. (1981). *Measurement and evaluation in teaching.* New York: Macmillan.

Guide for occupational exploration. (1979). Washington, DC: U.S. Government Printing Office.

Gurney, D. (1966). The effect of an individual reading program on reading level and attitude toward reading. *Reading Teacher, 19,* 277–279.

Hall, J. K. (1981). *Evaluating and improving written expression.* Boston: Allyn and Bacon.

Hall, R. V. (1971). *Managing behavior: Basic principles.* Austin, TX: Pro-Ed.

Hall, R. V. (1974). *Managing behavior: Applications in school and home.* Austin, TX: Pro-Ed.

Hall, R. V. (1983). *Managing behavior: The measurement of behavior.* Austin, TX: Pro-Ed.

Hall, R. V., & Hall, M. C. (1980a). *How to select reinforcers.* Austin, TX: Pro-Ed.

Hall, R. V., & Hall, M. C. (1980b). *How to use planned ignoring.* Austin, TX: Pro-Ed.

Hall, R. V., & Hall, M. C. (1982). *How to negotiate a contract.* Austin, TX: Pro-Ed.

Hammill, D. (1986). *Assessing for instructional purposes. A practical manual for educators, psychologists, speech pathologists, and diagnosticians.* Austin, TX: Pro-Ed.

Hammill, D. D., Brown, L. L., & Bryant, B. (1986). *A consumer's guide to tests in print.* Austin, TX: Pro-Ed.

Hammill, D. D., & Larsen, S. (1983). *The Test of Written Language.* Austin, TX: Pro-Ed.

Hammill, D. D., Larsen, S., & McNutt, G. (1977). The effects of spelling instruction: A preliminary study. *The Elementary School Journal, 78,* 67–72.

Hammill, D. D., & Leigh, J. (1983). *Basic School Skill Inventory—Diagnostic.* Austin, TX: Pro-Ed.

Hammill, D. D., & Wiederholt, J. L. (1972). *The resource room: Rationale and implementation.* Philadelphia: Journal of Special Education Press.

Hanna, P. R., Hanna, J. S., Hodges, R. E., & Rudorf, E. H. (1966). *Phoneme-grapheme correspondences as cues to spelling improvement.* Washington, DC: Department of Health, Education, and Welfare.

Hanna, P. R., Hodges, R. E., & Hanna, J. S. (1971). *Spelling: Structure and strategies.* Boston: Houghton Mifflin.

Hanna, R., & Moore, J. T. (1953). Spelling—from spoken word to written symbol. *Elementary School Journal, 53,* 329–337.

Hansen, C. L. (1978). Writing skills. In N. G. Haring, T. C. Lovitt, M. D. Eaton, & C. L. Hansen (Eds.), *The fourth R: Research in the classroom.* Columbus, OH: Charles E. Merrill.

Hare, V. C., & Borchardt, K. M. (1984). Direct instruction of summarization skills. *Reading Research Quarterly, 20,* 62–74.

Harris, A. J. (1968). Diagnosis and remedial instruction. In H. M. Robinson (Ed.), *The sixty-seventh yearbook of the National Society for the Study of Education.* Chicago: University of Chicago Press.

Harris, A. J. (1970). *How to increase reading ability* (5th ed.). New York: David McKay.

Harris, T. L., & Herrick, V. E. (1963). Children's perception of the handwriting task. In V. E. Herrick (Ed.), *New horizons for research in handwriting* (pp. 159–184). Madison: University of Wisconsin Press.

Harth, R. (1966). Changing attitudes toward school, classroom behavior, and reaction to frustration of emotionally disturbed children through role-playing. *Exceptional Children, 33,* 119–120.

Hathaway, S. R., & McKinley, J. L. (1967). *Minnesota Multiphasic Personality Inventory.* New York: Psychological Corporation.

Hawisher, P. (1975). *The resource room: Access to excellence.* Lancaster, SC: S.C. Region V Educational Service Center.

Heddens, J. W., & Smith, K. J. (1964). The readability of elementary mathematics textbooks. *The Arithmetic Teacher, 11,* 466–468.

Hodges, R. E. (1981). The language base of spelling. In V. Froese, and S. B. Straw (Eds.), *Research in the language arts.* Austin, TX: Pro-Ed.

Hodges, R. E., & Rudorf, E. H. (1965). Searching linguistics for cues for the teaching of spelling. *Elementary English, 42,* 529–533.

Holland, J. L. (1973). *Making vocational choice: A theory of careers.* Englewood Cliffs, NJ: Prentice-Hall.

Holland, J. L. (1974). Vocational guidance for everyone. *Educational Researcher, 3*(1), 9–15.

Hollander, E. P. (1965). Validity of peer nominations in predicting a distant performance criterion. *Journal of Applied Psychology, 49,* 434–438.

Horn, E. (1926). A basic writing vocabulary: 10,000 words most commonly used in writing. University of Iowa Monographs in Education, First Series, No. 4, Iowa City, Iowa.

Horn, E. (1957). Phonetics and spelling. *Elementary School Journal, 57,* 424–432.

Hough, J. B. (1967). An observation system for the analysis of classroom instruction. In E. J. Amidon & J. B. Hough (Eds.), *Interaction analysis: Theory, research, and application.* Reading, MA: Addison-Wesley.

Hresko, W. P., & Brown, L. (1984). *Test of Early Socioemotional Development.* Austin, TX: Pro-Ed.

Hunt, K., & O'Donnell, R. (1970). *An elementary school curriculum to develop better writing skills.* Tallahassee: Florida State University. (U.S. Office of Education Grant No. 4-9-08-903-0042-010)

Iano, R. P. (1972). Shall we disband our special classes? *Journal of Special Education, 6,* 167–178.

Idol-Maestas, L. (1981). Increasing the oral reading performance of a learning disabled adult. *Learning Disability Quarterly, 4,* 294–301.

IRA Computer Technology and Reading Committee. (1984). Guidelines for educators on using computers in the schools. *Reading Research Quarterly, 20,* 120–122.

Irwin, J. W., & Davis, C. A. (1980, November). Assessing readability, the checklist approach. *Journal of Reading,* 129–130.

Isaacson, L. (1978). *Career information in counseling and teaching.* Boston: Allyn & Bacon.

Iwata, B., & Bailey, J. (1974). Reward versus cost token systems: An analysis of the effects on students and teachers. *Journal of Applied Behavior Analysis, 7,* 567–576.

Jastak, J. F. (1972). *Wide range employability sample test.* Wilmington, DE: Jastak Associates.

Jastak, J. F., & Jastak, S. R. (1965). *Wide Range Achievement Test.* Wilmington, DE: Guidance Associates.

Johnson, D. D. (1971). The Dolch list re-examined. *Reading Teacher, 24,* 455–456.

Johnson, D., & Myklebust, H. (1967). *Learning disabilities: Educational principles and practices.* New York: Grune & Stratton.

Johnson, M. S., & Kress, R. A. (1969). *Informal reading inventories.* Newark, DE: International Reading Association.

Junkala, J. (1970). Teacher evaluation of instructional materials. *Teaching Exceptional Children, 2,* 73–76.

Kaluger, G., & Kolson, C. J. (1978). *Reading and learning disabilities.* Columbus, OH: Charles E. Merrill.

Kazdin, A. E. (1975). *Behavior modification in applied settings.* Homewood, IL: Dorsey.

Kazdin, A. E. (1977). *The token economy.* New York: Plenum.

Kelley, T., Madden, R., Gardner, E., & Rudman, H. (1964). *Stanford Achievement Tests.* New York: Harcourt, Brace and World.

Kessler, J. W. (1966). *Psychopathology of childhood.* Englewood Cliffs, NJ: Prentice-Hall.

Klare, G. R. (1976). A second look at the validity of readability formulas. *Journal of Reading Behavior, 8,* 129–252.

Kliebhan, M. C. (1955). *An experimental study of arithmetic problem-solving ability of sixth grade boys.* Washington, DC: The Catholic University Press.

Kohfeldt, J. (1974). *Contracts.* Wayne, NJ: Innovative Educational Support Systems.

Kokaska, C. J., & Brolin, D. E. (1985). *Career education for handicapped individuals.* Columbus, OH: Charles E. Merrill.

Kolstoe, O. P. (1976). Developing career awareness: The foundation of a career education program. In G. B. Blackburn (Ed.), *Colloquium series on career education for handicapped adolescents.* West Lafayette, IN: Purdue University.

Komiski, P. K. (1984). Educational computing: The burden on insuring quality. *Phi Delta Kappan, 66,* 244–249.

Kottmeyer, W. (1959). *Teacher's guide for remedial reading.* New York: McGraw-Hill.

Kottmeyer, W., & Claus, A. (1984). *Basic goals in spelling.* New York: McGraw-Hill.

Kramer, E. (1971). *Art therapy with children.* New York: Schocken.

Kramer, K. (1970). *The teaching of elementary school mathematics.* Boston: Allyn and Bacon.

Kroth, R. (1973a). The behavioral Q-sort as a diagnostic tool. *Academic Therapy, 8,* 317–330.

Kroth, R. (1973b). *Target behavior.* Bellevue: WA: Ed-Mark.

Lambert, N. M., Hartsbough, C. S., & Bower, E. L. (1979). *Pupil Behavior Rating Scale.* Monterey, CA: CTB/McGraw-Hill.

Lane, P., Pollack, C., & Sher, N. (1972). Remotivation of disruptive adolescents. *Journal of Reading, 15,* 351–354.

Lankford, F. S. (1974). What can a teacher learn about a pupil's thinking through oral interviews? *Arithmetic Teacher, 21,* 26–32.

LaPray, M., & Ross, R. (1969). The graded word list: A quick gauge of reading ability. *Journal of Reading, 12*(4), 305–307.

Larsen, S. C. (1986). *Assessing writing.* Austin, TX: Pro-Ed.

Larsen, S., & Hammill, D. D. (1986). *The Test of Written Spelling.* Austin, TX: Pro-Ed.

Laten, S., & Katz, G. (1975). *A theoretical model for assessment of adolescents: The ecological behavioral approach.* Madison, WI: Madison Public Schools, Special Educational Services.

Lazar, M. (1957). Individualized reading: A dynamic approach. *Reading Teacher, 11,* 75–83.

Lazarus, A. (1971). *Behavior therapy and beyond.* New York: McGraw-Hill.

Leon, J. A., & Pepe, H. J. (1983). Self-instructional training: Cognitive behavior modification for remediating arithmetic deficits. *Exceptional Children, 50,* 54–60.

Levitt, E. E. (1957). Results of psychotherapy with children: An evaluation. *Journal of Counseling Psychology, 25,* 189–196.

Lilly, S. M. (1970). Special education: A teapot in a tempest. *Exceptional Children, 37,* 43–48.

Limbacher, W. (1969). *Dimensions of personality.* New York: Pflaum.

Lindquist, M. M., Carpenter, T. P., Silver, E. A., & Matthews, W. (1983). The third national mathematics assessment: Results and implications for elementary and middle schools. *Arithmetic Teacher, 31,* 14–19.

Lindzey, G., & Borgatta, E. F. (1954). Sociometric measurement. In G. Lindzey (Ed.), *Handbook of social psychology.* Reading, MA: Addison-Wesley.

Lloyd, J. (1980). Academic instruction and cognitive behavior modification: The need for attack strategy training. *Exceptional Education Quarterly, 1,* 53–63.

Lloyd, J. W., Hallahan, D. P., Kosiewicz, M. M., & Kneedler, R. D. (1982). Reactive effects of self-assessment and self-recording on attention to task and academic productivity. *Learning Disability Quarterly, 5,* 216–227.

Long, N. J., & Newman, R. G. (1980). Managing surface behavior of children in schools. In N. J. Long, W. C. Morse, & R. G. Newman (Eds.), *Conflict in the classroom* (4th ed.). Belmont, CA: Wadsworth.

Loper, A. B., Hallahan, D. P., & Ianna, S. O. (1982). Meta-attention in learning disabled and normal students. *Learning Disability Quarterly, 5,* 29–36.

Losen, S. M., & Diament, B. (1978). *Parent conferences in the schools.* Boston: Allyn and Bacon.

Lovitt, T. C. (1975a). Applied behavior analysis and learning disabilities. Part I. Characteristics of ABA, general recommendations, and methodological limitations. *Journal of Learning Disabilities, 8,* 432–443.

Lovitt, T. C. (1975b). Applied behavior analysis and learning disabilities. Part II: Specific research recommendations and suggestions for practitioners. *Journal of Learning Disabilities, 8,* 504–518.

Maier, H. W. (1969). *Three theories of child development.* New York: Harper and Row.

McCallon, E., & McCray, E. (1975). *Planning and conducting interviews.* Austin, TX: Learning Concepts.

McCarney, S. B., Leigh, J. E., & Cornbleet, J. (1983). *Behavior Evaluation Scale.* Columbia, MO: Educational Services.

McCracken, R. A., & McCracken, M. J. (1978). Modeling is the key to sustained silent reading. *Reading Teacher, 31,* 406–408.

McGinty, R. L., & Meyerson, L. N. (1980). Problem solving: Look beyond the right answer. *Mathematics Teacher, 73,* 501–503.

McIntyre, R. B. (1970). Evaluation of instructional materials and programs: Application of a systems approach. *Exceptional Children, 37,* 213–220.

McLeod, T. M., & Armstrong, S. W. (1982). Learning disabilities in mathematics-skill deficits and remedial approaches at the intermediate and secondary level. *Learning Disability Quarterly, 5,* 305–311.

McLoughlin, J. A., & Lewis, R. B. (1986). *Assessing special students.* Columbus, OH: Charles E. Merrill.

Means, B., & Roessler, R. (1975). *Personal achievement skills training.* Fayetteville: Arkansas Rehabilitation Research and Training Center.

Meichenbaum, D. (1975). *Toward a cognitive theory of self-control* (Research Report No. 48). Waterloo: Department of Psychology, University of Waterloo, Ontario.

Meichenbaum, D. H. (1977). *Cognitive behavior modification.* New York: Plenum Press.

Meichenbaum, D. H. (1983). Teaching thinking: A cognitive-behavior approach. In *Interdisciplinary voices in learning disabilities and remedial education.* Austin, TX: Pro-Ed.

Meighen, M., & Pratt, M. (1964). *Phonics we use.* Chicago: Lyons and Carnahan.

Mellon, J. C. (1969). *Transformational sentence-combining: A method for enhancing the development of syntactic fluency in English composition* (Research report, No. 10). Urbana, IL: National Council of Teachers of English.

Michel, D. E. (1971). *Music therapy: An introduction to therapy and special education through music.* New York: Day.

Miller, L. K. (1975). *Principles of everyday behavior analysis.* Monterey, CA: Brooks Cole.

Miller, S. K. (1985). Computers and writing. *Direct Instruction News, 4*(3), 12–13.

Miller, S. K., & Engelmann, S. (1980). *Cursive writing program.* Tigard, OR: C. C. Publications.

Minton, M. J. (1980). The effect of sustained silent reading upon comprehension and attitudes of ninth graders. *Journal of Reading, 23,* 498–502.

Moffett, J. (1973). *A student-centered language arts curriculum.* Boston: Houghton Mifflin.

Moore, J. C., Jones, C. J., & Miller, D. C. (1980). What we know after a decade of sustained silent reading. *Reading Teacher, 33,* 445–450.

Moreno, J. L. (1946). *Psychodrama.* New York: Beacon House.

Moreno, J. L. (1953). *Who shall survive? Foundations of sociometry, group psychotherapy, and sociodrama* (2nd ed.). New York: Beacon House.

Mosenthal, P., & Na, T. J. (1980). Quality of children's recall under two classroom testing tasks: Towards a socio-psycholinguistic model of reading comprehension. *Reading Research Quarterly, 15,* 504–527.

Moyer, S. S. (1982). Repeated reading. *Journal of Learning Disabilities, 15,* 619–623.

Murray, H. A. (1943). *Thematic Apperception Test.* Cambridge, MA: Harvard University Press.

Myklebust, H. R. (1965). *Development and disorders of written language.* New York: Grune and Stratton.

National Commission on Excellence in Education. (1983). *A nation at risk: The imperative for educational reform.* Washington, DC: U.S. Government Printing Office.

National Council of Teachers of Mathematics. (1980). *An agenda for action: Recommendations for school mathematics of the 1980's.* Reston, VA: NCTM.

Naumberg, M. (1973). *An introduction to art therapy.* New York: Teachers College Press.

Newcomer, P. L. (1980). *Understanding and teaching emotionally disturbed children.* Boston: Allyn and Bacon.

Newcomer, P. L. (1986). *The Standardized Reading Inventory.* Austin, TX: Pro-Ed.

Newcomer, P. L., & Curtis, D. (1984). *Diagnostic Achievement Battery.* Austin, TX: Pro-Ed.

Newland, T. E. (1932). An analytical study of the development of illegibilities in handwriting from the lower grades to adulthood. *Journal of Educational Research, 26,* 249–258.

Nicholson, T. (1980). Why we need to talk to parents about reading. *Reading Teacher, 34,* 19–21.

Nickse, R. (1977). *Assessing adult life skills competencies: The New York external state high school diploma program.* New York: The Adult Education Research Conference.

Niedermeyer, F. C. (1973). Kindergarteners learn to write. *Elementary School Journal, 74,* 130–135.

Nihira, K., Foster, R., Shellhaas, M., & Leland, H. (1975). *AAMD Adaptive Behavior Scales, public school version.* Washington, DC: American Association on Mental Deficiency.

Noble, J. K. (1966). *Better handwriting for you.* New York: Noble and Noble.

NOMOS Institute. (1978). *Adult competencies, categories, definitions, and specific statements.* Berkeley, CA: NOMOS Institute.

Nordoff, P., & Robbins, C. (1971). *Music therapy in special education.* New York: Day.

Northcutt, N. W. (1975). Functional literacy for adults. In D. M. Neilsen & H. F. Hjelm (Eds.), *Reading and career education.* Newark, DE: International Reading Association.

O'Hare, F. (1973). *Sentence-combining: Improving student writing without formal grammar instruction* (Research report No. 15). Urbana, IL: National Council of Teachers of English.

O'Leary, K. D., & Becker, W. C. (1967). Behavior modification of an adjustment class: A token reinforcement program. *Exceptional Children, 33,* 637–642.

O'Leary, K. D., & O'Leary, S. G. (1977). *Classroom management: The successful use of behavior modification* (2nd ed.). New York: Pergamon.

Olson, D. (1972). On a theory of instruction: Why different forms of instruction result in similar knowledge. *Interchange, 3,* 9–24.

Otto, W., & Smith, R. J. (1980). *Corrective and remedial teaching* (3rd ed.). Boston: Houghton Mifflin.

Palomares, V. H., & Ball, G. (1974). *Human development program.* La Mesa, CA: Human Development Training Institute.

Pany, D., Jenkins, J. R., & Schreck, J. (1982). Vocabulary instruction: Effects on word knowledge and reading comprehension. *Learning Disability Quarterly, 5,* 202–215.

Panyan, M. (1980). *How to use shaping.* Austin, TX: Pro-Ed.

Papert, S. (1980). *Mindstorms: Children, computers, and powerful ideas.* New York: Basic Books.

Parker, R. (1982). *Occupational Aptitude Survey and Interest Schedule.* Austin, TX: Pro-Ed.

Perline, I. H., & Levinsky, D. (1968). Controlling behavior in the severely retarded. *American Journal of Mental Deficiency, 73,* 74–78.

Petty, W. T., & Jensen, J. M. (1980). *Developing children's language.* Boston: Allyn and Bacon.

Piaget, J. (1960). *Language and thought in the child.* New York: Meridian Books, New American Library.

Piaget, J. (1965). *The child's conception of number.* New York: W. W. Norton.

Piaget, J. (1967). *Six psychological studies.* New York: Vintage Books, Random House.

Piaget, J., & Inhelder, B. (1963). *The child's conception of space.* London: Routledge and Kegan Paul.

Pierce, M. McN., Stahlbrand, K., & Armstrong, S. B. (1984). *Increasing student productivity through peer tutoring.* Austin, TX: Pro-Ed.

Piers, E. V., & Harris, D. B. (1969). *The Piers-Harris Children's Self-Concept Scale.* Nashville, TN: Counselor Recordings and Tests.

Pitman, J. (1963, October 30–November 1). The future of the teaching of reading. Paper presented at the Educational Conference of the Educational Records Bureau, New York.

Plattor, E. E., & Woestehoff, E. S. (1971). Toward a singular style of instruction in handwriting. *Elementary English, 48,* 1009–1011.

Polloway, E. A., Patton, J. R., & Cohen, S. B. (1981). Written language for mildly handicapped students. *Focus on Exceptional Children, 14*(3), 1–16.

Polloway, E. A., & Smith, J. E. (1982). *Teaching language skills to exceptional learners.* Denver: Love Publishing.

Pooley, R. C. (1960). Dare schools set a standard in English usage? *English Journal, 49,* 179–180.

Porter, R. B., & Cattell, R. G. (1975). *The IPAT Children's Personality Questionnaire.* Champaign, IL: Institute for Personality and Ability Testing.

Powell, G. C. (1972). An attitude scale for reading. *The Reading Teacher, 25,* 442–447.

Proff-Witt, J. (1978). *Speed spelling.* Tigard, OR: C. C. Publications.

Proff-Witt, J. (1979). *Advanced speed spelling.* Tigard, OR: C. C. Publications.

Pumerey, D., & Elliott, C. D. (1970). Play therapy, social adjustment and reading attainment. *Journal of Educational Research, 12,* 183–193.

Quay, H. C., & Peterson, D. R. (1979). *Behavior problem checklist.* New Brunswick, NJ: School of Professional Psychology, Rutgers University.

Rashotte, C. A., & Torgesen, J. K. (1985). Repeated reading and fluency in learning disabled children. *Reading Research Quarterly, 20,* 180–188.

Reder, S. (1978). *Internal draft documents of the functional literacy project.* Portland, OR: Northwest Regional Educational Laboratory.

Redl, F. (1959). The concept of a therapeutic milieu. *American Journal of Orthopsychiatry, 29,* 721–734.

Redl, F., & Wattenberg, W. (1959). *Mental hygiene in teaching.* New York: Harcourt, Brace and World.

Redl, F., & Wineman, D. (1957). *The aggressive child.* New York: Free Press, 1957.

Reger, R., Schroeder, W., & Uschold, K. (1968). *Special education: Children with learning problems.* New York: Oxford University Press.

Reid, D. K., Hresko, W., & Hammill, D. (1981). *Test of Early Reading Ability.* Austin, TX: Pro-Ed.

Reinert, H. J. (1980). *Children in conflict* (2nd ed.). St. Louis: C. V. Mosby.

Reisman, F. K. (1972). *A guide to the diagnostic teaching of arithmetic.* Columbus, OH: Charles E. Merrill.

Reisman, F. K. (1977). Diagnostic teaching of elementary school mathematics: Methods and content. Chicago: Rand McNally.

Reisman, F. K. (1984). *Sequential Assessment in Mathematics Inventory (SAMI).* Columbus, OH: Charles E. Merrill.

Reisman, F. K., & Kauffman, S. H. (1980). *Teaching mathematics to children with special needs.* Columbus, OH: Charles E. Merrill.

Reynolds, H. H. (1966). Efficacy of sociometric rating in predicting leadership success. *Psychological Reports, 19,* 35–40.

Riley, J. E. (1971). *Animal Picture Q-Sort.* Denton: Texas Woman's University.

Roberts, G. H. (1962). The failure strategies of third grade arithmetic pupils. *Arithmetic Teacher, 15,* 442–446.

Roe, A. (1956). *The psychology of occupations.* New York: John Wiley and Sons.

Rorschach, H. (1966). *The Rorschach Inkblot Test.* New York: Grune and Stratton.

Rothman, E. P., & Berkowitz, P. H. (1963). *Buttons: A projective test for preadolescent and adolescent boys and girls.* Los Angeles: Western Psychological Services.

Rotter, J. B. (1954). *Social learning and clinical psychology.* Englewood Cliffs, NJ: Prentice-Hall.

Ruddell, R. B. (1976). Psycholinguistic models. In H. Singer and R. Ruddell (Eds.), *Theoretical models and processes of reading.* Newark, DE: International Reading Association.

Ruedy, L. R. (1983). Handwriting instruction: It can be part of the high school curriculum. *Academic Therapy, 18*(4), 421–428.

Rumelhart, D. E. (1977). Toward an interactive model of reading. In S. Dornic (Ed.), *Attention and performance.* Hillsdale, NJ: Lawrence Erlbaum.

Sabatino, D. A. (1971). An evaluation of resource rooms for children with learning disabilities. *Journal of Learning Disabilities, 4,* 84–93.

Salend, S. J., & Salend, S. M. (1985). Implications of using microcomputers in the classroom. *Journal of Learning Disabilities, 18,* 51–53.

Salvia, J., & Ysseldyke, J. E. (1985). *Assessment in special and remedial education,* 2nd ed. Boston: Houghton Mifflin.

Samuels, S. J. (1981). Some essentials of decoding. *Exceptional Education Quarterly, 4,* 11–25.

Saxe, G., & Shaheen, S. (1981). Piagetian theory and the atypical case: An analysis of the developmental Gerstmann syndrome. *Journal of Learning Disabilities, 14,* 131–135.

Scheidlinger, S., & Rauch, E. (1972). Group psychotherapy with children and adolescents. In B. Wolman (Ed.), *Handbook of child psychoanalysis.* New York: Van Nostrand Reinhold.

Schneider, M. J., & Ferritor, D. E. (1982). The meaning of work. In B. Bolton (Ed.), *Vocational adjustment of disabled persons.* Austin, TX: Pro-Ed.

Schwejda, P., & Vanderheiden, G. (1982, September). Adaptive-firmware card for the Apple II. *Byte,* 276–314.

Selg, N. A., & Jones, J. S. (1980). *Functional competencies in occupational adaptability and transferrable skills.* Columbus, OH: National Center for Research in Vocational Education.

Serio, M. (1968). Cursive writing. *Academic Therapy, 4,* 67–70.

Shaw, H. (1971). *Spell it right!* New York: Barnes and Noble.

Silbert, J., Carnine, D., & Stein, M. (1981). *Direct instruction mathematics.* Columbus, OH: Charles E. Merrill.

Silvaroli, J. N. (1973). *Classroom Reading Inventory* (2nd ed.). Dubuque, IA: William C. Brown.

Silver Burdett Spelling. (1983). Morristown, NJ: Silver Burdett. (Series unauthored.)

Simon, S. B., Howe, L. W., & Kirschenbaum, H. (1978). *Values clarification.* New York: Hart.

Singer, H. (1978, May). Active Comprehension: From answering to asking questions. *Reading Teacher, 903.*

Skinner, B. F. (1953). *Science and human behavior.* New York: Macmillan.

Smith, B., & Fry, R. (1978). *Instructional materials in independent living.* Stout, WI: Materials Development Center.

Smith, C. T. (1978). Evaluating answers to comprehension questions. *Reading Teacher, 31,* 896–900.

Smith, F. (1971). *Understanding reading.* New York: Holt, Rinehart and Winston.

Smith, F. (1983). How children learn. In D. Carnine, D. Elkind, A. D. Hendrickson, D. Meichenbaum, R. L. Sieben, & F. Smith (Eds.), *Interdisciplinary voices in learning disabilities and remedial education.* Austin, TX: Pro-Ed.

Smith, J. (1967). *Creative teaching of the language arts in the elementary school.* Boston: Allyn and Bacon.

Smith, J. O. (1962). Group language development for educable mental retardates. *Exceptional Children, 29,* 95–101.

Soar, R., Soar, R., & Ragosta, M. (1971). *The Florida climate and control system.* Gainesville: Institute for the Development of Human Resources, College of Education, University of Florida.

Spalding, R. B., & Spalding, W. T. (1969). *The writing road to reading* (2nd ed.). New York: William Morrow.

Sparrow, S. S., Balla, D. A., & Cicchetti, D. V. (1984). *Vineland Adaptive Behavior Scales.* Circle Pines, MN: American Guidance Service.

Special Education Instructional Materials Center. (1972). *Instructional materials and resource material available to teachers of exceptional children and youth.* Austin, TX: Special Education Instructional Materials Center, University of Texas.

Spivak, G., & Spotts, J. (1966). *The Devereux Child Behavior Rating Scale.* Devon, PA: Devereux Foundation.

Spivak, G., Spotts, J., & Haimes, P. E. (1967). *The Devereux Adolescent Behavior Rating Scale.* Devon, PA: Devereux Foundation.

Spivak, G., & Swift, M. (1967). *The Devereux Elementary School Behavior Rating Scale.* Devon, PA: Devereux Foundation.

Spivak, G., & Swift, M. (1973). Classroom behavior of children: A critical review of teacher-administered rating scales. *Journal of Special Education, 7*, 55–89.

Steffe, L. P. (1968). The relationship of conservation of numerousness to problem-solving abilities of first-grade children. *The Arithmetic Teacher, 15*, 47–52.

Stephens, T. M. (1970). *Directive teaching of children with learning and behavior handicaps.* Columbus, OH: Charles E. Merrill.

Stern, C. (1965). *Structural arithmetic.* Boston: Houghton Mifflin.

Sternberg, L. (1976). *Patterns Recognition Skills Inventory.* Northbrook, IL: Hubbard Scientific.

Stewart, C. J., & Cash, W. B. (1976). *Interviewing: Principles and practice.* Dubuque, IA: W. C. Brown.

Striefel, S. (1981). *How to teach through modeling and imitation.* Austin, TX: Pro-Ed.

Strong, W. (1973). *Sentence combining: A composing book.* New York: Random House.

Sucher, F., & Allred, R. (1971). *Screening students for placement in reading.* Provo, UT: Brigham Young Press.

Sulzbacker, S. I., & Hauser, J. E. (1968). A tactic for eliminating disruptive behavior in the classroom: Group contingent consequences. *American Journal of Mental Deficiency, 73*, 88–90.

Sulzer-Azaroff, B., & Mayer, G. (1977). *Applying behavior analysis procedures with children and youth.* New York: Holt, Rinehart and Winston.

Super, D. E. (1957). *The psychology of careers.* New York: Harper and Row.

Super, D. E. (1976). Career education and the meanings of work. *Monographs on career education.* Washington, DC: U.S. Department of Health, Education and Welfare, U.S. Office of Education.

Swirsky, J., & Vandergoot, D. (1980). *Placement assessment resources.* Albertson, NY: National Center on Employment of the Handicapped.

Taber, F. M. (1983). *Microcomputers in special education: Selection and decision making process.* Reston, VA: ERIC Clearinghouse on Handicapped and Gifted Children, Council for Exceptional Children.

Texas State Learning Resource Center. (1976). *Career/vocational education bibliography.* Austin, TX: TSLRC.

Thomas, J. L. (1972). Tutoring strategies and effectiveness: A comparison of elementary age tutors and college age tutors. *Dissertation Abstracts, 32*, 3580–A.

Thompson, R., & Quinby, S. (1981). *Individualized interest area contracts.* East Aurora, NY: United Educational Services.

Thorndike, E. L. (1917). Reading as reasoning: A study of mistakes in paragraph reading. *Journal of Educational Research, 8*, 323–332.

Thorndike, R. L., & Hagen, E. (1977). Measurement and evaluation in psychology and education (2nd ed.). New York: John Wiley.

Thorpe, L. P., Clark, W. W., & Tiegs, E. W. (1953). *California Test of Personality manual.* Los Angeles: California Test Bureau.

Thorpe, L. P., Lefever, D. W., & Naslund, R. A. (1969). *SRA achievement series in arithmetic.* Chicago: Science Research Associates.

Thurber, D. N. (1981). *D'Nealian handwriting.* Glenview, IL: Scott, Foresman.

Tiegs, E. W., & Clark, W. W. (1970). *California Arithmetic Test.* Los Angeles: California Test Bureau.

Treacy, J. P. (1944). The relationship of reading skills to the ability to solve arithmetic problems. *Journal of Educational Research, 38,* 86–96.

Trieschman, A. E. (1969). Understanding the stages of a typical temper tantrum. In A. E. Trieschman, J. K. Whittaker, & L. K. Brendtro (Eds.), *The other 23 hours.* Chicago: Aldine.

Ullmann, L. P., & Krasner, L. (1975). *A psychological approach to abnormal behavior* (2nd ed.). Englewood Cliffs, NJ: Prentice-Hall.

Ulman, E., & Dachinger, P. (Eds.).(1977). *Art therapy in theory and practice.* New York: Schocken.

Urban, W. H. (1963). *The Draw-A-Person Test.* Los Angeles: Western Psychological Corporation.

U.S. Office of Education. (1969). *Standard terminology for curriculum and instruction in local and state school systems* (State Educational Records and Report Series: Handbook VI). Washington, DC: U.S. Government Printing Office.

U.S. Office of Education. (1972). *Career education: A handbook for implementation.* Washington, DC: U.S. Government Printing Office.

Valletutti, P., & Bender, M. (1982). *Teaching interpersonal and community living skills.* Austin, TX: Pro-Ed.

Vaughn, J. L., Jr. (1980). Affective measurement instruments: An issue of validity. *Journal of Reading, 24,* 16–19.

Ventura, M. F. (1980). *The selection and evaluation of instructional materials: A review of the literature.* Unpublished document.

Voorhis, T. G. (1931). *The relative merits of cursive and manuscript writing.* New York: Teachers College, Columbia University.

Wadsworth, H. O. (1971). A motivational approach toward the remediation of learning-disabled boys. *Exceptional Children, 38,* 33–42.

Walker, H. M. (1970). *Walker problem behavior checklist.* Los Angeles: Western Psychological Corporation.

Walker, H. M., & Buckley, N. K. (1974). *Token reinforcement techniques.* Eugene, OR: E-B Press.

Walker, H. M., McConnell, S., Holmes, D., Todis, B., Walker, J., & Golden, N. (1983). *Walker social skills curriculum: The ACCEPTS program.* Austin, TX: Pro-Ed.

Wallace, E. E. (1984). *The Riverside spelling program.* Chicago: Riverside.

Wallace, G., & Larsen, S. C. (1978). *Educational assessment of learning problems.* Boston: Allyn and Bacon.

Ward, T. (1968). Questions teachers should ask in choosing instructional materials. *Teaching Exceptional Children, 1,* 21–23.

Watson, B., & Van Etten, C. (1976). Materials analysis. *Journal of Learning Disabilities, 9,* 408–416.

Weber, R. M. (1968). The study of oral reading errors: A survey of the literature. *Reading Research Quarterly, 4,* 96–119.

Weber, R. M. (1970). A linguistic analysis of first-grade reading errors. *Reading Research Quarterly, 5,* 427–451.

Wechsler, D. (1949). *Wechsler Intelligence Scale for Children.* New York: Psychological Corporation.

Weinstein, G., & Fantini, M. D. (1970). *Toward humanistic education: A curriculum of affect.* New York: Praeger.

West, W. W. (1966). *Developing writing skills.* Englewood Cliffs, NJ: Prentice-Hall.

Westerman, G. (1971). *Spelling and writing.* San Rafael, CA: Dimensions.

Wiederholt, J. L. (1971). Predictive validity of Frostig's constructs as measured by the Developmental Test of Visual Perception. *Dissertation Abstracts, 33,* 1556–A.

Wiederholt, J. L. (1985). *The Formal Reading Inventory.* Austin, TX: Pro-Ed.

Wiederholt, J. L., Cronin, M. E., & Stubbs, V. (1980). Measurement of functional competencies and the handicapped: Constructs, assessments, and recommendations. *Exceptional Education Quarterly, 1,* 69–74.

Wiederholt, J. L., Hammill, D. D., & Brown, V. L. (1983). *The resource teacher: A guide to effective practices* (2nd ed.). Austin, TX: Pro-Ed.

Wiederholt, J. L., & Larsen, S. C. (1983). *Test of Practical Knowledge.* Austin, TX: Pro-Ed.

Williams, G. H., & Wood, M. M. (1981). *Developmental art therapy.* Austin, TX: Pro-Ed.

Williams, J. (1977). Building perceptive and cognitive strategies into a reading curriculum. In A. S. Reher & D. L. Scarborough (Eds.), *Toward a psychology of reading.* Hillsdale, NJ: Lawrence Erlbaum.

Williams, J. P. (1973). Learning to read: A review of theories and models. *Reading Research Quarterly, 8,* 121–146.

Winefordner, D. (1978). *Worker trait group guide.* Bloomington, IL: McKnight Publishing.

Wolpe, J. (1976). *Theme and variations: A behavior therapy casebook.* New York: Pergamon.

Woltmann, A. G. (1971). The use of puppetry in therapy. In N. J. Long, W. C. Morse, & R. G. Newman (Eds.), *Conflict in the classroom* (pp. 223–227). Belmont, CA: Wadsworth.

Wood, M. M. (Ed.). (1981a). *Developmental therapy sourcebook: Volume I, music, movement, and physical skills.* Austin, TX: Pro-Ed.

Wood, M. M. (Ed.). (1981b). *Developmental therapy sourcebook: Volume II, fantasy and make-believe.* Austin, TX: Pro-Ed.

Workman, E. A. (1982). *Teaching behavioral self-control to students.* Austin, TX: Pro-Ed.

Workman, E. A., & Hector, M. (1978). Behavioral self-control in classroom settings: A review of the literature. *Journal of School Psychology, 16,* 227–236.

Wrenn, C., & Schwarzrock, S. (1984). *The coping with series.* Circle Pines, MN: American Guidance Service.

Yee, A. (1966). The generalization controversy on spelling instruction. *Elementary English, 43,* 154–161.

Zaner-Bloser Staff. (1974). *Evaluation scale.* Columbus, OH: Zaner-Bloser.

Zionts, P. (1985). *Teaching disturbed and disturbing students.* Austin, TX: Pro-Ed.

Author Index

Subject Index

410

About the Authors

Donald D. Hammill

Before earning his doctorate degree from The University of Texas, Dr. Hammill worked in the Texas Public Schools for five years as a teacher and a speech therapist. He has served on the teaching staffs of Wichita State University and Temple University. In 1976–1977, he was President of The Council for Learning Disabilities. Presently he is President of Pro-Ed, Inc., a company that specializes in psychoeducational testing materials and professional books in the area of special and remedial education. He is author of sixty articles published in journals having peer review. He is the publisher of two journals, *Remedial and Special Education* (RASE) and *Topics in Early Childhood Special Education* (TECSE), and he serves on the professional advisory board of *Learning Magazine*. He has written seven textbooks and monographs, including *The Resource Teacher: A Guide to Effective Practices*, also published by Allyn and Bacon. In addition, he has participated in the development of sixteen diagnostic, norm-referenced assessment tests, including the Detroit Tests of Learning Aptitude (DTLA-2), Test of Language Development (TOLD), and the Test of Written Language (TOWL).

Nettie R. Bartel

Dr. Bartel received her Ph.D. from Indiana University. She has served as President of the Teacher Education Division of the Council for Exceptional Children (CEC) and, most recently, as Executive Secretary of the Commission for Commonwealth Universities, Pennsylvania Association of Colleges and Universities. A recipient of numerous awards and much recognition for outstanding achievement in special and higher education, Dr. Bartel is currently Professor of Special Education at Temple University. In addition, she is coordinator of the Faculty Seminar—a group of seventy senior university faculty members researching and implementing a new model of higher education. Professor Bartel has published several books, monographs, and major review chapters, as well as numerous articles in education journals.

418